Colonial Mediascapes

Colonial Mediascapes

SENSORY WORLDS OF THE EARLY AMERICAS

Edited and with an introduction by
Matt Cohen and Jeffrey Glover

Foreword by Paul Chaat Smith

University of Nebraska Press
Lincoln and London

Parts of chapter 4 were previously published in Birgit Brander Rasmussen's "Writing in the Conflict Zone: Don Felipe Guaman Poma de Ayala's *El primer nueva corónica y buen gobierno*," in *Queequeg's Coffin: Indigenous Literacies and Early American Literature*, 79–110 (Durham: Duke University Press, 2012). Copyright © 2012 by Duke University Press, all rights reserved. Republished by permission of the copyright holder (www.dukepress.edu).

An expanded version of chapter 7 originally appeared in Peter Charles Hoffer's *Sensory Worlds in Early America*, 22–76 (Baltimore: Johns Hopkins University Press, 2005). Reprinted courtesy of Johns Hopkins University Press.

Chapter 8 was previously published in Jon T. Coleman's *Vicious: Wolves and Men in America*, 19–36 (New Haven: Yale University Press, 2004). Reprinted courtesy of Yale University Press.

Publication of this volume was assisted by the Virginia Faulkner Fund, established in memory of Virginia Faulkner, editor in chief of the University of Nebraska Press.

Library of Congress Cataloging-in-Publication Data
Colonial mediascapes: sensory worlds of the early Americas / edited and with an introduction by Matt Cohen and Jeffrey Glover; foreword by Paul Chaat Smith.
pages cm.
Includes bibliographical references and index.
ISBN 978-0-8032-3239-6 (cloth: alk. paper)—ISBN 978-0-8032-4999-8 (pbk.: alk. paper)—ISBN 978-0-8032-5441-1 (epub)—ISBN 978-0-8032-5442-8 (mobi)
1. Indians of North America—Communication. 2. Indians of Mexico—Communication. 3. Indians of South America—Communication. 4. First contact of aboriginal peoples with Westerners—America—History—17th century. 5. Communication—America—History—17th century. 6. Literacy—America—History—17th century. 7. Books and reading—America—History—17th century. 8. Oral tradition—America—History—17th century. 9. United States—History—Colonial period, ca. 1600–1775. 10. Great Britain—Colonies—America. 11. Spain—Colonies—America. I. Cohen, Matt, 1970–
E98.C73C65 2014   973.3—dc23   2013035773

Set in Adobe Caslon by Laura Wellington. Designed by J. Vadnais.

Contents

Illustrations

MAP

FIGURES

Foreword

Colonial Mediascapes is a bold and ambitious project that proposes new ways of thinking about books, technology, and American Indians.

When the old ways of thinking are filled with rusted and corroding words, sometimes the new ways require new words. New words are usually off-putting, and in fact the clumsy word for new words (neologism) is itself a perfect example. However, the argument in the pages that follow is so groundbreaking, and so profound and disorientating, that it justifies the creation of new names for new things.

Let me crudely characterize the existing discourse. The winter count calendar is (kind of) like a book. The quipu is (kind of) like a computer. The petroglyph is (kind of) like words. The subtext is not so buried; what we're really talking about is this: Indians are, on a good day, (kind of) like Europeans. Just as the structure of these sentences about books and computers embeds a clear point of view on what is understood to be superior, the underlying assumption applies to the users of these things as well.

As a curator at the Smithsonian's National Museum of the American Indian, I always felt these well-intentioned comparisons were a trap. I never thought it was quite believable that some ugly ball of yarn was really an indigenous UNIVAC, or at least an abacus. That isn't to say I thought it wasn't those things; just that in an exhibition format, no text label making such a comparison would be convincing. Yet even if one had the expertise and real estate to build a compelling, smart exhibition that would persuade skeptics that those ratty-looking Peruvian strings contained mathematical genius, what did that really get us? Since a microscopic fraction of Indians who ever lived used such a device, I suggest we get the exception that proves the rule, that's what.

The chapters that follow demonstrate how these things are not approximately similar but fundamentally different, and they begin to explode the notion of technological determinism that shapes much of the current discourse about the past five centuries of American history.

True, "objects of knowledge transfer" doesn't roll off the tongue, and time will tell if "mediascapes" gains traction as a way to think about these questions, which is just fine. The ideas, though, I am certain are going to be around a long time.

Paul Chaat Smith
September 2010

Acknowledgments

We are most of all grateful to all of our contributors, for their generosity, care, and patience. For the existence and much of the quality of this book, we owe a debt to our anonymous readers and the editorial staff at the University of Nebraska Press, and to Matt Bokovoy in particular for his good guidance on the design of the introduction. For their contributions to the discussions and the symposium that started this project we would like to thank Gonzalo Lamana, Walter Mignolo, Elizabeth Fenn, Orin Starn, John David Miles, and Frank Salomon. For institutional support at Duke University of that symposium— "Early American Mediascapes," on February 15, 2008—we are grateful to the Arts and Sciences Research Council; Information Science and Information Systems; the John Hope Franklin Humanities Institute; the Department of History; the Department of Cultural Anthropology; the Program in Literature; and Rare Books, Manuscripts, and Special Collections at Duke Libraries.

Matt Cohen would like to thank, for their intellectual and professional guidance, Carolyn Podruchny, Kenneth Mills, Priscilla Wald, Kenneth Price, Doug Armato, Fredrika Teute, and Ralph Bauer. Roanne Kantor is an excellent translator and helped out at a key moment. Better critics and supporters than Jace Everett, Bob Gross, Phil Round, Rob Nelson, Rob Mitchell, John Miles, Lauren Coats, Bart Keeton, Elizabeth Cullingford, Orin Starn, Luis Cárcamo-Huechante,

Tom Ferraro, Russ Leo, Kinohi Nishikawa, Lars Hinrichs, and Christopher Labarthe would be hard to find. For more than can be written, thank you, Nikki Gray, Dan Cohen, Michael Cohen, Katharine Cohen, and Marian Sherwood Weston.

Jeffrey Glover would like to thank Elizabeth Maddock Dillon and Wai Chee Dimock for their support and encouragement at the beginning of this project. Matt Cohen, Hsuan Hsu, Elliott Visconsi, and Michael Warner offered many helpful criticisms of an early draft of chapter II, as did the participants in the "Early American Mediascapes" symposium. Karen Kupperman, Kelly Wisecup, and Jodi Schorb also offered helpful comments at the "Early American Borderlands" conference. Mark Lebetkin came through at a key moment with characteristic generosity. Ashlee Humphreys and Jan and Carl Glover were always there.

Colonial Mediascapes

Introduction

Matt Cohen and Jeffrey Glover

New World colonialism catalyzed an extraordinary range of controversies and theories about humanness and history, many of which centered on the question of communication—and writing in particular.
Could a people without what Westerners recognized as "writing" know
their own history? Could they be converted to Christianity, and if so,
what would be the proper means of doing so? Such questions evolved
in eighteenth-century Europe and its colonies into debates about the
patterns of human history and the possibility of a universal language,
and in the nineteenth, into arguments about human evolution and the
relationships between race and writing. As many critics have pointed
out, in the wake of theories of writing such as Isaac Taylor's *The History of the Alphabet* (1899), a stadial notion of media development held
strong sway in the twentieth century. The oral and gestural, it was argued, evolved into hieroglyphics or writing, then manuscript, then
print, in a cultural progression sometimes coupled to the development
of science and technology, human consciousness, or visions of global
rational governance. A host of ideas about what made humans distinctive or about the destiny of the human race were hitched to the
evolution of writing, and Amerindian evidence was important to most
of them.[1] In our own time, the most powerful means of storing and

retrieving information is neither image-based nor text-based but relies on binarized electrical signals. Yet the oral-literate explanatory structure persists, as does a technological determinism that rationalizes the outcomes of settlement history in terms of guns, germs, steel, or economics.

Against this conception of media and the notions of history that follow from it, thinkers across many disciplines have proposed alternatives. There is Sandra Gustafson's notion of "emerging media" ("the ongoing technological, cultural, and ideological transformations that affect all media, whether 'old' or 'new'"), N. Katherine Hayles's notion of "intermediation," or Martin Lienhard's argument for the "multimedia literacy" of indigenous worlds.[2] These scholars focus on inscriptions, supports, and performances rather than teleologically organized stages of development. Their work has brought new urgency to the study of printed or written artifacts that circulated in contexts shaped by different forms of media. It has also furnished tools for accessing resistant and alternative public worlds that defy description within hierarchies of orality and literacy.

In assembling *Colonial Mediascapes* we have tried not to define writing, textuality, or literacy but rather to exhibit some recent, influential evolutions of the conversation about communication in colonial America, broadly conceived. "The cross-fertilization of cultures takes many forms, leaving behind many records, language being only one of them, and often not the primary one," writes Wai Chee Dimock; "there is no reason to think of language as self-sufficient."[3] A focus on textuality has sometimes hampered the understanding of communication systems themselves as contentious sites for the unfolding of colonization. By looking at text together with what we might call "other-than-text"—or modes of inscription or expression that are not linguistic—the discussion enacted in this book tends to understand inscription as happening, and as being received, in relation to multiple, sometimes simultaneous modes of communication. Assembled under this principle, the essays here open new understandings of how media made history before the Revolutionary era in the Americas.[4]

There are two principal scholarly occasions for this volume. The first is the friction we perceive between the theorization of writing and coloniality in Latin America, which has embraced indigenous communication practices, and that in North America, where the focus has remained on the traditional objects of the history of the book—and to an extent on Western conceptions of history itself.[5] The second occasion is the hemispheric trend in early American studies, which seems to offer excellent opportunities to put indigenous systems and intercultural colonial communications episodes into the same critical space, if not fully into dialogue. For a long time, the history of the book in New England and its attendant intellectual and social history and the extraordinarily rich debates about what Lux Vidal described as *grafismo indígena* in Mesoamerica and the Andes have orbited each other, seldom crossing paths.[6] Book studies has been particularly fertile in the evidentiary ground of New England; it is unsurprising, then, that many of the essays here are based in that space. From book history—and from textual scholarship more broadly—many essayists take the notion that medium shapes, but does not determine, meaning in communication. But we also draw, as our title suggests, on postcolonial anthropology and on historical media studies, in which the redefinition of media categories offers ways to resist the magnetism of teleological stories of cultural development that follow from the valorization of writing and print.[7]

One of the most influential redefinitions of writing in the American colonial context came with Elizabeth Boone and Walter Mignolo's edited collection *Writing without Words* in 1994. Boone and Mignolo concluded that, to quote the latter, "the history of writing is not an evolutionary process driving toward the alphabet, but rather a series of coevolutionary processes in which different writing systems followed their own transformations."[8] Boone and Mignolo's definition of writing was challengingly broad: "the communication of relatively specific ideas in a conventional manner by means of permanent, visible marks." This definition was designed to focus on "communication, on the structured use of conventions, and on the element of permanency."[9]

For the critics in *Writing without Words*, as Joanne Rappaport put it, "the power of European institutions was constituted and maintained through the spread of literacy in indigenous communities from the late sixteenth to early nineteenth centuries."[10] The legacy of the insistence by the contributors to *Writing without Words* on the political nature of any representation of indigenous communication resonates in each of the essays here, despite important differences in methodology and political orientation.

Boone and Mignolo focused on writing for good reason: to undermine the evolutionist and Western colonialist equation, deeply rooted through academic study and publication, of alphabetic writing with higher consciousness and human capacity. We think it is time, thanks to their influential work, to try out *media* as an organizing frame. Western theories and practices of evidence, property, and sovereignty are today less dependent upon notions of writing and increasingly dependent upon theories of media. Studies of performance and other-than-textual communication and reconstructions of impermanent media have broadened the archive of colonial studies and called attention to the way archival practices dating to the colonial period shape current disciplinary boundaries. A shift from "writing" to "media" sets up a relay with contemporary communications controversies and with studies in other fields that productively disrupt progressive, linear thinking about communication history. The idea of media, not just colonial discourse, is important to us here, because we feel that the focus on the linguistic should be one part of a larger attempt to understand scenes of communication (or publications, in a much older and broader sense of the term) as events that not only shaped settlement history but also conditioned access to the past.

This introduction surveys the archival history of indigenous representation, with its multiple—though sometimes surprisingly coincident—temporalities. Our attempt is to trace some of the long history of conversations about indigenous American media to situate the appearance of this collection in the *longue durée*. In this we apply the lessons of many teachers, from Mignolo and Boone to Jill Lepore, Lisa

Introduction

Brooks, Paul Chaat Smith, Jace Weaver, Joanna Brooks, Jean O'Brien, Craig Womack, James Clifford, and George Tinker, all of whom question how history is conceptualized in discussing indigenous representation.

In that spirit, we want to say a word about the title of this book. We've borrowed the term *mediascapes* from Arjun Appadurai. Working at the nexus of area studies and anthropology, Appadurai's work attempts to understand how groups in today's world imagine themselves into being, without fixed spaces and through a swarm of media and communications devices, during what Appadurai argues is the staggering final stage of the collapse of the nation-state form. Long-distance community formation, a challenging new media realm, reconfigurations of economy and governance, the constant encounter with different ethnicities, and a fragmented, highly localized set of power negotiations—Appadurai's modernity sounds familiar to students of early colonialism.[11]

Mediascape is one of five "scapes" that Appadurai posits as tools for analyzing how individuals and groups imagine self-determination today. Together with ethnoscapes, technoscapes, financescapes, and ideoscapes, mediascapes are "cultural flows" that take on local meaning in specific times and places, and through which communities and individuals refract each of the other "scapes." Mediascape refers more specifically to the distribution of the ability to create and spread information as well as the contents of that dissemination. Mediascapes are made up of both a set of images or stories about people—true or false—and the means by which those images or stories are transmitted. They are perspectival, local, often rapidly evolving sets of systems, protocols, and ways of speaking about others (33–36).

Such a way of understanding the importance of media both follows the lead of *Writing without Words* in focusing on power and the social embodiment of media practices and moves us beyond the paradigm of writing into an analytic that encourages us to consider colonial relations as they are constituted across media. It also leverages some of the powerful insights offered by postcolonial studies into the ways uses of media become in themselves contests for power in the hands of subalterns. But there are also problems with the term. It is good to recall first that Appadurai intended each of the "scapes" as "building blocks," not as determinants, of political cultural analysis; mediascapes are a starting point, not a telos (33). Second, the tempo of the world Appadurai describes is much more rapid than that of the colonial world. For all that we share with the past a state of heterochronicity, nearly instantaneous global communication competes more heavily with natural time scales and forces than in the colonial era. Too, the global imagination is much more fundamentally shaped by ideas like race than in the colonial world; colonization and empire may not have established "civilization" everywhere, but their political products have spiraled wide and deep. And finally, Appadurai's work posits the existence of what he terms "diasporic public spheres"—a contentious notion in colonial studies, and one that Appadurai would argue might be an anachronistic way of understanding long-distance relations in the colonial era.[12] So it is as an analytical spur, and perhaps a transdisciplinary invitation, that we propose mediascapes as a way of understanding how we have conceptualized this book.

The approach to mediascapes suggested by Appadurai does not lend itself to the kinds of grand, linear narratives that organized media history in the nineteenth century and before. The essays in *Colonial Mediascapes* offer divergent and conflicting approaches to the project of telling literary history in new ways. The first part, "Beyond Textual Media," presents essays that address the mediation of early American archives. For centuries, scholars and archivists of early American history have focused on the codex form and its many permutations, organizing libraries, canons, archives, and syllabi around the concept of the book. The essays in part 1 grapple with the consequences of book-based archival practices for the study of the many early American people who recorded history without writing. Part 2, "Multimedia Texts," looks at the relationship between written texts and other kinds of communication. These essays suggest the ways in which a broader understanding of communication can transform received understandings of textuality. Part 3, "Sensory New Worlds," features essays that consider the interface between media and the senses in American encounters. These essays describe how struggles over soundscapes and other sensory phenomena shaped settlement outcomes. The concluding section, "Transatlantic Mediascapes," examines intersections of indigenous and transatlantic forms of communication. Often, the contact zone between Europeans and Native people is viewed as a localized space. These essays show how struggles over media in the colonies shaped the political and intellectual history of European powers.

Western interest in non- or paralinguistic indigenous representation in the Americas has been intense from the earliest days of encounter, though the occasions and uses of recoveries of Mexican maps and codices, or of paleolithic inscriptions by Native North Americans, were various and often conflicted. In their original contexts, many of these media were themselves tools of empire and the maintenance of hierarchies; sometimes they were deliberately constructed to cross linguistic and cultural boundaries, and at other times they reified governmental or local communal control by stifling such transmissions. The media of the pre- and early colonial period in America that have attracted the most attention, both archival and scholarly, include the codices and maps of Mesoamerica; the khipus of the Inca empire; the wampum, winter counts, and birchbark scrolls of North America; and the languages, architecture, and stone inscriptions of all of these areas. Less emphasized but no less subject to collecting and museumification have been song, fabrics, basketry, pottery, weaponry, and burial objects. More elusive to commodification but increasingly of interest to scholars today have been dance, tattoos, and the physical layout of communities, shrines, and pathways.[13]

These media were, to use Jay Bolter and Richard Grusin's term, "remediated" by Europeans in many ways. Such remediations extended from the physical extraction to Europe of artifacts, documents, and people; to the creation of syllabaries; to the representation in book form of codices, architecture, totemic signatures, tattoos, and other inscribed forms. Such remediations also happened the other way: indigenous people throughout the continent appropriated European media. Doubtless these practices illustrate an appreciation by the Americans of the importance that books, letters, coins, jewelry, and other inscribed objects held for newcomers, but evidence of long-distance trade prior to colonization also suggests that such enfolding of the media of others was in many groups a long-standing practice. The remediation of American indigenous representations, then, proceeded under a complex state of interchange. European controversies simultaneously fueled the spread of indigenous communications practices and obscured their functioning and contexts.

"The most frequently published and widely circulating works on America over the entire century," Rolena Adorno points out, "were the epic poems of conquest."[14] The generic expectations of these works allowed for representations of indigeneity that would not have been possible in other genres more tightly regulated by church or state, as they were indirect, artful, and formulaic representations of customs rather than historical ones. While more direct representations, such as the codices, seem preferable to the refraction of epic poetry, there too the story is complex. The mass destruction of such documents by Spaniards like Fray Diego de Landa went hand in hand with their recognition as significant. "These people used certain characters or letters," wrote Landa, "with which they wrote in their books about their antiquities and their sciences; with these, and with figures, and certain signs in the figures, they understood their matters, made them known, and taught them."[15] Certain "*signs* in the *figures*": the mixture of codes became, very early on, part of the European calculus of the significance of indigenous American representation. Moreover, the Mexica *amoxtli*, or painted histories, were designed to be performed; the content and composition were assembled with oral and gestural performance in mind.

Yet it is to the Spanish administration that we owe the existence of the majority of known Mesoamerican codices. José Rabasa reminds us that "although the missionaries burned native writings in the early years of the conquest, by the early 1540s Spanish administrators were encouraging and even sponsoring the production of texts using glyphs." As Rabasa compellingly puts it, "What could more powerfully constitute a link between the *encomienda* and tribute patterns before the conquest than an indigenous pictographic record?"[16] Codices also served as legal evidence in land disputes.[17] This resurgence and transformation of other-than-textual signification simultaneously inscribes indigenous inclinations and Spanish governmental objectives. For Rabasa, this means not just that Amerindian ways were being adapted but also that Spanish authorities were "committing themselves to dwell in both worlds," the Nahua and the Spanish New World, "at least from a hermeneutic necessity, though not from an affective affinity."[18] He argues that the same is true of early indigenous uses of European writing, such as the Nahuatl *Historia de Tlatelolco desde los tiempos más remotos*, written around 1528 using the Latin alphabet and part of a massive outpouring of texts from the missionaries working among the Aztecs.

Indigenous mapping practices and ways of understanding landscape were also preserved by and refracted through Spanish administrative demands. The *relaciones geográficas* were created around 1580 based on a royal Spanish questionnaire. The maps they included—sometimes called *lienzos* when painted on canvas—each covered a small town or province within the *gobierno* of New Spain, and most were created by indigenous people. Barbara Mundy shows that in many cases, particularly in outlying areas, maps still remained from the precolonial era, and in some cases these may have been copied in response to the questionnaire. These maps survived because, unlike religious almanacs, "community maps were recognized as secular documents by Europeans and never specifically earmarked for destruction," an argument that Jorge Cañizares-Esguerra makes about codices as well.[19] Native painters still used traditional indicators for landforms and pathways, included details such as the roots of plants, and depicted social relations or the comparative importance of resource areas using indigenous rules for scale and position rather than a Euclidean projection—techniques that Mundy terms "communicentric projection."[20] The church, too, was an important vector for the maintenance of indigenous visual traditions, as Mundy's work shows. The church was also a site of the transmission of language, rhetorical codes, gestures, and histories—and for the archiving of indigenous representational practices considered demonic.

The khipu is an interesting exception to—in ways showing the limits of—the European fascination with indigenous American nontextual representation. Khipus are bundles of multicolored knotted strings, used to regulate the Inca empire and its sophisticated tributary economies. As Frank Salomon puts it, they are "one aspect of America that Europe never really discovered."[21] Spanish writers gave credence to the khipu, but they appear never to have tried hard to figure out how khipus worked. Were they code? Were they text? Were they indecipherable outside of a performance or a ritual context? Did their uses vary by region and historically, or were they designed to bridge space, time, and dialect? In many ways, Salomon suggests, the problem of the khipu raises some of the most persistent questions about human communications systems more broadly. Gary Urton's work has focused on decoding khipu morphology. He argues convincingly for a variety of bureaucratic, record-keeping uses of the strings, for keeping track of tribute, for example. Salomon, while agreeing that in the past "the cord system articulated political life as organized by corporate kinship groups," shows this by exploring its continued use into the contemporary era in certain Andean contexts (*Cord Keepers* 3). He also goes so far as to suggest that uses of the khipu may have been heterogeneous and that it might have been designed to mimic forms of action other than speech.[22] In part because of the khipu's methodological and historiographical importance, most of the essays in *Colonial Mediascapes* that take up Hispanophone contexts involve the khipu, approaching it from a variety of formal standpoints as a transmedia device.

What Mundy argues of Mesoamerican maps, in most analysts' accounts, holds true for other indigenous forms of inscription south of the Rio Grande. "Indigenous maps began to change," she writes, "when the understanding of space held by their makers did, most visibly when Spanish programs of land use and urbanization forced them into different relationships with their environment. In addition, both within the indigenous community and outside of it, new types of writing and literacy undercut the authority that native maps once had."[23] It is certainly the case that the production of new codices and khipus using traditional symbolic systems dwindled as the seventeenth century wore on. Simultaneously, these forms saw increasing reproduction in European contexts, for a variety of reasons.

Just as the ecclesiastical and governmental institutions of New Spain fostered a complicated dynamic of elimination, preservation, and transmission of American representation, so too did that dynamic function through antiquarian collecting, travel literature, museum building, and historical and natural philosophical research in Europe. It would be risky, then, to speak of *an* or *the* "archive" of indigenous colonial representation, if by that term we take even Derrida's broad sense of a place, articulated to authority production, where documents that are to shape the future are selected and preserved. Both the situations and the forms of authority that attach to the places where indigenous inscription appear are multifarious and multidimensional— and they show a long history of contentious relation. Indigenous representation as an imaginary, or Borgesian, archive, then, might be thought of as a key shaper of the human sciences, continuously, since the beginning of the sixteenth century.

There is disagreement on the question of how seriously, and in what way, Spanish intellectuals and authorities took Amerindian writing. Scholars seem to concur that in general, a strong analogical optic encouraged Spanish authorities to deprecate indigenous writing as generally a product of collaboration with, or even a direct creation of, the devil. "The model of writing and the book imbedded in the European mind during the Renaissance," Mignolo summarizes, "erased many of the possibilities for missionaries and men of letters to inquire into different writing systems and sign carriers rather than simply describe them by analogy with their own model."[24] There were exceptions: José de Acosta, in book 6 of his *Historia natural y moral de las Indias* (1590), compares Amerindian writing systems not just with the European alphabetic system but with Chinese writing. Acosta suggests broad encoding power for the khipu, among other things, though without, as we will see, offering a detailed description of khipu encoding or interpretation.[25]

It was not only obscure historians such as Francesco Patrizi (in the sixteenth century) but also Amerindians (in the seventeenth) such as Fernando de Alva Ixtlilxochitl and Francisco de San Antón Muñon Chimalpain Cuauhtlehuanitzin, trained by humanist friars, who challenged the notion that indigenous forms of inscription carried no historical weight. Juan de Torquemada, in his *Monarchía indiana* of 1615, wrote that the Mexicans "kept very good knowledge" of the acts of Spanish conquest and "recorded them as history, first using figures and characters and later alphabetical writing."[26] Cañizares-Esguerra argues that the perceived genres of the inscriptions were important to Europeans. If they treated cosmological matters, they were false and dangerous; if they treated historical matters, they were perhaps controversial, but not risky. As we saw, Diego de Landa burned Mayan ritual books and tortured Amerindians to death for paganism—but he also was so convinced by Mayan calendrical sophistication that he searched the Yucatán systematically for stelae, on which he felt the history of the previous kingdoms had been written.[27]

The story is complicated by the history of publication and republication of the codices and other accounts; for example, most of the important Spanish histories of Peru before the arrival of Europeans that were written in the 1500s went unpublished during their authors' lives—sometimes for centuries, as in the case of Pedro Cieza de León's *El señorío de los Incas*. And yet, parts of *El señorío* appeared, recast, in Antonio de Herrera y Tordesillas's *Historia general de los hechos de los castellanos* (1605–15). Parts of these works and of the codices were also published and republished at different times in languages other than Spanish, sometimes, as in the case of the Codex Mendoza in the

Englishman Samuel Purchas's *Hakluytus Posthumus* (1625), for the first time.

"Renaissance scholars thought that indigenous scripts, however limited, registered historical events," Cañizares-Esguerra argues, while "Enlightenment literati thought that scripts were material evidence upon which to reconstruct conjectural histories of the development of the mind."[28] Fray Diego Durán consulted Amerindian-authored accounts in Mexica script for his history of the Mexicas in the late sixteenth century, but by the eighteenth century such sources were deprecated, particularly by English historians. Interestingly, even in Cañizares-Esguerra's account, it is clear that some historians, such as Francisco Xavier Clavijero, were still taking indigenous sources seriously, and it was not long before creole American intellectuals began to make nationalist claims for the importance of indigenous writing systems as such in deliberate contradistinction to the European intellectual demotion of the American past (as primitive) and present (as degenerate). Such a tendency overlapped with North American trends; it was not long after this that North American students of indigenous languages such as John Heckewelder and, a little later, Henry Rowe Schoolcraft began to take a serious interest in all forms of American Indian inscription, and a similar effort at recovering and reprinting Indian documents from the early colonial era began in the United States. This does not undermine Cañizares-Esguerra's larger observation that Walter Ong, Jack Goody, Ian Watt, and other theorists of the development of literacy understood the significance of "primitive" inscription methods in a way that descends from this tendency.[29]

And on this both Mignolo and Cañizares-Esguerra agree. As early as the sixteenth century, American hieroglyphs were considered as a primitive form of writing rather than a divinely inspired form of communication. But whether arguing for an occult significance to symbolic scripts or arguing for a stadial model, like Giambattista Vico's, that positioned writing in a Christian historical evolution, or searching for evidence that climactic change caused degeneration, as Cornelius de Pauw claimed, the images and scripts of America remained a key evidentiary basis for epistemological conflict.[30] Even John Wilkins, early in a series of theorists of a universal language that would both transcend nationality and obviate falsehood, insisted on hieroglyphics—both Egyptian and Mexican—as a negative example, proof of an earlier, and thus failed, approach to communication. And the patriotic creole elites of the late eighteenth and early nineteenth centuries made such documents central to their arguments, precisely because the international epistemological controversies around Amerindian scripts (or, for example, the images at the ruins of the Mayan city of Palenque) made American inscriptions crucial to ongoing debates about the human condition that were situated at the nexus of nationalism, religion, and the need to maintain settler and creole legal hegemony—what Rolena Adorno terms "the polemics of possession."[31]

In the nineteenth century, Mignolo writes, "ancient writing systems became the treasure trove of and a commodity for travelers and businessmen for whom the economic expansion of their countries allowed a transformation of cultural legacies into exotic commodities."[32] But collectors and states also moved indigenous objects—sometimes even people—into museums as part of a new "scientific" orientation toward history and human capacity and a post-Revolutionary claim to a national past. The nineteenth century, with its celebration of the four hundredth anniversary of Columbus's voyage, saw a surge in the publication of so-called Mexican antiquities that did not abate until the 1920s. Alfredo Chavero's two-volume 1892 edition *Antigüedades mexicanas* contains lithographs of *lienzos* and other visual documents.[33] Manuel Orozco y Berra's work, beginning in the 1860s, focused on indigenous cartography, as did that of Antonio Peñafiel from the 1880s. This too was a fertile period for book-historical study; José Toribio Medina's eight-volume *La imprenta en México* was published in 1912.[34] Revolutionary centennials were occasions to remediate the indigenous past and assert the modernity of American nationhoods. Sometimes paradoxically, such memorializations even confirmed postcoloniality. Creole nationalism was rhetorically rooted in indigenous particularities, now organized within a progressive temporality that kept them safely in the past—yet this modernness was sustained by a repressive dynamics that brought Native forms back to light again obsessively. New media allowed for new forms of remediation: photography and film, in particular, became dominant new modes of representing indigenous peoples, growing alongside the increasing professionalization of both history and anthropology. The republication of codices and lienzos, together with the photographing and filming of ruins and engravings, now functioned in the context of a scientific exploration into primitivism and an often universalizing ethnography.

The 1940s saw a tendency in scholarship on the colonial era to attempt to counteract the "Black Legend." But in the late 1940s and early 1950s a more fundamental shift away from the dynamic of national hagiography or critique began; as Rolena Adorno put it, "the dichotomy of victor and vanquished was no longer an adequate description" of the conquest of America.[35] The publication of codices, archaeological studies, and other discussions of indigenous Central and South American media helped build new interpretations of colonization in the works of John V. Murra, Miguel León-Portilla, Ángel María Garibay, and many others—interpretations that centered Native perspectives and social structures or that demonstrated the multiplicity of influences on the political and economic unfolding of Spanish colonization.[36]

In many cases these republications and archivizations have been put by indigenous people to uses that their curators might never have imagined possible, particularly in the wake of increasing global activism and efforts at self-determination by indigenous peoples beginning in the 1960s.[37] Academic work that took up colonial texts from indigenous standpoints flowered during this time, which also saw the linguistic turn in the humanities, the rise of cultural studies and New Historicism, the return of the political to scholarly work, and, broadly, an increasing pressure on traditional historical method. The historiography traced above, routed through the works of major Hispanists concerned with the question of indigenous media, is a product of this more recent context. Surveying the bibliographies of *Writing without*

Words and Mundy's study of maps, one finds a clear surge in reissues or new editions of Central and South American indigenous-made documents in the 1960s and 1970s, with at least seventeen codices and maps edited and interpreted during these decades and the production at the University of Texas Press of the multivolume *Handbook of Middle American Indians* (beginning in 1964).[38] Interest in the codices was geographically widespread: the publications in Mundy's bibliography are from across the Americas and Europe.

Frank Salomon's discovery and discussion of the sustained use of khipus for community organization in the Huarochirí province in Peru brings us back both to the tricky temporality of the colonial archive and to fundamental questions about how to analyze American communication forms. If the question of early American signifying systems was once how writing produces higher consciousness, for Mignolo, Boone, Rappaport, Rabasa, and other Hispanists of the past few decades, the guiding question has been how writing produces subalternity. With Salomon, we suggest tweaking the question in order to produce methodological leverage and new questions: How do different media become political and social facts? The colonial Americas, when the media of both Native Americans and Amerindians are considered, not only exemplify the complexities of answering such a question but offer an account of the history of present-day media archives and discourses.

The archive of colonial North American literary scholarship has also recently expanded to include a broader range of communication practices. Yet scholars of North American literature have confronted a different set of methodological problems. While Latin American archives have historically preserved materials that incorporated elements of indigenous textual traditions such as khipus, illustrated books, and pictographs, the North American archive largely consists of the written and printed records of political and religious elites. In attempting to recover oppositional and alternative cultures of information, scholars have used these elite materials to reconstruct communication practices that operated beyond the domain of writing and print. This has involved widening the category of "literature" to include practices such as oratory, performance, and ritual.[39] And, as in the Central and South American cases, it has involved a heightened awareness of how the archival records of colonial states still condition contemporary scholarly labor.

The earliest extensive records of indigenous communication practices in North America were produced by English and Dutch joint-stock companies trading along the North Atlantic coast. For these early commercial ventures, manuscript accounts of coastal languages and other communication ways served as a means to facilitate exchange and promote trading ventures to metropolitan stakeholders. At first, the incredible variety of Native languages and dialects thwarted European attempts to produce any reliable account of coastal languages.[40] A bewildered traveler with the Dutch West India Company observed that languages in the Hudson River Valley alone "vary frequently not over five or six leagues; forthwith comes another language; if they meet they can hardly understand one another."[41] Early European observers differed in their strategies for mapping this confusing linguistic terrain. William Wood optimistically hoped that the apparent array of American tongues might only reflect differences in dialect, which, like the unruly tongues of the British Isles, would disappear when tribes were brought under a centralized imperial government. Wood observed, "Every [American] country differ[s] in their speech, even as our northern peoples do from southern, and western from them."[42] Other travelers thought linguistic diversity among tribal groups indicated underlying tensions that could be exploited for European ends. Traveling in the Carolinas, John Lawson wrote that "difference of speech causes jealousies and fears amongst [Indians], which bring wars, wherein they destroy one another."[43] In the earliest stages of colonization, many Native groups attempted to prevent settlers from overhearing proper tribal languages. Observing that the Delawares only spoke to Europeans using the "shortened words" of a pidgin tongue, the Dutch trader Jonas Michaëlius complained that the Indians tried to "conceal their language from us [rather] than to properly communicate it."[44] While such observations represented distinctly European expectations about linguistic homogeneity and national unity, they also reflected indigenous commitments to preserving difference, or at the least a form of strategic leverage, in the face of imperialist encroachments.

Many early promotional narratives portrayed communication with Native people in terms of gestures and hand signs.[45] Accounts of gestural communication served to reassure investors in England and the Netherlands who feared that the difficulty of learning Indian languages might stall trade or lead to political tension. In an early sixteenth-century account of an exploratory venture in the mid-Atlantic, Giovanni da Verrazzano described the potentially pacifying effects of gestural imitation on Indians, writing, "By imitating their signs, we inspired them in some measure with confidence."[46] In an account of George Waymouth's 1605 voyage to New England, James Rosier reported that signs and gestures had been perfectly suitable for carrying out economic exchanges with Indians. "I signed unto them," he wrote, "that if they would bring me such skins as they ware I would give them knives. . . . This I did to bring them to an understanding of exchange, and that they might conceive the intent of our comming to them to be for no other end."[47] While such descriptions served to promote commercial ventures, other travelers made less extravagant claims about the cross-cultural intelligibility of gestures. Casting doubt on the claims of commercial agents such as Rosier, the Royalist castaway Henry Norwood found the "insignificant signs" of Maryland Indians "as hard to be interpreted as if they had expres'd their thoughts in the *Hebrew* or *Chaldean* tongues."[48] Such divergent experiences reflected not only regional differences among Native groups but also the competing agendas of different settlement ventures. While the promoters of financial ventures expressed confidence about the cross-cultural intelligibility of gestural communication, those with no financial interest in the American trade offered less optimistic opinions about New World communication.

To forestall skepticism about their ability to communicate across cultural lines, many English ventures sought to record and publish Indian languages in systematic form, often with the assistance of "go-betweens" or cross-cultural interpreters acquired through kidnapping or adoption.[49] Before traveling to America as the official chronicler of a voyage to Roanoke, Thomas Harriot learned parts of the Carolinian Algonquian dialect from Manteo and Wanchese, two coastal Indians brought to England by Sir Walter Raleigh in 1584. On his return from Virginia, Harriot produced "An universall Alphabet conteyninge six & thirty letters" (1585), the result of his efforts "to seeke for fit letters to expresse the Virginian speche."[50] The alphabet included pronunciation instructions for Algonquian phonemes, offering potential readers the chance to sound out Indian tongues for themselves from the comfort of transatlantic distance. The voyage also employed the painter John White to capture visual records of coastal lifeways. White depicted Indians with indecipherable tattoos that suggested the variety and complexity of coastal textual practices.[51]

While Harriot recorded Chesapeake languages using models derived from natural philosophy, other writers used different formats, often compiling linguistic information with other kinds of materials, and in the process making divergent arguments about the importance of indigenous languages. Many of these reports, such as Johannes Megapolensis's account of the Mohawk and Mahican languages, circulated in manuscript among governmental officials, company agents, and missionaries.[52] Yet print publications from John Smith, Thomas Gage, and William Wood also included vocabulary lists of Indian words modeled after manuals of trade jargon, emphasizing how knowledge of Native languages might yield financial profit for travelers, planters, and adventurers for hire. Controversies over the accuracy of these materials quickly became part of struggles for resources and political power. When Roger Williams petitioned the parliamentary Committee for Foreign Plantations for a charter for the independent settlement community Providence Plantations, he supported his appeal with the phrasebook *A Key into the Language of America* (1643), which he published in part to correct the "grosse *mis-takes*" in current English understandings of Algonquian tongues.[53] Far from offering a unified imperial or cultural judgment of Indian signification as inferior or savage, then, accounts of Indian languages and communication systems offered dissenters like Williams the opportunity to challenge reports from the politically dominant colonies such as Massachusetts Bay and to gain credibility in the metropolis by positioning themselves as alternative sources of information about American politics.[54] Natives gained politically from these transatlantic missions as well. From the sixteenth century onward, many Native people traveled to England with returning colonists. Sometimes they traveled as captives; at other times they came voluntarily and enjoyed audiences with colonial or government officials interested in the progress of English colonial endeavors. Pocahontas, the daughter of Wahunsunacawh, paramount chief of the Chesapeake Bay Powhatans, enjoyed an audience with King James during her visit to England in 1616, sitting at the king's side during a performance of a Twelfth Night masque.[55] Other Native people used English transatlantic routes to communicate with English governmental officials in writing. In 1646, several sachems of the Narragansett tribe of southern New England conveyed an "Act of Submission" to English authorities by way of an English traveler. The sachems signed the document with pictographs. In response to the tribe's submission, Parliament extended the tribe the protection of the English crown.[56] While the Narragansetts were successful in their attempt to form an alliance with the English crown, most Native people who attempted to communicate with European governments were ignored, and many who traveled across the Atlantic never returned home.

Just as theological concerns had shaped Spanish responses to and controversies about Amerindian representation, debates over Native languages took on added urgency in North American evangelical ventures. In the seventeenth century, English efforts at missionary outreach were narrower in scope than those of their Spanish counterparts. Still, the Anglican Church devoted significant attention to Indians in

Introduction

Virginia.[57] And, while lacking state funding, later Puritan efforts received considerable support from philanthropic societies such as the Society for the Propagation of the Gospel. These missionary endeavors produced an extensive archive of indigenous texts. Early English evangelism of Algonquian-speaking peoples was largely directed by John Eliot, a Cambridge-educated minister who immigrated to Boston as part of the Great Migration. Rejecting the commonly held notion that Native languages were too primitive to communicate religious concepts, Eliot viewed Algonquian languages as a potential channel for converting Native people. Starting in the late 1640s, Eliot learned to speak Massachusett by living among Christian converts in southern New England. In the 1650s he translated the Bible into the Massachusett language and printed several hundred copies on colonial presses (this Bible, titled *Mamusse Wunneetupanatamwe Up-Biblum God*, was the first Bible to be printed in the English colonies). While the immediate intended audience for these publications consisted of "praying Indians," or Native converts to Christianity, Eliot's printed materials also circulated among colonial Puritans and financial supporters in England, who rewarded his progress with donations. While Eliot's linguistic labors were accompanied by concerted efforts to eradicate other aspects of Algonquian culture, such as customary dress, diet, and religious practices, Eliot's mission offered an important venue for Native expression. As well as learning Massachusett from Native people who listened to his preaching, Eliot hired Native people as translators and typesetters and submitted the manuscript of his Massachusett-language Bible to Native converts for review. Indigenous collaborators such as James Printer, John Sassamon, and Job Nesutan profoundly shaped the printed output of Eliot's mission. Eliot also arranged for the publication of religious confessions in indigenous voices in an attempt to prove to ministerial elites that Natives were genuine converts. The Eliot archive has been a site of scholarly contest for some time; early historians of the colonial period such as Cotton Mather argued about the meaning of Eliot's legacy for later generations of Puritans, while antiquarians collected and sold Eliot's books and archived them in university and state libraries. More recently, a new generation of scholars has used Eliot's archive to expand the concepts of authorship and literacy to include Native contributions and ways of reading.[58]

Though involving cooperation between Native converts and English ministers, Eliot's publishing ventures were hardly insulated from the tense and often violent politics of the North American frontier. Eliot viewed print as a vehicle for God's Word, but other English and Indians saw the intercultural circulation of printed materials as a potentially threatening development.[59] However much Puritans berated Catholics for what they considered superficial conversion tactics, the English, French, and Spanish shared a common association of books and writing with imperial power. Roger Williams reported that the Narragansetts had neither "*Clothes, Bookes*, nor *Letters*, and conceive their *Fathers* never had; and therefore they are easily perswaded that the *God* that made *English* men is a greater *God*, because Hee hath so richly endowed the *English* above *themselves*."[60] The anxieties and aspirations that surrounded print as a sign of European cultural superiority came to a head during King Philip's War (from roughly 1675 to 1676), which was in part triggered by the murder of John Sassamon, one of Eliot's collaborators. Eliot's communities of praying Indians were subject to violent reprisals by both sides and eventually resettled at the behest of Eliot and other sympathetic ministers. Warring parties also apparently perpetrated similar violence on Eliot's Bibles. In a letter written in the 1680s, Eliot lamented that "all the Bibles and Testaments were carried away and, burnt or destroyed" in the war.[61] The decision to target printed materials reveals the religious and cultural meanings attached to print culture by both English and Indian groups. Recent archaeological excavations of Algonquian burial grounds have also found pieces of English religious materials incorporated into Native funerary culture, suggesting the numerous kinds of symbolic value that could attach to printed and written materials as they were transmitted across cultural and racial boundaries.[62]

French settlers and Iroquois-allied Native groups in the Great

Lakes region also struggled over the meaning of writing and the role of communication technologies in political and religious rituals. While English missions were constrained by lack of funding and waning metropolitan interest, Jesuit priests in New France received steadier state endorsement and from 1611 to 1811 continuously published accounts of their interactions with the Iroquois and other groups. Eventually collected and printed in the late nineteenth century, *The Jesuit Relations* have begun to receive renewed interest from scholars as a multigeneric archival record of European and indigenous interactions. They also provide a glimpse of the way missionaries and colonists recognized and even valorized Native political media for strategic purposes.[63] Writing about treaty negotiations in 1645, for example, a Jesuit priest drew an analogy between writing and wampum, arguing that the strings of beads serve "the same function as writing and contracts among us."[64] Iroquois leaders conferred a similar recognition on European accounting technologies, citing the "Pen-and-Ink Work" of Jesuit scribes. The reflexive attention to communication in French, English, Dutch, and other northern European government archives suggests the extent to which struggles over the medium of record keeping were often bound up with conflicts over the terms and scope of political alliances.

As with codices and other Amerindian records, written accounts of European and indigenous interactions gained considerable currency in European philosophical and scientific circles. The European encounter with Native North America unfolded against the backdrop of renewed inquiries by many early modern thinkers into the link between language and cultural difference. Many of these thinkers viewed linguistic variation as a result of God's toppling of the Tower of Babel and the splintering of an ancient, universal language into mutually incomprehensible offshoots. The vernacular languages of European nations were seen as inferior or debased tongues that had lost the unity between word and object that had characterized sign systems before the Fall. To many European theorists, the sprawling linguistic diversity of the Americas seemed to supply a missing link that could be used to trace language back to its primeval form.[65] European in-tellectuals scanned indigenous texts for resemblances to ancient lan-guages. Surveying reports from the colonies, Thomas Thorowgood saw similarities between Algonquian languages and Old Testament He-brew, observing that "very many of [the Indians'] words are like the Hebrew," while Thomas Morton found that "the Natives of this coun-try, doe use very many wordes both of Greeke and Latine, to the same signification that the Latins and Greeks have done."[66] Observations of Indian rituals, sign languages, and other forms of communication seemed to have biblical resonance as well. In the late sixteenth cen-tury, treatises on the arts of gestural rhetoric such as Guillaume Tar-dif's *Rhetorice artis ac oratorie facultatis compendium* (1475) were translated into multiple languages, as Reformed intellectuals sought to trace contemporary gestural and sign systems back to their roots in biblical systems of communication. Colonial writers pointed to ges-tural communication between Europeans and Indians as evidence of a residual, universal language of signs gradually degraded by the way-ward course of postlapsarian history. Such links between indigenous and biblical sign systems only increased the sense of apocalyptic ur-gency already felt by many Reformed thinkers and philosophers.

Debates over evangelical communication on the frontier coincided with changes in the way many European philosophers understood the concept of language and its relationship to history. As Edward G. Gray has shown, while many Reformed thinkers saw European and Amer-ican languages as deriving from a single prelapsarian source, in the eighteenth century, Enlightenment thinkers increasingly came to view language as a social convention that varied in complexity and reflected different levels of national and cultural attainment. Accounts of Amer-ican languages served as the basis for arguments about the environ-mental basis of human capacities and cultures.[67] In *An Essay Concerning Human Understanding* (1690), John Locke cited the radical difference of indigenous tongues from European counterparts as evi-dence that language was a contingent and local phenomenon rather than a medium for articulating innate concepts. Locke pointed to the supposed simplicity of indigenous languages as a counterargument against claims for the prehistoric unity of language. "The terms of [English] law," he wrote, "will hardly find words that answer them in the Spanish or Italian, no scanty languages; much less, I think, could any one translate them into the Caribbee or Westoe tongues."[68] Linguistic hierarchies also informed Enlightenment philosophies of history. In his *Scienza Nuova* (1725), Giambattista Vico pointed to the poetic nature of American Indian languages as evidence that early peoples understood the world in terms of divine rather than rational order. "This is now confirmed by the American Indians," he wrote, "who call gods all the things that surpass their small understanding."[69] For Vico and other Enlightenment thinkers, comparisons between European and Indian languages offered a glimpse into the historical emergence of supposedly civilized cultures from backward and savage ones.

The philosophical interest in Native languages in Enlightenment circles created publishing opportunities for American thinkers located at the margins of European academic discourse. With the rise of American literary, historical, and anthropological studies in the nineteenth century, philosophers and scientific investigators increasingly came to view indigenous materials as objects of ethnographic inquiry. In *Notes on the State of Virginia* (1785), Thomas Jefferson drew on seventeenth-century surveys by the Virginia Assembly to provide European readers with a map of North American indigenous politics and languages. Jefferson emphasized his own location on formerly indigenous-owned territory in order to add credibility to his account of indigenous languages and history, even going so far as to describe personally unearthing a barrow or Indian mound in order to supply answers to archaeological speculation. "I first dug superficially in several parts of [the mound]," he wrote, "and came to collections of human bones, at different depths, from six inches to three feet below the surface."[70] Jefferson's decision to focus on funerary practices ironically reflected the ways archaeological scrutiny denied the existence of contemporary Indian groups. Jefferson decried the lost ethnographic opportunities occasioned by the displacement of Indian tribes. "It is to be lamented," he wrote, "that we have suffered so many of the Indian tribes already to extinguish, without our having previously collected and deposited in the records of literature, the general rudiments at least of the languages they spoke."[71] Colonial and early national officials collected wordlists of Indian languages in order to ameliorate the loss of ethnographic information that accompanied Indian removal. These vocabularies were the subject of fierce debate among various communities of investigators. While Jefferson argued that the astounding variety of American languages was the result of the ancientness of American civilizations, ethnologists such as Benjamin Barton argued that all indigenous languages came from "one great stock," with differences instead reflecting the environmental shaping of human cultures.[72] Underlying such debates was the assumption that Indian languages reflected historically backward peoples and therefore offered a window into the distant origins of American civilization.[73]

In addition to sparking the imagination of Jefferson and other learned inquirers, the record of the continent's first inhabitants also inspired antiquarian interest. Shortly after the American Revolution, newly formed organizations such as the American Antiquarian Society and the Massachusetts Historical Society began to catalog and print colonial materials in an effort to document the prehistory of the United States. These nationalist collections retroactively framed early colonial history as the origin point of U.S. democratic institutions and reprinted colonial materials in order to "trace the progress of society in the United States."[74] The indigenous contents embedded in colonial materials, such as pictographic signatures or transcriptions of Native languages, were framed as relics of vanished peoples whose disappearance was the precondition for the emergence of the U.S. state. The Massachusetts Historical Society printed numerous colonial texts with indigenous materials, including Daniel Gookin's manuscript account of the history of New England's praying Indians as well as Williams's *A Key into the Language of America*. The society also formatted other kinds of indigenous-authored materials for print publication, such as an inscription copied from a gravestone at Gay Head and letters to colonial governors from King Philip and the Sakonnet sachem Awashonks. These collections privileged print as a mode for preserving historical documents. The "Introductory Address" to the first volume of the Collections of the Massachusetts Historical Society, penned by Jeremy Belknap, argued that "the art of printing affords a mode of preservation more effectual than Corinthian brass or Egyptian marble; for statues and pyramids which have long survived the wreck of time, are unable to tell the names of their sculptors, or the date of their foundations."[75] Like ancient techniques for preserving historical information, the indigenous languages and communication practices depicted in colonial texts stood in contrast to the progressive archival institution of print publication, which was portrayed as secure from historical obsolescence. The documentary collections of the Massachusetts Historical Society and New England Genealogical Society were models for the publications of other state and regional historical societies later founded in the American South and Midwest, which reprinted indigenous materials alongside other forms of historical miscellany. They also inspired accounts of Native America in popular fiction and poetry by professional writers such as Henry Wadsworth Longfellow, James Fenimore Cooper, and John Augustus Stone, who saw the "vanishing Indian" of early national ethnography as a theme for a uniquely American literature.[76] Many of these organizations are still active today, and they sponsor much early American research; the archival politics of today's work on the colonial era are intertwined with the imperatives of these organizations and their histories in ways that have yet to be fully articulated.

The state and federal bureaucracies created to manage political relations with Indian tribes were important venues for the publication of many kinds of Native materials. Throughout the nineteenth century, agents and missionaries working with government agencies collected vocabularies, oral stories, maps, and representational objects such as blankets, pipes, and ceramics. These items often served as the basis for ethnological accounts that in turn informed federal policy. The missionary John Heckewelder used his government offices to collect information about Northeastern groups, eventually publishing his *Account of the History, Manners, and Customs of the Indian Nations Who Once Inhabited Pennsylvania and the Neighboring States* (1818). The Indian agent Henry Rowe Schoolcraft collaborated with his wife, the Ojibwe Jane Johnston Schoolcraft, on collections of Ojibwe stories as well as volumes of ethnological research. The Schoolcrafts' work sought to codify indigenous storytelling as an "oral imaginative lore" that existed alongside print-bound European literary traditions.[77] The conclusion of the Indian Wars and the closing of the frontier created numerous documentary opportunities for investigators working in other media as well. Painters, photographers, and stage performers followed settlers and expanding government agencies to western territories and collected material culture, stories, and songs and recorded scenes from plains life.[78] These books, images, and performances often used printed and photographic representations of indigenous oral culture and traditional practices to critique white modernity and overdevelopment. They also made celebrities of prominent figures in the Indian Wars, such as Black Elk, who toured the United States and Europe re-creating Plains rituals and performances as popular entertainment for mass audiences.

Federal policy shaped Native self-representation as well. While government agents, missionaries, and anthropologists published versions of Native languages and communication ways, Native people authored manuscript and printed accounts of their own cultures for both white and indigenous reading publics. Native authors such as William Apess, David Cusick, and William Warren circulated and published histories that rebutted claims of Native "disappearance" and asserted the historical continuity of indigenous nations. As the literary historian Maureen Konkle has shown, this counter-historiographic movement challenged federal removal policy by using printed renditions of storytelling and ritual traditions to assert tribes' status as sovereign nations with valid claims to land tenure.[79] In 1825 the Cherokee Nation adopted an alphabetic system devised by Sequoyah and later began printing the *Cherokee Phoenix*, a dual-language newspaper that circulated among Cherokee towns in North Carolina, Virginia, Alabama, and elsewhere. The newspaper reported on laws, government proceedings, land transactions, and other features of Cherokee nationhood that mirrored those of Western nation-states. It also included accounts of religious practices, oral stories, and poetry and fiction authored by members of the tribe. Yet in most places there were severe constraints on the access of Native people to the print public sphere. Recent scholarship has pointed to the necessity of looking at diaries, religious confessions, student work from reservation boarding schools and missions, illustrations, and marginalia in religious and pedagogical materials in order to recover the broadest possible archive of nineteenth-century Native American writings.[80]

The twentieth and twenty-first centuries have seen a flowering of indigenous self-representation across the Americas, often in oppositional public spheres that coalesced around movements for sovereignty, territorial reclamation, and citizenship rights. As José Rabasa has pointed out, these new frameworks for thinking about indigenous symbolic systems and their politics—particularly the notion of resistance and domination working in complex, interlaced ways—"could not have been formulated before the dissolution of the colonial world after World War II and the postcolonial condition of thought we associate with Frantz Fanon and, in general, with the emergence of a native intellectual elite that contests the historical and epistemological privileges of the metropolis."[81] The latter, of course, happened in the United States and Canada under a continuing state of colonial relations—one that, with the rise of reservation gaming in the United States, has forced a considerably more complex engagement with different theories of sovereignty. In North America this has often taken the form of a valorization and remediation of oral tradition, in forms ranging from recorded music and film to every genre (and emerging genres) of published, often popular, imaginative writing. But just as often, both in tribal museums (or the new National Museum of the American Indian) and in cultural festivals and powwows, challenging state-to-reservation relations has involved foregrounding other-than-textual media such as dance, song, music, film and video, and a broad range of material arts. The Native American Graves Protection and Repatriation Act, passed in 1990, seems to reverse the nineteenth-century terms of museum remediation, putting the question of who owns Native representations of and from the past at the center of a series of important lawsuits that have altered attitudes toward indigenous signifying practices and caused controversies about the curatorship of the past. The Indian Arts and Crafts Board of the U.S. Department of the Interior places two-page spreads in in-flight magazines, reminding Indian art buyers that their activity is regulated by the state to ensure that "the Native American heritage and tribal affiliation of the producer" are "marketed truthfully."[82] This policy reflects a collaboration between sovereignty objectives and commercial strategies characteristic of many of the legal compromises of the past few decades that have brought some indigenous North American groups to renewed cultural, economic, and political power. In this way, private, public, and academic archives of indigenous representation continue to evolve under changing political conditions and in a shifting relationship to ongoing Native signification.

From the most recent of these conditions and relationships emerge a series of questions taken up in the essays that follow. How did colonial societies understand the relationship between indigenous information technologies and social power? What would literary studies look like—more precisely, what new questions and problems could be identified—if we embrace nontextual media and move beyond the oral-literate dynamic? How did power relations within and between colonial societies shape themselves through questions about and competing (or sometimes harmonious) theories of communication? And given that, as we have seen above, indigenous Indian, Amerindian, African, and other cultures' forms of representation early became the occasion for a series of global-scale arguments about human progress, race, and national destiny—indeed, even the idea of "the human" itself—what might be gained from raising these questions in a series of colonial places across the Americas?

Hemispheric treatment of colonization can bring great leverage to bear on old problems and, as we have been suggesting, can allow us to ask new questions. But there are important caveats to be considered when employing such analyses. Because of intense imperial competition, religious differences, and trade restrictions, comparison has been an important modality of scholarly approaches to colonization. The history of interactions among indigenous groups complicates the picture more; Daniel Richter, among others, goes so far as to suggest we might understand the North American wars of the eighteenth century as in no small way playing out long-standing American Indian intergroup tensions, not just French, Dutch, English, and Iberian claims to Indian territory. As Ralph Bauer observes, early Americanists taking a hemispheric approach "typically juxtaposed two or more texts originating from throughout the Western hemisphere either on the basis of larger, transnational generic, formal, or aesthetic movements (as did Owen Aldridge), or on the basis of some common historical experiences in the New World (racial and cultural encounters and mixtures, for example, or the experience of creole settler colonialism)."[83]

There have been objections to this formal or experiential comparative model. Cañizares-Esguerra has argued that comparisons sometimes fall into an exceptionalist or essentialist reification of categories that are themselves products of colonialism—such as an imagined impermeable imperial membrane between Protestantism and Catholicism—and that instead we should focus on a shared Christian ontology.[84] Mignolo's *The Darker Side of the Renaissance* questions the comparative frameworks in which studies of American colonization proceed, unfolding through concepts like the book, genres, history, religion, property, or geography.[85] It is easy to find analogues across cultures for all of these concepts, but doing so hazards mismatching (even at times erasing) important ways of seeing and being. At the same time, such analogies risk, inasmuch as they work from one cultural location toward others, blindness to non-analogical features across cultures. Attention to the processes and locations of comparison, then, becomes central. The essays in this volume describe, in different ways, colonial communications exchanges and their predicates and reflect on our ways of describing them. They draw differing conclusions about the values and risks of intercultural analysis in the colonial relation; the tension between these conclusions, we hope, will not merely represent different critical attitudes but serve the purpose of fueling our readers' awareness of those locations and processes of comparison that constitute fields of study at this moment in time.

Another complication of doing comparisons is the difference between legal cultures. A focus on formal continuities in literature and religion stops short of addressing this difficulty. Rabasa's blanket declaration that "laws determine texts that organize the world for colonization" isn't entirely true: that would be to swing all the power of determination to law and writing—to re-create the problem of technological determinism on the humanistic end of the spectrum.[86] One must confront the importance of differences in major approaches to law; Patricia Seed's discussion of the unharmonious ways colonizing powers laid claim to property is a good example. But we must also attend to the ways those laws evolved in complex, rich local settings of adaptation, non-enforcement, and precedence.[87]

Rabasa mentions the difficulty of understanding the collective quality of many Amerindian utterances or inscriptions.[88] This is a widespread dynamic across American cultures—but often the locally specific class or role of the writers matters as much as anything else in understanding the social force of a document or statement. Formal analysis of indigenous representation may be usefully rooted less in romantically unified communities than in specific understandings of how boundaries or interests *within* those communities are constructed, as well as that community's relations with perceived-to-be-outside audiences. To complicate matters, the "oral" is valorized by many indigenous collectivities as a cultural possession, a mark of distinction and formal uniqueness. Critiques of the oral-literate divide from the academy must confront the fact that for contemporary tribes within the United States, "oral culture" is often an important form of evidence for proving a tribe's historical existence and initiating legal challenges to state and federal governments. The contested history of terms such as "oral culture" suggests the extent to which media categories are the products of inter- and intracultural struggle as much as of the triumph of colonial classification systems.[89]

Another commonality of the many forms of indigenous media is that they tend to speak to one or another major question in anthropology or history—wampum to the political history of northeast North America; codices to the history of Mesoamerica; khipus to the question of how a vast empire was managed without writing. Seen in this larger perspective, the recognition of indigenous communication practices *as systems*—cultural and political expressions at the level of forms and protocols, not just content—is central to continuing struggles over sovereignty across the Americas. Hitherto that discussion has taken place on Western terms; nation-states have been viewed as expanding entities within a global order, while tribes are rooted in specific territories and local political spheres. Appadurai suggests that with challenges to the nation-state form, different accounts of media and systems of cultural differentiation may emerge from a broader crisis in Western understandings of the complexity and historical duration of nation-states. The reconfigurations of state order that have accompanied globalization have provoked remappings of indigenous communication systems beyond the public spheres of the "domestic dependent nation," with its implied localism and explicit relation to a paternalistic state. The reconstitution of historical tribes from geographically dispersed descendants and the emergence of indigenous groups as major forces in the global tourism and gaming industries have led to a redefinition of tribes as potentially global entities. They have also led to a corresponding revival of extra-local possibilities within historically indigenous communication systems.

"At this point," Mignolo writes, "the question is no longer how to use the enlightening guidance of Western notions of rationality in order to understand colonial, postcolonial, and Third World experiences but, rather, how to think from hybrid conceptual frameworks and spaces in between."[90] New media conditions can help us talk differently about the colonial period—though thinking from between spaces is difficult, not least because it foregrounds the question of the locations of our own academic or personal politics just at the moment we would hope to offer a model for transcending such politics. We now accept alternative literacies as an idea, yet we have few means for engaging them institutionally in the United States. Colonial negotiations and appropriations remain a vital place for rethinking representation and power, as much as for unearthing violent pasts—for changing how we speak, from particular places and archives.

Notes

1. Isaac Taylor, *The History of the Alphabet: An Account of the Origin and Development of Letters*, 2 vols. (London: Kegan Paul, Trench, 1883–99).
2. Sandra M. Gustafson, "The Emerging Media of Early America," *Proceedings of the American Antiquarian Society* 115.2 (October 2005): 205–50, quote on 229; N. Katherine Hayles, *My Mother Was a Computer: Digital Subjects and Literary Texts* (Chicago: University of Chicago Press, 2005), esp. 15–61; Martin Lienhard, "Las prácticas textuales indígenas: Aproximaciones a un nuevo objeto de investigación," *Nuevo Texto Crítico* 7.14–15 (1994–95): 78; and the special issue of *Ethnohistory* edited by Frank Salomon and Sabine Hyland on the topic of "Graphic Pluralism: Native American Systems of Inscription and the Colonial Situation," *Ethnohistory* 57.1 (Winter 2010). For other important media studies interventions see Lisa Gitelman, *Always Already New: Media, History, and the Data of Culture* (Cambridge: MIT Press, 2006); Jay David Bolter and Richard Grusin, *Remediation: Understanding New Media* (Cambridge: MIT Press, 2000); and Friedrich Kittler, *Discourse Networks, 1800/1900* (Stanford: Stanford University Press, 1992).
3. Wai Chee Dimock, *Through Other Continents: American Literature across Deep Time* (Princeton: Princeton University Press, 2008), 157.
4. In this we follow, among other leads, Frank Salomon's encouragement of "a more omnidirectional model of inscription." Salomon, *The Cord Keepers: Khipus and Cultural Life in a Peruvian Village* (Durham: Duke University Press, 2004), 6.
5. See Matthew P. Brown, "The Tiger's Leap and the Dog's Paw: Method, Matter, and Meaning in the History of the Book," *Early American Literature* 44.3 (2009): 657–75.

6. Lux Vidal, *Grafismo indígena: Estudios de antropología estética* (São Paulo: Livros Studio Nobel, 1992).

7. Other scholars have asserted genealogical connections between the information age and structural precedents in the colonial era; see Bernhard Siegert's argument about the bureaucratic "rasterization" of Spanish colonial settlement, historiography, and the development of information technology in *Passage des Digitalen: Zeichenpraktiken der neuzeitlichen Wissenschaften, 1500–1900* (Berlin: Brinkmann & Bose, 2003), esp. 65–119; and in the North American context see Albert Borgmann, *Holding On to Reality: The Nature of Information at the Turn of the Millennium* (Chicago: University of Chicago Press, 1999).

8. Walter Mignolo, "Literacy and Colonization: The New World Experience," in *1492/1993: Re/discovering Colonial Writing*, ed. René Jara and Nicholas Spadaccini, Hispanic Issues 4 (Minneapolis: Prisma Institute, 1989), 51–96, quote on 62.

9. Elizabeth Hill Boone, introduction to *Writing without Words: Alternative Literacies in Mesoamerica and the Andes*, ed. Elizabeth Hill Boone and Walter Mignolo (Durham: Duke University Press, 1994), 15.

10. Joanne Rappaport, "Object and Alphabet: Andean Indians and Documents in the Colonial Period," in Boone and Mignolo, 271–92, quote on 271. See also Joanne Rappaport, *The Politics of Memory: Native Historical Interpretation in the Colombian Andes* (Cambridge: Cambridge University Press, 1990); and Joyce Marcus, *Mesoamerican Writing Systems: Propaganda, Myth, and History in Four Ancient Civilizations* (Princeton NJ: Princeton University Press, 1992).

11. Arjun Appadurai, *Modernity at Large: Cultural Dimensions of Globalization* (Minneapolis: University of Minnesota Press, 1996). Today, the nation-state is still going strong; a reflection on the way nation-states emerged out of the fragmentation of the colonial era might suggest the form's potential for surviving the new electronic and culturalist landscape.

12. Appadurai, *Modernity at Large*, 21. Still, there are important examples of the attempt to bring something like Jürgen Habermas's notion of the "public sphere" into the discussion of colonization before 1700; see, e.g., Phillip Round, *By Nature and by Custom Cursed: Transatlantic Civil Discourse and New England Cultural Production, 1620–1660* (Hanover NH: University Press of New England, 1999); and Jonathan Beecher Field, *Errands into the Metropolis: New England Dissidents in Revolutionary London* (Hanover NH: University Press of New England, 2009).

13. See, e.g., Hilary Wyss and Kristina Bross, *Early Native Literacies in New England: A Documentary and Critical Anthology* (Amherst: University of Massachusetts Press, 2008); and Greg Sarris, *Mabel McKay: Weaving the Dream* (Berkeley: University of California Press, 1997).

14. Rolena Adorno, "Literary Production and Suppression: Reading and Writing about Amerindians in Colonial Spanish America," *Dispositio* 11.28–29 (1986): 6. A revised version of this essay is chapter 8 in Adorno's *The Polemics of Possession in Spanish American Narrative* (New Haven: Yale University Press, 2007).

15. Diego de Landa, *Yucatan before and after the Conquest* (ed. 1978), chapter 41, quoted in Walter Mignolo, "Signs and Their Transmission: The Question of the Book in the New World," in Boone and Mignolo, *Writing without Words*, 220–70, quote on 223.

16. José Rabasa, *Writing Violence on the Northern Frontier: The Historiography of Sixteenth-Century New Mexico and Florida and the Legacy of Conquest* (Durham: Duke University Press, 2000), 9. Rabasa's study, like Frank Salomon's, was published in the series Latin America Otherwise: Languages, Empires, Nations, one of several that link critical studies of language and representation to the study of empires and colonialism, and coedited by Walter Mignolo. See also Serge Gruzinski, *Conquest of Mexico: The Incorporation of Indian Societies into the Western World, 16th-18th Centuries* (Cambridge, U.K.: Polity Press, 1993).

17. Jorge Cañizares-Esguerra, *How to Write the History of the New World: Histories, Epistemologies, and Identities in the Eighteenth-Century Atlantic World* (Stanford: Stanford University Press, 2001), 74.

18. Rabasa, *Writing Violence*, 18.

19. Barbara Mundy, *The Mapping of New Spain: Indigenous Cartography and the Maps of the Relaciones Geográficas* (Chicago: University of Chicago Press, 1996), 92; Cañizares-Esguerra, *How to Write the History*.

20. See also Marion Oettinger Jr., *Lienzos coloniales: Una exposición de pinturas de terrenos communales de México, siglos XVI–XIX* (Mexico City: UNAM, Instituto de Investigaciones Antropológicas). Many of these maps are in the Benson Latin American Collection at the University of Texas at Austin; some are in Spain at the Real Academia de la Historia in Madrid and the Archivo General de Indias in Seville; others are in the Archivo General de la Nación in Mexico; and there are scattered examples elsewhere.

21. Salomon, *Cord Keepers*, xvii.

22. Salomon asserts that, with the exception of the work of Carlos Radicati di Primeglio, "khipu studies . . . have erred by ignoring material traces of use as opposed to design" (*Cord Keepers*, 16); see also Gary Urton, *Signs of the Inca Khipu: Binary Coding in the Andean Knotted-String Records* (Austin: University of Texas Press, 2003). Interestingly, there may be parallel long-term uses of the *mapas* and *lienzos* echoing from the days of the *relaciones geográficas*. See Marion Oettinger Jr. and Fernando Horcasitas, *The Lienzo of Petlacala: A Pictorial Document from Guerrero, Mexico* (Philadelphia: American Philosophical Society, 1982), which suggests the Petlacala *lienzo* may have been updated until at least the 1950s.

23. Mundy, *Mapping of New Spain*, xx.

24. Mignolo, "Signs and Their Transmission," 234.

25. See Mignolo, "Signs and Their Transmission," 235.

26. Jaun de Torquemada, *Monarquía indiana*, 4th ed., Biblioteca Porrúa, vols. 41–43 (Mexico City: Porrúa, 1969), 1:418.

27. Cañizares-Esguerra, *How to Write the History*, 67.

28. Cañizares-Esguerra, *How to Write the History*, 68.

29. Marshall McLuhan made perhaps the most influential formulation of the relationship between alphabetic print systems and modernity; "Typography ended parochialism and tribalism," he claimed, and "had psychic and social consequences that suddenly shifted previous boundaries and patterns of cultures." McLuhan, *Understanding Media: The Extensions of Man* (London: Sphere, 1967), 94. John Halverston has deconstructed Goody's "literacy thesis," including the notion that abstract thought and logical structures emerge from writing; Halverston, "Goody and the Implosion of the Literacy Thesis," *Man* 27 (1992): 301–17; Jack Goody and Ian Watt, "The Consequences of Literacy," *Comparative Studies in Society and History* 5.3 (1963): 304–45. See also Maurice Bloch, "Literacy and Enlightenment," in *Literacy and Society*, ed. Karen Schousboe and Mogens Trolle Larsen (Copenhagen: Akademiske Forlag, 1989), 15–37. Other important studies of writing include Ignace J. Gelb, *A Study of Writing*, 2nd ed. (Chicago: University of Chicago Press, 1963); and Walter Ong, *Orality and Literacy: The Technologizing of the Word* (New York: Methuen, 1982).

30. Giambattista Vico, *The New Science of Giambattista Vico*, trans. Thomas Goddard Bergin and Max Harold Fisch (Ithaca NY: Cornell University Press, 1948); Cornelius de Pauw, *Recherches philosophiques sur les Américains* (London: 1771).

31. Adorno, *The Polemics of Possession*.

32. Walter Mignolo, "Afterword: Writing and Recorded Knowledge in Colonial and Postcolonial Situations," in Boone and Mignolo, *Writing without Words*, 309. On collecting Amerindian scripts and images see also Paula Findlen, *Possessing Nature: Museums, Collecting, and Scientific Culture in Early Modern Italy* (Berkeley: University of California Press, 1994).

33. Alfredo Chavero, *Antigüedades mexicanas publicadas por la Junta Colombina de Mexico en el cuarto centenario del descubrimiento de América*, 2 vols. (Mexico City: Oficina Tipográfica de la Secretaría de Fomento, 1892). For a similar conjunction of celebrating the quatercentenary with indigenous media history in the United States, see Garrick Mallery, *Picture-Writing of the American Indians*, 2 vols. (Washington DC: Smithsonian, 1893). For more on centennials and indigeneity, see the special issue edited by Luis Cárcamo-Huechante and Álvaro Fernández Bravo of the *Revista de Crítica Literaria Latinoamericana* 71 (2010): esp. the editors' introduction, "Re-visiones Críticas: Independencias, Centenarios y Bicentenarios," 11–26.

34. José Toribio Medina, *La imprenta en México (1539–1821)*, 8 vols. (Santiago de Chile: Casa de Medina, 1912).

35. Rolena Adorno, introduction to *Books of the Brave: Being an Account of Books and of Men in the Spanish Conquest and Settlement of the Sixteenth-Century New World*, by Irving A. Leonard (Berkeley: University of California Press, 1992), ix–xl, quote on xi.

36. See, e.g., John V. Murra, *Formaciones económicas y políticas del mundo andino* (1956; Lima: Instituto de Estudios Peruanos, 1975); Miguel León-Portilla, *The Broken Spears: The Aztec Account of the Conquest of Mexico*, trans. Lysander Kemp (Boston: Beacon Press, 1962); Ángel María Garibay Kintana, *Historia de la literatura Nahuatl*, 2 vols. (Mexico City: Porrúa, 1953–54); and Edmundo O'Gorman, *The Invention of America: An Inquiry into the Historical Nature of the New World and the Meaning of Its History* (Bloomington: Indiana University Press, 1961),

37. For an overview of the Latin American context and an argument that relates such activism to long-standing local networks, see Deborah J. Yashar, "Contesting Citizenship: Indigenous Movements and Democracy in Latin America," *Comparative Politics* 31.1 (October 1998): 23–42.

38. Fray Bernardino de Sahagún, *Florentine Codex: General History of the Things of New Spain*, trans. Arthur O. J. Anderson and Charles E. Dibble (Salt Lake City and Santa Fe: University of Utah Press and School of

American Research, 1950–82); Bartolomé de Las Casas, *In Defense of the Indians*, trans. Stafford Poole (De Kalb: Northern Illinois University Press, 1974); and see in general the work of Howard F. Cline, George Kubler, and Donald Robertson.

39. See, e.g., Sandra M. Gustafson, *Eloquence Is Power: Oratory and Performance in Early America* (Chapel Hill: University of North Carolina Press, 2000); Joshua David Bellin, *Medicine Bundle: Indian Sacred Performance and American Literature, 1824–1932* (Philadelphia: University of Pennsylvania Press, 2008); and Susan P. Castillo, *Colonial Encounters in New World Writing, 1500–1786: Performing America* (New York: Routledge, 2006).

40. In what follows, we draw on Lois M. Feister, "Linguistic Communication between the Dutch and Indians in New Netherland, 1609–1664," *Ethnohistory* 20.1 (1973): 25–38; Edward G. Gray, *New World Babel: Languages and Nations in Early America* (Princeton NJ: Princeton University Press, 1999), 8–27; and James Axtell, "Babel of Tongues: Communicating with the Indians in Eastern North America," in *The Language Encounter in the Americas, 1492–1800*, ed. Edward G. Gray and Norman Fiering (New York: Berghahn Books, 2000), 15–60.

41. J. Franklin Jameson, ed., *Narratives of New Netherland* (New York: Scribner, 1909), 72; qtd. in Feister, "Linguistic Communication," 30.

42. William Wood, *New England's Prospect*, ed. Alden T. Vaughan (1634; reprint, Amherst: University of Massachusetts Press, 1977), 10; qtd. in Gray, *New World Babel*, 13.

43. John Lawson, *A New Voyage to Carolina* (1709; reprint Chapel Hill: University of North Carolina Press, 1967), 239; qtd. in Gray, *New World Babel*, 19.

44. Jameson, *Narratives of New Netherland*, 126; qtd. in Axtell, "Babel of Tongues," 36.

45. Karen Ordahl Kupperman, *Indians and English: Facing Off in Early America* (Ithaca NY: Cornell University Press, 2000), 83–84; Feister, "Linguistic Communication," 26–28.

46. Feister, "Linguistic Communication," 27.

47. James Rosier, "A True Relation of the Voyage of Captaine George Weymouth," in *Dawnland Encounters: Indians and Europeans in Northern New England*, ed. Colin G. Calloway (Hanover NH: University Press of New England, 1991), 39-40.

48. Henry Norwood, "A Voyage to Virginia. By Colonel Norwood" [1649], in *Tracts and Other Papers Relating to the Origin, Settlement, and Progress of*

the Colonies in North America, ed. Peter Force (Washington DC: 1836–47), vol. 3, no. 10, 39; qtd. in Axtell, "Babel of Tongues," 28.

49. For accounts of these figures, see Stephen Greenblatt, *Marvelous Possessions: The Wonder of the New World* (Chicago: University of Chicago Press, 1992), 119–51; and Frances Karttunen, "Interpreters Snatched from the Shore," in Gray and Fiering, *The Language Encounter*, 215–29.

50. Kupperman, *Indians and English*, 81.

51. See Michael Gaudio, *Engraving the Savage: The New World and Techniques of Civilization* (Minneapolis: University of Minnesota Press, 2008). See also Diana DiPaolo Loren, *In Contact: Bodies and Spaces in the Sixteenth- and Seventeenth-Century Eastern Woodlands* (Lanham MD: AltaMira Press, 2007), which discusses the importance of media such as tattoos and beadwork in articulating individual and group identities.

52. See Feister, "Linguistic Communication," 32–33.

53. Roger Williams, *A Key into the Language of America* (London, 1643), A2v.

54. See Field, *Errands into the Metropolis*, esp. 26–47.

55. Alden T. Vaughan, *Transatlantic Encounters: American Indians in Britain, 1500–1776* (Cambridge: Cambridge University Press, 2006), 87.

56. See Jenny Hale Pulsipher, *Subjects unto the Same King: Indians, English, and the Contest for Authority in Colonial New England* (Philadelphia: University of Pennsylvania Press, 2005), 30. See also Field, *Errands into the Metropolis*, 48–71.

57. Louis B. Wright, *Religion and Empire: The Alliance between Piety and Commerce in English Expansion, 1558–1625* (Chapel Hill: University of North Carolina Press, 1943).

58. Sacvan Bercovitch, *The American Jeremiad* (Madison: University of Wisconsin Press, 1978); Michael P. Clark, *The Eliot Tracts: With Letters from John Eliot to Thomas Thorowgood and Richard Baxter* (New York: Praeger, 2003); Kristina Bross, *Dry Bones and Indian Sermons: Praying Indians in Colonial America* (Ithaca NY: Cornell University Press, 2004; and Matthew P. Brown, *The Pilgrim and the Bee: Reading Rituals and Book Culture in Early New England* (Pennsylvania: University of Pennsylvania Press, 2007). For accounts that emphasize the Native acquisition of alphabetic literacy, see Hilary E. Wyss, *Writing Indians: Literacy, Christianity, and Native Community in Early America* (Amherst: University of Massachusetts Press, 2003); and Hilary E. Wyss, *English Letters and Indian Literacies: Reading, Writing, and New England Missionary Schools, 1750–1830* (Philadelphia: University of Pennsylvania Press, 2012).

59. Jill Lepore, *The Name of War: King Philip's War and the Origins of American Identity* (New York: Vintage, 1999).

60. Williams, *Key*, A4.

61. *Journal of Jasper Danckaerts, 1679–1680*, ed. Bartlett Burleigh James and J. Franklin Jameson (New York: Barnes and Noble, 1913), 264; qtd. in Gray, *New World Babel*, 78–79.

62. See e.g., Hugh Amory, "The Trout and the Milk: An Ethnobibliographical Essay," in Amory, *Bibliography and the Book Trades: Studies in the Print Culture of Early New England*, ed. David Hall (Philadelphia: University of Pennsylvania Press, 2004), 11–33.

63. Reuben Gold Thwaites, ed., *Jesuit Relations and Allied Documents*, 73 vols. (Cleveland: Burrows, 1898–1901); Birgit Brander Rasmussen, "Negotiating Peace, Negotiating Literacies: A French-Iroquois Encounter and the Making of Early American Literature," *American Literature* 79.3 (2007): 445–73.

64. Thwaites, ed., *Jesuit Relations*, 40:164; qtd. in Rasmussen, "Negotiating Peace," 445.

65. Gray, *New World Babel*, 28–55.

66. Thomas Thorowgood, *Jewes in America, or, Probabilities that the Americans are of that Race* (London: T. Slater, 1650), 15; qtd. in Gray, *New World Babel*, 24. Thomas Morton, *The New English Canaan*, in Force, *Tracts*, vol. 2, no. 5, 15; qtd. in Gray *New World Babel*, 25.

67. Gray, *New World Babel*, 85–111.

68. John Locke, *An Essay Concerning Human Understanding*, ed. Peter H. Nidditch (Oxford: Oxford University Press, 1975), III, v, 8; qtd. in Gray, *New World Babel*, 89.

69. Vico, *New Science*, 104–5.

70. Thomas Jefferson, *The Portable Thomas Jefferson*, ed. Merrill Peterson (New York: Penguin, 1977), 139.

71. Thomas Jefferson, *Notes on the State of Virginia*, ed. William Peden (New York: Norton, 1972), 101; qtd. in Gray, *New World Babel*, 114.

72. Benjamin Barton, *New Views of the Origin of the Tribes and Nations of America* (Philadelphia, 1797), lvi; qtd. in Gray, *New World Babel*, 130.

73. Gray, *New World Babel*, 112–58.

74. *Collections of the Massachusetts Historical Society* 1 (1792): 1.

75. *Collections*, 4.

76. See Alan Trachtenberg, *Shades of Hiawatha: Staging Indians, Making Americans, 1880–1930* (New York: Hill and Wang, 2004). For an account

of New England historical societies, see Jean M. O'Brien, *Firsting and Lasting: Writing Indians out of Existence in New England* (Minneapolis: University of Minnesota Press, 2010).

77. Henry Rowe Schoolcraft, *Algic Researches: Comprising Inquiries Respecting the Mental Characteristics of the North American Indians*, vol. 1, *Indian Tales and Legends* (New York, 1839), 31.

78. Philip J. Deloria, *Playing Indian* (New Haven: Yale University Press, 1999); Michael A. Elliott, *Custerology: The Enduring Legacy of the Indian Wars and George Armstrong Custer* (Chicago: University of Chicago Press, 2008); Mick Gidley, *Edward S. Curtis and the North American Indian, Incorporated* (New York: Cambridge University Press, 1998); and Joel Pfister, *Individuality Incorporated: Indians and the Multicultural Modern* (Durham: Duke University Press, 2004).

79. Maureen Konkle, *Writing Indian Nations: Native Intellectuals and the Politics of Historiography, 1827–1863* (Chapel Hill: University of North Carolina Press, 2006); Lisa Brooks, *The Common Pot: The Recovery of Native Space in the Northeast* (Minneapolis: University of Minnesota Press, 2008).

80. See Wyss, *Writing Indians*; Phillip Round, "Indigenous Illustration: Native American Artists and Nineteenth-Century U.S. Print Culture," *American Literary History* 19.2 (2007): 267–89; and Robert Warrior, *The People and the Word: Reading Native Nonfiction* (Minneapolis: University of Minnesota Press, 2005).

81. Rabasa, *Writing Violence*, 16.

82. Southwest Airlines, *Spirit*, November 2009, 52–53, quote on 53.

83. Ralph Bauer, "Early American Literature and American Literary History at the 'Hemispheric Turn,'" *American Literary History* 22.3 (2010): 250–65, quote on 219. Examples include Gordon Sayre, *Les Sauvages Américains: Representations of Native Americans in French and English Colonial Literature* (Chapel Hill: University of North Carolina Press, 1997); Jorge Cañizares-Esguerra, *Puritan Conquistadors: Iberianizing the Atlantic, 1550–1700* (Stanford: Stanford University Press, 2006); Susan Castillo and Ivy Schweitzer, *The Literatures of Colonial America: An Anthology* (London: Blackwell, 2001); and stretch back at least to Alfred Owen Aldridge's collection *Early American Literature: A Comparatist Approach* (Princeton NJ: Princeton University Press, 1982). See also David Boruchoff, "New Spain, New England, and the New Jerusalem: The 'Translation' of Empire, Faith, and Learning (translatio imperii, fidei ac scientiae) in the Colonial Missionary Project," *Early American Literature* 43.1 (2008): 5–34; Ralph Bauer,

"Notes on the Comparative Study of the Colonial Americas: Further Reflections on the Tucson Summit," *Early American Literature* 38.2 (2003): 281–304; and, for a recent overview of hemispheric approaches from an American studies–based standpoint, Caroline Levander and Robert S. Levine's introduction to their edited volume, *Hemispheric American Studies* (New Brunswick: Rutgers University Press, 2008), 1–17.

84. See Cañizares-Esguerra, *Puritan Conquistadors*.

85. Walter Mignolo, *The Darker Side of the Renaissance: Literacy, Territoriality, and Colonization* (Ann Arbor: University of Michigan Press, 1995). Mignolo's book is surprisingly undercited in American Indian intellectual work, considering how it articulates together concerns with territory and concerns with representation.

86. Rabasa, *Writing Violence*, 25.

87. See Patricia Seed, *Ceremonies of Possession in Europe's Conquest of the New World, 1492–1640* (Cambridge: Cambridge University Press, 1995); and Lauren Benton, *A Search for Sovereignty: Law and Geography in European Empires, 1400–1900* (Cambridge: Cambridge University Press, 2009).

88. Rabasa, *Writing Violence*, 13.

89. See also Matthew Sparke, "A Map That Roared and an Original Atlas: Canada, Cartography, and the Narration of Nation," *Annals of the Association of American Geographers* 88.3 (1998): 463–95; and the critique of oralism in Christopher Teuton, *Deep Waters: The Textual Continuum in American Indian Literature* (Lincoln: University of Nebraska Press, 2010), esp. 16–17.

90. Mignolo, *Darker Side*, 331.

PART I
BEYOND TEXTUAL MEDIA

I

Dead Metaphor or Working Model?

"THE BOOK" IN NATIVE AMERICA

Germaine Warkentin

A multidisciplinary convergence appears to be forming
towards a new narrative in which the last 30,000 years
of human cultural life are perceived . . . against the
background of evolutionary time rather than as the obscure
backdrop of ethnocentric conceptions of historical times—
the unfathomable night that preceded the rise
of civilization.

—PAUL BOUISSAC[1]

On July 12, 1562, Diego de Landa (1524–79), the bishop of Yucatán, ordered the friars at the Franciscan mission in Mani to put to the torch
a quantity of Mayan "idols," calendar scrolls (*katuns*), and "books." In
his 1566 *Relación de las cosas de Yucatán*, Landa observed of the *katuns*
that they must have been invented by the devil, or by some idolator
convinced of all the "principal deceits, divinations and delusions" under which, in his view, the benighted Mayans suffered. As for the "libros," he wrote,

these people also used certain glyphs or letters, in which they wrote down their ancient history and sciences in their books; and by means of these letters and figures and by certain marks contained in them, they could read about their affairs and taught others to read about them too. We found a great number of these books in Indian characters and because they contained nothing but superstition and the devil's falsehoods we burned them all; and this they felt most bitterly and it caused them great grief.

Unmoved by their grief, Landa also disinterred and burned the bones of a number of the Mayans themselves.[2]

Despite the physical differences between the familiar European codex and the novel Mayan artifacts, between the European alphabet and the Mayan glyphs, Landa clearly had no difficulty identifying the manuscripts he was burning as powerful objects of knowledge transfer, nor understanding the threat they posed to his duty to transform the inhabitants of Yucatán into good Christians. Thanks to him, only three of the pre-Hispanic Mayan books survive (plus the expected colonial documents), in libraries very far from Yucatán, a survival rate pattern resembling that of the Aztec and Mixtec codices.[3] Fair warning: that awkward phrase "objects of knowledge transfer" will occur again, as I struggle to avoid prejudicing my argument by using the term "book." I detest jargon, and have waited in vain for some more suitable term to occur to me, but perhaps it's just as well. My purpose in this essay is to defamiliarize the concept of "the book" so as to look with a different perspective on what explanatory capacity it offers, what (at the moment) it lacks, and how, if refreshed, it might throw open a door to new work on the many different types of objects used by Native peoples to record and transfer knowledge in the Americas. My focus on the materiality of books rather than the text (of whatever sort) inscribed in them is intentional, as will emerge; though Landa's aim was to destroy the Mayan texts, it was the physical objects he felt he had to burn in order to do it.

The bonfire of the Mayan codices is a notorious episode in the his-

Germaine Warkentin

tory of colonialism. It is also an important episode in the history of the book, the field in which I work. By "the book" we usually intend the wide range of portable objects in alphabetic symbols that European culture has produced over more than two millennia, everything from Graeco-Roman scrolls to eighteenth-century octavos to Victorian three-decker novels to modern newspapers. Intellectually, we tend to be settled comfortably in the area we call "print culture," studying the social practices of writing, production, circulation, and reading. We do so chiefly in terms of the book as a material object; reading cannot take place without an inscription to be read, but obviously nothing can be inscribed unless you have some material or other—the bibliographic term is *substrate*—on which to inscribe it. So evident does the priority of the book's materiality seem that it has been little theorized until the recent influence of poststructuralism, where epistemological doubts about the nature of material evidence have loomed large.[4] Textual critic Peter Shillingsburg, for example, began an influential 1991 article by stating the skeptical view that "objectivity is a chimera and that statements about facts, history and truth are relative—not actually 'knowable'—because of the gap in perception between object and subject (an inability to verify correspondence between mental constructs and 'real' objects)."[5]

Arjun Appadurai's essay "Disjuncture and Difference in the Global Cultural Economy" puts this uneasy sense of cognitive dissonance another way. "It takes only the merest acquaintance with the facts of the modern world," he observes, "to note that it is now an interactive system in a sense which is strikingly new."[6] The term "mediascape" is the second of the five "scapes" he proposes as an elementary framework for understanding the new phenomenon of information distribution in "a world in which both points of departure and points of arrival are in cultural flux, and thus the search for steady points of reference . . . can be very difficult."[7] His vision—on the face of it characteristically postmodernist—is of a world of disjunctive global flows that constantly present the individual with a radical experience of contingency. To the book historian, however, this picture of the operation of the media (of which books, of course, are part) seems neither postmodernist nor even particularly modern. In the history of the book as we know it, at least three such transformations have produced similar destabilizing effects: the shift from scroll to codex in the second and third centuries CE, the inception of printing with movable type in fifteenth-century Europe, and the digital revolution going on today. The difference between them is chiefly one of scale, for in all three cases our concept of what constitutes a "book" has had to be redefined. This has never been an easy task. In the fifteenth century the Duke of Urbino refused to permit a printed book to enter his library of beautiful manuscripts; in the twenty-first, Amazon's Kindle threatens settled assumptions about the material book we have entertained since the invention of printing in the West.

One of these assumptions was my own. More than a decade ago, as a book historian writing "In Search of 'The Word of the Other,'" I argued that the various objects of knowledge transfer used in the early Americas, despite their physical differences, could be linked together conceptually by the fact that in one way or another all of them—codices, wampum, khipu, birchbark scrolls, petroglyphs, painted skins—served the same social functions that in Europe were served by the book.[8] Lately I've been pondering the extent to which I might have ironized, perhaps even abandoned, my "social" interpretation in the face of the challenge to explanation posed not by *likeness* but by *unlikeness*: the extreme variation in materials, form, types of inscription, and function that in the Americas distinguishes these objects of knowledge transfer not just from the European book but from each other. Their material differences radically disrupt the narrative that the European codex historically represents, challenging us to revisit our settled concept of what constitutes a book, even to entertain the possibility that the European codex, despite its cultural dominance, is an exception to the norm rather than the norm itself. Perhaps book history needs a new model, one that would accept and develop the book's tendency to metamorphose into various forms, making it possible to penetrate more deeply the complex origins and functions of

Germaine Warkentin

knowledge transfer using material objects, not only in the Americas but elsewhere. To develop such a model would broaden the scope of book history beyond its present parameters. And it would enable the pre-contact Americas (and non-European societies in general) to re-enter book history not as a puzzling exception to the rules but as a fully conceptualized, indeed transformative, aspect of them. In this essay I suggest a direction we might take. I will be examining the codex as metaphor, the supposedly fractured memories of early Native life, the function of Appadurai's "cultural flux" in human experience, and the epistemological issues that raises. I then want to consider the evolutionary and archaeological resources for constructing a model of "the book" that will bring the European definition of the book and the textuality of the early Americas into fruitful dialogue.

The Codex as Metaphor

The European book in codex form was central to the Christian religion of which Landa was an emissary. In the second century CE the codex—parchment leaves, folded and sewn along the spine—became the preferred medium for the recording and dissemination of the texts of the new religion, eventually supplanting the classical scroll with its limited capacity, less convenient handling, and fragile papyrus substrate. So effective an image did the codex become that in the thirteenth century, Dante, in a famed passage near the end of the *Paradiso*, would use the metaphor of the book to describe the whole of God's universe, "legato con amore in un volume" (bound up by love in a single book) (canto 33, line 86). First material object, then privileged text, and finally powerful metaphor, the European codex in Landa's day was the dominant object of knowledge transfer across much of the then-known world, and has remained so until the coming of the digital revolution. And as a metaphor, the book brought other metaphors with it: "reading" broadly conceived as any sort of visual interpretation (one can "read" a painting or a building, for example), and "library" as any systematic collection of objects (compact discs, DNA markers) that stores information for later reference.

Thus it is not surprising that the term "codex" has almost invariably been used to describe the Mesoamerican artifacts Landa was burning. Bibliographically speaking, however, they are not codices at all, as John B. Glass pointed out nearly four decades ago in the *Handbook of Middle American Indians* where—more recent breakthroughs in decipherment having yet to occur—he carefully referred to them as "pictorial manuscripts."[9] Glass distinguished five basic forms: the *Tira* or roll, which is occasionally found folded; the screenfold proper (a deliberately pleated Tira); the *Lienzo*, a sheet of cloth that is the usual medium for maps and documents; the single sheet or panel; and the *Mapa*, a broadly used but inexact term for other single-panel artifacts. Methods of reading them vary considerably and depend very much on the format of the material; a Tira might be read up, down, left, or right, but the screenfolds are chiefly horizontal, though some have to be read boustrophedon style (left to right, then right to left). The contrast with the linear reading necessitated by the layout and sequential pages of the European codex could not be more obvious.

The hegemony attained by the codex is only partly a matter of the dominance of alphabetic symbols and the linear reading they bring with them. Books are bearers of power; Landa may represent the archetype of the European oppression of Native information systems, but internal events in Mesoamerica produced the same drive toward textual dominance. On December 3, 735 CE, Seibal (a city in today's Guatemala) and its king, Yich'ak-Balam, were conquered by the third king of the dynasty that ruled the nearby city of Dos Pilas. Linda Schele and Peter Mathews write, "The Dos Pilas victors gloated over their defeat of Yich'ak-Balam on stelae at Dos Pilas and Aguateca, and they erected a Hieroglyphic Stairway at Seibal registering its new vassal status."[10] Mayan hieroglyphic stairways are generally devoted to the recording of incidents of warfare and the capture of enemies by the kings who erected them.[11] The stairway at Seibal and the related stelae even record the destruction of the historiographic records of the predecessor kingdom: "they chopped the writing of the statues that were made," according to one stela.[12] Such ruthless exploitation of

Germaine Warkentin

textual dominance paradoxically means that, according to Schele and Mathews, "the Maya [have] an unbroken written history that started before the beginning of the Christian era and continues today."[13]

Faced with systems of knowledge transfer at variance with its own, European book culture, itself originating in the texts and accounts recorded on Babylonian clay tablets, has generally granted to the scrolls of the Chinese a status equivalent to that of the codex. China, however different it was from Europe, had to be acknowledged as a complex, advanced civilization. It possessed a sophisticated book culture of scrolls and painting brushes, one that invented printing well before Europeans did, and for a long time didn't bother to develop it further, because its manuscript traditions nicely suited the practices of its already highly developed social culture.[14] But whether European or Asian, the concept of the book is handicapped in dealing with a culture that uses solid material objects to communicate, lacks what we understand to be texts and accounts, and may not be a settled one— for example, a hunter-gatherer society. As a result, non-European systems of knowledge transfer have often been dismissed as the improvisations of cultures that were either primitive or dying: oral, nonliterate societies unlike those that are evolved, complex, and implicitly "superior." The esteemed historian of rhetoric George Kennedy fell into this trap with his well-meant but flat-footed *Comparative Rhetoric: An Historical and Cross-Cultural Introduction* (1998). Scott Richard Lyons (Leech Lake Ojibwe), though respectful toward Kennedy's formidable contributions to the study of Greek and Roman rhetoric, produced a withering Native critique of his classification of rhetoric into two sections, the oral and the literate, and the "evolutionary" reading he then produced of its development from animal utterances to those of "oral" indigenous people, thence "upwards" to the literacy of Egyptians, Chinese, and South Asians.[15]

In many cases non-European systems of knowledge transfer have simply not been recognized as systems at all, as D. F. McKenzie showed in his influential study of the writing and printing of the 1840 Treaty of Waitangi, "The Sociology of a Text: Oral Culture, Literacy and Print in Early New Zealand." In the drafting of the treaty as eventually signed by the Maoris, a "Maori" text was carefully provided, but it was written not in the language as actually used but in "Protestant, Pakeha, Missionary Maori," English words in Maori form that would have frustrated many of the Maoris signing the treaty. Furthermore, the version they did sign was written and presented to them without taking into consideration the Maoris' sophisticated oral consultation process.[16] In a groundbreaking study of Great Lakes kinship networks and pictographic treaty signatures, Heidi Bohaker demonstrates the extent to which we have been blind to the specifically material differentiation of non-European information systems. Richard White had argued in his classic *The Middle Ground* (1991) that documentation of Great Lakes peoples in the seventeenth century is "a historical landscape that consists largely of dim shadows . . . a fractured society has been preserved in fractured memory. To pretend otherwise is to deceive."[17] Bohaker, however, shows in detail how richer histories could be written if historians "embraced as potential source material the wide range of media on which Anishinaabe (and other aboriginal peoples) left behind assertions of their collective and individual identities" (51). We will shortly examine just such a range of media in considering what a book historian sees when she examines the winter counts of the Plains Natives.

In the 1980s and 1990s, scholars of the Americas such as Gordon Brotherston, Walter Mignolo, Keith Basso, and Elizabeth Hill Boone began to mount a serious challenge to the Eurocentric concept of the book and the historical reluctance to apply it to non-European and non-Asiatic civilizations.[18] Since then, scholars like Frank Salomon, Thomas H. Guthrie, Lesley and David Green, Galen Brokaw, Angela Haas, and Barbara Risch have continued to probe the issues in a new and radical way, as have the essayists collected in this volume and those in a recent special issue of *Ethnohistory* devoted to Native inscription and the colonial situation.[19]

Indeed, writers and scholars from other Native traditions have begun to take ownership of the concept of the codex in its Mesoameri-

Germaine Warkentin

can form. Seeking an ancestry for their various nations' specific practices, and increasingly opposed to the line drawn between "oral" aboriginal culture and "literate" European and settler culture laid down by Europeans (and sometimes too readily adopted by aboriginals), Craig Womack (Creek) asserts that for a Native literary tradition the codices are foundational: "The . . . Mayan codices, written in Mayan pictoglyphic symbols before contact, and in Mayan in the Latin alphabet afterward, are a fascinating study . . . [opening up] a space for Native intellectual discussion, in the form of textual production, in contact, not in competition, with the oral tradition."[20] In her demonstration of the hypertextuality of wampum, Angela Haas (Eastern Cherokee) regards the codices as important related objects.[21] Lisa Brooks (Abenaki) wryly relates how the very materiality of the Mayan codices wove itself into her book *The Common Pot* (2008):

> We are sitting on the grass, stretching our legs, talking about birchbark scrolls, Mayan codices, and the intertwining of writing and the oral tradition. . . . We think of those libraries, burned by the Spanish priests. And we think of the birchbark that we gathered yesterday to start our cookfire, the birchbark that can be used to make canoes, baskets, homes . . . and books. We think of how it is the best thing to use to start a fire. We think of those scrolls . . . we think of the priests. We think of how easy it would have been.[22]

Lightly, Brooks lets the moment of resistance to colonialism pass, but the ambiguity invoked by the metaphor of the book has rarely been so deftly exploited since Ray Bradbury's novel about book-burning, *Fahrenheit 451* (1951).

"Dim Shadows . . . Fractured Memory"

Native writers like these look back to the Mesoamerican screenfolds as offering, for them at least, a coherent historiographical foundation, rich in possibilities. Nevertheless, an unbroken, centuries-long written history like that of the Mutul kingdom is difficult to find north of the Rio Grande, where the many Native systems of knowledge transfer vary so greatly in their symbolic expression, easily degradable materials, and social functions that, taken as a group, they make an explanatory theory based on traditional concepts of "the book" almost useless. For the European book, alphabetic literacy is both a practical necessity and a social ideal. To produce an object like the one in which you are reading this essay requires a complex technology and the commodification that goes with it; so reified do these conditions seem to scholars in the field that much current book history currently describes itself as "print culture." None of this is the case with the Mesoamerican artifacts, nor indeed with other objects in the early Americas that function to transfer knowledge. Khipu, wampum, birchbark scrolls, petroglyphs, painted skins—each represented symbolically mediated behavior. But in most cases their authority rarely extended very far beyond the cultural group that employed the artifact, and the kinds of "reading" they required had nothing to do with the dominant system of the alphabet. Though wampum was involved in complex rituals of exchange, commodification in the Marxist sense of the term did not become a factor in its role until settler Europeans began to reinterpret it in terms of their system of economic exchange. Inscriptions on stone aside, the most technically complex may be systems that require beading and fine needlework; in the early contact period, instruments for making better beads were eagerly seized on by Native nations, and metal needles and awls were coveted trade goods.[23] At this remote distance from the European codex—bound at the spine, filling great libraries and archives, ruling the conceptual space even as we argue today about whether or not the book is "dead"—the metaphor of the book is stretched to the breaking point.

Anthropologists Frank Salomon and Sabine Hyland have faced a similar problem of synthesis as they attempt a coherent approach to the multiple systems of inscription—on whatever substrate—in the early Americas. They point to the "conceptual discord" resulting from

Germaine Warkentin

the unambiguous application of European-derived concepts to such writing:

> The unintended consequence . . . was to narrow grammatology down to studying "civilization" and phonetic writing, rather than the vast range of graphic behaviour. . . . [S]ystems using other principles, or conveying information in ways other than verbal equivalence, were considered less worthy of study. These languished, defined only by what they were not, namely a part of the grand genealogy of "letters" enshrined in the humanities.[24]

Their conclusion is that "we do not yet have any consensual basis for sorting the cases or even agreement on what the analytical axes might be" (3). To deal with this situation, they have devised the useful investigative concept of "graphic pluralism." The book historian, however, encounters pluralism at an even more fundamental level, for as has already been pointed out, no inscription can exist without a substrate, a material upon which it can be inscribed. This raises the same problem of analysis, and in an even more discouraging form because of the multiple media used in North America for the storage and transfer of information.[25]

There is, however, at least one North American Native medium of communication that provides a richly textured example of what can happen when the making of objects of knowledge transfer meets with the recurring transformations, devastations, and innovations of human history. This is pictographic communication as practiced on the interior plains by Arapahos, Assiniboines, Cheyennes, Kiowas, Lakotas, Nez Percés, and other Plains peoples. Its purposes included depictions of the natural and supernatural worlds, the celebration of heroic deeds by individuals and groups, the hunt, community life, and the marking of passing years.[26] Such communication was widespread, used varying media, is well documented, and covers a long historical period. It also represents a signal encounter with the problem of cultural flux.

The documentable tradition of pictographic inscription begins with the petroglyphs that are to be found in many places in the West and were first studied by Colonel Garrick Mallery in the nineteenth century.[27] Those that have survived weathering and vandalism are so fluent and exuberant that they imply the existence of a thriving preexisting graphic tradition. In an important systematic analysis of archaeological, cultural, and historical data from the great wall of petroglyphs found at Writing-on-Stone along the Milk River in Alberta, Martin Magne and Michael Klassen demonstrate that certain "classic" pictographs date from the pre-contact period because they bear no evidence of European influence—horses, guns—and depict the body shields used by Plains Natives before they adopted the horse. They are "probably the result of hundreds of years of artistic tradition, indicated by the strongly conventionalized depiction of the entire anthropomorph, and in particular anatomical details such as genitals and heartlines."[28] Magne and Klassen stress the way in which the development of these and other pictographs represents both the continuity of rock art traditions and the way the development of motifs reflects ongoing changes in Plains culture.

The pictographic tradition, as Howard Rodee and James D. Keyser have argued, is continued in the painted skins, robes, and tipis of the early contact period, the calendrical winter counts clustered in the period 1775–1900, and the ledger-book drawings of the 1860s–1930s.[29] The book historian, however, looks less at the pictographic figures than *through* them to the successive media on which they have been inscribed: stone, hide, and eventually paper. The Battiste Good winter count is a good example because of its long historical frame and its willed connection to the earlier petroglyphs. Like many other winter counts, it exists in variant copies on different materials.[30] Battiste Good (1821–1908; Brulé, Dakota), the "keeper" of this particular count, included in the version held at the Smithsonian the image of a vision he experienced in the Black Hills, in which he "saw prints of a man's hands and horse's hoofs on the rocks," thus deliberately linking his count with the petroglyph tradition.[31] The calendar itself begins in the

Germaine Warkentin

mythological time of the Dakotas (from about 900 CE), depicted in twelve successive camp circles, and after 1700 continues with a pictograph for each year up to 1879. Good's own version was inscribed on cloth, but he drew a copy in a sketchbook for the collector William H. Corbusier; later his count was redrawn (with important omissions) when Garrick Mallery published it in 1893. There are variant copies by Good's son High Hawk (one on large paper), two other book copies, and yet another on several sheets of paper.

This metamorphic quality is symptomatic of the tradition itself. Good's winter count is only one example of a tradition of pictographic inscription in which a number of Plains nations participated and which was sustained over many years as they fought their enemies, were massacred, suffered relocation, and lost control of the very world their images described and chronicled. Notwithstanding the oppression they suffered, the Plains Natives continued to paint and draw on whatever medium became available. Used to carving on rock and painting on hides of all sorts, they adapted fluently to the new media—autograph books, sketchbooks, ledger books, and many types of notepaper and stationery—that white armies and settlers brought with them. Between 1875 and 1878 at Fort Marion in Florida, Cheyenne, Kiowa, and Arapaho prisoners even filled with their sketches some small drawing books they had been given, and the results were sold to tourists.[32] Christina E. Burke describes the complex textual record that the winter counts developed as a result of the succession of "keepers" of a given count, the advent of alphabetic script (sadly, Mallery thought Good's inclusion of European inscriptions degraded the original),[33] and the multiple copies on cloth or paper that circulated in family groups and were later made for white collectors and tourists.[34] To the historian these objects record a cruel experience of continual loss, but to the book historian they represent, despite that undeniable tragedy, a remarkable record of achievement plucked from adversity. The adoption of modern media that the ledger and drawing books represent can be seen from one point of view as the nostalgic fantasy of humans in a hopeless situation, suffering in the aftermath of a cultural disaster. Looked at another way, it represents an innovative solution to an acute experience of contingency.

Occurring at a critical moment of cultural transition, these winter counts and ledger books may be objects of deep longing, yet at the same time they are full of energy. Like the twentieth-century development of samizdat, they show us a culture under heavy stress responding with a method of information transfer that, despite the fragmenting effects of geographical and cultural distance and political disruption, brings the technologies involved in substrate and inscription into a fertile new relationship. Contingencies resulting either from a fractured historical experience or from the sheer indeterminacy of material conditions do not seem to quench the human capacity to rethink, rework, and reintegrate. As we will see, the section of the mediascape occupied by the book seems to possess the same capacity to reinvent itself in the face of apparently unmasterable cultural change. One of those changes has been the testing of critical discourse not only by the salutary collapse of old disciplinary boundaries but by more troubling epistemological doubts about the human capacity to draw verifiable conclusions about experience.

The Uses of Contingency

Appadurai's account of the contemporary mediascape is only one of many initiatives in cultural studies (hardly summarizable here) assessing the networks that transport information across increasingly permeable boundaries. In book history, challenged by work like McKenzie's, the book historian's former reluctance to move beyond the systems of print culture and national boundaries—technological in one case and political in the other—is breaking down under the pressure of an emerging concern with "transnational" studies and the challenge of the digital revolution.[35] At the same time, a movement in the history of science, medicine, and technology is attempting to work across boundaries, fueled in this case by the need to integrate non-Western science into the discipline.[36] As we will shortly see, biologists are in dialogue with archaeologists as both explore the begin-

Germaine Warkentin

nings of language, social life, and the exploitation of material objects during the development of behaviorally modern humans in the Middle and Upper Palaeolithic. Evidently, some form of the "multidisciplinary convergence" that Paul Bouissac envisions so eloquently in my epigraph is coming about.

Such initiatives, however, are confronted by what Appadurai bravely acknowledges as "the great traditional questions of causality, contingency, and prediction in the human sciences," though his view is that "in a world of disjunctive global flows, it is perhaps important to start asking them in a way that relies on images of flow and uncertainty, hence 'chaos,' rather than on older images of order, stability and systematicity."[37] Students of the book cannot skirt such questions, for the book is patently a material object, and thus it poses, as Peter Shillingsburg (already quoted) points out, the knotty epistemological problem of verification. How do we experience such objects—whether European or not—in a world of flow and uncertainty, and how can we verify our experience of them? Can we be sure the conclusions we draw are not simply constructions resulting from historical and social conditions we can never step outside of? Dealing with material objects poses a classic problem in the philosophy of mind, in its most familiar form the dualism of the seventeenth-century philosopher René Descartes. There is no need to give examples of the way the long history and postmodern avatars of Cartesianism have affected research and interpretation in recent decades. On one hand are the rigorous objectivists, often fueled by extremely naive ideas about science; on the other are not Berkeleian idealists so much as ruthless skeptics, convinced that in the end, as Richard Rorty held, it's all just conversation.[38]

But what is going on during that conversation? Increasingly, epistemologists, anthropologists, and biologists are attempting to escape this profitless debate and the Cartesian body/mind disjunction that in part underlies it.[39] Neither objectivism nor skepticism, for example, has proved to have sufficient explanatory power to deal with physically material objects that at the same time have demonstrably cultural roles.[40] Equally important for my argument, they take no account of the function of the constant human experience of cultural disruption in understanding the world about us. To think about contingency in this way, I will suggest, invokes not just the kind of disjunction discussed by Appadurai but the kind of correlative movement toward dealing with disruption that we have seen among the Plains Natives.

One of Battiste Good's contemporaries, the nineteenth-century pragmatist philosopher C. S. Peirce (1839–1914), made a particularly fertile attempt to bypass the Cartesian categories. In an essay that appeared in *Popular Science* in 1878, Peirce described very simply the problem to which he would devote his life: "What sort of conception we ought to have of the universe, how to think of the *ensemble* of things, is a fundamental problem in the theory of reasoning."[41] Peirce approached his problem not only as a philosopher but as a mathematician, arguing calmly that induction was a matter of probability and that reasoning produced not definitive knowledge but "an inference of possibility."[42] He could do this without a disabling skepticism because his philosophical system was not binary, like Descartes', but triadic. That is, he saw human cognition as action working upon objects to produce thought. Peirce's system, extrapolated in many forms over a long lifetime, constantly explains itself in terms of such triadic relationships. The best known, as he described it in his highly personal taxonomy, is the triad of *token* or *symbol* (for Peirce, a conventional indicator of something existing), *index* (which points to the symbol without acting upon it), and *icon* (a sign of resemblance linking token and index through resemblance).[43] Here, as in his other triads, the third term is always in a condition of acting upon the other two.

The consequence is a fresh conception of "truth"; no longer is it framed as some final and definitive result of thought, nor is it disablingly skeptical. Rather, the mind is constantly engaged in the discovery of the state of things, and engaged likewise in constantly adapting to new information. The historian Carlo Ginzburg situates this kind of knowing in a social framework that might have appealed to Peirce when he terms our routine confidence in the human capac-

Germaine Warkentin

ity to test and evaluate "the evidential paradigm," writing that it "can be found throughout the world, with no limits of geography, history, ethnicity, sex or class." Far removed from the higher forms of knowledge possessed by the elites, it is the property "of hunters, of sailors, of women. It binds the human animal close to other animal species."[44]

Peirce and his heirs in this century such as Susan Haack represent only one example of the search for an integrative method, a way of thinking about the ensemble of things that seeks an open and exploratory approach to verification and thus confronts the human experience of the evidential paradigm head-on. For Haack, explanation is the product of a whole web of more or less mutually supportive beliefs, at the center of which is situated a human subject with a psychology that can be experimentally tested and whose process of verification constitutes a probing, constantly evaluative procedure that draws on a wide range of comparative materials to risk conclusions possibly trustworthy enough to act upon. Haack assigns a role to the experience of contingency, not because it represents a substantive position about the disjunctive character of knowledge, but as a methodological precondition for effective explanation.

The anthropologists John Tooby and Leda Cosmides argue in fact that the capacity to perceive alternative worlds, to risk the testing of solutions, has a specific evolutionary function. Humans, they write,

> are radically different from other species in the degree to which we use contingently true information—information that allows the regulation of improvised behavior that is successfully tailored to local conditions. . . . When hominids evolved or elaborated cognitive adaptations that could use information based on relationships that were only 'true' temporarily, locally, or contingently rather than stably and across the species range, this opened up a new and vastly enlarged universe of potentially representable information for use. . . . giving human life its distinctive complexity, variety and relative success. . . . Managing these new types of information adaptively required the evolution of a large set of

specialized cognitive adaptations [including] the evolution of new information formats . . . that tag and track the boundaries within which a given set of representations can safely be used for inference or action.[45]

The experience of contingency as humans have evolved, they argue, is the fertile source of our very capacity to create and use information and the multitude of formats it has historically taken and will take.

"The *Ensemble* of Things"

Can we produce a model for understanding objects of knowledge transfer that takes this improvisatory capacity into account? We are returned to the central concern of this essay: to propose an integrative framework for understanding both the European and the non-European book, neither as culturally predatory nor historically marooned, but with equal status as objects of knowledge transfer. Evolution is one of the richest areas available to us for investigating how humans have used material objects to exchange information. The semiotician Paul Bouissac, in the passage that forms the epigraph to this essay, foresees the development of a new narrative about human cultural life, one in which the *longue durée* is represented by an evolutionary time frame rather than a historical one devised to fulfill the grand plan of one or another dominant culture. Central to such a development would be a fuller understanding of the biological foundations of reading and writing. Humans, it seems, will read anything—weather signs, three-volume novels, the tracks left by an animal. That capacity appears to be buried deep in the fabric of the brain, as Mark Changizi has demonstrated in his study of how humans recognize optical images—road signs, Chinese characters, landscape.[46] As Barbara Risch observed, however, as she studied the Lakota winter counts, "humans are text-producing creatures."[47] That is, it is not enough simply to recognize objects; they must be construed as symbolically mediated in some way.

Bouissac crisply summarizes the rigorous biomechanical conditions

Germaine Warkentin

in which symbolically mediated behavior of any sort might be generated: the capacity to represent, to have ideas, to devise goal-directed messages, and to make sense of messages received.[48] A long list of biologists, neurologists, and evolutionary anthropologists has been examining how this might happen, though in the case of reading they are backing into it by trying to figure out what happens when we *can't* read, as when we suffer from dyslexia.[49] Their various proposals, however, depend on an important prior condition: the ability to mark symbolically mediated information upon objects of some sort. At some point in our career as tool-makers, *homo sapiens sapiens* (fully modern humans) began to sense that material objects could be used for the storage and exchange and communication of information. The recognition that objects could be made to represent symbolic information is thus one of the most remarkable insights humans have ever had.

What evidence do we have of how and when humans began to demonstrate such capacities? Excavating since 1991 in a small cave at Blombos in South Africa, the archaeologist Christopher Henshilwood has uncovered decorative beads and at least two inscribed lumps of red ocher that have proved to be the earliest well-attested examples of deliberate human *marks made upon objects.* They are indeed deliberate, as rigorous scientific analysis of the knife marks has shown.[50] At approximately 80,000 years, they prove to be almost 50,000 years older than the oldest known cave paintings, those at Chauvet in the Ardèche, which date from about 32,000 BCE. Francisco d'Errico, the scientist who analyzed the knife markings, published his findings in *Rock Art Research*, but he carefully titled his report "Microscopic and Statistical Criteria for the Identification of Prehistorical Systems of *Notation*" (my emphasis), thus effectively circumventing the too-easy categorization of any and every kind of prehistoric marking as "art." No one yet knows what the marks mean, and perhaps we never will, so Henshilwood is extremely cautious about whether they represent symbolically mediated behavior. Nevertheless, the conclusion to the most recent of his many reports on his team's findings is worth quoting in full:

In this study we demonstrate, for the first time, the presence of a tradition in the production of geometric engraved representations in the MSA [Middle Stone Age];[51] second, that this tradition goes back in time to at least 100 ka [100,000 years] ago; and third, that the tradition includes the production of a number of different patterns. From the evidence, we cannot determine the context in which these engravings were used or why they were abandoned. We also cannot be sure whether the engraved ochres from Blombos were created as non-objective or expressive designs. The fact that they were created, that most of them are deliberate and were made with representational intent, strongly suggests that they functioned as artefacts within a society where behaviour was mediated by symbols.[52]

Henshilwood's discoveries and his analysis of them are part of ongoing research and evaluation in the field, but whatever advances occur, they are destined to play an important role in defining the criteria for the beginning of the human exchange of information in material form.

The need to conduct such exchanges is being studied by the evolutionary anthropologist Robin Dunbar and his team at the British Academy project "From Lucy to Language: The Archaeology of the Social Brain." Dunbar's influential article "The Social Brain Hypothesis" argues that the human brain did not evolve—as had long been thought—to recognize and remember facts, but rather to *produce and exchange information*. Brutally simplified, Dunbar's hypothesis is that social relationships, with their need to store and communicate information, drove the evolution of cognition, and with it language.[53] The archaeologist Steven Mithen similarly holds that sometime in the early Upper Palaeolithic period, when humans began to make tools and live in collaborative social groups with their need for information storage and exchange, they discovered how to use external material objects to create art, and thus extend their range, power, and capacity. In doing so they created what the psychologist Merlin Don-

Germaine Warkentin

ald calls "external symbolic storage." Donald's concept is something like the biologist Richard Dawkins's "extended phenotype," a physical object that some biological creature devises to extend its range, power, and capacity. Dawkins's delightful and apposite example is the beaver dam.[54]

The effect of such work (a rich literature well beyond what I can briefly review here) is to defamiliarize the Eurocentric concept of the book with a vengeance. By following the genesis of information transfer using material objects through human evolutionary history, we find ourselves with a model that attends to the process of change through time not as disjunctive, but as a normal diversification of functions. What I find as I explore this topic is something like what evolutionists call descent with modification. In my application, it's simply a model (Blombos may be only one instance among multiple discoveries of communication using material objects), but it is a useful model. Ways of storing information on material objects were born, served their social function, and died—or sometimes just lived on as "survivor technologies" in some smaller but still useful niche. Wampum and khipu continue to serve ceremonial functions for the Iroquois and Andeans, but the clay tablets of the Babylonians are, so far as one can tell, a dead technology; in Darwinian terms, they did not survive the process of selection. (The printed codex is being tested in this way today by the advent of Kindle and devices like it.) As descent with modification took place, different usages took up separate existences, and we ceased to classify them together: for example, the modern person of Europeanized culture thinks of painting pictures as belonging to an entirely different category from writing text, but in aboriginal cultures, particularly those of the Plains Natives, painting and textuality tend to represent points on a single unifying spectrum.

Employing the classic model of the evolutionary tree, we might envision the European codex as constituting merely one branch of that tree. Or perhaps a distributive model is better, where the threads of a network are distributed across an area in relative independence from each other yet continue to interact. The multifarious non-European versions of information exchange all diversify if not from that ocher plaque in the cave at Blombos then from some object like it. In the Americas the Mesoamerican tradition represents one thread, the Andean khipu another, and in North America a particularly rich pattern of diversification emerges. In such models the practice of information transfer in the early Americas is liberated from the straitjacket of colonialized categories and takes the place it deserves in Peirce's "*ensemble* of things," where we can assess without prior prejudice its function in the cultures it serves. Different as the books of Native America are from each other, and different as they are from the European codex that has colonized them, they become part of a coherent account that contains but also accepts those differences, indeed is built upon them. And of course a model exploiting Dunbar's "social brain hypothesis" would renovate and restore to use the argument I originally made that Native objects of knowledge transfer served the same social function as the European book.

"Books in Indian Characters"

We return to the codices that Diego de Landa burned, the "books in Indian characters" that he recognized as a threat to the forms of belief he represented. They were indeed a threat, and remain so even in the fragmented forms in which we now possess them. The Mesoamerican codices are foundational because they have changed the game, initiating the slow but inevitable adjustment that re-situates both the European book and Native objects of knowledge transfer in a larger and more reasoned setting. That setting, I hope, will be an integrative process of inquiry that functions politically, empirically, and biologically: politically because it refuses the historically conditioned distinctions between primitive and civilized, oral and literate; empirically because it accepts the risk of testing, of the heuristic method with its plunge into contingency; and biologically because it attends to what we know or may learn about the development of the species. It is this concept of the "*ensemble* of things" toward which I think a renovated concept of the book as an object of knowledge transfer might reach, and of

Germaine Warkentin

which the aboriginal achievement in the Americas, because of the challenge it offers to conventional thinking, is an essential, indeed priceless component.

Notes

1. Paul Bouissac, "Probing Pre-Historic Cultures: Data, Dates and Narratives," *Rock Art Research* 23.1 (2006): 95; see esp. section 3, "Marks as Symbols? Toward an Early Writing Systems Hypothesis."

2. A. R. Pagden, ed. and trans., *The Maya: Diego de Landa's Account of the Affairs of Yucatan* (Chicago: J. Philip O'Hara, 1975), 13.

3. These are the Dresden, Paris, and Madrid codices; see John B. Glass, "A Survey of Native Middle American Pictorial Manuscripts," in *Handbook of Middle American Indians*, ed. H. F. Cline, 16 vols. (Austin: University of Texas Press, 1964–76), 14:12–13, and esp. his cautionary note (n12) regarding the problem of dating.

4. The importance of this to the history of the book is exemplified in some famous—perhaps infamous—words by the distinguished bibliographer W. W. Greg: "Let it then be granted that bibliography is the study of books as material objects. . . . [W]hat the bibliographer is concerned with is pieces of paper or parchment covered with certain written or printed signs. With these signs he is concerned merely as arbitrary marks; their meaning is no business of his." Few of us have that much rigor, but in this 1932 statement Greg got to the heart of the matter: books are material objects, and we have to keep that in mind when we start trying to explain them. Greg, "Bibliography—An Apologia," in *Collected Papers*, ed. J. C. Maxwell (Oxford: Clarendon Press, 1966), 241, 247. One group of scholars concerned about the materiality of the book is, unexpectedly, following the development of digital textuality. Among them, Jerome McGann is particularly aware of the complexity of these issues; see McGann, "Our Textual History," *Times Literary Supplement*, November 20, 2009, 13–15.

5. Peter Shillingsburg, "Text as Matter, Concept, and Action," *Studies in Bibliography* 44 (1991): 31.

6. Arjun Appadurai, "Disjuncture and Difference in the Global Cultural Economy," *Public Culture* 2.2 (1990): 1.

7. Appadurai, "Disjuncture and Difference," 18. The five "scapes," that is, the dimensions of global cultural flow, are ethnoscapes, mediascapes, technoscapes, financescapes, and ideoscapes (6–7).

8. Germaine Warkentin, "In Search of 'The Word of the Other': Aboriginal Sign Systems and the History of the Book in Canada," *Book History* 2 (1999): 13.

9. Glass, "Survey," 14:8–9.

10. Linda Schele and Peter Mathews, *The Code of Kings* (New York: Scribner, 1998), 177–78.

11. David Stuart, "'The Fire Enters His House': Architecture and Ritual in Classic Maya Texts," in *Function and Meaning in Classic Maya Architecture*, ed. Stephen D. Houston (Washington DC: Dumbarton Oaks Research Library and Collection, 1988), 414.

12. Schele and Mathews, *The Code of Kings*, 177 and fig. 5.3.

13. Schele and Mathews, *The Code of Kings*, 196.

14. See T. H. Barrett, *The Woman Who Discovered Printing* (New Haven: Yale University Press, 2008).

15. Scott Richard Lyons, "Rhetorical Sovereignty: What Do American Indians Want from Writing?" *College Composition and Communication* 51.3 (February 2000): 459.

16. Donald F. McKenzie, "The Sociology of a Text: Oral Culture, Literacy and Print in Early New Zealand," in McKenzie, *Bibliography and the Sociology of Texts* (Cambridge: Cambridge University Press, 1999), 113–17. First published in *The Library*, 6th ser., 6 (December 1984), and often reprinted.

17. Heidi Bohaker, "*Nindoodemag*: The Significance of Algonquian Kinship Networks in the Eastern Great Lakes Region, 1600–1701," *William and Mary Quarterly*, 3rd ser., 63.1 (January 2006): 30 (hereafter cited parenthetically in the text). Bohaker is quoting Richard White, *The Middle Ground: Indians, Empires and Republics in the Great Lakes Region, 1650–1815* (Cambridge: Cambridge University Press, 1991), 2.

18. The work of these scholars is discussed in Warkentin, "In Search of 'The Word of the Other,'" 5 and n17.

19. See, e.g., Galen Brokaw, "Indigenous American Polygraphy and the Dialogic Model of Media," *Ethnohistory* 51.1 (Winter 2010): 119–33; Lesley J. F. Green and David R. Green, "Space, Time and Story Tracks: Contemporary Practices of Topographic Memory in the Palikur Territory of Arukwa, Amapá, Brazil," *Ethnohistory* 56.1 (Winter 2009): 163–85; Thomas H. Guthrie, "Good Words: Chief Joseph and the Production of Indian Speech(es), Texts and Subject," *Ethnohistory* 54.3 (Summer 2007): 509–46; Angela M. Haas, "Wampum as Hypertext: An American Indian Intellectual Tradition of Multimedia Theory and Practice," *Studies in American In-*

Germaine Warkentin

dian Literatures 19.4 (Winter 2007): 77–102; Barbara Risch, "A Grammar of Time: Lakota Winter Counts, 1700–1900," *American Indian Culture and Research Journal* 24.2 (2000): 23–48; and Frank Salomon and Emilio Chambi Apaza, "Vernacular Literacy on the Lake Titicaca High Plains, Peru," *Reading Research Quarterly* 41.3 (July–September 2006): 304–26.

20. Craig S. Womack, *Red on Red: Native American Literary Separatism* (Minneapolis: University of Minnesota Press, 1999), 15–16.

21. Haas, "Wampum as Hypertext," focuses her argument on wampum, but see esp. n5.

22. Lisa Brooks, *The Common Pot: The Recovery of Native Space in the Northeast* (Minneapolis: University of Minnesota Press, 2008), xx. All ellipses except the first are the author's.

23. For the pre-contact history of wampum beads see Lynn Ceci, "Tracing Wampum's Origins: Shell Bead Evidence from Archaeological Sites in Western and Coastal New York," *Proceedings of the 1986 Shell Bead Conference: Selected Papers*, ed. Charles F. Hayes and Lynn Ceci (Rochester NY: Rochester Museum and Science Center, 1988), 63–80; in the same volume see also Richard W. Yerkes, "Shell Bead Production and Exchange in Prehistoric Mississippian Populations," 113–23.

24. Frank Salomon and Sabine Hyland, "Guest Editors' Introduction" to the special issue "Graphic Pluralism: Native American Systems of Inscription and the Colonial Situation," *Ethnohistory* 57.1 (Winter 2010): 2 (hereafter cited parenthetically in the text). I am grateful to Frank Salomon for giving me advance access to this important introduction.

25. Participants in the Great Lakes Research Alliance for the study of Aboriginal Arts and Cultures (GRASAC) have undertaken a large-scale, systematic study of the Native artifacts of their area that have been scattered because archives and museums customarily divide and re-categorize heritage materials according to their own institutional practices. Book historians look forward to working on the material their innovative website and international collaborative team will bring together. See the GRASAC website, https://grasac.org/gks/gks_about.php.

26. For a useful thematic analysis, see Risch, "A Grammar of Time," 29–31.

27. Garrick Mallery, *Picture-Writing of the American Indians*, 2 vols. (1893; New York: Dover, 1972).

28. Martin P. R. Magne and Michael A. Klassen, "A Multivariate Study of Rock Art Anthropomorphs at Writing-on-Stone, Southern Alberta," *American Antiquity* 56.3 (July 1991): 410.

29. Howard D. Rodee, "The Stylistic Development of Plains Indian Painting and its Relationship to Ledger Drawings," *Plains Anthropologist* 10.30 (November 1965): 218–19; James D. Keyser, "Lexicon for Historic Plains Indian Rock Art: Increasing Interpretative Potential," *Plains Anthropologist* 32.115 (1987): 44.

30. Battiste Good's superb winter count begs to be edited by a scholar with both ethnographical insight into its origins and the bibliographic experience to sort out and describe the various versions.

31. Candace S. Greene and Russell Thornton, eds., *The Year the Stars Fell: Lakota Winter Counts at the Smithsonian* (Washington DC and Lincoln: Smithsonian Institution and University of Nebraska Press, 2007), esp. 42–43, plates 12 and 13. Good's vision is described on 293. The Smithsonian version is in book form, and it is supposed to be read from back to front, consequently the vision depiction appears at the end.

32. Janet Catherine Berlo, "Drawing and Being Drawn In: The Late Nineteenth-Century Plains Graphic Artist and the Intercultural Encounter," in *Plains Indian Drawings, 1865–1935: Pages from a Visual History*, ed. Berlo (New York: Harry N. Abrams for the American Federation of Arts and The Drawing Center, 1996), 12–14.

33. Mallery, *Picture-Writing*, 1:288.

34. Christina E. Burke, "*Waniyetu Wówapi*: An Introduction to the Lakota Winter Count Tradition," in Greene and Thornton, *The Year the Stars Fell*, 2–3.

35. See Sydney Shep, "Books without Borders: The Transnational Turn in Book History," in *Books without Borders*, vol. 1, *The Cross-National Dimension*, ed. Robert Fraser and Mary Hammond (Basingstoke: Palgrave Macmillan, 2008), 13–37.

36. See, e.g., *Beyond Borders: Fresh Perspectives in History of Science*, ed. Josip Simon, Néstor Herren, et al. (Newcastle: Cambridge Scholars Publishing, 2008).

37. Appadurai, "Disjuncture and Difference," 20.

38. Rorty thinks that whatever we know is so entirely context-bound that justification can only be a matter of "conversation," of social practice. "We understand knowledge when we understand the social justification of belief," he writes, "and thus have no need to view it as accuracy of representation." Richard Rorty, *Philosophy and the Mirror of Nature* (Princeton NJ: Princeton University Press, 1979), 170.

39. For a comprehensive recent survey of these problems see Margaret

Germaine Warkentin

Boden's provocatively titled *Mind as Machine: A History of Cognitive Science*, 2 vols. (Oxford: Clarendon Press, 2006), esp. chapter 16 (2:1334–1443). Unsurprisingly, Boden concludes her vast and entertaining survey with the words, "In sum, the relation between mind and life is still highly problematic. . . . The common-sense view is that one (*life*) is a precondition of the other (*mind*). But there's no generally accepted way of proving that to be so" (1443). The late Francisco Varela argued, however, that body and mind are continuous and that the human cell functions by autopoesis (ongoing self-organization). His work on dynamic embodiment is being pursued by the philosopher of cognition Evan Thompson; see his *Mind in Life: Biology, Phenomenology and the Sciences of Mind* (Cambridge: The Belknap Press of Harvard University Press, 2008). See also the relationship between knowing and the body argued in George Lakoff and Mark Johnson, *Metaphors We Live By* (Chicago: University of Chicago Press, 1980) and *Philosophy in the Flesh: The Embodied Mind and Its Challenge to Western Thought* (New York: Basic Books, 1999).

40. Examples of this difficulty can be found in Scott Atran, *Cognitive Foundations of Natural History: Towards an Anthropology of Science* (Cambridge: Cambridge University Press, 1990), 3–4; and Gerald L. Edelman and Giulio Tononi, *A Universe of Consciousness: How Matter Becomes Imagination* (New York: Basic Books, 2000), chapter 17. Both books wrestle unsuccessfully with the epistemological status of metaphor, Atran with symbolic or non-propositional utterance (3–4), Edelman and Tononi with the "multiple ambiguous references" of poetry (222). A different and in my view more profitable approach to the relationship between sense information and culture is outlined by Carlo Ginzburg; see note 44 below.

41. Charles Sanders Peirce, "The Order of Nature," *Popular Science Monthly*, June 9, 1878, reprinted in *The Essential Peirce: Selected Philosophical Writings*, ed. Nathan Houser and Christian Kloesel, 2 vols. (Bloomington: Indiana University Press, 1992), 1:171.

42. Peirce, "The Order of Nature," 1:177.

43. Peirce, "On the Algebra of Logic: A Contribution to the Philosophy of Notation," *American Journal of Mathematics* 7 (1885): 180–202, reprinted in *Essential Peirce*, 1:225–28.

44. Carlo Ginzburg, "Clues: Roots of an Evidential Paradigm," in *Clues, Myths and the Historical Method*, trans. John and Anne C. Tedeschi (Baltimore: Johns Hopkins University Press, 1989), 125.

45. John Tooby and Leda Cosmides, "Does Beauty Build Adapted Minds? Toward an Evolutionary Theory of Aesthetics, Fiction and the Arts," *SubStance* 94/95 (2001): 19–20.
46. Mark A. Changizi et al., "The Structure of Letters and Symbols throughout Human History Are Selected to Match Those Found in Natural Objects," *American Naturalist*, May 2006, E129. I am indebted to Douglas Galbi for drawing my attention to this paper.
47. Risch, "A Grammar of Time," 25.
48. Paul Bouissac, "Interspecific Communication," in *Semiotik/Semiotics: Ein Handbuch zu den zeichentheoretischen Grunlagen von Natur und Kultur/A Handbook on the Sign-Theoretic Foundations of Nature and Culture*, ed. R. Posner, K. Robering, and T. A. Sebeok, vol. 4 (Berlin: Walter de Gruyter, 2004), 3391.
49. Mark Changizi's work (see note 46, above) is an exception, but almost all the experts in cognition that I have studied interpret the project of discovering how humans read as discovering how they read alphabetic script, and because that script is of recent invention they treat reading as a cultural phenomenon rather than as either genetically based or an adaptation. See Stanislas Dehaene et al., "The Neural Code for Written Words: A Proposal," *Trends in Cognitive Sciences* 9.7 (July 2005): 335–41. Simon Fisher's discovery in 2002 of a mutation on the FOXP2 gene for the first time confirmed by experiment the link between a physical property of the brain and a perceptual capacity, more correctly in this case the *incapacity* known as dyslexia. See W. Enard et al., "Molecular Evolution of FOXP2, a Gene Involved in Speech and Language," *Nature* 418 (2002): 869–72. As for writing, as recently as 1999 Dan Sperber and Lawrence Hirschfeld observed, "writing—which is so important to cognitive and cultural development . . . is a form of expertise, although it has become so common that we may not immediately think of it as such. It would be of the utmost interest to find out to what extent this expertise is grounded in specific psychomotor evolved adaptations." Dan Sperber and Lawrence Hirschfeld, "Culture, Cognition, and Evolution," in *MIT Encyclopedia of the Cognitive Sciences*, ed. Robert Wilson and Frank Keil (Cambridge: MIT Press, 1999), http://cognet.mit.edu.myaccess.library.utoronto.ca/library/erefs/mitecs/cultureintro.htmln.
50. Francesco d'Errico, "Microscopic and Statistical Criteria for the Identification of Prehistorical Systems of Notation," *Rock Art Research* 8.2 (1991): 83–93.

51. "Middle Stone Age" is South African archaeological nomenclature for what is elsewhere termed the Middle Palaeolithic.

52. Christopher S. Henshilwood, Francesco d'Errico, and Ian Watts, "Engraved Ochres from the Middle Stone Age Levels at Blombos Cave, South Africa," *Journal of Human Evolution* 57 (2009): 45.

53. Robin M. Dunbar, "The Social Brain Hypothesis," *Evolutionary Anthropology* 6 (1998): 178–90; Robin M. Dunbar, "The Social Brain: Mind, Language and Society in Evolutionary Perspective," *Annual Review of Anthropology* 32 (2003): 163–81. See also the proceedings of the 2008 British Academy conference *Social Brain, Distributed Mind*, ed. Robin Dunbar, Clive Gamble, and John Gowlett (Oxford: Proceedings of the British Academy/Oxford University Press, 2009). The website of Dunbar's project is "From Lucy to Language: The Archaeology of the Social Brain," http://www.liv.ac.uk/lucy2003/.

54. Stephen Mithen, *The Prehistory of the Mind: The Cognitive Origins of Art and Science* (London: Thames and Hudson, 1996), esp. chapter 9, "The Big Bang of Human Culture: The Origins of Art and Religion"; Merlin Donald, *Origins of the Modern Mind: Three Stages in the Evolution of Culture and Cognition* (Cambridge: Harvard University Press, 1991); Richard Dawkins, *The Extended Phenotype: The Long Reach of the Gene* (Oxford: Oxford University Press, 1982).

2

Early Americanist Grammatology

DEFINITIONS OF WRITING AND LITERACY

Andrew Newman

The Problem with Writing

In *The Legacies of Literacy: Continuities and Contradictions in Western Culture and Society*, Harvey Graff points out that "virtually all" discussions of literacy "founder because they slight efforts to formulate consistent and realistic *definitions of literacy*, have little appreciation of the *conceptual complications* that the subject presents, and ignore the vital role of *sociohistorical context*."[1] Yet within the mainstream of literacy studies, the issue has been less to define literacy than to establish a standard or norm for the application of an existing definition, which corresponds to the lay understanding of literacy as "the ability to use reading and writing" (*OED*). The prevailing question has been *how much* such ability qualifies an individual as literate, or perhaps whether that ability might inhere only in reading (as a minimum threshold), which is understood as the ability to decode writing (or phonetic script). This question is political in that it helps determine literacy rates, which affect policy and funding decisions.[2] For scholarly methodology, a consistent standard such as Graff's "basic or primary levels of reading and writing" allows for comparisons between contexts "over time and across space."[3] Such comparisons undermine the broad, optimistic generalizations about the cognitive and societal "consequences" of literacy that flourished during a previous generation of scholarship by illuminating the vast discrepancies in the uses and distribution of literacy in societies that have been qualified as "literate."[4] Yet by any standard, this underlying definition of literacy, with the definitions of reading and writing so conventional as to go unstated, scarcely applies to the preColumbian Americas or to the colonial Americas beyond the missionary fringe of Graff's "Western Culture and Society." Thus within these sociohistorical contexts, the "conceptual complications" attending the use of the term *literacy* abound.

Increasingly, scholars have argued for revised and expanded definitions of "writing," "literacy," and "books" that would include a wide array of Native American media. This essay critiques this intervention. I hope readers will find it to be a sympathetic critique. I share the goal of establishing indigenous media as an important object of early American, early modern, and Native studies, and I reject the proposition that unless a specific medium corresponds to a Eurocentric understanding of the term it is definitively *not* writing. But I argue against the application of such prescriptive, a priori definitions, whether broad or narrow, to what the editors of this collection have aptly characterized as colonial mediascapes.

Until recently, the terms *literacy* and *writing* passed easily and unexamined from general scholarly and common usage into scholarship on the indigenous, colonial, and early national Americas, particularly outside of Mesoamerica. They designated practices and technologies brought over by the European colonists, not indigenous communications. Indeed, these practices were definitively European; the colonists themselves used them to define European identity over and against American. Therein lies the origin of the problem. Samuel Purchas's oft-cited claim that, alongside Europeans, "the Americans" were "as speaking Apes" is altogether representative of the colonists' attitudes: literacy was a marker of cultural superiority.[5]

The boom in academic scholarship on literacy in the 1960s, in which several prominent scholars converged on the idea that alphabetic literacy was the key, causal component of Western civilization, did more to clarify and codify such age-old prejudices than to correct them. Indeed, Walter Ong's characterization of the cognitive consequences of literacy and the "psychodynamics of orality" bears a striking resemblance to Purchas's elaboration of the European's "litterall advantage": "by speech we utter our minds once, at the present, to the present, as present occasions move (and perhaps unadvisedly transport) us: but by writing Man seems immortall."[6] For Ong, Eric Havelock, Jack Goody, and others, the adoption of a phonetic alphabet engendered the capacities for historical consciousness, abstract thought, and, on a collective level, bureaucratic organization. The attribution of these supposed advances to the adoption of an alphabet had the ineluctable corollary of leaving those without an alphabet behind, occasioning a "Great Divide," as this school of thought has been labeled, between so-called literate and so-called oral societies.

The subsequent generation of literacy scholars assiduously dismantled the Great Divide theories, querying their technological determinism by examining the interrelated "uses" of written and spoken language in context, and invalidating many of their generalizations about "literacy" and "orality" as descriptors of culture. Similarly, applications of the Great Divide typology in early American studies drew substantial critique. These include Tzvetan Todorov's unfortunate claim in *The Conquest of America* that the Spaniards enjoyed a decisive *cognitive* advantage over, in order, the Mayas, the Aztecs, and the Incas. According to Todorov, these civilizations were ranged at increasing degrees of distance from the evolutionary goal of alphabetic literacy; he considers "writing as an index of the evolution of mental structures."[7] Less prominently, James Axtell argued in "The Power of Print in the Eastern Woodlands" that the Indians were universally awed by the magic of European literacy, an impressionability that the Jesuits capitalized upon and the Puritans neglected.[8] Critics have agreed that such arguments have little basis outside of the Great

Andrew Newman

Divide theories themselves. Peter Wogan argues that the numerous European reports of Native awe at literacy are more reliably indicative of "European ideologies of writing" than of Native perceptions.[9] Stephen Greenblatt suggests that the "narcissism that probably always attaches to one's own speech was intensified by the possession of a technology of preservation and reproduction."[10]

Early colonial accounts also narcissistically reported the Native Americans' admiration for and awe at other European technologies. Yet no one questions, or attempts to redefine, the initial exclusivity of firearms, or horses, or navigational instruments, which also functioned as markers of difference.[11] Literacy is arguably more constitutive of the identities of the colonial authors, as well as those of the colonialist scholars who read them. A better comparison might be to agriculture, which is linked to literacy through the metaphorical extension of *cultivation*.[12] Perhaps more so than literacy, colonists considered their practice of sedentary agriculture as definitive of their difference from the Native Americans. At least, it was more integral to their legal justifications for dispossessing the Indians of their supposedly uncultivated land. Yet as Stuart Banner notes, the preconception that the Natives were savages—meaning that they did not practice cultivation—was "quickly contradicted by experience." Colonial writers sent back many reports observing indigenous agricultural practices. Similarly, although when soil became depleted the Indians would relocate their villages and reapportion plots of land, it became apparent that the Indians had a "system of property rights" associated with their agricultural practice: "if the Indians' property system was not exactly like the English system, it clearly *was* a property system."[13] These realizations had legal implications, and the Europeans adjusted accordingly. Nevertheless, the categorical distinction between Indian hunters and European farmers remained intact through and beyond the colonial era. Among countless expressions of this perception is Crevecoeur's famous fear ("once hunters, farewell to the plough") that backwoodsmen will degenerate into "new made Indians."[14] To whatever extent colonists acknowledged that Indians drew subsistence from agriculture, they did not consider it to be definitive of Native American culture in the sense that hunting was.

Similarly, although colonists readily recognized that the Iroquois and Algonquians had communicative media, especially pictographs (or "hieroglyphics") and wampum, that filled functions analogous to the European alphabet, Indians and Europeans alike perceived, according to James Merrell, not a "spectrum of communicative forms" but a "divide separating peoples that could read and write from those that could not."[15] But was the perception of this divide a product of the failure to recognize that although indigenous writing systems were not exactly like European ones, they nevertheless were writing systems? Have colonialist scholars reproduced this error?

Redefinitions

One way to reconceptualize the definition of literacy (the ability to use reading and writing) so as to include the use of Native American sign systems is to revise our understanding of writing. Most laypersons and scholars, when they use the word *writing*, refer to the use of alphabetic script. Many scholars of writing, or grammatologists, have defined writing as the visual representation of spoken language and consider alphabetic systems the most efficient form of such representation—the pinnacle of the evolution of writing. Other visual or tactile semiotic systems are either subordinate categories of writing or rudimentary forms that lie outside the category. In his tendentious *Visible Speech: The Diverse Oneness of Writing Systems*, John DeFrancis parses the grammatological debate over where to bound the concept of writing as pitting "inclusivists," for whom "writing includes *any* system of graphic symbols that is used to convey *some amount of thought*," against "exclusivists," for whom "writing includes *only* those systems of graphic symbols that convey *any and all thought*."[16] Peter T. Daniels provides a representative exclusivist definition in *The World's Writing Systems* (1996): writing is "*a system of more or less permanent marks used to represent an utterance in such a way that it can be recovered more or less exactly without the intervention of the ut-*

Andrew Newman

terer."[17] This definition, a theoretical description of the operation of alphabetic systems, corresponds to the widespread and conventional understanding of writing. For the purposes of this essay I will employ the exclusivist/inclusivist binary, which I feel is an apt if imperfect characterization of the different sides in the debate.

According to Elizabeth Hill Boone, exclusivist definitions "summarily dismiss the indigenous Western Hemisphere."[18] As she points out, the only indigenous writing included within *The World's Writing Systems* is Mayan, which is both pictographic and phonetic.[19] Boone's introduction to the collection *Writing without Words: Indigenous Literacies in Mesoamerica and the Andes* has been the fountainhead for an Americanist inclusivist argument that, roughly speaking, began with the most obvious candidates for inclusion and has progressed outward, conceptually and geographically, progressing along Todorov's evolutionary hierarchy from the Mayan to the Aztec to the Incan empires and then beyond the systems of the great Mesoamerican and Andean civilizations to those employed by what Eric Cheyfitz describes as the "kinship cultures" of America north of Mexico.[20]

Boone's approach is to take a category that was both outlined and marginalized by the grammatologists Ignace J. Gelb and Geoffrey Sampson, to question its subordination to phonetic writing, and to urge its inclusion within an expanded definition of writing: "*the communication of relatively specific ideas in a conventional manner by means of permanent, visible marks.*"[21] This definition, then, would include not only phonetic systems but also "semasiographic" ones that do not represent language (or "words"); they represent ideas. They therefore disrupt what is commonly thought to be a coextensive relationship between writing and spoken language. Boone gives examples of extant and quotidian semasiographic systems, such as the "conventional" notational systems for music, math, and chemistry and mostly "iconic" systems such as road signs. In pre-Columbian America, she considers the Aztec pictographs and the Peruvian knotted cords, or khipu, to be semasiographic in function.[22]

Boone highlights the advantages of semasiographic systems over the language-bound phonetic ones.[23] She points to the deficiencies of speech, and therefore of phonetic systems, in conveying "ideas of a musical, mathematical, or visual nature."[24] Far from evolutionary precursors, semasiographs are increasingly the medium of the future; as "our culture becomes more visual" and, implicitly, global, we grow more reliant on "largely iconic systems that carry meaning without a detour through speech." Importantly, these systems are not fully iconic; that is, the images are not simply visual depictions of their referents. Rather, their communication of meaning involves convention and context. (She gives the example of an instruction panel for a hand dryer in a public bathroom.) As with alphabetic writing, meaning emerges through the "interplay" of the elements: they have a grammar. Readers familiar with the images, the grammar, and the context usually "understand the meaning at a glance."[25]

Exclusivists counter that compared with phonetic systems, which have the full semantic (not to say expressive) range of spoken language, semasiographic systems are limited in the volume and complexity of the information they convey. According to DeFrancis, nonphonetic symbol systems, or "codes," are necessarily limited in scope; if they qualify as writing, they do not qualify as comprehensive systems. He distinguishes between "partial" and "full" writing.[26] Similarly, Steven Roger Fischer, in *A History of Writing*, distinguishes between "complete" and "incomplete" writing. For exclusivist grammatologists, pictography, knot records, and other "primitive" Native American media fall under the latter category.[27]

Yet as with the proponents of the thesis that literacy begets civilization, the exclusivists might be discomfited to find their arguments anticipated in colonial discourse. Samuel Purchas was actually more ecumenical in his definition of writing than proponents of the visible speech construct might assume; he acknowledged not only phonetic and logographic systems (in which the symbol stands for a word) but also semasiographic ones. He also imposed a steep hierarchy. According to Purchas, peoples wrote "with Quippos in Stones and Threads, as in Peru; with Pictures as in Mexico, and the Egyptian Hieroglyph-

Andrew Newman

ikes; with Characters, each expressing a word or thing, not a letter, as the Chinois, Japonites, and our Arithmeticians and Astronomers in the figures of their Arts . . . the most have used letters, which by Art are disposed to frame all words, and hath beene the most complete kind of writing which ever was."[28] In the context of an enormous compilation celebrating the project of empire building, Purchas's grammatological hierarchy clearly fits with the imperialist ideology of the *translatio imperii et studii*—the conquest by "the culture-bringers."[29]

The exclusivists try to shed such ideological baggage by assuming a posture of objectivity. With J. Marshall Unger, DeFrancis complains that the inclusivist definition of writing is "so vague as to be useless as a technical term—not all gesture is dance; not all landscapes are maps; not all human noises are music. Why must all intentional visible marks be writing?"[30] As Kathryn Woolard explains in the introduction to *Language Ideologies: Theories and Practice*, however, the "definition of what is and what isn't literacy is never purely technical but always a political matter."[31] The exclusivists seem willfully obtuse to this point, and to the arbitrariness of their placement of a boundary between what is and what isn't "true" writing. Boone might argue that the vagueness they object to is simply the price one must pay for a rigorous examination of the assumptions underlying definitions—a familiar corollary of poststructuralism, which is full of inconveniences to anyone attempting a straightforward argument. Yet her imperative that "it is essential that we . . . include" semasiographic systems in the "definition of writing" seems to be driven more by ideology than by methodology. It is indeed important to "recognize supralinguistic ways of presenting knowledge," but why must that recognition entail a designation as "writing"?[32]

The controversy over Incan khipu is especially instructive, because the impetus to classify the khipu as writing seems to come as much from a perceived need to legitimize the Incan civilization as from a desire to understand the khipu. "The Inka have, for too long, been set apart as the one civilization without writing," wrote Robert Ascher in

"Inka Writing" in 2002.[33] "People feel this great need to pump up the Inca by indicating that the khipu were writing," Patricia J. Lyon of the Institute of Andean Studies at Berkeley said to the *New York Times*, commenting on Gary Urton's book *Signs of the Inka Khipu: Binary Coding in the Andean Knotted-String Records* (2003).[34] Yet apparently, with the khipu, the Incas had a complex, if now largely indecipherable, record-keeping system that fulfilled the administrative needs of a massive and complex social organization. Calling it writing does not make it any more sophisticated, and it does not make the Incan civilization any more advanced. Urton himself, assessing the complications of definitions of writing that either conflate or distinguish between "sound-based" and "meaning-based" "sign systems," calls the khipu writing "primarily for want of a better term."[35] In 2005, with Carrie Brezine, Urton announced a significant step in understanding how the khipu carried meaning, determining that each khipu in a set encoded "place identifiers."[36] As a "binary coding" system, the khipu are possibly more analogous to digital media than to writing. Is digitization a form of writing? Conceivably the answer is yes, but there is no ideological imperative to make that case.[37]

Nor is there a methodological imperative. The usefulness of "writing" as a conceptual lens for analyzing Native media is mixed. According to Boone, "art and writing in pre-Columbian America are largely the same thing."[38] She discusses the resulting difficulty in categorizing pre-Columbian sign systems, but she does not explain the decision to employ a single English term. (Indeed, recent scholarship suggests that during the colonial period the European concept of writing was more easily contained by indigenous categories than vice versa.)[39] The title of the roundtable that led to *Writing without Words* was "Art and Writing: Recording Knowledge in Pre-Columbian America." For Boone, the conjunctive phrase "Art and Writing" is misleading, suggesting a gap between the concepts where none existed. With the final publication title, however—*Writing without Words: Alternative Literacies in Mesoamerica and the Andes*—Boone and Mignolo choose to incorporate the fission between "Art" and "Writing" into "Writing" and "Literacies" in order to "explode" the "assumptions" underlying the common usage of those terms.[40] Yet perhaps this intervention is not entirely compatible with the goal of understanding pre-Columbian record keeping. (The publication's previous working title, "Records without Words," seems more straightforwardly accurate.) The terms "Writing" and "Literacies" (and "Book") may even push back against their radical dilation, constraining the conceptions of forms that they do not quite comprehend.

Extensions and Applications

Scholars have taken up the inclusivist argument in ways that are unanticipated by Boone's essay. For example, in "Pictures, Gestures, Hieroglyphs: 'Mute Eloquence' in Sixteenth-Century Mexico," Pauline Moffit Watts, "extrapolating from Boone's definition of writing," arrives at a formulation of "literacies" that resembles those proposed by educational theorists such as James Paul Gee and the New London Group. Gee argues that the restrictive understanding of literacy depends on a mistaken perception of "reading and writing as decontextualized and isolable skills"; by contrast, he defines "literacies" as competencies in the systematic and multimodal "ways of being in the world" that he calls "discourses."[41] For Gee, a given literacy may involve reading and writing, but it invariably involves many more modalities. Similarly, the New London Group proposes a pedagogy of "multiliteracies," which "focus on modes of representation much broader than language alone. These differ according to culture and context and have specific cognitive, cultural, and social effects."[42] Watts points out that while a majority of people in both Renaissance Europe and early colonial Mexico did not read and write, in the narrow sense, they were "literate in various visual, tactile, *and performative* systems of recording and transmitting information."[43]

This insight, which can certainly be extended to America north of Mexico, closes the supposed gap between indigenous and Western cultures of communication and diminishes the significance attached to the presence or absence of any single communicative medium. Yet the insight is not dependent on a redefinition of literacy; it is not necessary to characterize communicative systems as "literacies" in order to study them, comparatively or otherwise. The major thrust of literacy scholarship, inside and outside of early American studies, has been to elaborate the social contexts—including other media—for "uses" of literacy, narrowly defined, and to move beyond the "autonomous model" characteristic of the literacy thesis. Gee is mistaken in assuming that an understanding of literacy as the ability to read and write entails a perception of literacy as a decontextualized skill. Thus thinking of the ability to read and write as one of many possible communicative competencies or "literacies," and thinking of "literacy" (or the ability to read and write) as one of many possible communicative competencies, may be interchangeable propositions—except for that issue of politics. Yet the political correctness is also double-edged: the choice is between denying to Native media a title with as much clout as literacy, or subsuming Native media under a category that traditionally and etymologically refers to a single Western form.[44] Why *literacy*?

The usage of "literacies" in the subtitle of *Writing without Words* corresponds not to the concept of "multiliteracies" but rather to the more narrowly "pluralist" definition of literacies that recognizes "distinct *forms* of reading and writing."[45] As scholars have extended Boone's definition of writing into Native America north of Mexico, however, the two meanings have partly converged, insofar as the categorization of different sign systems may involve the recognition of their embeddedness in multimedia contexts for communication. As Hilary Wyss observes in "Indigenous Literacies: New England and New Spain," New English colonists less readily acknowledged the Native communicative practices they encountered as literacy because they were not so much repositories of information as tools for the activation of communal meanings: "Images on baskets, pictographs, the mats that lined the interiors of wigwams, and utensils all reinforce oral exchanges whose functions are extremely varied but always include a community element."[46]

At first glance, the systems used by Native Americans north of

Andrew Newman

Mexico before the arrival of European colonists seem beyond the scope of any definition of writing. Unlike the Inca Empire, which, as Galen Brokaw notes in this volume, "has always been something of an embarrassment to the theory that the development of complex socioeconomic and political institutions requires the existence of writing," the peoples north of Mexico seemed consistent with this theory: no writing, no civilization.[47] Like the Natives of Mesoamerica, those of North America practiced pictography, but there was a difference in scale, both in the number of pictographic texts and the scope of those texts. DeFrancis, critiquing scholars who considered the winter counts or "chronological records of the Dakotas" as writing, claimed that "such pictographs are no more informative than the depicted objects themselves. They are not writing." He adds that more substantive pictographic records are "very few in number" and that inclusivist scholars keep trotting out the same "two or three examples."[48]

Germaine Warkentin points out that even Gordon Brotherston's inclusivist *Book of the Fourth World* "concentrates on Latin America, reaching north only to draw the mound-builders of the Ohio and Mississippi Rivers (Turtle Island) and the early history of the Algonquins and Lenape into a discussion dominated by the written culture of peoples farther south."[49] By referring to Brotherston's discussion of "the early history of the Algonquins and Lenape," Warkentin unintentionally exemplifies the problem she is addressing, because the text he adduces is the *Walam Olum*, a pictographic migration epic that recounts ninety generations, or successions of "Kings."[50] The 1921 *Cambridge History of American Literature* describes the *Walam Olum* as "the one native record that could be called, in our fashion, a book."[51] Yet the *Walam Olum* has proven to be apocryphal.[52] As Warkentin points out in this volume, such a "unbroken, centuries-long written history" is "difficult to find north of the Rio Grande, where the many Native systems of knowledge transfer vary so greatly in their symbolic expression, easily degradable materials, and social functions that, taken as a group, they make an explanatory theory based on traditional concepts of 'the book' almost useless."[53]

Similarly, the indigenous media of what is now the United States and Canada strain the capacity of inclusive—much less "traditional"—concepts of writing, such as those provided by Ignace J. Gelb and Augustine Gaur. Gelb proposes a definition of writing as "a system of human intercommunication by means of conventional marks." He classifies pictography and mnemonic media such as tallies as "Forerunners of Writing" and, like others, posits an evolutionary schema in which the "phonetization of the script" was the great leap forward.[54] For Gaur, writing is "information storage" in which "the information is stored mechanically, on an independent object, and can be retrieved and used at the same time, in any place (in the case of moveable objects such as books etc.) by all those who are able to consult and decode it." Gaur contradicts herself, first stating that writing demands memory only insofar as users need to remember the signification of the signs (whether phonetic or ideographic) but then listing memory aids or mnemonic devices as forms of writing.[55] Yet the wampum belts exchanged in Iroquoian and Algonquian diplomacy cannot be sufficiently characterized as either storage systems or memory aids: they marked and substantiated the delivery of orations; like contracts, they enforced and commemorated verbal agreements.[56]

Wampum was also a medium of exchange. Gordon Sayre, also extending Boone's definition of writing to the Eastern Woodlands, suggests that the encounter with Iroquoian and Algonquian cultures "confounded" European notions "of writing, money, and clothing as separate systems."[57] Similarly, Warkentin wonders if "the European definition of the 'written' in fact may involve some sort of category mistake."[58] But the question is circular: to include "wampum and other Native signification systems" is to redefine the category. Warkentin brings nuance to the inclusivist argument by recognizing the potentially reductive effect of Western classifications for indigenous media: "I am not thus consenting to yet one more act of appropriation that would reduce a Native category to a European understanding of it."[59] Yet she suggests that the redefinition of writing might have profound and positive political and juridical implications: it might, for example,

Andrew Newman

give wampum belts equal weight with print records in suits over centuries-old land transactions. This important claim, however, comes at the cost of a concession to the forensic bias toward written records over oral ones. Carried from the courtroom into scholarly practice, this argument would have the corollary of diminishing the evidentiary value of Native histories that were not accompanied by some sort of material sign system.

Moreover, whatever the status of written evidence in the courtroom, and despite the continuing privileging of "documentary evidence" in scholarship, a categorization as "writing" is not a prerequisite for the academic analysis of indigenous media from what is now the United States and Canada. Birgit Brander Rasmussen proposes that her definition of writing—the *"communication of relatively specific ideas transmitted across space and/or time by use of a conventionalized system of visual or tactile marks understood by a given community of readers"*—makes it "possible to move from monologic to dialogic studies of colonial conflict."[60] Yet there have been countless studies of intermediality—for example, of the interchange between poetry and music—that have not found it necessary or productive to extend the definition of one medium to include the other. Contrary to Rasmussen's premise, it is not necessary to accept her "redefinition of writing" to appreciate her insights, nor those of other recent research that takes a media-studies approach to colonial encounters.[61] As Jens Schröter suggests, it is precisely by studying the dynamic interactions among media that we come to understand their commonalities and differences; we might therefore arrive at definitions instead of beginning with them.[62]

Any definition of writing will leave some media, some people, out. "Just as there is no people without history," writes Arnold Krupat, "so too, is there no people without writing." Yet his list of forms of "Native *writing*" is drastically insufficient to sustain such a claim. In its entirety, it includes "such things as the 'string balls' of various material constructed by Yakima girls from their early childhood and the birchbark scrolls of the Chippewa *mite* priests. There are Iroquois wampum strings which, as Sir William Johnson wrote in 1753, 'they

look upon as we our letters, or rather bonds.' There are Plains pictographs painted on tipis, robes, and shirts, and Lakota winter counts
which we shall consider further."[63] The necessary "and so on" is weakly implied, but Krupat has nearly exhausted the gamut of Native
North American candidates for inclusion in the category of writing,
and there are plenty of "people" who have not been matched up with
a sign system.

But what does it mean to say that a people is with or without writing? Even in the case of alphabetic scripts, the issue is much more
complex than the dispute over definitions makes it seem. A famous
study by Sylvia Scribner and Michael Cole is particularly relevant. The
Vai people of Liberia used three different scripts: a native syllabary,
Arabic, and English. Scribner and Cole's analysis of those who were
literate in one or more of these scripts revealed that each was associated with different uses and specific use-related cognitive skills.[64] Thus
it is not tenable to generalize about the uses and significances of different phonetic scripts even within a culture. In that regard, the argument that we should consider wampum as a form of writing becomes
an unnecessary distraction from the study of the uses of wampum in
indigenous and colonial contexts.

The irony of the impulse to confer the title "writing" upon any and
all indigenous media is that it actually upholds, and even inflates, the
prestige of writing as a cultural credential. I agree with Boone that the
exclusivist discussion of non-alphabetic sign systems is marked by an
"insidious pejorative tone," but the argument that it is derogatory *not*
to classify a medium as writing reinforces the very value judgment it
contests.[65] Viewed as language ideologies, exclusivism and inclusivism share a Eurocentric emphasis on the importance of possessing a
writing system.

"Indian Writing"

In this essay I have argued that the prescriptive application of an inclusive definition of "writing" to the media of the indigenous Americas is of dubious methodological value, and that even its ideological

Andrew Newman

thrust goes awry. Yet disputing the proposition that not recognizing wampum or pictography as writing constitutes a dismissal or failure is not to deny the usefulness of comparison. The comparison to European writing, despite the pitfalls of cultural translation, is one of the limited means available to scholars of indigenous peoples and colonialism for understanding so-called alternative literacies. As scholars like Rasmussen have demonstrated, the colonists and Native Americans employed communicative media in ways that are both analogous and distinct, and their uses and forms were altered and adapted through colonial interaction or "dialogization."[66]

Historical actors and observers, Europeans and Native Americans alike, also availed themselves of this comparison. For example, the Moravian missionary John Heckewelder, whose *Account of the History, Manners and Customs of the Indian Nations who Once Inhabited Pennsylvania and the Neighboring States* (1819) is in part an impassioned defense of Native American cultures of communication against charges of inferiority, drew an analogy between the use of diplomatic wampum, in strings and belts, and the keeping of written records. Describing the practice of "the turning of the belt," he explained that when it "is done properly, it may be as well known by it how far the speaker has advanced in his speech, as with us on taking a glance at the pages of a book or pamphlet while reading; and a good speaker will be able to point out the exact place on a belt which is to answer to each particular sentence, the same as we can point out a passage in a book."[67]

In his chapter on "Signs and Hieroglyphics," Heckewelder allows that the Indians "do not possess our art of writing," which he defines as the use of "alphabets, or any mode of representing to the eye the sounds of words spoken."[68] He insists, however, that they have a communicative system that is in some respects more ideal than phonetic script. His ensuing description of "Indian writing" is similar to Boone's discussion of semasiography in that he suggests the advantages of independence from spoken language. He explains that Indians use "hieroglyphics" or "Indian writing" to "describe facts in so plain a manner, that those who are conversant with those marks can understand them with the greatest ease, as easily, indeed, as we can understand a piece of writing." For example, "marks" traced by a war party on the stripped side of a tree can convey "all necessary information" to those coming the same way: the tribal affiliation of the chief and warriors, the days spent coming and going, the number of fatalities and of scalps and prisoners taken, and so on: "all which, at a single glance, is perfectly well understood by them . . . all Indian nations can do this, although they have not all the same marks; yet I have seen the Delawares read with ease the drawings of the Chippeways, Mingoes, Shawanos, and Wyandots, on similar subjects."[69] Implicitly, the pictographic system, like the system of gestures or "signs," is more immediate and efficient, and less inhibited by cultural difference, than phonetic language because it represents meaning "without a detour through speech."[70]

Heckewelder concludes this chapter with an "anecdote" to "shew how expressive and energetic is this hieroglyphic writing of the Indians":

A white man in the Indian country, met a Shawanos riding a horse which he recognised for his own, and claimed it from him as his property. The Indian calmly answered "Friend! after a little while, I will call on you at your house, when we shall talk of this matter." A few days afterwards, the Indian came to the white man's house, who insisting on having his horse restored, the other then told him: "Friend! the horse which you claim belonged to my uncle who lately died; according to the Indian custom, I have become heir to all his property." The white man not being satisfied, and renewing his demand, the Indian immediately took a coal from the fire-place, and made two striking figures on the door of the house, the one representing the white man taking the horse, and the other, himself, in the act of scalping him; then he coolly asked the trembling claimant "whether he could read this Indian writing?" The matter thus was settled at once, and the Indian rode off.[71]

Andrew Newman

The humor of the anecdote comes from role reversal: more typically, in the experience of both Indians and colonists, colonists used writing to authorize their dispossession of Indian property. In that regard, the Shawnee's drawing is comparable to a European document not in terms of its semiotic operation but in terms of its use to enforce a property claim. In this particular context, the "white man in the Indian country" could hardly afford to fail to recognize the drawing as writing.

For the purposes of scholarship, however, the analogy is better conceived of as a starting point. The comparative framework can enhance our understanding of both indigenous and European media. A value to the inclusivists' intervention is that it should compel colonialist scholars to think about what they mean when they refer to writing and literacy and books. With regard to a context such as the Puritan communities in colonial New England, the boundaries demarcating these concepts may feel close at hand. Yet when we turn our attention to indigenous media we reach for these boundaries—and find that they don't actually exist.

Notes

1. Harvey J. Graff, *The Legacies of Literacy: Continuities and Contradictions in Western Culture and Society* (Bloomington: Indiana University Press, 1987), 3.
2. Peter Roberts, "Defining Literacy: Paradise, Nightmare or Red Herring?" *British Journal of Educational Studies* 43.4 (December 1995): 113.
3. Graff, *The Legacies of Literacy*, 3.
4. For an example of the methodological problem of varying standards ("definitions") of alphabetic literacy, see Javier Nuñez Errazuriz, "Signed with an X: Methodology and Data Sources for Analyzing the Evolution of Literacy in Latin America and the Caribbean, 1900–1950," *Latin American Research Review* 40.2 (2005): 118.
5. Samuel Purchas, *Hakluytus Posthumus, or Purchas His Pilgrimes: Contayning a History of the World in Sea Voyages and Lande Travells by Englishmen and Others*, 20 vols. (Glasgow: James MacLehose and Sons, 1905), 1:486. I discuss this use of literacy, narrowly conceived, by the authors of captivity narratives in "Captive on the Literacy Frontier: Mary Rowlandson, James Smith and Charles Johnston," *Early American Literature* 38.1 (2003): 31–65.

6. Purchas, *Hakluytus Posthumus*, 1:486; Walter Ong, *Orality and Literacy: The Technologizing of the Word* (New York: Methuen, 1982), 31–65.

7. Tzvetan Todorov, *The Conquest of America: The Question of the Other* (New York: Harper & Row, 1984), 81–82.

8. James Axtell, *After Columbus: Essays in the Ethnohistory of Colonial North America* (Oxford: Oxford University Press, 1988), 86–99.

9. Peter Wogan, "Perceptions of European Literacy in Early Contact Situations," *Ethnohistory* 41.3 (Summer 1994): 410.

10. Stephen Greenblatt, *Marvelous Possessions: The Wonder of the New World* (Chicago: University of Chicago Press, 1991), 9. Also on Todorov, see Eric Cheyfitz, *The Poetics of Imperialism: Translation and Colonization from "The Tempest" to Tarzan* (New York: Oxford University Press, 1991), xxiv–xxv; Dennis Tedlock, "Dialogues between Worlds: Mesoamerica after and before the European Invasion," in *Theorizing the Americanist Tradition*, ed. L. P. Valentine and R. Darnell (Toronto: Toronto University Press, 1999), 163–80. On Axtell and Wogan, see Phillip H. Round, *Removable Type: Histories of the Book in Indian Country, 1663–1880* (Chapel Hill: University of North Carolina Press, 2010), 11.

11. Bernal Díaz describes Hernán Cortes's theatrical use of cannon and horse to awe the Natives in *The Conquest of New Spain* (New York: Penguin Classics, 1963), 78–80. John Smith reports that, after his initial capture, he gained the advantage by producing his compass: "Much they marvailed at the playing of the Fly and Needle, which they could see so plainely, and yet not touch them, because of the glass that covered them." He uses the instrument as a pretext for what, in his view, is an awe-inspiring discourse on European cosmographic knowledge. John Smith, *Captain John Smith: A Select Edition of His Writings*, ed. Karen Ordahl Kupperman (Chapel Hill: University of North Carolina Press, 1988), 80. Andrew Lipman puts the "brazen claims of European superiority" in context by distinguishing "between 'common' navigation, meaning coastal piloting and relative positioning with the age-old techniques of local knowledge and dead reckoning, and 'grand' navigation, meaning sailing courses out of sight of land with the aid of charts and global-positioning devices such as compasses, sextants, and astrolabes." "Murder on the Saltwater Frontier: The Death of John Oldham," *Early American Studies: An Interdisciplinary Journal* 9.2 (2011): 274.

12. Richard Waswo, *The Founding Legend of Western Civilization: From Virgil to Vietnam* (Hanover NH: University Press of New England [for] Wesleyan University Press, 1997), xiii, 15–20.

Andrew Newman

13. Stuart Banner, *How the Indians Lost Their Land: Law and Power on the Frontier* (Cambridge: Harvard University Press, 2005), 19–20.

14. J. Hector St. John De Crevecoeur, *Letters from an American Farmer and Sketches of Eighteenth-Century America* (New York: Penguin Classics, 1981), 44.

15. James H. Merrell, *Into the American Woods: Negotiators on the American Frontier* (New York: Norton, 1999), 215.

16. John DeFrancis, *Visible Speech: The Diverse Oneness of Writing Systems* (Honolulu: University of Hawaii Press, 1989), 4.

17. Peter T. Daniels, "The Study of Writing Systems," in *The World's Writing Systems*, ed. Peter T. Daniels and William Bright (New York: Oxford University Press, 1996), 3.

18. Elizabeth Hill Boone, "Introduction: Writing and Recording Knowledge," in *Writing without Words: Alternative Literacies in Mesoamerica and the Andes*, ed. Elizabeth Hill Boone and Walter Mignolo (Durham: Duke University Press, 1994), 9.

19. See Martha J. Macri, "Maya and Other Mesoamerican Scripts," in Daniels and Bright, *The World's Writing Systems*, 172–88.

20. Cheyfitz, *The Poetics of Imperialism*, xxiv.

21. Boone, "Introduction," 15.

22. Boone, "Introduction," 16.

23. Boone, "Introduction," 7.

24. Boone, "Introduction," 9.

25. Boone, "Introduction," 10, 16–17.

26. DeFrancis, *Visible Speech*, 20–64.

27. Steven Roger Fischer, *A History of Writing* (London: Reaktion, 2001), 11–33.

28. Purchas, *Hakluytus Posthumus*, 1:492.

29. See Waswo, *Founding Legend*, 29–37.

30. J. Marshall Unger and John DeFrancis, "Logographic and Semasiographic Systems: A Critique of Sampson's Classifications," in *Scripts and Literacy: Reading and Learning to Read Alphabets, Syllabaries, and Characters*, ed. Insup Taylor and David R. Olson (Dordrecht: Kluwer, 1995), 46.

31. Kathryn A. Woolard, "Introduction: Language Ideology as a Field of Inquiry," in *Language Ideologies: Theory and Practice*, ed. Bambi B. Schieffelin, Kathryn A. Woolard, and Paul V. Kroskrity (New York: Oxford University Press, 1998), 23.

32. Boone, "Introduction," 17.

33. Robert Ascher, "Inka Writing," in *Narrative Threads: Accounting and Recounting in Andean Khipu*, ed. Jeffrey Quilter and Gary Urton (Austin: University of Texas Press, 2002), 103.

34. John Noble Wilford, "String, and Knot, Theory of Inca Writing," *New York Times*, August 12, 2003, sec. Science.

35. Gary Urton, *Signs of the Inka Khipu: Binary Coding in the Andean Knotted-String Records* (Austin: University of Texas Press, 2003), 27–28.

36. Gary Urton and Carrie J. Brezine, "Khipu Accounting in Ancient Peru," *Science* 12.309 (August 2005): 1065–67.

37. For further discussion of the qualification of khipu as writing, see in the present volume the chapters by Ralph Bauer and Galen Brokaw.

38. Boone, "Introduction," 3; see also Walter D. Mignolo, "Afterword: Writing and Recorded Knowledge in Colonial and Postcolonial Situations," in Boone and Mignolo, *Writing without Words*, 293–94.

39. According to Lisa Brooks, "the Abenaki word *awikhigan*, which originally described birchbark messages, maps, and scrolls, came to encompass books and letters." *The Common Pot: The Recovery of Native Space in the Northeast* (Minneapolis: University of Minnesota Press, 2008), xxi. I take a similar lesson from Galen Brokaw's contribution to this volume.

40. Boone, "Introduction," 3.

41. James Paul Gee, *Social Linguistics and Literacies: Ideology in Discourses*, 3rd ed. (New York: Taylor & Francis, 2007), 176, 210.

42. Bill Cope, Mary Kalantzis, and New London Group, *Multiliteracies: Literacy Learning and the Design of Social Futures* (London: Routledge, 2000), 5.

43. Pauline Moffitt Watts, "Pictures, Gestures, Hieroglyphs: 'Mute Eloquence' in Sixteenth-Century Mexico," in *The Language Encounter in the Americas, 1492–1800: A Collection of Essays*, ed. Edward G. Gray and Norman Fiering (New York: Berghahn Books, 2000), 82.

44. As Anthony Webster points out in a relevant discussion, "etymology, the search for a word's 'true meaning,' is a linguistic ideology." Anthony K. Webster, "Keeping the Word: On Orality and Literacy (With a Sideways Glance at Navajo)," *Oral Tradition* 21.2 (2007): 296. My point is that a term's traditional connotations may interfere with new applications; the inclusivists seem only to acknowledge the reverse.

45. Roberts, "Defining Literacy," 420.

46. Hilary E. Wyss, "Indigenous Literacies: New England and New Spain," in *A Companion to the Literatures of Colonial America*, ed. Susan P. Castillo

and Ivy Schweitzer, Blackwell Companions to Literature and Culture (Malden MA: Blackwell, 2005), 394.

47. Brokaw, "Semiotics, Aesthetics, and the Quechua Concept of *Quilca*," 167.

48. DeFrancis, *Visible Speech*, 35.

49. Germaine Warkentin, "In Search of 'The Word of the Other': Aboriginal Sign Systems and the History of the Book in Canada," *Book History* 2 (1999): 35.

50. Gordon Brotherston, *Book of the Fourth World: Reading the Native Americas through Their Literature* (New York: Cambridge University Press, 1992), 191–92; see also Gordon Brotherston, "The Time Remembered in Winter Counts and the Walam Olum," in *Circumpacifica: Festschrift für Thomas S. Barthel* (Frankfurt: Peter Lang, 1990), 2:307–37.

51. Mary Austin, "Non-English Writings II: Aboriginal," in *The Cambridge History of American Literature*, ed. W. P. Trent et al. (New York: Putnam, 1921), 612.

52. David M. Oestreicher, "Unmasking the Walam Olum: A 19th-Century Hoax," *Bulletin of the Archeological Society of New Jersey* 49 (1994): 1–44. For a discussion of the reception of the Walam Olum and the desire to attribute literacy to Native Americans, see Andrew Newman, *On Records: Delaware Indians, Colonists, and the Media of History and Memory* (Lincoln: University of Nebraska Press, 2012), 36–54.

53. Germaine Warkentin, "Dead Metaphor or Working Model? 'The Book' in Native America," 55–56.

54. Ignace J. Gelb, *A Study of Writing: The Foundations of Grammatology* (Chicago: University of Chicago Press, 1952), 12, 24–59.

55. Augustine Gaur, *A History of Writing* (London: British Library, 1984), 14–17.

56. Michael K. Foster, "Another Look at the Function of Wampum in Iroquois-White Councils," in *The History and Culture of Iroquois Diplomacy: An Interdisciplinary Guide to the Treaties of the Six Nations and Their League*, ed. Francis Jennings (Syracuse: Syracuse University Press, 1985), xviii, 278; Birgit Brander Rasmussen, *Queequeg's Coffin: Indigenous Literacies and Early American Literature* (Durham: Duke University Press, 2012).

57. Gordon Sayre, *Les Sauvages Américains: Representations of Native Americans in French and English Colonial Literature* (Chapel Hill: University of North Carolina Press, 1997), 186.

58. Warkentin, "In Search of 'The Word of the Other,'" 12.

59. Warkentin, "In Search of 'The Word of the Other,'" 20.

60. Rasmussen, *Queequeg's Coffin*, 33.

61. For example, Lisa Brooks explores "the ways in which the writing that came from Europe was incorporated into" a "Native space" characterized by the circulation of "Birchbark messages" and "wampum records." *The Common Pot*, 13. According to Matt Cohen, "books, paths, letters, vistas, ceremonial posts, recipes, body decoration, purges, trees, and animals and their sounds all [took] on new signifying powers" through the encounter between English colonists and the native inhabitants of "the Algonquian east coast." *The Networked Wilderness: Communicating in Early New England* (Minneapolis: University of Minnesota Press, 2010), 26. Jeffrey Glover compares the representations of indigenous media in Dutch and English colonial documents in "Channeling Indigenous Geopolitics: Negotiating International Order in Colonial Writing," *PMLA* 125.3 (May 2010): 589–605. Phillip Round discusses how both "oral traditions" and "a wide array of sign systems" "mediated Native use of and reaction to European print." *Removable Type*, 11.

62. Jens Schröter, "Discourses and Models of Intermediality," *CLCWeb: Comparative Literature and Culture* 13.3 (September 1, 2011), http://docs.lib. purdue.edu/clcweb/vol13/iss3/3.

63. Arnold Krupat, *Red Matters: Native American Studies* (Philadelphia: University of Pennsylvania Press, 2002), 66.

64. Sylvia Scribner and Michael Cole, *The Psychology of Literacy* (Cambridge: Harvard University Press, 1981).

65. Scribner and Cole, *Psychology of Literacy*, 7.

66. Rasmussen, *Queequeg's Coffin*, 72.

67. John Heckewelder, *An Account of the History, Manners and Customs of the Indian Nations who Once Inhabited Pennsylvania and the Neighboring States* (Philadelphia: A. Small, 1819), 93–94, as seen in eHRAF World Cultures.

68. Heckewelder, *Account*, 117.

69. Heckewelder, *Account*, 117–18.

70. Boone, "Introduction," 16.

71. Heckewelder, *Account*, 118–19.

Andrew Newman

3

Indigenous Histories and Archival Media in the Early Modern Great Lakes

Heidi Bohaker

For historians seeking to understand indigenous responses to colonialism in early America, or indigenous histories more broadly, the necessity of relying exclusively on sources authored by colonists has proved a frustrating limitation. In recent decades, scholars have thought carefully about the reliability of European-authored sources for the writing of indigenous histories. These researchers have integrated methodologies from comparative literature and history to understand their sources as constructions of European imaginations and discursive practices.[1] Few have arrived at so extreme a conclusion as literary critic Stephen Greenblatt, who argues in his study of the Columbian voyages that the lens through which readers attempt to view "the natives" in European writing is entirely opaque.[2] But Greenblatt and others have done such a thorough job analyzing the many problems of these European-authored sources that the utility of the sources for understanding indigenous histories has been called into question. For the earliest periods of encounter, where such sources are thinnest, the problem is magnified. As Richard White plainly put it in *The Middle Ground*, what historians have been able to reconstuct of the mid-seventeenth-century conflicts in the Great Lakes region is about people who "either had Jesuit missionaries among them or lived beside neighbours that did."[3] This raises a question: Are people who did not create archives of alphabetic writing inherently less knowable than those who did? If so, what is the historian to do? The reality is that indigenous peoples of the Great Lakes region did not produce such documentary records of alphabetic texts written in their own language in any significant quantity until the nineteenth century.[4] Are we therefore left, as Richard White claims, to write about "a historical landscape that consists largely of dim shadows"?[5]

I argue instead that we should move beyond European and colonist-authored print and manuscript sources to study those that indigenous cultures created themselves. We can locate an indigenous-authored archive and use it productively in historical writing if we can redefine our concept of what an archive might be and what sources it might contain. To do so we must consider the worldview behind the sources, make room for culturally distinct ways of recording and communicating information about the past, and consider how such sources are understood within the society that created them. This includes allowing for the possibility that in some worldviews some sources are understood as having agency, and indeed might even be considered persons, as is the case of the *aadizookaanag* (sacred stories) of the Algonquian-speaking Anishinaabeg in the Great Lakes region. The *aadizookaanag*, or grandfathers, are both narratives *and* a class of persons. Such narratives carry knowledge, as do grandparents, and they are recognized as having power and life of their own. Such an archive would therefore include all the ways in which people recorded information and communicated with one another and, by extension, with other-than-human persons.[6] This kind of archive would go far beyond collecting written or print sources, or even looking for their analogues. Instead, it would consider the capacities for recording and transmitting information (and to whom, and for whom) from within the cultural tradition.

It is in this imagining of an expanded archive that the concept of an early American "mediascape" can be a useful theoretical tool. Arjun

Heidi Bohaker

Appadurai developed the concept as part of a larger explanatory framework to theorize the movements of peoples (ethnoscapes), ideas (ideoscapes), technologies (technoscapes), and wealth (financescapes) in the twenty-first-century "global cultural economy." Appadurai chose the suffix "-scape" to explain abstract concepts and relationships between these concepts as a kind of topography in the physical world: real, and yet irregular, loosely bounded areas in contrast with the precision of geometric forms. For Appadurai, the common suffix -scape serves the inclusive purpose of indicating "that these are not objectively given relations which look the same from every angle of vision, but rather that they are deeply perspectival constructs, inflected by the historical, linguistic and political situatedness of different sorts of actors: nation-states, multinationals, diasporic communities, as well as sub-national groupings and movements (whether religious, political or economic), and even intimate face-to-face groups, such as villages, neighbourhoods and families."[7] While Appadurai envisions mediascapes as consisting primarily of electronic communications and "the images of the world created by these media," he does include "preelectronic" hardware as part of this concept.[8] In adapting Appadurai's construct to the early modern Americas, we consider the (clearly) "preelectronic" media on or through which information is produced and exchanged and, at the same time, the images, ideas, and concepts expressed on or through that media. The concept of mediascape is a useful one because it invites historians to seek sources beyond the confines of print culture in order to identify, historicize, and understand the media produced within indigenous cultures.

While indigenous peoples of the Great Lakes region did not begin to produce a significant quantity of writing on paper in alphabetic text until the nineteenth century, they certainly left an inscribed record, where meaning was transmitted from writer to reader through the use of both iconic and symbolic imagery on a diverse range of media. They employed this non-alphabetic semiotic system for both private and public communication. Images of icons and symbols appear on sacred scrolls, wampum, travelers' messages, treaty documents, petitions, weapons, ceremonial objects, tattoos and other body art, community signposts, boundary markers, and grave posts. Today one can find examples of these icons and images in archives, museum collections, and parks on a range of media, including rock, birchbark, paper, wood, and clothing.[9] But these examples, while diverse, are in fact analogues or near analogues of European writing systems. The concept of a mediascape suggests we should cast an even wider net and include other Great Lakes communicative practices like music and sound, the decorative arts, oral tradition, and the use of tobacco smoke as a medium for communication between humans and other-than-human beings in our archive of potential primary source material.[10] This essay will demonstrate the usefulness of a mediascape for the history of this region by describing the rich range of indigenous Great Lakes communication practices and technologies that can be included under this broad conceptual canopy, as well as the implications of using these primary sources in our historical writing.

As Walter Mignolo aptly noted, a great paradox in historical writing is that those people who were most rooted in and deeply aware of the human history in the Americas were themselves perceived by Europeans as not having any history at all, as being "pre-history," because they lacked a system of alphabetic writing.[11] This view, still evident in some recent histories, is increasingly being challenged, and a growing body of scholarship, most notably coming from the disciplines of anthropology and archeology and from the fields of Mesoamerican and South American studies, is calling for recognition of indigenous semasiographic systems as writing.[12] Andrew Newman's essay in this collection, "Early Americanist Grammatology: Definitions of Writing and Literacy," argues that the word *writing* has become overworked by the efforts of these inclusivists, and with not very satisfactory results, as some quite "non-writing" forms of communication and record-keeping technology such as wampum belts bend the definition of writing to the breaking point. Rather than take an inclusivist or exclusionist stance myself on, for example, the question of wampum, I consider it more important to think about wampum belts as a type

Heidi Bohaker

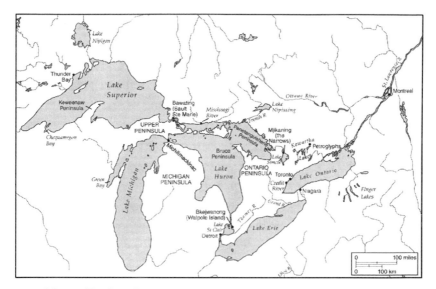

Map 3.1. The Great Lakes region. By Mariange Beaudry, Cartographer & GIS Analyst, Department of Geography, University of Toronto.

of recording device and a communications medium. Our expanded archive first needs a comprehensive inventory of the diverse ways in which people of the Americas thought of and expressed themselves as people with histories. As researchers then begin to build such archival inventories, we will be in a better position to think about ways in which we can interpret the information on these diverse media as historical sources.[13]

Thinking about material culture and art as potential historical sources makes the past less distant and disrupts the periodization of history in the Americas as beginning with the arrival of Europeans. For indigenous peoples of the Great Lakes region, as in the rest of the Americas, the word *early* defines a time well before the arrival of Spanish, French, Dutch, or English sailors. When evidence from oral traditions, archaeology, and linguistics is combined, the rich and millennia-old history of the Great Lakes region is clear. Indigenous oral traditions speak of in situ origins of discrete cultures, but there are histories of migration and relocation as well.[14] Continuous archaeological evidence of human occupation dates from the end of the last period of glaciation, approximately ten to twelve thousand years ago. A growing body of scholarship paints an increasingly detailed picture of major changes in daily life and the development and incorporation of new technologies, but much work remains to be done.[15]

More specifics are known about the history of the last millennia. By this period, speakers of three language families called the Great Lakes region home. Common diplomatic practices had matured, facilitating alliances and trading relationships among the following three culturally and linguistically distinct peoples: nations of Siouian speakers situated to the west and south of Lake Superior; nations (and in the later part of the period, political confederacies) of Iroquoian speakers in the southern Ontario peninsula, along the St. Lawrence and south and east of Lake Ontario; and Algonquian-speaking nations, the most widely distributed, north of Lakes Superior and Huron, south through the Michigan peninsula, and east past the Ottawa River. Archaeological evidence indicates that corn agriculture arrived more than two thousand years ago in the southern part of the Great Lakes most suitable to growing it.[16] Growing factionalism and violence between five Iroquoian-speaking nations south of Lake Ontario led to the formation of a new political organization, possibly as early as the twelfth century and certainly by the fifteenth.[17] Associated with the birth of this new political entity—the Haudenosaunee Confederacy, or "people of the completed longhouse"—is the use of belts and strings of shell wampum as gifts, markers of truth in diplomatic councils and alliance making, and archival records of the agreements they embody.[18]

This Great Lakes region, with its cultural, linguistic, and political complexity, also makes a fascinating case study for the larger project envisioned by another contributor to this volume, Germaine Warkentin. In "Dead Metaphor or Working Model? 'The Book' in Native America," Warkentin proposes a complete reconceptualization of the history of the book. She suggests shifting the focus to "objects of knowledge transfer." I agree with Warkentin in principle, but I further suggest that culturally and regionally specific case studies are neces-

Heidi Bohaker

sary for the construction of larger theoretical conversations; otherwise, the new terminology and thinking tools we construct risk being limited by our own cultural conventions. For example, in the Great Lakes region, cultural categories differ significantly between Haudenosaunee and Anishinaabe peoples and are often sharply different from European ones. In this world, thinking of media of any sort as an object (as in an "object of knowledge transfer") is a problem where the medium (or the substrate, as a bibliographer would say) is alive or has the quality of a living being. I include here not only tattoos and painting on human bodies but also writing on birchbark and painting on rocks. Irving Hallowell, the noted anthropologist of the Algonquian-speaking Anishinaabeg (Ojibwes), understood this worldview when he was told by one informant that some but not all stones were alive. As Hallowell explains, "the Ojibwe are not animists in the sense that they dogmatically attribute living souls to inanimate objects such as stones. . . . Whereas we should never expect a stone to manifest animate properties of any kind under any circumstances, the Ojibwe recognize, *a priori*, potentialities for animation in certain classes of objects under certain circumstances."[19] Scholars need to be mindful of the tension between Western ontological categories and indigenous ones in the classification and analysis of media. Following Appadurai, media must therefore be understood as "deeply perspectival constructs" and be studied within and as part of the cultures that created them.[20] In the Great Lakes region, the medium itself could shape or determine the message.

Categories and Inventories

Mapping the mediascape of the Great Lakes region is an enormous project, and one that is complicated by Western institutional traditions and disciplinary practices. Archives typically store documents, while museums house material culture. While present-day archivists and curators are certainly aware that documents have their own materiality and that material culture can have textual qualities, institutional structures continue to promote the divide. Privileging the time

Fig. 3.1. The "Peace Path" belt: a loom-woven wampum belt recording an alliance relationship. The three diamonds represent nations united together on the path of peace, symbolized by the white line. Belt of white and purple shell beads, twine, nettlestock fiber, and leather, 9.4 x 61 cm, Edward Burnett Tylor Collection, PRM 1896.7.8, Pitt Rivers Museum. Material analysis and interpretation courtesy Great Lakes Research Alliance for the Study of Aboriginal Arts and Culture, record 64. Courtesy Pitt Rivers Museum, University of Oxford.

of "contact" between American and European cultures further reinforces a disciplinary boundary mirrored by many institutions. Material culture collected in an archaeological context, or material culture associated with the time before European contact, is typically stored separately from ethnology collections in museums. Complicating this practice is the fact that archaeologists have traditionally been hired to manage archaeology collections and ethnologists to manage ethnology collections, even when the materials in question pertain to the same peoples or are part of the same continuum of cultural practice. Such institutional habits further fragment knowledge, reinforce the idea of "contact" as a historically significant, nearly impenetrable divide, and make it difficult for scholars to see and appreciate indigenous cultural and political continuities over time, especially in the face of colonization and conquest in more recent centuries.

A practical example of this problem is the challenge faced by historians attempting to compile the communications record of a single late-eighteenth-century land transaction or alliance agreement negotiated between colonial officials and indigenous peoples in the Great Lakes region. Oral tradition of the event may survive in community memory, but that corporate memory could be scattered across several distinct reservations (or reserves in Canada). Just as likely, the oral history has been lost as a result of Canadian and American programs of residential schooling and assimilation that began in the late nineteenth century, which resulted in significant indigenous language loss in many

Heidi Bohaker

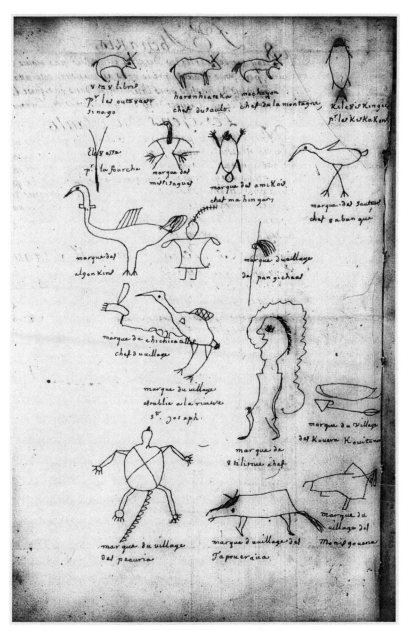

Fig. 3.2. 1701 Great Peace of Montreal. Clerk's copy, second signature page, showing pictographic images of *doodem* and village identity. The original treaty document is no longer extant. Courtesy Archives nationales d'outre-mer, Aix-en-Provence, France. COL C11A 19/Fo 41–44. All rights reserved.

communities. Official "treaty texts" are housed in British and French colonial archives, in a separate Indian Treaties and Surrenders collection of the Library and Archives Canada, or in the ratified treaties collection of the U.S. National Archives and Records Administration. Minutes of council meetings taken at negotiations are typically located in the private papers of whatever colonial official(s) attended, when such minutes were kept and if they have survived (see fig. 3.2). The gifts, including wampum belts (fig. 3.1) and the wampum strings that formed an integral part of eastern Great Lakes diplomacy, can be found, if they have survived, rarely in indigenous hands but most often in the vaults of European and North American museums. In these last cases, the gifts and wampum belts are often without provenance, making their association with specific treaty events difficult to determine.[21] The collectors who purchased or were given these items typically valued them for their "exotic" qualities, not for the significance of the messages that they contained.[22]

To address these and similar problems, a group of interested researchers from indigenous cultural centers, museums, archives, and universities has formed the Great Lakes Research Alliance for the Study of Aboriginal Arts and Cultures (GRASAC). GRASAC emerged out of a question the principal collaborators asked initially in 2004: Can digital technology be deployed to reunite objects from Great Lakes peoples' heritage that are currently scattered across museums and archives in North America and Europe, guided by and in dialogue with aboriginal community knowledge, memory, and perspectives? Pursuing this question (still a work in progress) has resulted in the creation of a network of more than seventy Great Lakes researchers who contribute their knowledge to a database residing at Carleton University in Ottawa, Canada.[23] Our rapidly growing database of nearly four thousand records is the result of multiple team field trips to museums and archives in Canada, the United States, and Europe.[24] It is because of these on-site collaborative, interdisciplinary, and cross-cultural research endeavors that as a historian I can begin to address larger questions about the communication practices of Great Lakes

Heidi Bohaker

peoples. In the remainder of this essay I introduce some of the numerous and varied practices of the region, discussing first those that fit into more conventional Western categories of notational and mnemonic practices and concluding with a discussion of practices that cross, blur, and complicate these categories.[25] In doing so my intention is to demonstrate the usefulness of building comprehensive media inventories and engaging in regional and culture- or community-specific case studies to both historical studies and larger theoretical conversations about communication practices in the Americas.

Notational Practices

Notational practices in the Great Lakes region formed a vital component of the area's communication systems and are the closet analogues to European practices of writing. Communication in this category includes pictographic representation of kinship network or village identity on a range of media, messages left for fellow travelers, grave markers, and public art celebrating martial accomplishment. At the heart of these practices were images used to assert the identity of the writer, author, artist, or inscriber. From this starting point, other signs or marks were used to communicate additional information: for example, people used tick marks on bark or wood to indicate the number of travelers in a party. All these notational practices must be understood within their respective and highly distinctive cultural contexts.

The Anishinaabeg, for example, were organized politically from at least the sixteenth to the nineteenth centuries by their *doodem* identities.[26] Inherited from their fathers and fathers' fathers, this crucial cultural category connected those who shared the same identity in a geographically expansive yet tightly bound sense of family that guaranteed the hospitality due family members. Anishinaabe women kept their *doodem* identities when they married, thereby providing their families with a second set of kin connections on which to rely. Evidence from the field of linguistics corroborates the importance of this identity as a kinship network and establishes it as an old structure, one that clearly predates early seventeenth-century contact with Europe-

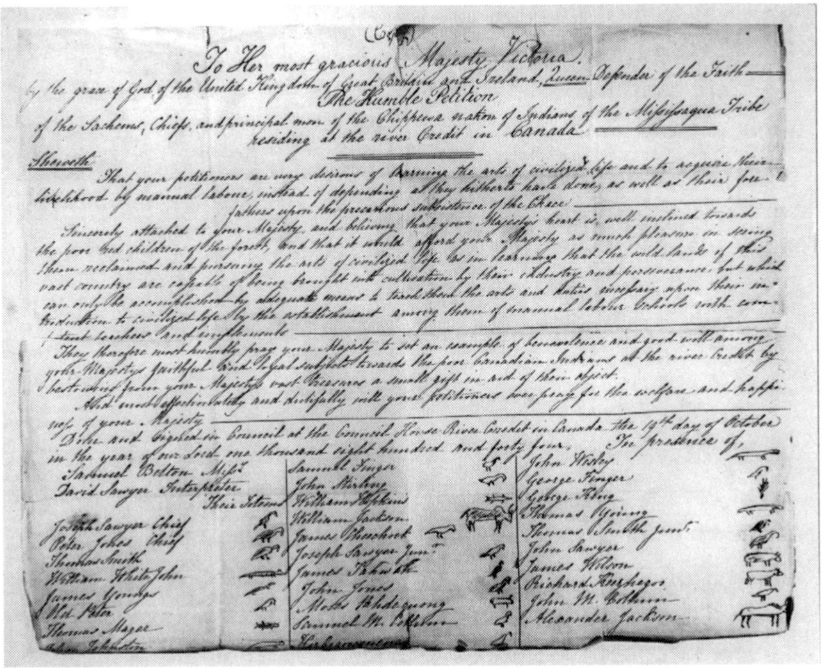

Fig. 3.3. Petition to Queen Victoria from the Chippewa nation of Indians of the Mississauga Tribe, October 19, 1844 (Peter Jones fonds, Box 1, Folder 9), showing continuity of signing with *doodem* images. Courtesy Victoria University Library Special Collections (Toronto).

ans. The root of *doodem* is "ote/ode," which means "heart"; this concept also metaphorically expresses kinship and was sometimes expressed graphically by making the outline of the heart visible. The "m" suffix is a marker for a particular type of dependent noun that cannot actually appear without a possessive pronoun—not "brother" but "my brother" or "her brother." There was no way in Anishinaabemowin to express kinship as a concept without expressing relationship at the same time.[27]

The Anishinaabeg communicated *doodem* identity in many ways, both symbolically and through iconic pictographs. They left a graphic record: on rock art, material culture, treaty and land-surrender documents, and petitions they consistently signed with the marks of their *doodemag* (*doodem* is the singular) as a simultaneous expression of both

Heidi Bohaker

their personal identities and their connection to their larger extended kinship networks (see fig. 3.3). In more recent periods, Anishinaabe peoples sometimes wore (as some still do) a pictographic image of their *doodem* identities on their clothing.[28] The potential archive for this kind of notational writing is therefore relatively large. While material examples are rare before the late eighteenth century, descriptive examples are found in the writings of Europeans from the seventeenth century; the presence of similar images on rock art dating before the seventeenth century further establishes continuity of this notational practice over a long period among the Anishinaabeg.[29]

Members of the Huron-Wendat and Haudenosaunee Confederacies also used kinship networks as a fundamental unit of political and social organization, but their kinship relationships were defined differently and deployed in distinctive ways. Among these Iroquoian-speaking peoples, their clan or *otara* identity was inherited from the mother and passed down through women to subsequent generations. *Otara*, which means "land, clay, earth," connects people to place. As Mohawk historian Deborah Doxtater explains, "when one asks an individual what clan they belong to (*oh nisen'taroten*) one is literally asking 'what is the outline or contour of your clay?'"[30] In his 1666 memoir on the "families of the Iroquois," the Jesuit priest Joseph Chaumonot gave a graphic representation of these images in use. The political complexity of the Haudenosaunee Confederacy, however, meant that depending on the context, other identities could be and were represented. Members of the confederacy belonged not only to *otara* but also to villages and nations. *Otara* identity cut across nations and villages, so it was and is possible, for example, to be either a Mohawk or an Oneida of the Wolf clan. On the 1701 Great Peace of Montreal, some Haudenosaunee delegates signed with the mark of their nation, while others used the mark of their village. Members of the Wendat Confederacy appear to have used an image representing their town or village on their shields in the period before 1650, prior to their dispersal from their home on the Penetanguishine peninsula of southern Ontario.[31]

Descriptive examples shed light on the diversity and extent of these notational practices, which appear, for example, in messages left for travelers and on weapons, clothing, and grave markers. During his 1609 trip down the Richelieu River, French cartographer Samuel de Champlain observed that scouts traveled ahead, looking for messages left by others. As Champlain wrote, "they know by certain marks by which the chiefs of one nation designate those of another, notifying one another from time to time of any variations of these. In this way they recognize whether enemies or friends have passed that way." In 1624 the Recollect Gabriel Sagard noticed that his Wendat companions did much the same thing, leaving a message on birchbark that included the "armorial bearings of their town." In war the Wendats carried "a round-piece of tree-bark, with the armorial bearings of their town or province painted upon it, and fastened to the end of a long stick, like a cavalry pennant." Nearly two centuries later, in 1793, a man named Major Littlehales accompanied Upper Canada's first lieutenant governor, John Graves Simcoe, on a journey from Niagara to Detroit and observed more evidence of these practices. Within a few miles of the Delaware Indian village southwest of the present-day city of London, Littlehales "observed many trees blazed, and various figures of Indians returning from battle with scalps, and animals drawn upon them descriptive of the Nations, Tribes and numbers that had passed—many of them well drawn, especially a Bison." Farther west toward Detroit, Littlehales observed additional examples of the same practice.[32]

North of Lake Superior in Lake Nipigon country, Scottish fur trader Duncan Cameron's 1801 journal provides additional insight into the ways in which the Anishinaabeg used traveling messages for those following on the route. Cameron referred to the pictographic representation of *doodem* identity as a "totem":

By these totems they are enabled to leave letters or marks on their way as they travel, by which other of their acquaintances who may travel the same way afterwards can immediately tell who

Heidi Bohaker

they are and which way they went. By these means, when they
wish to meet, they are never at a loss to find each other; the traveler will take a piece of birch rind, and with coal or the point of
a knife will design his totem, that of his wife and of any other
persons in the band, the number of males and females of each
such totems, designing each according to their importance. The
wife never takes the husband's mark, but retains that of her family, and the children of both sexes take the father's mark. They
leave these marks fastened to a pole and pointed in the direction
they are going; if in summer, they will leave a bunch of green
leaves, which will, from their withered state, give a pretty good
idea of the time they passed. If any of the family died lately, he
is represented without a head, or laying on the side.[33]

Use of images in this context was an effective way to communicate
additional information to other travelers. Ethnologist Francis Densmore recorded examples of the same type used in a Minnesota Anishinaabe community in the early twentieth century, demonstrating
the continuity of the practice and offering a graphic example of the
family structure described by Cameron. As figure 3.4 reveals, Densmore explained that the first canoe contained a father who had the
Bear as his *doodem*, the mother as a Catfish, with the three children
bearing the *doodem* of their father. The second canoe illustrates the
same pattern: the father and his children were Eagle (or Eagle-as-
thunderbird), while the mother was a Bear.[34] Women generally pad-
dled in the stern of the canoe, and as Cameron noted, they kept their
doodem identity when they married. Figure 3.4 thus represents two
households traveling together.

The use of pictographic images to communicate information about
the deceased on grave markers is another notational practice sustained
over time. In his 1613 visit to the Ottawa River communities, Champlain observed the use of markers on graves on which images were
drawn: "If it is a man they put up a shield, a sword with a handle such
as they use, a club, a bow and arrows; if it is a chief, he will have a

Fig. 3.4. "Figure 16—native drawing. Two families in canoes"; traveling message recorded by Francis Densmore in her 1929 ethnography of the Anishinaabeg in Minnesota. From Francis Densmore, *Chippewa Customs* (St. Paul: Minnesota Historical Society Press, 1979), 177; originally published by the Smithsonian Institution Bureau of American Ethnology, *Bulletin* 86 (1929).

bunch of feathers on his head and some other ornament or embellishment; if a child, they give him a bow and arrow; if a woman or girl, a kettle, an earthen pot, a wooden spoon, and a paddle."[35] A Jesuit priest gave another seventeenth-century example: "when any person of eminence has died in his country, those who can best use the knife and hatchet cut out his likeness, as well as they can, and fix it upon the grave of the deceased,—anointing and greasing this man of wood as if he were alive. They call this figure Tipaiatik: as if they said, 'the head or portrait of one deceased.'" On his 1793 journey mentioned above, Major Littlehales also observed a cemetery, while en route from Niagara to Detroit in the Ontario peninsula. West of the Grand River, near a branch of the Thames, on February 12 of that year, he saw a "burying ground of earth raised neatly, covered with leaves and wickered over, adjoining it a large pole with painted hieroglyphics on it, denoting the Nation, Tribe and achievements of the deceased, either as Chiefs, Warriors, or Hunters." Densmore also witnessed this notational mortuary practice in Minnesota, as did the anthropologist William Jones at Mille Lacs.[36]

Among the Anishinaabeg, expression of *doodem* identity also occurs in more symbolic ways that make sense in a social and cultural context in which people were frequently on the move. The Anishinaabeg participated in widespread, but seasonally expected, politically negotiated movement, often through the territories of others. They transitioned seasonally from small extended-family winter hunting camps to large

Heidi Bohaker

summer gatherings of several hundred to a thousand or more people.[37] This was not a world of bounded spaces but one of webs, of networks, of interaction. And in this world, the public and immediately visible communication of political identity was paramount. It was vitally important in this region to achieve "at-a-glance" and "from-a-distance" recognition of just whom one was meeting: friend, family, or enemy. Recognition of a person's *doodem* identity was crucial in determining the character of the encounter. Examples from a range of sources give insight into this complex, visually coded world. While these practices are still notational, it is difficult to conceive of them as a kind of "writing" in the same way that inscribed pictographs on grave markers and travelers' messages could be seen. In these other cases, people used a particular material, such as fur or feathers, to communicate their clan identities to their reading audience. The French Jesuit Louis Nicolas noted that those of the Hare family communicated their *doodem* identity through the clothing they wore. Nicolas noted the eldest of the family was "always dressed or surrounded by a robe of rabbit skins which needed to be killed in times of snow so that these rare furs have become totally white." The elder of the family of the Great Hare always wore these white winter pelts of the Great Hare.[38] Nearly three centuries later, the noted Canadian anthropologist Diamond Jenness observed similar practices on Parry Island in Georgian Bay in 1929, observing that "loon people attached the head of a loon" to their clothing as a marker of their *doodem* identity.[39]

One 1736 census of France's indigenous allies in the Great Lakes gives further insight. In this document the author attempts to explain the system of visual communication to his superiors, both by identifying the locations of people with specific *doodem* identities and by explaining how each identity was communicated. He explains that one could distinguish between Great Lakes Anishinaabeg by the way each person belonging to a different *doodem* had of making his "mark, of making the huts, of cutting their hair, by the differences in the weapons, the arrows . . . by the snowshoes, by the canoes, by the paddles and by other indications that they leave on their routes."[40] The author of that census indicated that if one was trained to read this system, the clues combined would place each Anishinaabe person in his or her proper sociopolitical context. But knowledge of this visual system was complicated and hard to obtain, he noted, without a lifetime of immersion in the culture. As these and more recent sources indicate, some of this communication happened in quite subtle ways—subtle at least from the perspective of an outside observer. University of British Columbia law professor Darlene Johnston reported that her grandmother trimmed her winter moccasins with otter fur to indicate her *doodem* identity.[41] Such use of fur or feathers is intended as notational communication, but it is not graphic, not inscription, not writing. And yet it is an articulation of a central aspect of identity; interpretations stumble in our failure to see and make use of the sources in this archive.

Mnemonic Practices

While historicially one can say that Great Lakes peoples privileged orality and human memory for record keeping, they had a longstanding practice of using pictographs, inscriptions, and other mnemonic devices to support oral recitations. It was in this context that people interpreted alphabetic writing brought by Europeans. Indigenous people were certainly interested in European communication technologies. In his 1635 field report to his superior, Jean de Brebeuf reported that people at the village of Tonaché (part of the Huron-Wendat Confederacy) were intrigued by some of the technologies that the Jesuits had brought with them, studying the clock to determine how it could make sound, and carefully observing the Jesuits to ensure that none of the priests were somehow shaking it. Brebeuf reported that alphabetic writing was also a source of fascination, "for they could not conceive how, what one of us, being in the village, had said to them, and put down at the same time in writing, another, who meanwhile was in a house far away, could say readily on seeing the writing." Brebeuf further noted that people attempted to replicate this feat: "I believe they have made a hundred trials of it."[42] Some indigenous

Heidi Bohaker

peoples learned to write in roman orthography in both their own languages and in French. Writing in this way was also explicitly taught to the small number of indigenous children who came to schools at seminaries and convents at Quebec.[43]

Nevertheless, orality remained dominant through the nineteenth century, even shaping how people described the act of reading alphabetic texts. "It is an excellent word that they have employed to signify that one knows how to read, *ninisitawabaten*," the Jesuit Jérôme Lalemant observed in 1646 of the Algonquian-speaking Atticamegue (Whitefish) people; "this correctly means, 'I hear,' and *Niwabaten*, 'I see;' from these two words they compose one which signifies 'I hear by seeing:' that is to say, 'I read well,' 'I know what I see.'"[44] To read, then, was to listen with the eyes, to use and decode visual symbols in support of speech. This was a long-standing practice, as people had customarily used[45] mnemonic devices such as wampum belts and strings as well as pictographic notations on bark scrolls to remember and convey accurately long narrations for diplomatic or ceremonial purposes.

Wampum and message belts are the classic and most widely known examples of mnemonic devices deployed by Great Lakes peoples.[46] Strings and belts of wampum "carried the words" spoken in council. In this way wampum was conceptualized by indigenous peoples as a recording device that had its own agency. As many who work in this field have come to recognize, belts were explained as receiving the words when they were, as Mary Druke has described it, "read . . . in the presence of an ambassador or messenger who memorized them and repeated them at his destination, but it was the wampum that carried them."[47] In other words, the belts were understood more as a recording medium than an aid to memory. They could have an agency all their own—they contained words and could speak for themselves. It is in this context that indigenous understandings of alphabetic literacy must be interpreted. When a man from the Whitefish people visited the French in 1646, he observed the priest read a prayer in his language from a piece of paper. The man asked to see the paper himself; when the priest replied, "thou wouldst understand nothing upon it," the man countered, "How so? . . . it speaks my language."[48] His expectation was that alphabetic writing would perform and function as wampum and other indigenous media did.

While the broad purpose of the belt's message can be read by a wider community, since color and graphic symbolism were deployed in a relatively consistent manner, the specific terms of each agreement had to be memorized by those charged with keeping the belt. As Mary Druke notes, "to 'read' a belt was not primarily to explain the significance of individual emblems, though this sometimes was done, but rather to relate the speeches associated with the wampum. A belt without emblems might therefore represent as rich a record of council proceedings as a belt with figures."[49] Sometimes more than one belt could be associated with a particular agreement. The few extant examples of belts from the seventeenth century suggest that icons were used less frequently than symbols in this period, and such belts appear to contain fewer symbols than later ones. Those commissioned in the mid-eighteenth century by British Indian Department superintendent Sir William Johnson, for example, were typically bigger and deployed a wider range of imagery, including sometimes the names of individuals and dates of the event being commemorated.[50] In so doing, the British inserted their own preferences for record keeping into Great Lakes practices.

Other mnemonic practices were specific to their distinctive Great Lakes cultural traditions. The Grand Council of the Haudenosaunee Confederacy used (and still uses) a mnemonic device known as a condolence cane as part of its formal political process. The cane contains pegs representing the fifty hereditary chiefs and their titles in the council. When a chief dies or when a new chief is installed, the cane itself is read in council.[51] Among the Anishinaabeg, members of the Midewiwin use pictographs on birchbark scrolls as part of their ceremonial practices. Much Anishinaabe rock art can be included in the category of mnemonic practice as elders use the images as memory aids and guides in the transmission of important knowledge to the next generation.[52] Both notational and mnemonic communicative

Heidi Bohaker

practices were widespread throughout the region and are the most obvious and visible components of the indigenous mediascapes of the Great Lakes region.

Blurring Categories: Extending the Mediascape of the Great Lakes Region

The strict use of notational and mnemonic categories obscures other important aspects of Great Lakes indigenous communicative practices, but the concept of mediascapes allows us to include these other aspects in our virtual archive. First of all, some inscribed items are both mnemomic and notational in purpose, such as weapons. The political identity of the owner might be incised in a weapon's handle; a turtle, for example, representing the clan identity of its early nineteenth-century original owner, appears carved in the handle of a ball-headed club at the Detroit Institute of Arts (fig. 3.5). Or the political identity might be asserted as part of the sculptural form of the weapon itself, as in the case of a weapon in the British Museum whose handle is carved in the shape of an eagle—an eagle wearing belts of wampum.[53] But warriors also carved their weapons with pictographs that served private, mnemonic functions. These might record dream imagery, convey power to the owner, or both.

Art historian Ruth B. Phillips supports the interpretation that these images are related to dream experiences. She notes that "artistic expression in such a context must respond to two contradictory imperatives; visionary experience had to be given concrete visual form in order to retain the blessing of the guardian spirit, yet the vision had, at the same time, to be kept private lest its power be forfeited. Ambiguity of visual imagery was thus necessary and desirable."[54] Anishinaabe warriors entered battle armed with a formidable physical arsenal charged in addition with spiritual powers. They wielded their autobiographies as weapons and works in progress, aiming to record new accomplishments upon the same item. Decorated as such, the weapon could become a kind of "calling card," intentionally left behind after combat.[55] At the turn of the eighteenth century, the Jesuit

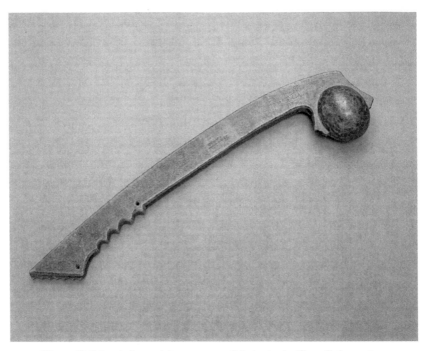

Fig. 3.5. Ball-headed war club, a weapon of choice in the Great Lakes region; these weapons were carved from hardwood, with the ball carved out of a knot, the densest part of the tree. This particular piece is inscribed with two thunderbirds, *manidoog* of the upper world, and one image of *michi-bizhu*, the Great Lyn, *manidoo* of the underwater world. Anonymous artist, Eastern Woodlands, 1800–1840, 12.6 x 7.3 x 59 cm, gift of the Natural History Society of Montreal, M15891. Courtesy McCord Museum, Montreal QC.

father Antoine Silvy observed war clubs filling this function. A typical weapon (a ball-headed club), Silvy described, is constructed as follows: "the shape of a jaw, is made of hardwood, is heavy and has a lump or ball at the end. On top they put their godhead, their name sign, which is usually a beaver, otter, or some other animal or bird. They also represent their face, the number of men they have killed and prisoners taken. They leave for the sake of glory, similar tomahawks in places where they make expeditions, this is so their enemies will know who killed there and from what nation."[56] By godhead, Silvy is most likely describing either pictorial representation of Anishinaabe *doodem* or Haudenosaunee otara—an expression of kinship identity. While

Heidi Bohaker

Fig. 3.6. Pipe carved in the style of a ball-headed weapon; pictographs on the stem are of floral designs and what appears to be a war record, including two human figures, warriors with two feathers each in their respective headdresses, shooting a catfish, with bow and arrows. Anonymous artist, Eastern Woodlands, first half of the nineteenth century, gift of the Natural History Society of Montreal, M15889, 10.5 x 6 x 57.5 cm. Courtesy McCord Museum, Montreal QC.

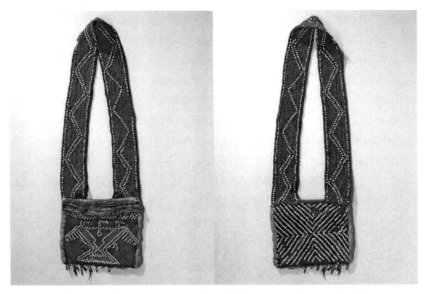

Figs. 3.7 and 3.8. Finger-woven bag (likely eighteenth century) with thunderbird motif on one side, chevrons on the reverse, and zigzag lines evoking lightning or power lines on the strap. Bead infil with resist dying, size 6 pony beads, woolen yarn edged with worsted yarn or bison hair, brass cones with red-dyed animal hair and porcupine quill wrapping around base of cones, decorative strip of black-dyed hide with quillwork. Material analysis and interpretation courtesy Great Lakes Research Alliance for the Study of Aboriginal Arts and Culture, record 956. A.1894.269; photograph courtesy National Museums Scotland.

some of the other inscriptions were likely private, others (or the body of work as a whole) could be taken together to identify the owner uniquely.

Other communicative practices in the Great Lakes region defy strict Western categorization but make sense within the context of their respective indigenous cosmological and ontological categories. Imagery on a rich range of material culture reflects and reminds its readers of important oral histories. Indeed, knowledge of respective oral histories and the central organizing principles of each indigenous cultural tradition often makes the cultural attribution of a material culture item possible. Often what appears to be a merely decorative geometric pattern on an item of clothing or a bag conveys great meaning.

Heidi Bohaker

Fig. 3.9. Finger-woven eighteenth-century bison or cattle hair bag decorated with white glass beads; showing five human figures joining hands and horizontal zigzag lines possibly representing power lines of the upper and underwater worlds, respectively. PRM 1884.69.15; transferred to the Pitt Rivers Museum from the South Kensington Museum in 1884. Material analysis and interpretation courtesy Great Lakes Research Alliance for the Study of Aboriginal Arts and Culture, record 105. Photograph courtesy Pitt Rivers Museum, University of Oxford.

Phillips has demonstrated the consistent relationship between distinct icons of thunderbeings (*animikiig*), the hourglass or triangle form, and the chevron as all referencing the Upper or Sky world of the Anishinaabeg. In contrast, references to the Underworld, or more precisely the underwater world, can be represented by an iconic image of the underwater *manidoog* (typically in the form of a long-tailed lynx or snake) and triangles or wavy lines intended to evoke waves. The presence of both these images on an item, typically one on each side, evokes narratives of the great cosmic struggles between underwater and upper-world *manidoog*, even as at the same time these two images together represent the important Anishinaabe cultural priorities of balance, harmony, and reciprocity, as in figures 3.7 and 3.8.[57] While

Fig. 3.10. Clay pipe from the Dawson site, in downtown Montreal, dating to the fifteenth century. This pipe has two faces and is inscribed with nested chevrons, possibly power lines. Anonymous artist, Eastern Woodlands, 1475–1525, 5.5 x 10.5 cm, purchased from the Natural History Society of Montreal, M4243. Courtesy McCord Museum, Montreal QC.

thunderbirds are well known in other cultural traditions in the Americas, it is the combination and position of these birds on such pieces that clearly reference Anishinaabe narratives. In the pipe bag example shown in figure 3.9, human figures holding hands occupy the middle of the design field. The zigzag lines above and below reference the underwater and sky realms.

Some communicative practices stand entirely outside the categories of mnemonic and notational. It takes only a little familiarity with Great Lakes indigenous cultures to realize the importance of tobacco, and in particular the smoking of tobacco, to regional communicative practices. Ceramic and stone pipe bowls and stems are a common feature of Great Lakes archaeological sites.[58] Tobacco smoke is without question a central indigenous medium of communication in the Great Lakes region. The smoke has multiple purposes; it can be used to clear and calm people's minds, to cement agreements, and to convey messages between humans and other-than-human persons. Although the most common association of pipe smoking is with peace negotiations, people used a variety of pipes for different purposes beyond peace negotiations. Pipes could be fashioned with or without stems. Those

Heidi Bohaker

Fig. 3.11. Effigy pipe bowl, carved, painted, and incised with lead and brass inlays. A pipe of this high quality would likely have been used in diplomatic contexts. Anonymous artist, Eastern Woodlands, 1760–1780, 9 x 3.5 x 17.5 cm, gift of the Natural History Society, Montreal, M11030. Courtesy McCord Museum, Montreal QC.

without stems were typically used for personal smoking (see fig. 3.10), while those with stems were more typically used as part of ceremonies. Pipe bowls themselves were also a medium on which specific messages could be conveyed or narratives referenced (fig. 3.11). As with other forms of material culture, Great Lakes people could and did use pipes as a substrate on which to inscribe messages. Thus I would argue that both pipes and the smoke that they produced form a central component of indigenous communicative practices and should be studied as such.

Implications and Conclusions

At the beginning of this chapter I suggested that scholars of indigenous histories not only need to work with an expanded archive, but that in order to use such an archive productively we need detailed regional case studies to better understand the richness and full extent of local communication practices. By doing so we will be able to write richer histories of "early" America and to read old sources with fresh understandings. There are significant implications here for the writing of histories of colonialism and imperialism as well. In the Great Lakes region of North America, the direct, daily impact of colonialism on indigenous lives was not felt until the nineteenth century.[59] For two centuries before, as Richard White established in *The Middle Ground*, European colonists and indigenous nations coexisted in a state in which power relations were roughly balanced.[60] This apparent balance of power sometimes operated under great tension. While Europeans were unable to conquer, convert, and assimilate the peoples of the Great Lakes in this period, many of these newcomers certainly desired to do so. Beginning with the arrival of the first Catholic missionaries in the St. Lawrence valley at the start of the seventeenth century, indigenous peoples became the targets of campaigns intended to assimilate them entirely into the lower orders of French and later English social hierarchies. For the most part, these programs succeeded only in places and at times in which indigenous nations experienced crises due to epidemic disease and warfare. Where societies remained relatively intact, they could and did successfully navigate the multifarious assimilative efforts of newcomers.[61]

While Great Lakes peoples were on the whole successful at protecting their political and cultural autonomies through the nineteenth century, that reality is not always evident in those historical sources authored by Europeans. In their production of documents, both French and later English colonial officials did in texts what they could not do in person: they practiced colonization on paper. They made maps in which they claimed indigenous territory as their own long before they possessed the military power or authority to make their desires reality; they made claims in reports and publications about successes they had not achieved. In this way, seventeenth- and eighteenth-century writers and cartographers laid a documentary foundation for their nineteenth- and twentieth-century descendants to imagine that earlier colonization efforts had been more effective than they actually were.[62]

Historians of "early modern" America have much to gain by jettisoning Western conceptions of what constitutes history and historical sources in favor of categories grounded in indigenous epistemological frameworks. Appadurai's expansive definition of a mediascape that

Heidi Bohaker

includes "pre-electronic" hardware allows scholars to explore the full range of indigenous expressive technologies as potential historical sources. Museum collections, both archaeological and ethnological, are important sites for this research, but such efforts will be futile if they are not combined with knowledge of indigenous languages, cosmological beliefs, and epistemological frameworks and the rich corpus of oral narratives. This work requires a different way of thinking about historical sources. While as a researcher one may never know the exact date a particular pipe was made, or the name of the artist who made it, the pipe did have a maker and was fashioned at a particular moment in time. Attending instead to the messages that the artist or inscriber sought to communicate or to the meaning conveyed by the use of a material medium opens our eyes to indigenous understandings of historical experience.

Such work has immediate implications for historians. In the Canadian context in which I work, eighteenth-century treaties live in the present day as part of ongoing court cases over land claims, access to resources, and legal rights. Debates over the legitimacy of indigenous communication practices therefore have deep significance outside the confines of the academy. In 1982 the new Canadian Charter of Rights and Freedoms recognized existing treaty obligations between the Crown and First Nations as well as the preexistence of certain aboriginal rights in places where those rights had not yet been ceded or altered by treaty. Widespread concerns over the lack of specificity with respect to the definition of "aboriginal rights" has led to the imposition of specific tests by the Canadian Supreme Court. In 1996 the Van Der Peet decision required that indigenous people who wanted to assert an aboriginal right (to hunt or fish, for example) had to establish that they have both remained in the same geographic location and practiced the activity being claimed from the time of "contact" (which a later decision defined as 1603—the year Champlain sailed up the St. Lawrence River as far as the Lachine Rapids near present-day Montreal).[63] This requirement to "litigate aboriginality," as Anishinaabe legal historian Darlene Johnston describes the situation, has sent claimants hurrying off to conventional archives, attempting to establish that the name by which their people are now known can be linked with a name and a place in British or French colonial records or the writings of the Jesuits.[64] Such work is complicated; it employs an entire and expensive army of researchers and lawyers who draw their evidence principally from the writings of Europeans. In 1997 the Supreme Court introduced a new challenge when it made another landmark decision (Delgamuukw) in which it ruled favorably on the (limited) admissibility of indigenous oral traditions as evidence.[65] While the Court demonstrated its willingness to hear new forms of evidence, this decision has nevertheless created new possibilities and new problems as the scholarship needed to support these cases struggles to catch up.[66] Historians remain preferred as expert witnesses, though, and the writings of Europeans are still privileged evidence, used now to corroborate oral traditions introduced into court. In these legal settings, the contest over communication technologies continues.

It is my hope that this work will one day be of use to scholars interested in larger theoretical and philosophical questions, such as those raised by other scholars in this volume. But in the short term, a more important goal is to contribute to new understandings of how colonialism operated in different times and places, by increasing access to indigenous-authored evidentiary streams that provide counternarratives or alternatives to the claims of Europeans. As Walter Mignolo persuasively argues in *The Darker Side of the Renaissance*, there is a deeply enmeshed relationship among communication systems, the practices of colonialism, and the writing of history. Although Great Lakes indigenous communities were not a colonized people during the seventeenth and eighteenth centuries, our historical narratives invariably draw on sources written by Europeans in the earlier period of coexistence, a period in which Europeans wanted to and were trying to colonize the region. If we want to make space for what Mignolo describes as "alternative discursive practices, parallel to both the offi-

Heidi Bohaker

cial discourses of the state . . . and the established discourses of official scholarship," we need to recover, understand, and make use of indigenous communicative practices as sources of indigenous voices and perspectives, thereby simultaneously refining our understanding of the diversity of American mediascapes.[67]

Notes

1. For New France and the Great Lakes region, see, e.g., Olive Patricia Dickason, *The Myth of the Savage and the Beginnings of French Colonialism in the Americas* (Edmonton: University of Alberta Press, 1984), 273–78; Gordon Sayre, *Les Sauvages Américains: Representations of Native Americans in French and English Colonial Literature* (Chapel Hill: University of North Carolina Press, 1997); and Allan Greer, "Colonial Saints: Gender, Race, and Hagiography in New France," *William and Mary Quarterly* 57.2–3 (April 2000): 323–48.

2. In *Marvelous Possessions: The Wonder of the New World* (Chicago: University of Chicago Press, 1991), Greenblatt argues that we can really study only European representational practices in texts that purport to tell us something about "the New World." Because Europeans were diverse in their cultures and religions and inconsistent in their representational practices, Greenblatt feels that we cannot develop a representational template that would allow us to "see through" to aboriginal peoples and their historical experiences. According to Greenblatt, "we can be certain only that European representations of the New World tell us something about the European practice of representation" (7–8).

3. Richard White, *The Middle Ground: Indians, Empires and Republics in the Great Lakes Region, 1650–1815* (New York: Cambridge University Press, 1991), 2.

4. See Alan Corbiere, "Exploring Historical Literacy in Manitoulin Island Ojibwe," *Papers of the Algonquian Conference* 34 (2003): 57–80.

5. White, *The Middle Ground*, 2.

6. Irving Hallowell described how the Anishinaabeg extended the concept of "personhood" to non-human beings. See Hallowell, "Ojibwe Ontology, Behaviour, and Worldview," in *Readings in Indigenous Religions*, ed. Graham Harvey (London: Continuum, 2002), 24.

7. Arjun Appadurai, "Disjuncture and Difference in the Global Cultural Economy," *Public Culture* 2.2 (Spring 1990): 7.

8. Appadurai, "Disjuncture and Difference," 9.

9. For examples of this semiotic system in practice in the Great Lakes region, see Joan Vastokas, "Ojibwe Pictography: The Origins of Writing and the Rise of Social Complexity," *Ontario Archaeology* 75 (2003): 3–16; Selwyn Dewdney, *The Sacred Scrolls of the Southern Ojibway* (Toronto: University of Toronto Press, 1975); and Thor Conway, "Ojibwa Oral History Relating to 19th-Century Rock Art," *American Indian Rock Art*, vol. 15 (Glendale AZ: American Rock Art Association, 1992), 11–25. In his analysis of rock art, Conway sees strong patterns of continuity between early (pre-seventeenth-century) and nineteenth-century practices. See also Grace Rajnovich, *Reading Rock Art: Interpreting the Indian Rock Paintings of the Canadian Shield* (Toronto: Natural Heritage/Natural History, 1994); and Ruth Bliss Phillips, "Dreams and Designs: Iconographic Problems in Great Lakes Twined Bags," in *Great Lakes Indian Art*, ed. David Penney (Detroit: Wayne State University Press, 1989), 53–68. For examples of wampum, see Francis Jennings and William Fenton, eds., *Iroquois Indians: A Documentary History of the Diplomacy of the Six Nations and Their League*, microform (Woodbridge CT: Research Publications, 1984). Germaine Warkentin discusses the performance of wampum during a treaty negotiation in 1645; see Warkentin, "In Search of 'The Word of the Other': Aboriginal Sign Systems and the History of the Book in Canada," *Book History* 2 (1999): 1–27. This is a tiny selection of archaeology, art history, and museology publications on the expressive culture of Great Lakes peoples.

10. Essays by Willard B. Walker ("Native Writing Systems," 158–84) and Allan R. Taylor ("Nonspeech Communication Sytems," 275–89) in Yves Goddard, ed., *Handbook of North American Indians*, vol. 17 (Washington DC: Smithsonian Institution, 1996), discuss indigenous writing practices separately from other communication techniques and technologies.

11. Walter Mignolo, *The Darker Side of the Renaissance: Literacy, Territoriality, and Colonization* (Ann Arbor: University of Michigan Press, 1995), 127–29.

12. See Elizabeth H. Boone, "Introduction: Writing without Words," in *Writing without Words: Alternative Literacies in Mesoamerica and the Andes*, ed. Elizabeth H. Boone and Walter Mignolo (Durham: Duke University Press, 1994), 3–26. Some are casting an even broader net. The January 2010 issue of *Ethnohistory* is a special issue devoted to the topic of graphic pluralism in the Americas that grew out of a day-long conference session in

2007. Contributors discuss a range of communication technologies from Mayan hieroglyphics to Andean *khipus*.

13. Anthropologist Joan Vastokas has demonstrated that there are multiple ways in which indigenous art, for example, can be used as a historical source. First, the items themselves are "historical documents . . . physical objects with distinctive material and formal characteristics that exist in real space and real time and which are more or less dateable." Second, art conveys specific information about worldviews and systems of knowledge. Third, many works of indigenous art are historical in that they contain references to major events in the lives of individuals and their communities. Fourth, such art may very well be or contain examples of semasiographic systems. Joan Vastokas, "History without Writing: Pictorial Narratives in Native North America," in *Gis Das Winan: Documenting Aboriginal History in Ontario*, ed. Dale Standen and David McNab, Occasional Papers of the Champlain Society no. 2 (Toronto: Champlain Society, 1996), 51–53.

14. For a discussion of the use of oral tradition as historical evidence, see Jan Vansina, *Oral Tradition as History* (Madison: University of Wisconsin Press, 1985). Vansina suggests that both migration stories and in situ creation narratives "should be understood as cosmologies" that contain important clues about a particular history, even if the events described in the narratives cannot be dated. "One can never conclude that certain events occurred," Vansina writes, "but the study of accounts of genesis and origin can lead to formulation of questions to be pursued by other means" (22–23).

15. Clearly, art and aesthetics were historically important, as people devoted considerable time and energy to the fabrication of beautiful ground stone carvings, incised bone combs for hair ornamentation, stamped and incised pottery, and painted and quilled clothing. Bone paint brushes and stamps survived in archaeological contexts, as do examples from the eighteenth century. See, e.g., Christopher J. Ellis et al., eds., *The Archaeology of Southern Ontario to A.D. 1650* (London, Ont: London Chapter, Ontario Archaeological Society, 1990); and Ronald F. Williamson and Christopher M. Watts, eds., *Taming the Taxonomy: Towards a New Understanding of Great Lakes Archaeology* (Toronto: Eastend Books, 1999).

16. For a more detailed survey of political and social changes in this region during this period, see the overview provided in Alice B. Kehoe, "Chapter 5: The Northeast," in *North American Indians: A Comprehensive Account*, 3rd ed. (New York: Prentice Hall, 2006), 206–21. Kehoe gives AD

1000 as the rough period for the introduction of corn agriculture. However, in recent decades new archaeological and paleo-botanical scholarship has revealed a dramatic new history of corn agriculture as a food
item incorporated by Great Lakes people much earlier than ever before
thought. See John P. Hart and William A. Lovis, "Reevaluating What
We Know about the Histories of Maize in Northeastern North America:
A Review of Current Evidence," *Journal of Archaeological Research* 21.2
(June 2013): 175–216.

17. Barbara A. Mann and Jerry L. Fields make a compelling argument for
the twelfth-century formation of this confederacy based on a known
eclipse. See "A Sign in the Sky: Dating the League of the Haudenosaunee," *American Indian Culture and Research Journal* 21.2 (1997): 105–63.
Daniel K. Richter, *The Ordeal of the Longhouse: The Peoples of the Iroquois
League in the Era of European Colonization* (Chapel Hill: University of
North Carolina Press, 1992), relies on earlier data to provide a fifteenth-
century date for the formation of the league (30–31). For a Haudenosaunee version of the origin story see Arthur Caswell Parker, *The
Constitution of the Five Nations or the Iroquois Book of the Great Law* (1969;
reprint, Oshweken: Iroqrafts, 2008).

18. Michael K. Foster, "Another Look at the Function of Wampum in
Iroquois-White Councils," in *The History and Culture of Iroquois Diplomacy:
An Interdisciplinary Guide to the Treaties of the Six Nations and Their League*,
ed. Francis Jennings (Syracuse: Syracuse University Press, 1985), 99–114.

19. Hallowell, "Ojibwe Ontology," 24.

20. Appadurai, "Disjuncture and Difference," 7.

21. See, e.g., Mary Druke, "Iroquois Treaties: Common Forms, Varying Interpretations," in Jennings, *The History and Culture of Iroquois Diplomacy*,
85–98.

22. See Ruth B. Phillips, *Trading Identities: The Souvenir in Native North
American Art from the Northeast, 1700–1900* (Seattle: University of Washington Press, 1998).

23. The database is still under development and at the time of writing is only
available to members who are actively contributing to it. See https://grasac
.org/gks. For a parallel effort in the world of Inka khipus, the Khipu Database Project, based at Harvard University, see http://khipukamayuq.fas
.harvard.edu/.

24. Heidi Bohaker and Ruth Phillips, "Bringing Heritage Home: Aboriginal
Perspectives in Western Repositories" (paper presented at the annual

Heidi Bohaker

meeting of the Canadian Anthropological Society, Ottawa, Ontario, May 2008).

25. Allan R. Taylor suggests that indigenous communicative practices, while not writing per se, could be grouped into two principal categories: notational and mnemonic. See Taylor, "Nonspeech Communication Systems," 283–84.

26. The Anishinaabeg include people who may also call themselves or were known historically as Ojibwes (mainly in Canada), Chippewas (principally in the United States), the Odawas or Ottawas, Mississaugas, Algonquins, or Pottawatomis. I use the term Anishinaabeg as a collective term of identity. When a more precise distinction is necessary, I use a compound form such as "Mississauga-Anishinaabeg." In previous publications I used *nindoodem*, retaining the first-person pronoun as a prefix, and in so doing following established linguistic conventions. But as this makes for awkward reading, and as increasingly other Anishinaabemowin vocabulary is being used in English, I have decided to drop the first-person prefix in favor of "doodem," which is the easier to read and pronounce.

27. Heidi Bohaker, "'*Nindoodemag*': Anishinaabe Identities in the Eastern Great Lakes Region, 1600 to 1900" (PhD diss., University of Toronto, 2006); J. Randolph Valentine, *Nishnaabemwin Reference Grammar* (Toronto: University of Toronto Press, 2001), 107–8.

28. See Cory Silverstein, "Clothed Encounters: The Power of Dress in Relations between Anishnaabe and British Peoples in the Great Lakes Region, 1760–2000" (PhD diss., McMaster University, 2000), esp. 97–105, and plates 477, 479, illustrating the use of pictographic imagery on clothing.

29. For an accessible guide to rock art in the Great Lakes region see Grace Rajanovich, *Reading Rock Art: Interpreting the Indian Rock Paintings of the Canadian Shield* (Toronto: Natural Heritage, 1994). This archive is discussed in detail in my forthcoming book *The Politics of Treaty Pictographs: Inscribing Anishinaabe Kinship Networks in the Eastern Great Lakes Region* (Toronto: University of Toronto Press).

30. Deborah Doxtator, "Inclusive and Exclusive Perceptions of Difference: Native and Euro-Based Concepts of Time, History, and Change," in *Decentring the Renaissance: Canada and Europe in Multidisciplinary Perspective, 1500–1700*, ed. Germaine Warkentin and Carolyn Podruchny (Toronto: University of Toronto Press, 2001), 42.

31. Gabriel Sagard, *The Long Journey to the Country of the Hurons* (Toronto: Champlain Society, 1939), 154. For histories of the Wendat Confederacy

to 1650, see Conrad E. Heidenreich, *Huronia: A History and Geography of the Huron Indians, 1600–1650* (Toronto: McClelland and Stewart, 1971); and Bruce Trigger, *The Children of Aataentsic: A History of the Huron People to 1660* (Kingston: McGill-Queen's University Press, 1976). Two recent studies shed new light on the social and political history of the Wendat: John Steckley, *Words of the Huron* (Waterloo, Ontario: Wilfred Laurier University Press, 2007); and Gary Warrick, *A Population History of the Huron-Petun, AD 500–1650* (Cambridge: Cambridge University Press, 2008).

32. Champlain, *The Works of Samuel de Champlain*, ed. George Wrong (Toronto: Champlain Society, 1922–36), 2:84; Sagard, *Long Journey*, 154; E. B. Littlehales, "Journal from Niagara to Detroit, 1793," in *The Correspondence of Lieut. Governor John Graves Simcoe*, ed. E. A. Cruikshank (Toronto: Ontario Historical Society, 1923–31), 4:289, 293.

33. Duncan Cameron, "The Nipigon Country, 1801," in *Les bourgeois de la Compagnie du Nord Ouest*, ed. Louis Masson (Quebec: De l'imprimerie générale, 1890), 231–300, quote on 246–47.

34. Frances Densmore, *Chippewa Customs* (Minneapolis: Ross & Haines, 1970), 177.

35. Champlain, *Works*, 2:279.

36. Paul Le Jeune, "Relation of 1635," in *Jesuit Relations and Allied Documents*, ed. Reuben Gold Thwaites, 71 vols. (Cleveland: Burrows, 1898–1901), 8:27; Henry Rowe Schoolcraft, *Historical and Statistical Information Regarding the History, Conditions, and Prospects of the Indian Tribes of the United States*, 5 vols. (Washington DC: Bureau of Indian Affairs, 1851–56), 1:420; Littlehales, "Journal from Niagara to Detroit," 4:289; William Jones, "Ethnographic and linguistic field notes on the Ojibwa Indians," folder 7, American Philosophical Society, Philadelphia.

37. "Relation of 1640–1641," in Thwaites, *Jesuit Relations*, 21:239–41. For biographies of Jérôme Lalemant and his brother Charles see *The Dictionary of Canadian Biography Online*, s.v. "Lalemant, Jérôme" (by Léon Pouliot) and s.v. "Lalemant, Charles," http://www.biographi.ca.

38. BNF, fonds français, vol. 24255, Nicolas, "Histoire naturelle," 62.

39. Diamond Jenness, "The Ojibwa Indians of Parry Island," *National Museum of Canada Bulletin* 78 (1935): 8.

40. In the original French: "chaque Nation par la facon de faire sa marque, de cabannes, de decouper les cheveux, par la différence des armes, fleshes . . . par les raquettes, par les canots, par les avirons, et par d'autres indices

qu'ils laissent sur les routes." ANF, CIIA, v.66 f.236–256v, "D'enombrement des nations sauvages," 1736, 234.

41. Darlene Johnston, "Litigating Identity: The Challenge of Aboriginality" (master's thesis, Faculty of Law, University of Toronto, 2003), 44–46.

42. Jean de Brebeuf, "Relation of What Occurred among the Hurons in the Year 1635," in Thwaites, *Jesuit Relations*, 8:113.

43. Claudio R. Salvucci, ed., *American Languages in New France: Extracts from the Jesuit Relations* (Bristol PA: Evolution Publishing, 2002), 12. While Salvucci offers a useful quick overview of the presence of indigenous languages in the *Jesuit Relations*, the extracts are sometimes incomplete and are not contextualized. The reader is advised to consult the original sources.

44. Lalemant, "Relation of 1645–46," in Thwaites, *Jesuit Relations*, 28:225.

45. See Foster, "Another Look." Wampum had two distinct functions: as a valued gift in and of itself and as a mnemonic device. Because of the intense labor involved in making belts, belts were more valuable as gifts than strings of beads, and larger belts were generally regarded as more valuable or important than smaller ones. While wampum was the preferred item of exchange to cement agreements and alliances, other gifts could be used. As historian Mary A. Druke notes, "what mattered most was the *process* of exchange of presents" ("Iroquois Treaties," 89). See also Jonathan Lainey, "Wampum Belts from Colonial Time to Today," *Recherches Amerindiennes au Quebec* 35.2 (2005): 61–73.

46. Foster, "Another Look," 104–5.

47. Druke, "Iroquois Treaties," 89.

48. Lalemant, "Relation of 1645–46," 225.

49. Druke, "Iroquois Treaties," 89.

50. Marshall Becker and Jonathan Lainey, "Wampum Belts with Initials and/or Dates as Design Elements: A Preliminary Review of One Subcategory of Political Belts," *American Indian Culture and Research Journal* 28.2 (2004): 25–45.

51. William Fenton and J. N. B. Hewitt, "Some Mnemonic Pictographs relating to the Iroquois Condolence Council," *Journal of the Washington Academy of Sciences* 35 (1945): 301. See also Bruce Elliott Johansen and Barbara Alice Mann, s.v. "Condolence Cane," *Encyclopedia of the Haudenosaunee (Iroquois Confederacy)* (Westport CT: Greenwood Press, 2000), 58. For a comparative case in South America see Frank Salomon, *The Cord Keepers: Khipus and Cultural Life in a Peruvian Village* (Durham: Duke University Press, 2004), 77–108.

52. See Dewdney, *Sacred Scrolls*; Conway, "Ojibwa Oral History." See also Rajnovich, *Reading Rock Art*; Michael Angel, *Preserving the Sacred: Historical Perspectives on the Ojibwa Midewiwin* (Winnipeg: University of Manitoba Press, 2002); Joan Vastokas, "Interpreting Birch Bark Scrolls," *Papers of the Fifteenth Algonquian Conference*, ed. William Cowan (Ottawa, Ontario: Carleton University, 1984), 425–44; Ruth B. Phillips, "Zigzag and Spiral: Geometric Motifs in Great Lakes Indian Costume," in Cowan, *Papers of the Fifteenth Algonquian Conference*, 409–24; and Phillips, "Dreams and Designs," 53–68.

53. The Jesuit Louis Nicolas observed in the second half of the seventeenth century that those who had the Hare as their *doodem* "put this image on their weapons." Joncaire documented that this identity was communicated through the weapons as well.

54. Phillips, "Zig-zag and Spiral," 418.

55. Scott Meachum, "'Markes upon Their Clubhamers': Interpreting Pictography on Eastern War Clubs," in *Three Centuries of Woodlands Indian Art*, ed. J. C. H. King and Christian F. Feest (Altenstadt: ZKF, 2007), 67–73.

56. Father Antoine Silvy, *Letters from North America*, trans. Ivy Alice Dickason (Belleville, Ontario: Mika, 1980), 123–24. I wish to thank Darlene Johnston for bringing this source to my attention.

57. Phillips, "Dreams and Designs"; see also the essays in King and Feest, *Three Centuries of Woodlands Indian Art*.

58. See, e.g., Peter G. Ramsden, "The Hurons: Archaeology and Culture History," *Archaeology of Southern Ontario to AD 1650*, OAS 5 (1990): 369; and the essays in Sean M. Rafferty and Rob Mann, eds., *Smoking and Culture: The Archaeology of Tobacco Pipes in Eastern North America* (Knoxville: University of Tennessee Press, 2004), esp. Rafferty, "'They Pass Their Lives in Smoke, and at Death Fall into the Fire': Smoking Pipes and Mortuary Ritual during the Early Woodland Period," 1–42; Penelope B. Drooker, "Pipes, Leadership, and Interregional Interaction in Protohistoric Midwestern and Northeastern North America," 73–124; and Neal L. Trubowitz, "Smoking Pipes: An Archaeological Measure of Native American Cultural Stability and Survival in Eastern North America, AD 1500–1850," 143–64.

59. Colonialism remains a reality for many indigenous peoples today. For an overview of the situation in Canada, see the final chapters of Olive Patricia Dickason and David T. McNabb, *Canada's First Nations: A History of Founding Peoples from Earliest Times* (Toronto: Oxford University Press,

2009). See also R. David Edmunds, "Native Americans and the United States, Canada and Mexico," in *A Companion to American Indian History*, ed. Philip J. Deloria and Neal Salisbury (London: Blackwell, 2004), 397–422.

60. White, *The Middle Ground*.

61. In addition to White's *The Middle Ground*, see Olive Patricia Dickason, *The Myth of the Savage*, 273–78; Bruce G. Trigger, *Natives and Newcomers: Canada's Heroic Age Reconsidered* (Kingston: McGill-Queen's University Press, 1985); and most recently, Neal Ferris, *The Archaeology of Native-lived Colonialism: Challenging History in the Great Lakes* (Tucson: University of Arizona Press, 2009).

62. Similar processes occurred in other colonial contexts. See, e.g., Sean Hawkins, *Writing and Colonialism in Northern Ghana: The Encounter between the LoDagaa and "The World on Paper"* (Toronto: University of Toronto Press, 2002).

63. R. v. Van der Peet, [1996] 2 S.C.R. 507; R. v. Adams, [1996] 3 S.C.R. 101.

64. See Johnston, "Litigating Identity."

65. Delgamuukw v. British Columbia, [1997] 3 S.C.R. 1010.

66. Heidi Bohaker, "Evidence and Language in Aboriginal Cases," presentation to the National Judicial Institute, Aboriginal Law Seminar, April 28, 2009.

67. Mignolo, *Darker Side*, 5.

PART II
MULTIMEDIA TEXTS

4

The Manuscript, the *Quipu*,
and the Early American Book

DON FELIPE GUAMAN POMA DE AYALA'S
NUEVA CORÓNICA Y BUEN GOBIERNO

Birgit Brander Rasmussen

In 1613, a Native American from the Andes who called himself Don
Felipe Guaman Poma de Ayala finished a 1,189-page manuscript titled
Nueva corónica y buen gobierno.[1] Addressed to King Phillip III of
Spain, this text represents an immensely ambitious effort to address
colonial Spain by an indigenous American writer who lived through
the aftermath of conquest. It has long been a centerpiece of colonial
Latin American studies, although there are no full translations that
would make Guaman Poma accessible to an anglophone audience.[2]
This unique book also deserves the attention of scholars of colonialism, American literature, and American book history beyond Latin
America.[3] It is from this context that I approach the manuscript. Although the Andes and Spanish-language literature are outside my
primary fields of training, I believe it is crucial to engage a text that
has so much to teach about the interanimation between European and
indigenous American forms of literacy, theorized by a native of the

region who attempted to navigate the two and produce a dialogue between them.[4]

The manuscript follows contemporary printing and typesetting conventions in detail, reflecting the author's knowledge of the European book and his near mastery of the form. Carefully paginated for publication, which the author explicitly requests, the text represents an effort to enter into the European world of print. The *Nueva corónica*, however, has a more local, formal antecedent as well, one that is important to a full understanding of Guaman Poma's literary achievement, namely the Andean *quipu*. Prior to the arrival of Europeans, the Incas and other Andean people used *quipus*, intricately knotted cords, to record and transmit knowledge. Analysis of Guaman Poma's manuscript reveals that the textual logic of *quipus* structures his manuscript in significant ways. His chronicle thus emerges out of and is shaped by two distinct textual traditions: the European book and the Andean *quipu*.

The organization of the manuscript reflects both the historical struggles of the region and the multiple textual principles brought into contact and conflict by Spanish conquest. The social and textual rupture brought on by conquest is marked in the manuscript by the division between two halves. The first part, "El primer nueva corónica," is a largely historical section that focuses on pre-Columbian history and customs and interweaves it with "European" (biblical) time and history. The second part, "Buen gobierno," details the arrival of the Spanish, the period of conquest, and subsequent colonial abuses along with Guaman Poma's recommendations for reform. Within these two segments of the manuscript are numerous subsections that range widely in both topic and genre—from the Inca bibliographies to an imagined dialogue with the Spanish king, from ethnographic passages to instructions to the reader. These various passages are shaped by Spanish and Andean literary conventions as well as by the intersection between the two. This effort to bring together European and Andean textual principles within the pages of a single manuscript parallels Guaman Poma's philosophical arguments for coexistence and balance in the region.

Birgit Brander Rasmussen

In order to trace the ways in which alphabetic and *quipu* forms of literacy shape the *Nueva corónica*, we must consider the book in the light of both Spanish and Andean textual traditions.[5] The book and alphabetic script will be familiar to all readers of this chapter, while *quipus* at this point remain relatively obscure and entirely opaque as texts because they can no longer be completely deciphered. This is a legacy of colonial violence. Spanish authorities banned *quipus* in the late sixteenth century because they were seen as idolatrous—a pattern common throughout "New Spain" where the destruction of indigenous records was widespread.[6]

As a consequence, knowledge of how *quipus* functioned before and at the point of contact has largely been lost. Scholars of writing have historically categorized them as mere mnemonic devices.[7] More recently, innovative scholarship has dramatically recast our understanding of *quipus* and revealed their continued relevance for Andean people and literary texts like the *Nueva corónica*.[8] Even so, the debate about what kinds of information *quipus* recorded, whether they were analogous to European written documents, and whether they were able to record language remains a lively and unresolved one.

Many early records of the encounter between Andean and European peoples, however, make reference to knotted cords, a widely used system of record keeping, in which Incan and other Andean peoples recorded information such as tax tributes, property rights, genealogy, myths, songs, history, and other narratives. José de Acosta's 1590 *História*, one of the most widely read Spanish chronicles at the time, notes that "Es increyble lo que en este modo alcaçaron, porque quanto los libros pueden dezir de historias, y leyes, y ceremonias, y cuentas de negocios, todo esso suplen los Quipos tan puntualmente que admira" (It is incredible what in this way they can grasp because all that books can say of histories and laws and ceremonies and business accounts, all this the *quipus* can supply in admirable detail).[9] The sense of a functional equivalence between European books and Andean *quipus* is corroborated by many other colonial sources and by Guaman Poma as well.

The failure or refusal to recognize indigenous forms of literacy as writing can be seen as a legacy of colonialism. It is well documented that early colonial agents, who saw indigenous texts as challenges to religious and civic authority, destroyed entire archives of literary cultures. In addition, Europeans and their descendants in the Americas developed a possessive investment in writing as a sign of cultural superiority. The colonial mythology of a conflict between literate Europeans and illiterate Native Americans was elaborated and maintained, in part, by philological and linguistic scholarship that relegated indigenous records to the realm of non-writing.[10]

It has become increasingly clear, however, that America's Native peoples possessed a diverse range of literary traditions and recorded their knowledge in textual forms that ranged from Ojibwe birchbark records to Mayan screenfold books, from Iroquois wampum to Andean *quipus*. These literary traditions are as important for early American studies as European books and alphabetic records. Even when knowledge of how to read such texts has been lost, innovative scholarship has explored methods for teasing out their textual logic and social functions, as well as tracing the ways in which these indigenous forms of literacy interacted with European alphabetism and continue to inform later alphabetic texts.[11] This volume is part of a growing corpus of scholarship that reveals how our understanding of textuality and the colonial sphere expands significantly, and in important ways, if we are willing to stretch definitions of writing and books beyond their traditional European referents.

Andean *quipus* encode information in strings and knots of various sizes and colors. They generally consist of a central cord to which a large number of smaller strings are attached. These cords use a wide variety of colors and knots to store information, although scholars do not know precisely how. Apart from the legacy of colonial destruction, there are other reasons why the "code of the *quipu*" has remained elusive.[12] For one thing, this complex semiotic system is radically different from most records known to scholars of writing. In contrast to paper, parchment, papyrus, and clay, *quipus* record meaning in three-

Birgit Brander Rasmussen

dimensional space rather than on a flat surface. Meaning is recorded through colors, types of knots, and the relative positions of those knots on the strings. The manner in which they were read seems to have been nonlinear, simultaneously tactile and visual, and organized according to a decimal principle in which information was organized and read in a mathematical fashion in units of ten.[13]

Did this pre-Columbian form of textuality inflect an alphabetic text like Guaman Poma's? If so, how? Indeed, dual Andean and European textual forms and conventions seem to organize the manuscript in a number of important ways; I will discuss one of them here in some detail. Given our limited understanding of *quipu* textuality, scholars have been more successful in mapping the presence of Spanish discursive genres and narrative conventions in the manuscript.[14] The structural principles of a distinctly Andean poetics, however, can be discerned by focusing on elements of the text that at first appear to reflect an inadequate grasp of Spanish textual conventions. Passages in the manuscript that seem poorly executed when measured by the standard of European languages and narrative genres may represent moments in which we can glimpse the Andean underpinnings of the manuscript.

This chapter approaches Guaman Poma's index as one such methodological entry point, so that "failure" in the text is recast analytically as a site where intercultural tensions and intertextual dialogue register in fascinating ways.[15] As others have noted, Guaman Poma's index does not correspond to the actual contents of the *Corónica*, seemingly indicating a failure to understand the purpose of an index.[16] The referent for this particular index, though, may lie beyond the pages of the book, for it seems to be organized by a decimal principle just as *quipus* were.[17] In fact, Brokaw has argued that Guaman Poma's final index is not meant to map the contents of the manuscript but rather to inscribe a decimal Andean textual and social logic at the conclusion of the text.[18] Brokaw's insight suggests the value of applying a structural analysis to Guaman Poma's text and linking its results to *quipu* scholarship. For example, Guaman Poma uses the designa-

tion "first" ("primer," "primero," and "primera") as an important organizing principle or marker within the manuscript. The peculiarity with
which he uses this designation becomes apparent when compared to
Spanish manuscripts such as Martín de Murúa's *Historia del origin y
genealogia real de los reyes Ingas del Pirú*, which Guaman Poma worked
on and to which he positioned himself as a corrective. Following European book conventions, Murúa appropriately uses the designation
"capítulo primero" for first chapters within major segments or parts of
the text. In contrast, Guaman Poma uses the designation "primer" to
mark various segments of the manuscript, to announce exposition, and
to organize the text in other ways.[19] "Primer" designates first chapters,
such as "primer capítvlo de los Yngas," in a manner similar to Murúa,
but it also marks singular elements, such as "El primer comienzo de
la dicha corónica," "Primer de generación indios," "La primera historia de las reinas," and "Primer capítvlo de palacios."[20] There is no "se-
gundo" (second) "capítvlo de palacios."[21] Instead, this "first" chapter is
followed by chapters titled "Estatvras," "Regalos," and "Depósitos."

What are we to make of this textual principle, and particularly of
the fact that while it is ubiquitous in the first half of the *Corónica*, the
"primer" designation is used only once in the second half, which follows conquest? This contrast is particularly marked if we compare two
segments dedicated to the months of the year. The first such segment,
located in the first half of the manuscript, begins with "El primero
mes, enero" (the first month, January), while the second such segment,
located toward the end of the second half, simply begins with "Enero"
(January). I propose that the first half of the manuscript, with its many
"primer" designations, corresponds to some aspect of *quipu* textuality,
which Guaman Poma abandons in the second half of the manuscript,
after conquest and the Spanish destruction of *quipus*. We might, then,
imagine the first half of the manuscript as a giant *quipu* superimposed
onto a book where multiple separate segments or chapters are like
strings attached to a central *quipu* cord, with each string marked by
the designation "primer." Each chapter thus corresponds to an imaginary *quipu* string that contains information organized again by the

Birgit Brander Rasmussen

first, second, third "visita," "inca," and so forth. The designation "primer" here marks not only a chapter but also a string on this imaginary *quipu*. Each element within a given chapter in turn represents subsidiary strings with the words like knots along these cords. While the entire manuscript is obviously composed in a European textual format, we may nonetheless see one half of the text corresponding to the form of the *quipu* and the other half corresponding to the form of the book.

The decimal logic of the final index may be seen as a reassertion of *quipu* textual principles after a period of great social and textual disruption. Or perhaps it is more accurate to see it as a marriage of Spanish and Andean textual forms brought into uneasy coexistence by Guaman Poma. This is a project that is far more ambitious than the production of an epic text written in a foreign language and script—itself an impressive achievement by any standard. But there is more at stake here for Guaman Poma than writing a corrective to colonial histories of the region. Indeed, the book represents an effort to instantiate, in textual terms, the kind of equilibrium that Guaman Poma argues for on a rhetorical and social level.

The division of the manuscript into two parts corresponds to the time before and after conquest. This structure is important because the principle of duality holds a particular significance in relation to *quipu* textuality and the social order in which it was embedded. Numerous colonial sources tell us that *quipus* usually functioned in pairs. It was standard practice in the courtroom to have at least two separate *quipucamayoc*, or clerks, working with a different *quipu*. These dual records were checked against each other in order to ensure narrative and quantitative accuracy. In the *Corónica*, Guaman Poma depicts a provincial administrator holding two such *quipus* (see fig. 4.1).[22]

The use of two interlinked *quipus* also corresponds to deeper social structures in Andean culture, where society itself was organized around the principle of complementary duality. After the Incas conquered the region, communities were divided into paired halves linked by their tribute obligations. According to Juan de Matienzo, each district was divided into two sectors, "one of which is called hanansaya, and the

Fig. 4.1. Incan official with two quipus. From Don Felipe Guaman Poma de Ayala, *El primer nueva corónica y buen gobierno*, page 348 [350]. Copenhagen, Det Kongelige Bibliotek, GKS 2232 4°. Courtesy of Det Kongelige Bibliotek/ The Royal Library of Denmark.

other hurinsaya."[23] A given district would divide its tribute obligations between these two related halves, each of which would record and track the information with its own *quipu*. While this dual social structure might have predated the Incas, Frank Salomon argues that it was the Inca empire that brought the *anan/urin* terminology and instituted a corresponding community tribute system.[24] The *anan/urin* division appears to be linked both to the sacred geography of the Inca and pre-Incaic worlds and also to the political and administrative structure of the Andes during Incan and Spanish rule. By the time the Spanish began to make their own tax records, the division had often been incorporated into community names like Anan Chillo and Urin Chillo.

Such communities were called *ayllus* or *parcialidades*. The Quechua term *ayllu* refers to a traditional Andean unit of political organization, ranging in size from a small hamlet to a village of several hundred individuals, often related and headed by a chief or noble. As the Incas established dominance in the region, they retained the term for administrative purposes. The Spanish in turn used the term *parcialidad*, and both words appear in the colonial literature. As two linked communities came together to divide the tax tribute burden, their respective *quipucamayoc* recorded the half due by each. When the tribute was delivered, it was checked against the records of each community. The two distinct *quipus* then functioned both individually as community records and collectively as a record of the larger whole of information, the tribute due from the entire *parcialidad*.

Lydia Fossa proposes that we understand this process not only as one of checks and balances but also as one of complementarity on a more abstract level.[25] Just as the two communities of Anan Chillo and Urin Chillo were parts of a larger whole, a given *parcialidad*, so the two *quipus* recording their taxes together represented a larger whole, a common register. Extending Fossa's insight, we can theorize that when two social units were linked by their tax obligations, a corresponding, distinct yet complementary relationship linked their *quipu* records. As two *quipus* were brought together, they became part of a larger whole during a process of reconciliation that seems to have been crucial not only to the process of calculating taxes but also to the social structure and to *quipu* textuality itself. Only with both *quipus* in operation, so to speak, could the larger whole of information and of the social fabric of the related units be reconstructed. The pairing of *quipus*, then, seems to correspond to a more general preference for balanced dualism in Quechua society. This dualism was part of a cosmological and social philosophy that structured Andean society around numerical principles meant to ensure balance and harmony.[26] Domingo de Santo Tomás, who also observed and wrote about *quipus*, particularly stresses the notion of "agreement" and even "conciliation" as key to that process in a more abstract sense.[27]

What does this have to do with the *Nueva corónica*? In fact, the drive toward reconciliation and the concept of complementary duality as metatextual principles rooted in the logic of *quipus* link Guaman Poma's text to broader Andean literary and social conventions.[28] In the manuscript, this drive to reconcile dual narratives operates on a number of levels. The division of the book into two major sections reflects, or even reproduces, the *quipu* convention of dual accounts that functioned as halves of a larger whole and that, in the process of coming together, had to be "consolidated." The first part describes a somewhat idealized, pre-conquest world of order and reason. This section "consolidates" Andean and Christian histories by knotting them together into a larger narrative whole that represents the two formerly separate worlds as distinct strands in a larger narrative and conceptual structure that conquest has now brought together.

Importantly, Guaman Poma represents the two worlds as coeval even before each becomes aware of the existence of the other and their destinies become forever intertwined. For example, his description of the birth of Jesus is embedded within his history of the Incas, in what he calls "Edad de Indios" (Age of the Indians). Guaman Poma makes the birth and crucifixion of Jesus contemporaneous with the reign of the second Inca, Cinche Roca Inca: "Del nacimiento de Nuestro Señor y Saluador del mundo Jesucristo: Nació en tienpo y rreyno *Cinche Roca Ynga* quando fue de edad de ochenta años. Y, en su tienpo de

Birgit Brander Rasmussen

Cinche Roca Ynga, padeció mártir y fue crucificado y muerto y sepultado y rresucitó y subió a los cielos y se asentó a la diestra de Dios Padre" (Of the birth of our Lord and Savior of the world Jesus Christ: he was born in the time and reign of *Cinche Roca Ynga* when he was of the age of eighty years. And, in his time of *Cinche Roca Ynga*, he suffered martyrdom and was crucified and died and interred and resurrected and ascended to the heavens and sat at the right side of God the Father) (*Guaman Poma*, 90). Similarly, depictions of Jesus, Mary, and Joseph, as well as the apostle San Bartolomé, occur between images of the second and third Incas. Refusing Spain ontological primacy, Guaman Poma represents the two worlds and their histories as linked and contemporaneous in both narrative and pictorial terms, even before contact.

The second part of the manuscript describes a post-conquest world of abuse and disorder, but it also attempts to consolidate that narrative with the possibility of reform and a return to order. In this section, Guaman Poma is not linking separate metanarratives or reconciling Andean and Spanish narratives of the past. Rather, he is joining together and attempting to bring into accord narratives of abuse and the possibility of reform. The two parts of the manuscript complement each other, providing distinct accounts that are held in a tense but dialogic relationship to provide a larger account of "one tenor."

Andean and Spanish accounts cannot, however, be in agreement the way that paired *quipus* traditionally were. In fact, the different histories and epistemologies that Guaman Poma engages are more often in conflict, and this tension cannot be easily resolved. While textual difference between paired *quipus* was traditionally resolved by a process of reconciliation that erased it, in the *Nueva corónica*, Guaman Poma negotiates difference of an entirely different magnitude, and he is in no position to offer clear reconciliation. Indeed, part of his project is to insist on the validity and viability of distinct Andean narrative and textual forms in the face of the Spanish drive to erase that Andean difference.

The structural division in the manuscript between two different textual regimes, the Inca *quipu* and the Spanish alphabetic book, is also reflected in Guaman Poma's illustrations. In the first section, Guaman Poma visually elaborates the various uses of *quipus* in Inca times.[29] In the second section, this preponderance of *quipus* has disappeared. Instead of a *secretario* wielding a *quipu* (*Guaman Poma*, 360), we see an administrative functionary with pen, paper, and ink writing alphabetic script (*Guaman Poma*, 828). The displacement of Andean textuality is incomplete, however, for traces remain. Earlier in the manuscript, Guaman Poma uses the term *quilca camayoc* to refer to pre-conquest *secretarios* who use *quipus* (*Guaman Poma*, 361). The use of an Andean term to describe a scene of alphabetic writing not only claims for Andean textuality an equivalence with alphabetic writing but also locates the latter within the logic of the former. Likewise, Guaman Poma's illustration of a pre-conquest *secretario* wielding two paired *quipus* (*Guaman Poma*, 350; fig. 4.1) is linked to a later image of a legal functionary holding a *quipu* and a book (*Guaman Poma*, 814; fig. 4.2). In the post-conquest Andean world, paired *quipus* have been replaced with a *quipu*-book pair. These two illustrations express the textual principle of complementary pairs and impose its logic onto the book. Taken together, they establish a continuity and a commensurability between *quipu* and book literacies and visually affirm the kind of post-conquest accommodation and coexistence to which the entire manuscript is committed.

Consolidated into one long narrative, the various parts of the manuscript all reinforce Guaman Poma's main argument: that social order is crumbling and that the way to restore justice and productivity to the region (to the benefit of both its people and the Spanish king) is to institute his recommendations for "buen gobierno."[30] For Guaman Poma, the tradition of consolidating *anan* and *urin* accounts represents a precedent to the problem of integrating distinct communities and their records, their versions of reality. Furthermore, this precedent offers the conceptual hope that bringing together and into dialogue distinct community records can produce a larger metanarrative that

Birgit Brander Rasmussen

Fig. 4.2. Incan official with quipu and book. From Guaman Poma de Ayala, *El primer nueva corónica y buen gobierno*, page 800 [814]. Copenhagen, Det Kongelige Bibliotek, GKS 2232 4°. Courtesy of Det Kongelige Bibliotek/The Royal Library of Denmark.

resolves contradictions within the subordinate accounts. Yet in place of the Andean convention of balancing accounts as a philosophical model of resolution, Guaman Poma offers the dialogic as a model of social and textual coexistence, in which the whole is constituted on numerous levels by halves that are sometimes complementary and sometimes in tension.

The attempt to reconcile distinct and at times radically incongruent dualities remains an important organizing principle in the manuscript, but in decidedly novel ways rooted in Guaman Poma's distinct historical moment and textual predicament. Within the manuscript, various sections represent the distinct worlds and narrative forms that Guaman Poma seeks to consolidate: Andean and Spanish, pre- and post-conquest, textual and pictorial, *quipu* and alphabetic. In order to accomplish this task of reconciliation, Guaman Poma turns to, and attempts to implement, principles of Andean numeracy related to social order and cosmic balance. According to the Quechua logic of dualism, singularity embodied by the number 1 is considered "incomplete and implies an imbalanced or even dangerous situation."[31] In contrast, the pair as represented by the number 2 constitutes a completed unit, a kind of cosmic balance that also reflects a process of rectification necessary to counteract the danger of "one" without its complementary second. From this perspective, the monologue of Spanish sources represented a dangerous singularity that could be balanced only by pairing (and balancing) it with an Andean perspective or narrative.

Of course, Guaman Poma is facing a very different situation than *quipucamayoc* who were reconciling presumably minor differences between two similar records, the way accountants might balance minor differences in ledger books. Instead, Guaman Poma brings together distinct literary traditions and perspectives that are often radically at odds with one another. He embodies them on the pages of his manuscript in order to bring them into dialogue and knot them together into a new narrative in which disparate perspectives and claims are reconciled into an admittedly uneasy coexistence. Whether on the micro-level of contemporary narratives such as Guaman Poma's and

Birgit Brander Rasmussen

Las Casas's version of the conquest and its implications, or on the macro-level of Andean and biblical creation stories, the dual rendering of narratives brought together and reconciled according to the logic of *quipu* textuality can be seen as an important organizing element in the manuscript.

Traditionally, the use of two *quipus* seems to have occurred when two distinct yet linked communities brought together separate records that had to be brought into agreement. It was standard that the preeminent community gave its account first. Guaman Poma's manuscript begins with the Christian creation story, which might indicate that he casts Spain as the preeminent of the two communities, according to *quipu* narrative conventions. That would certainly be strategic and appropriate given his interlocutor, the Spanish king, and his representation of himself as a loyal subject of the pope and Spain. Throughout the manuscript, however, Guaman Poma refuses to accord Europe primacy vis-à-vis Christianity. He represents the Andean people as more Christian than the Spanish, even before the arrival of missionaries. For example, after describing how the Incas used *quipus* in the administration of the region, Guaman Poma concludes by asserting their moral superiority as a form of lived, pre-contact Christianity: "Era cristianícimos" (They were exceedingly Christian) (*Guaman Poma*, 361). Hence, Guaman Poma claims Christianity as a third space of reconciliation, a distinct master narrative under which both Spanish and Inca claims can and must be subsumed. The convention of the dual *quipu* provided a precedent for conjoining more than one narrative as a prerequisite for a larger whole to emerge, in both narrative and social terms. And perhaps Christianity represented for Guaman Poma not only a utopian rhetorical and spiritual referent but also that larger truth which could emerge only in the painful juncture of Europe and the Americas, conceived as halves of a larger whole, two interlinked provinces under the dominion of the pope.

For unlike de Acosta and other European chroniclers, Guaman Poma's challenge is not simply to account for a previously unknown world within the logic of biblical authority. Rather, he must reconcile radically different worldviews, master narratives, and literary traditions from an Andean perspective, and in doing so he turns to both *quipus* and alphabetic script. Facing the enormous challenge of integrating distinct communities and narratives on a scale never faced by the *quipucamayoc*, Guaman Poma proposes a *quipu*-esque solution to an unprecedented philosophical and literary problem as he brings together the metanarratives and forms of the Andean and Spanish worlds within the pages of his manuscript.

While Spanish conquest initiated cataclysmic changes on an unprecedented scale, Andean people had lived through and negotiated conquest before when the Incas established dominion over the region. The principle of complementary duality and reconciliation that organized *quipu* textuality offered a precedent for how to resolve the monumental challenge posed by conquest and difference. As communities reconciled their *quipus* and narratives, they simultaneously established and maintained social harmony and became part of a larger whole. The conventions of *quipu* textuality provided a model for the simultaneous processes of ensuring social harmony and arriving at a more comprehensive and cooperative version of reality. In his manuscript, Guaman Poma joins together Spanish and Andean versions of reality, forcing them into dialogue and attempting to reconcile them, to bring them together to make a coherent whole in order to recuperate what Julio Ortega calls the "profound rupture of the conquest" and to create "the possibility that separate worlds will be legible to each other."[32]

It is not clear whether this is a conscious strategy on Guaman Poma's part, or even if he succeeds. Guaman Poma is no *quipucamayoc*, and unlike *quipus* of the past, his manuscript is not linked to a specific community or another *quipu*.[33] Detached in both temporal and material terms, the text floats loose in time and space in a manner decidedly antithetical to *quipu* logic. Indeed, its trajectory between the time it left Guaman Poma's hands and the time a German Peruvianist found the manuscript in the archives of the Royal Copenhagen Library almost four centuries later remains unknown. But even though the *quipu* drive toward reconciliation fails in Guaman Poma's narra-

Birgit Brander Rasmussen

tive, the process of dialogization succeeds, and we might call it proto-novelistic in its incorporation of different voices, perspectives, and languages.

In using this term, I do not mean to suggest that the text is more fiction than fact or history, but rather that it exhibits what Mikhail Bakhtin considers the central feature of novelistic discourse: dialogization. Whereas the *quipucamayoc* recorded and managed official narratives in the service of the Inca state, they were not authors in the modern sense. In the process of writing his manuscript, Guaman Poma draws on a multiplicity of narrative and rhetorical genres and textual forms and becomes something that did not exist in the pre-Hispanic world of the *quipucamayoc*: an author. This is a title he claims repeatedly and insistently in the manuscript, where he refers to himself as "autor" sixty-nine times. Thus, his *Corónica* is new not only vis-à-vis Spanish chronicles but also vis-à-vis the old histories contained in *quipus*. He is neither a *quipucamayoc* nor an *amauta*, but an *autor*. This is one of the ways in which Guaman Poma's manuscript is radically modern, a product of the new world that emerged out of the violent encounter between Europe and the Americas.[34] Attempting to insert an Andean perspective into early modern Europe, the manuscript offers an intercultural model of modernity. Narratively, the manuscript is oriented toward the future rather than toward the past, which is represented as unrecoverable. Instead, the narrative desire most palpable in the manuscript is the hope that it is still possible to imagine a different future and different terms of engagement. Guaman Poma's claim to the title "autor" marks that orientation. And his recommendation for "buen gobierno" is not a return to Incan rule but a move toward reconciliation and collaboration that can combine the best of Andean and Spanish worlds. Toward the end of the manuscript, Guaman Poma proposes the dialogue as a model for such collaboration, one that simultaneously instantiates the logic of dualism and proposes to turn the conflict zone into a zone of collaboration.

In the section titled "Pregunta su magestad" (His Majesty inquires), located toward the end of the manuscript, Guaman Poma offers the dialogue as a potential ideal model for the cross-cultural encounter. Here, Guaman Poma stages an imaginary conversation between himself and Philip III in which he serves as a sage adviser to a respectful king. Visually as well as narratively, Guaman Poma represents the two as potentially equal partners against the abuses of renegade colonial administrators. Following the second half of the manuscript, where Guaman Poma describes and condemns such abuses, this section imagines a series of questions and answers, exchanges between Guaman Poma and the king about how to reestablish justice in the region. With this imaginary conversation, Guaman Poma posits the dialogic as the ideal mode of interaction. He also insists, however, that a true dialogue must be collaborative, an exchange between two equal partners. Thus, while Guaman Poma accepts the authority of Philip III, the king in the imagined dialogue also respects Guaman Poma's authority. This is represented by the king's willingness to ask the questions prompted by the adviser. Narratively, however, this asymmetry eventually leads to a breakdown in the dialogic mode, as Guaman Poma has the king ask the exact questions suggested to him by Guaman Poma. As the dialogue progresses, the author, Guaman Poma, is entirely in charge of the narrative, as evident in the imperative: "Ask me now . . . ," where the dialogue becomes dictation. This breakdown does not necessarily indicate a failed belief in dialogue as a mode of exchange, but rather an insistence on the parameters of a true dialogue as the ideal mode of encounter.

In her book-length study of the manuscript, Rolena Adorno concludes that the text is about the impossibility of dialogue and cross-cultural understanding.[35] The despondency in the final account of Guaman Poma's journey to Lima does indeed suggest despair rather than hope. But would Guaman Poma compose a manuscript of over a thousand pages and carefully paginate it for publication (which he explicitly requests) in order to make the point that communication is hopeless and futile? More likely, the final sections of the manuscript serve as an injunction to take seriously the possibility and responsibility of dialogue. Such an exchange cannot be only imaginary, orches-

Birgit Brander Rasmussen

trated by one party, but must be a mutual and collaborative venture. This is Guaman Poma's invitation to the king and to any other reader of this manuscript which he wrote "para todo el mundo" and which today is available for all the world to engage, in printed form and on the Internet.

Hence, I read the dialogue between Guaman Poma and the king as simultaneously a failure and a model. For while the imagined dialogue marks a kind of failure, the failure of an actual exchange, it also provides a model of collaboration that must replace the dictatorial and monological nature of the colonial conflict zone. Such mutual recognition and understanding require a great deal of work by the reader as well as by Guaman Poma, who opens the manuscript by foregrounding the difficulty of his own project. Perhaps one purpose of Guaman Poma's description of his arduous journey is to share with his readers the magnitude of his own effort in order to ask of them that they meet him halfway. For, according to the metatextual principles of the Andes, the single author Don Felipe Guaman Poma de Ayala must not be left standing alone. Only by being joined by a reader can the completed unit required for narrative and cosmic balance emerge. The utopic hope embodied by the logic of complementary duality is also expressed in the decimal order of Guaman Poma's concluding table of contents. In these final pages of the manuscript, Guaman Poma marries European and Andean textual forms. The decimal logic of the Andes and their *quipus* is expressed in the European genre "table of contents," which can conform to and express Andean decimal principles. In the same way, the dialogue expresses the Andean logic of complementary duality embodied by the completed pair of the king and the author, a logic that Guaman Poma has managed to translate into a form that can make sense to his European readers.

Because it is marked by both Andean and Spanish literary conventions, the *Nueva corónica y buen gobierno* has much to teach us about indigenous Andean textual forms. On the pages of his manuscript, Guaman Poma brings multiple and often competing voices, narratives, histories, perspectives, and textual traditions into dialogue and uneasy coexistence. As signaled by its title, the *Nueva corónica* is self-consciously new in both its local and transnational contexts. This strangely modern text exhibits what Mikhail Bakhtin has called dialogization in its attempt to make the book a narrative space where Andean epistemology and *quipu* textuality can coexist with European cultural and narrative forms.[36] Thus, Guaman Poma's literary achievement goes beyond the mastery of a foreign system of literacy, namely alphabetism, as he brings radically different textual traditions into dialogue on the pages of his manuscript to produce a new chronicle of the colonial encounter between Spain and the Andes.

Acknowledgments

I would like to thank Ivan Boserup and the Royal Copenhagen Library for generously permitting me access to the original manuscript. I am most grateful to Frank Salomon and Russ Castronovo, as well as participants in the 2008 "Early American Mediascapes" symposium, for helpful feedback on my work. Thanks also to Jeffrey Glover and Matt Cohen for inviting me to participate in the symposium and contribute to this anthology.

Notes

1. The original title of the manuscript is *El primer nueva corónica y buen gobierno por Don Phelipe Gvaman Poma de Aiala.* Numerous contemporary editions are available; I found the digital version made available by the Royal Copenhagen Library particularly useful. See Felipe Guaman Poma de Ayala, *El primer nueva corónica y buen gobierno (1615/1616)* (København: Det Kongelige Bibliotek, GKS 2232 4°), http://www.kb.dk/elib/mss/poma/, hereafter cited parenthetically in the text as *Guaman Poma.*
2. For an abridged English translation of Guaman Poma's manuscript, see David Frye, ed. and trans., *Felipe Guaman Poma de Ayala: The First New Chronicle and Good Government* (Indianapolis: Hackett, 2006). Until 2006, the closest approximation to a translation was Christopher Dilke's *Letter to a King: A Peruvian Chief's Account of Life under the Incas and under Spanish Rule* (New York: Dutton, 1978). Scholarly work on Guaman Poma, primarily by Latin American scholars, began in the 1970s and re-

Birgit Brander Rasmussen

mains a growing body of work. For an overview of early scholarship see Charles R. Marsh, "Recent Studies on Guaman Poma de Ayala," *Latin American Indian Literatures* 6.1 (Spring 1982): 27–32. For an overview of recent scholarship see Rolena Adorno, *Guaman Poma and His Illustrated Chronicle from Colonial Peru: From a Century of Scholarship to a New Era of Reading/Guaman Poma y su crónica ilustrada del Perú colonial: Un siglo de investigaciones hacia una nueva era de lectura* (Copenhagen: Museum Tusculanum Press, University of Copenhagen, and The Royal Library, 2001).

3. I first became aware of Guaman Poma's work after reading Mary Louise Pratt, "Transculturation and Autoethnography: Peru, 1615/1980," in *Colonial Discourse, Postcolonial Theory*, ed. Francis Barker, Peter Hulme, and Margaret Iversen (Manchester: Manchester University Press, 1994), 24–46. For an important article that aims to introduce Guaman Poma's work to North American scholars of Native American literature, see Ralph Bauer, "'EnCountering' Colonial Latin American Indian Chronicles: Felipe Guaman Poma de Ayala's History of the 'New' World," *American Indian Quarterly* 25.2 (Spring 2001): 274–312.

4. "Interanimation" refers to the way in which two texts or forms of literacy become intertwined and mutually affect each other.

5. A great deal of study has been done on the ways in which Guaman Poma engages, replicates, and revises Spanish genres such as the *crónica de Indias*, as well as the *relación*. For an exhaustive study of genre in Guaman Poma's manuscript, see Rolena Adorno, *Guaman Poma: Writing and Resistance in Colonial Peru* (Austin: University of Texas Press, 1986). Fewer studies have focused on the ways in which Andean textual traditions structure the manuscript. See Galen Brokaw, "Transcultural Intertextuality and Quipu Literacy in Felipe Guaman Poma de Ayala's *Nueva corónica y buen gobierno*" (PhD diss., Indiana University, 1999); Galen Brokaw, "*Khipu* Numeracy and Alphabetic Literacy in the Andes: Felipe Guaman Poma de Ayala's *Nueva corónica y buen gobierno*," *Colonial Latin American Review* 11.2 (December 2002): 275–303; and Richard Luxton, "The Inca Quipus and Guaman Poma de Ayala's 'First New Chronicle and Good Government,'" Ibero-Americanisches Archiv N.F. Jg 5 H. 4 (1979), 315–41. On the interaction between Spanish and Quechua, see George L. Urioste, "The Spanish and Quechua Voices of Waman Puma," *Latin American Literature and Arts Review* 28 (January/April 1981): 16–19. On European and Andean artistic traditions in the manuscript, see R. Tom Zuidema, "Guaman Poma between the Arts of Europe and the Andes," *Colonial Latin American Review*

3.1–2 (1994): 37–86. On the subversive work performed by Guaman Poma in relation to Spanish writing, see Martin Lienhard, *La voz y su huella: Escritura y conflicto étnico-social en América Latina, 1492–1988* (Hanover NH: Ediciones del Norte, 1991), 149–69.

6. Following their third council, in Lima in 1583, Spanish bishops issued an edict banning *quipus* as "libros profanos y lascivos" (profane and lascivious books). See Francesco Leonardo Lisi, *El Tercer Concilio Limense y la Aculturacion de los Indígenas Sudamericanos: Estudio crítico con edición, traducción y comentario de las actas del concilio provincial celebrado en Lima entre 1582 y 1583* (Salamanca: Ediciones Universidad de Salamanca, 1990), 103. Similar campaigns of destruction were waged elsewhere. See, e.g., Diego de Landa, *Yucatan before and after the Conquest* (New York: Dover, 1978).

7. See, e.g., L. Leland Locke, *The Ancient Quipu or Peruvian Knot Record* (New York: American Museum of Natural History, 1923); and I. J. Gelb, *A Study of Writing* (Chicago: University of Chicago Press, 1963).

8. Key studies that have informed my understanding of *quipus* include Marcia Ascher and Robert Ascher, *Code of the Quipu: A Study in Media, Mathematics, and Culture* (Ann Arbor: University of Michigan Press, 1981); Gary Urton, *Signs of the Inca Khipu: Binary Coding in the Andean Knotted-String Records* (Austin: University of Texas Press, 2003); Gary Urton, "From Knots to Narratives: Reconstructing the Art of Historical Record Keeping in the Andes from Spanish Transcriptions of Inca Khipus," *Ethnohistory* 45.3 (Summer 1998): 409–38; Frank Salomon, *The Cord Keepers: Khipus and Cultural Life in a Peruvian Village* (Durham: Duke University Press, 2004); Frank Salomon, "How an Andean 'Writing without Words' Works," *Current Anthropology* 42.1 (February 2001): 1–27; and Jeffrey Quilter and Gary Urton, eds., *Narrative Threads: Accounting and Recounting in Andean Khipu* (Austin: University of Texas Press, 2002). Various sources and studies use the terms *quipu, quipo, khipu*, and *k"ipu.* I have followed Guaman Poma's terminology and used *quipu.*

9. José de Acosta, *Historia natvral y moral de Las Indias, en qve se tratan las cosas notables del cielo, y elementos, metales, plantas, y animals dellas: Y los ritos, y ceremonias, leyes, y gouierno, y guerras de los Indios* (Sevilla: Juan de Leon, 1590), 410. I have modernized the spelling slightly for clarity. For an accessible English translation, see José de Acosta, *Natural and Moral History of the Indies*, ed. Jane E. Mangan (Durham: Duke University Press, 2002).

Birgit Brander Rasmussen

10. I make this argument more extensively in *Queequeg's Coffin: Indigenous Literacies and the Making of Early American Literature* (Durham: Duke University Press, 2012). See also Lienhard on the "fetishism of writing" and "extreme valorization" of writing, particularly alphabetic script, in European culture at the time of contact. *La voz y su huella*, xvii, 4.

11. See, e.g., Lienhard, *La voz y su huella*; Salomon, *Cord Keepers*; James Lockhart, *The Nahuas after the Conquest: A Social and Cultural History of the Indians of Central Mexico, Sixteenth through Eighteenth Centuries* (Stanford: Stanford University Press, 1992), 326–73; and Hertha Wong, *Sending My Heart Back across the Years: Tradition and Innovation in Native American Autobiography* (New York: Oxford University Press, 1992).

12. I am referencing here the titles of two key studies of Amerindian forms of literacy. "Code of the *quipu*" is part of the title of the Aschers' seminal study of *quipus*. "The Maya code" is part of the title of Michael Coe's equally important study of Maya pictoglyphs, *Breaking the Maya Code* (New York: Thames and Hudson, 1999).

13. See Ascher and Ascher, *Code of the Quipu*, which analyzes a large body of extant *quipus*, for an important effort to trace this decimal logic.

14. See, e.g., Bauer, "'EnCountering'"; and Adorno, *Guaman Poma: Writing and Resistance*.

15. Even elements in the manuscript that seem to reflect European narrative conventions might either be more correctly understood as rooted in Andean textual traditions or might mark moments in which Poma successfully marries the two. For example, Bauer notes Poma's use of a five-part structure in his royal biographies and relates it to Renaissance literary conventions. The number 5, Brokaw notes, is key in the Quechua ontology of numbers. Brokaw, "Transcultural Intertextuality," 110–16. See also Gary Urton, *The Social Life of Numbers: A Quechua Ontology of Numbers and Philosophy of Arithmetic* (Austin: University of Texas Press, 1997).

16. To aid readers, Rolena Adorno and John Murra provide a more accurate index at the beginning of their edited version. See Felipe Guaman Poma de Ayala, *El primer nueva corónica*, ed. John V . Murra and Rolena Adorno (Mexico City: Siglo Veintiuno 1980).

17. See Brokaw, "*Khipu* Numeracy and Alphabetic Literacy," 291–92. I find convincing Brokaw's division of the text into ten key sections, indicated by the designation "primer" or "primero." The "'first chapter' convention" seems to function as a key organizational principle in the text, which would correspond to a metatextual principle rooted in decimal logic. In

his analysis of the structure of the manuscript, Brokaw identifies not only ten key segments or "books" but also seventy chapters, which constitute seven "complete decimal units" (299). Thus, Brokaw finds a decimal principle at work on both primary and secondary levels.

18. Brokaw, "*Khipu* Numeracy and Alphabetic Literacy," 299.

19. Rolena Adorno and Ivan Boserup, "Gua Poma and the Manuscripts of Fray Martín de Murúa: Prolegomena to a Critical Edition of the *Historia del Perú*," *Fund og Forskning i Det Kongelige Biblioteks Samlinger* 44 (2005): 217.

20. Adorno, *Guaman Poma and His Illustrated Chronicle*, 15, 48, 120, 330.

21. Adorno and Boserup, "Gua Poma and the Manuscripts," 217.

22. Adorno, *Guaman Poma and His Illustrated Chronicle*, 350. Salomon notes that the two *quipus* in this image have matching end knobs, which may suggest they are related. Salomon, *The Cord Keepers*, 144.

23. Juan de Matienzo, *Gobierno del Perú* (Lima and Paris: Institut français d'études andines, 1967 [1567]), 20, as cited and translated by Frank Salomon, *Native Lords of Quito in the Age of the Incas: The Political Economy of North Andean Chiefdoms* (Cambridge: Cambridge University Press, 1986), 174.

24. See Salomon, *Native Lords of Quito*, 116–42. John Howland Rowe defines an *ayllu* as a kin group that owned a definite territory. For discussion of ayllus in pre-Incaic and modern Andean society, see Rowe, "Inca Culture at the Time of the Spanish Conquest," in *Handbook of South American Indians*, vol. 2, *The Andean Civilizations*, ed. Julian H. Steward (New York: Cooper Square, 1963), 253–56.

25. Lydia Fossa, "Two Khipu, One Narrative: Answering Urton's Questions," *Ethnohistory* 47.2 (2000): 453–68.

26. See Urton, *The Social Life of Numbers*, 218–19.

27. See Fossa, "Two Khipu, One Narrative," 460.

28. Rolena Adorno has traced the centrality of the anan/urin division in Guaman Poma's images, as well as his attempt to reconcile the contradiction between Andean and Spanish notions of history. See Adorno, "The Language of History in Guaman Poma's *Nueva Corónica y Buen Gobierno*," in *Oral to Written Expression: Native Andean Chronicles of the Early Colonial Period*, ed. Rolena Adorno (Syracuse: Maxwell School of Citizenship and Public Affairs, Syracuse University, 1982), 109–37.

29. *Guaman Poma*, 337, 350, 360, 362.

30. Incidentally, Juan Polo de Ondegardo agreed with Guaman Poma and

Birgit Brander Rasmussen

argued in his report that maintaining the Native system instituted by the Incas (themselves conquerors and extractors of tribute) would be of greatest benefit to the Spanish, because this system had worked for centuries and made theft impossible due to the dual records/checks and balances process inherent in the *quipu* system. Polo de Ondegardo, *Notable daño que rresulta de no guardar a estos yndios sus fueros* (Madrid: Biblioteca Nacional de Madrid, 1990 [1571]), 119 (ms 2821), as cited in Fossa, "Two Khipu, One Narrative," 454.

31. Brokaw, "*Khipu* Numeracy and Alphabetic Literacy," 286. Brokaw is paraphrasing Urton, *The Social Life of Numbers*, 218–19.

32. Julio Ortega, "Transatlantic Translations," *PMLA* 118.1 (2003): 25–40.

33. Juan M. Ossio and Richard Luxton both suggest that Guaman Poma tries to position himself as, or reclaim a hereditary position as, a *quipucamayoc*. See Luxton, "The Inca Quipus and Guaman Poma"; and Ossio, "The Idea of History in Felipe Guaman Poma de Ayala" (B. Litt. thesis, Oxford University, 1970).

34. I am grateful to Henry Turner, who invited me to be part of the University of Wisconsin-Madison Center for Early Modern Studies. These discussions prompted me think about the relationship between modernism and Guaman Poma's work.

35. Adorno, *Guaman Poma: Writing and Resistance*, 33.

36. Mikhail Bakhtin, *The Dialogic Imagination: Four Essays by M. M. Bakhtin*, ed. Michael Holquist, trans. Caryl Emerson and Michael Holquist (Austin: University of Texas, 1981), 427.

5

Semiotics, Aesthetics, and the Quechua Concept of *Quilca*

Galen Brokaw

European societies have always seen writing as an important indicator of "civilization." Even today, many scholars seem to feel compelled
to pronounce on whether or not the cultures they study possessed a
form of writing. One could argue on a number of different grounds
that such statements are inaccurate, but disagreements of this kind
ultimately come down to how one defines writing. The problem with
pronouncements about the absence of writing is not that they are in-
correct but rather that the terms and conditions that make them correct are determined by a sociocultural, political, and historical context
that is incompatible with the objects and practices developed by other cultures. Linguistic terms and their associated concepts develop in
dialogue with the social, economic, and political institutions that
emerge along with them. This does not necessarily mean that human
societies do not exhibit certain universal tendencies or some kind of
common, underlying cognitive substrate, but such universals are not
always indicated in any transparent way by the surface phenomena of
linguistic terms and their associated mental concepts. To say that another society did not possess a form of writing has very little descrip-

tive value. Furthermore, the perspective that informs such statements sets parameters that make it difficult, if not impossible, to understand the conceptual frameworks of other cultures and how they relate to material practices. This problem has been particularly acute in the study of Andean cultures and the media they employed.

The Inca empire has always been something of an embarrassment to the theory that the development of complex socioeconomic and political institutions requires the existence of writing. While the Incas undeniably created complex socioeconomic and political institutions, scholars generally claim that they did not possess a writing system. The most common solution to this "paradox" has been to treat the Inca empire as an exception: a society that managed to achieve a high level of complexity through the use of a system of knotted, colored cords known as the quipu, which, while not writing, fulfilled some of writing's basic functions. The fact that the inadequacy of this solution does not always generate the kind of critical response for which it cries out attests to the epistemological constraints of our modern alphabetically conditioned mentality. Some have argued that the Incas actually did employ a writing system, but the very terms and parameters of such arguments derive from an alphabetic perspective.

This alphabetic bias has contributed to the difficulty in deciphering the quipu, because it conditions not only the way we think about how an individual medium functions but also the way we think of semiosis more generally. One of the reasons that the quipu has proved so impervious to decipherment is that, unlike traditional writing systems, it employs multiple codes that record different types of information: the knots recorded numbers, the colors of the cords signaled information categories, and other dimensions of the quipu may have encoded other types of data. A complete reading of a quipu would involve the decoding and coordination of each of the various codes. In fact, this semiotic heterogeneity characterized Andean society in general, whose semiotic activities involved a number of different media. Of course, all societies employ multiple media, but in early modern Europe the importance of other media tended to diminish significantly or diverge into separate areas of social production (such as art). In the Inca empire, the quipu acquired a prominence and ubiquity that may have been analogous in some ways to the dominance of alphabetic script in European cultures. The quipu, however, was not always the ubiquitous medium that it became under the Inca administration. The general absence of the quipu from the archaeological record prior to the Wari and Inka periods suggests that it did not play such a prominent role in earlier Andean societies. And even after the emergence of the quipu as an essential feature of the Inca administration, the norm still seems to have been a multimedia context in which the secondary semiosis of social, economic, and political interaction took place through various media: architecture, sculpture, ceramic painting, and textiles. Several if not all of these media appear to have been informed in one way or another by similar semiotic principles. The quipu may have been merely one manifestation, albeit an important one, of much broader semiotic practices.

For lack of a better term, I refer to "semiotic practices," but this may not be the most felicitous way to designate Andean media. I do not reject out-of-hand the use of Western terms and concepts in the analysis of other cultures, particularly in theoretical work that deals with issues or phenomena that are not known to have been thematized organically by the society in question. But here the nature of the investigation itself is to explore the organic conceptual field to which indigenous media belong, and this demands a redefinition of familiar terms, if not a complete rejection of them. I will continue to refer to Andean media in terms of semiosis, for they were certainly involved in the transmission of meaning. But I would argue that the Quechua term *quilca* corresponded to an organic conceptualization of Andean media that calls into question the very distinction between semiotic, or what we might call "rational" or "conceptual," and nonsemiotic or "aesthetic" media. Even in European societies, this opposition should not be understood in an overly rigorous way. All conceptual communication has an aesthetic dimension, and aesthetic experience can be conceptual and communicative. Since it would be impossible for us

Galen Brokaw

to simply abandon the notions of reason/concept and aesthetics, it may be useful to think of them heuristically in terms of a continuum in which different media occupy unique positions indicating a particular relationship between, or configuration of, rational/conceptual and aesthetic thought. The infinite possibilities of such a continuum reveal the inadequacy of any kind of Manichaean opposition between "reason/conceptuality" and "aesthetics," "writing" and "non-writing," and so forth.

The Quechua concept designated by the term *quilca* has received relatively little attention from scholars. This term does not appear in colonial chronicles describing indigenous cultural practices until the end of the sixteenth century, and even then it is not thematized directly.[1] Throughout most of the sixteenth century, the term *quilca* appears almost exclusively in dictionaries. It first appears in Domingo de Santo Tomás's *Lexicon o vocabulario de la lengua general del Perú*, published in 1560, where it is defined as "libro" (book), "carta" (letter), and "letra" (letter [of the alphabet]). The additional meanings "escribir" (to write), "dibujar" (to draw), "bordar con colores" (to embroider with colors), and "teñir de colores" (to dye) appear in the entry for the verbal form *quellcani*.[2] The *Vocabulario y phrasis de la lengua general de los indios del Perú*, published by Antonio Ricard in 1586, adds "pintar" (to paint) and "esculpir" (to sculpt).[3] Diego González Holguín's *Vocabulario* (1608) defines *quilca* or *quellcca* as "papel carta, o escriptura" (paper letter, or writing); but definitions of other derivative versions of this term include "to draw or paint."[4] These dictionary definitions suggest that the semantic field associated with the term *quilca* includes a wide range of different media. ⟶ to represent a concept in a symbolic fashion?

The difference between the Andean and European conceptual frameworks associated with their respective media and the way in which each culture distributed semiotic and aesthetic functions among them makes the translation of such terms problematic. The concepts conveyed by the European terms *writing, book, painting, sculpture,* and so forth had no exact equivalents in Quechua or other indigenous Andean languages. By the same token, Andean concepts conveyed by such terms as *quilca* and *quipu* defied translation into Spanish. In the case of a physical object like the quipu, the Spaniards solved this problem by adopting the Quechua word itself. But even so, the problem of translation is evident in a symptomatic ambivalence characterizing the Spaniards' attempts to describe quipu practices. Ironically, the prominence in the Andes of the material medium of the quipu may have exacerbated the difficulties in understanding the semiotic practices associated with it by obscuring its role within a larger conceptual domain and its relationship to other forms of Andean media. The concept conveyed by the Quechua term *quilca* proved elusive to Spanish chroniclers, perhaps precisely because it was not initially associated with any single object or practice. The dictionary definitions cited above suggest that the term *quilca* referred to a more general field of semiosis/aesthetics in which a variety of media participated. At stake here, then, is not merely the referent of a discrete term but rather an entire framework of interrelated objects and practices.

Many scholars have accepted the direct and indirect association between "quilca" and "pintura" (painting) as evidence of the existence of a form of Inca painting, and some see this alleged Inca painting tradition as constituting a form of writing. Raúl Porras Barrenechea, for example, maintains that two distinct forms of media developed in the Andes: the quipu, which was primarily numeric in nature, and the quilca, which was pictographic.[5] Carlos Radicati seizes upon Domingo de Santo Tomás's definition of *quilca* as "writing" as proof that there existed a writing system.[6] One of the problems that has plagued such arguments about indigenous media and writing is that either they do not always define exactly what they mean by "writing" or they fail to recognize the viability of alternatives to alphabetic script. Radicati, for example, does not define what he means by "writing." If he does not equate writing with phonography, that is to say, the representation of speech, then he must define it in such a way that it includes the semiotic nature of the quipu, about which we know relatively little, or the quilca, about which we know even less. If he defines writing as

Galen Brokaw

phonography, then his argument is specious at best, not because his conclusion is *necessarily* false but because his reasoning is fallacious: he presents no evidence to support this assertion, and he does not take into account the issues of cultural contact and translation. Porras Barrenechea, on the other hand, clearly defines writing as phonography, and he argues that neither the quipu nor the quilca was phonographic; still, he does not consider the possibility that non-phonographic forms of semiosis might develop analogous levels of sophistication.

Victoria de la Jara analyzes more extensive linguistic evidence in colonial dictionaries, and makes a similar argument; but her work suffers from the same kind of fallacious reasoning, obscuring what otherwise is a valuable analysis. Jara claims, for example, that the colonial definition of *quilca* as "writing" proves the existence of an Andean form of writing but not necessarily of an Inca writing system. She points out that the Quechua language is much older than the Inca empire and argues therefore that the term *quilca* refers to a pre-Inca writing system.[7] Like Radicati, Jara assumes that the translation of *quilca* as "writing" by sixteenth-century Spaniards is transparent and that the term "writing" is unproblematic.

To accept uncritically that a colonial translation indicates an equivalence between the referents of the Spanish and indigenous terms and concepts is to misunderstand the nature of both translation and cultural difference. A Spanish translation of a Quechua word does not guarantee an equivalence to the original Andean referent, especially when dealing with something as complex as a semiotic and/or aesthetic medium. Furthermore, the definitions of *quilca* in colonial dictionaries would have been based on actual usage at the time. No evidence suggests that the Incas maintained anything analogous to dictionaries that would have been conducive to the preservation of archaic forms of Quechua words; nor do Quechua oral traditions appear to have involved the kind of rote memory that might have helped preserve archaic vocabulary. This is not to say that they could not have maintained memory of a past writing system; but if it no longer existed, it is unlikely that the meaning of any term in use at the time of the conquest corresponded to its meaning from that bygone era. Even if we take the translation of these terms at face value, therefore, they would not have referred in any transparent way to some ancient practice that was no longer in use. Absent the textual authority embodied in a dictionary, stable authoritative texts, or rote ritual oral performances, the meaning of linguistic terms is determined by their use. Jara may have been attempting to imply that the derivatives of the term *quilca* are merely vestiges referring to related practices that persisted after the alleged loss of the writing system, but this does not explain the apparently continued use of the non-derivative form of the term *quilca* itself; nor does it resolve the issue of translation.

The presence of the term *quilca* in early colonial dictionaries clearly indicates that the Spaniards had been exposed to it in a number of different contexts. Although the Spaniards never adopted the term to refer to any indigenous objects or practices, native Quechua speakers used it to refer to alphabetic writing, painting, and the other activities noted above. The term never appears in early Spanish chronicles, because, unlike the quipu, the various Andean objects and practices to which it referred were easily translatable into a variety of other terms. Thus, in many cases where Spanish terms such as "pintura" (painting), "bordado" (embroidery), "escultura" (sculpture), and so forth appear in colonial documents in reference to indigenous Andean society, the original Quechua word from which they were translated was likely often *quilca* or a compound containing *quilca*, particularly in the case of references to "painting."

In many cases, particularly after the early 1550s, references to Inca painting may be based on an assumption that the colonial practice of European-style indigenous painting derives in one way or another from a pre-Hispanic tradition.[8] The earliest reference to an indigenous form of painting appears in Juan de Betanzos's *Suma y narración de los Incas* in an episode that would have been transcribed from an oral account by a native Andean informant. Betanzos describes a context in which a recently conquered non-Inca group rendered account to the Incas with quipu and paintings.[9] Based on what later Quechua dic-

Galen Brokaw

tionaries translate as "painting," the original Quechua term here would have been *quilca*. Neither colonial chronicles nor the archaeological record, however, contain any substantive evidence of an Inca practice that would resemble European mimetic painting. Thus if *quilca* was not referring to the particular nature of the quipu itself, the Native informants upon whom Betanzos relied must have been referring to some other medium.

The implicit and explicit connections between *quilca* and the various media referenced in colonial dictionaries may explain why the Quechua term does not appear in descriptions of Andean cultural practices until the very end of the sixteenth century. There must have been a stronger basis for identifying *quilca* with European concepts than was the case for other terms for which there was no real translation, such as *quipu*. In other words, colonial writers may have been translating *quilca* without the kind of ambivalent equivocation that often occurs with other indigenous terms and concepts, and the European term used to translate *quilca* was probably "painting." But the convincing portion of Jara's research focusing on definitions in colonial vocabularies suggests that in addition to its association with the concepts of painting and writing, the semantic field of *quilca* and its verbal derivatives include the following: (1) "to embroider or work cloth"; (2) "to paint, to draw, to dye"; and (3) "to sculpt and work in wood, stone, or metals."[10] Jara concludes that the term *quilca* or *quelca* had a general meaning that encompassed a variety of more specific activities which had their own specific terms.[11] Unfortunately, her eagerness to "prove" her hypothesis that *quilca* referred to an ancient Andean writing system led her to gloss over several of the details in these sources and to miss the more nuanced implications of the lexical and semantic data she collected. The evidence, including references to quilca in colonial chronicles, does lend support to Jara's more conservative argument that the term *quilca* was related to semiotic (and aesthetic) practices.

The closely related late-sixteenth- and early-seventeenth-century chronicles produced by Martín de Murúa and Felipe Guaman Poma de Ayala include far more detailed descriptions of Andean culture and society than most previous chronicles. Furthermore, indigenous informants, including Guaman Poma, participated directly in the production of Murúa's chronicle, and Guaman Poma's own project appears to have been motivated in part by his discontent with Murúa. Although Guaman Poma does not thematize quilca directly, he refers to it in his descriptions of Andean socioeconomic and political institutions. Of course, Guaman Poma was writing around 1600 from a context in which indigenous cultural concepts and practices were often enmeshed with Spanish ones. Thus his references to quilca evince the same kind of tangled relationship with European ideas that served as the basis for Jara's argument about an Andean writing system. Guaman Poma applies the term *quilca* to the paper with which the Spanish conquistadores produced speech,[12] but he also links it to the quipu. In the section on Inca ordinances, Guaman Poma includes a list of officials, giving the name first in Quechua, then in Spanish. One of the offices that appears in this list is *quilca camayoc*, which translates loosely as "quilca maker" or "quilca steward" and more literally as "he who animates quilca"; but Guaman Poma renders the Spanish translation as "escriuano de quipo, cordel" (scribe of the quipu, cord).[13] Later, in the section dealing with the colonial administration, Guaman Poma describes the office of the "escribano de cabildo" (town scribe) using the Spanish term, but in the drawing that accompanies the text he also includes the label "quilcaycamayoc" underneath the Spanish title and next to the scribe.[14] In the pre-Hispanic era, the equivalent function was filled by the *quipucamayoc*, and even in the colonial period the Spanish administration recognized this by ordering that the *quipucamayoc* serve as the town scribe in indigenous communities.[15] Furthermore, in the earliest Quechua dictionary, Domingo de Santo Tomás includes an entry for *quillca quippo*, which he defines as "libro de cuentas" (book of accounts).[16]

The essential question here is whether this association between *quilca* and *quipu* developed before or after contact with the Spaniards. As Thomas Cummins explains, the meaning of the term *quilca*

Galen Brokaw

changed immediately after the conquest to refer to graphic inscriptions produced by the Spaniards, making it difficult to determine exactly how it was used in the pre-Hispanic period.[17] The use of the word *quilca* to refer to paper, books, writing, and painting, however, implies that native Andeans identified some common denominator between the original conceptual domain of the Andean term and writing or painting on paper. As many chroniclers point out, the object most analogous to alphabetic writing in terms of function was the quipu, but this medium had little else in common with alphabetic writing or painting. Thus, quilca must have been identifiable with writing and painting in terms of the materiality of the media, the practices associated with them, a larger conceptual domain, or a combination of these three things.

Rocío Quispe-Agnoli develops a more nuanced version of Jara's argument to suggest that *quilca* did not refer to any particular system of notation or representation but rather to the semiotic act or its product, and that this is what made it so easily applicable to the European notions of writing and painting.[18] This might explain the paradoxical fact that, on the one hand, colonial chroniclers apparently felt that their translation of this term was not problematic, and on the other hand, the exact definition was, and continues to be, so hard to nail down. And Quispe-Agnoli's proposal that *quilca* be understood as a general, abstract concept rather than a specific medium or a particular set of conventions would make sense in the context of a self-consciously multimedia society.

The definitions in colonial dictionaries and Guaman Poma's use of *quilca* are not inconsistent with Jara's understanding of this concept as encompassing a variety of media and Quispe-Agnoli's suggestion that it refers to semiotic practices and products; but the various media that qualify as quilca may also share certain kinds of conventions. Carlos Radicati argues for a more specific understanding of this term as referring to a semiotic system consisting of color sequences or patterns that could be incorporated into a number of different media.[19] The various media that appear to fall under the *quilca* concept may have emerged originally from the use of common conventions of color sequence, and these conventions may have been the original basis for the broader notion of *quilca* in use at the time of the Spanish conquest.

As indicated above, any analysis that uses evidence from colonial dictionaries must take into account the colonial context and the way in which words change in such contexts. However, the earliest efforts to compile dictionaries of Quechua may evince fewer of the transformations that would appear in later ones, because they rely upon Native informants who originally acquired their vocabularies prior to the Spanish invasion. In Santo Tomás's 1560 *Lexicon* the entries for the Spanish term "bordar" (to embroider) are particularly revealing. Santo Tomás includes two entries; the first gives "bordar, o broslar" as "compani." The second specifies a particular type of "embroidery" using color, "Bordar con colores" (to embroider with colors), and the Quechua translation is given as "quilcani."[20] The *Lexicon* therefore draws a distinction between *compa*, as a generic type of embroidery, and *quilca*, as specifically an embroidery with colors. In the Quechua-Spanish section, the *Lexicon* defines "Quillcani" more generally as "labrar alguna obra con colores generalmente."[21] Although awkward, the best translation for this Spanish definition would be "to work a work, generally with colors." The redundancy is important to convey the broad nature of both "labrar" and "obra." The general term "labrar" can refer to any type of work that in some way transforms the object worked upon. It can mean "to cut," "to carve," "to sculpt," "to polish," and even "to sew" and "to embroider."[22] Thus *quilca* may have referred both metonymically to specific media employing visual conventions of color and to a more general notion or principle of semiosis and aesthetics.

While the term *quilca* appears in contexts that ostensibly do not necessarily involve color (such as sculpture), such references may be metonymic or metaphoric extensions of the meaning related to an aesthetic and symbolic use of color developed originally in other Andean media such as those cited above. One of the media associated with both quilca and quipu that does not necessarily involve color is the accounting device and practice known as *yupana*. The word *yupa-*

Galen Brokaw

Fig. 5.1. Yupana device. Courtesy of Museo Larco, Lima, Peru.

na is related to the verb *yupay*, which can mean "to count," "to consider," "to esteem," "to value," "to register," and so forth.[23] Colonial documents that record the accounting of tribute attest to the use of yupana practices in conjunction with quipu.[24] As a material object, the yupana is often identified with archaeological objects made from blocks of stone that have been sculpted to form a series of trays (fig. 5.1), an image of which also ostensibly appears alongside Guaman Poma's drawing of a *quipucamayoc* (fig. 5.2).[25]

Other colonial sources corroborate the association between quipu and yupana evident in Guaman Poma's drawing, and they indicate a further connection to quilca. González Holguín's dictionary, for example, establishes a connection between both of these media and quilca: "Yupana qquellca, o qquipu. Las quentas por ñudos, o por escrito"

Fig. 5.2. Quipu accountant with yupana. Guaman Poma de Ayala, *El primer nueva corónica y buen gobierno*, page 362 [360]. Courtesy of Det Kongelige Bibliotek/The Royal Library of Denmark, Copenhagen.

(Yupana qquellca, or qquipu. The accounts using knots, or writing).[26] In the list of terms that Jara extracts from González Holguín, she curiously omits the "or qquipu" portion of this entry.[27] The disjunctive "o" (or) in the Quechua entry does not make it clear whether or not the "Yupana" portion of the expression is distributive. In other words, the equivalent terms in the definition might be (1) "yupana qquellca" and "qquipu" (non-distributive) or (2) "yupana qquellca" and "yupana qquipu" (distributive). Other entries in González Holguín's *Vocabulario* indicate the latter. Another entry on the same page and using a form of the same word (*yupa*), for example, illustrates the point: "Yumaquey yupa, o rantin. El que esta en lugar de mi padre como tal" (Yumaquey yupa, o rantin. He who is in place of my father as such).[28] Here "Yumaquey" refers to "father" while "yupa" conveys the notion of consideration. Together they refer to a person who is not one's father but who is counted or considered as such. The term "rantin" can mean to trade, take the place of, or acquire the qualities of.[29] In the context of this expression, "rantin" is equivalent to "yupa," and thus the term "Yumaquey" is distributive: the disjunction is between "Yumaquey yupa" and "[Yumaquey] rantin." Thus the same model would apply to other entries. So in the case of the *yupana* entry, it should be understood as "yupana qquellca, or yupana qquipu." In Quechua, adjectives precede nouns,[30] so in noun-noun constructions like this one, the first noun functions as an adjective much as in English. The equivalence of "yupana qquellca" and "yupana qquipu" then implies that in certain contexts *quilca* and *quipu* are synonymous. And the use of the term *quipu*, then, to refer to the system of colored, knotted strings may actually be an abbreviation of "yupana quipu," which would serve to distinguish when necessary between the base referent of *quipu*, which was "knot," and the larger device or practice of the colored, knotted string system or perhaps a particular genre of this medium.

Contact between Spaniards and Andeans inevitably affects the language of each. The application of Native words to European objects and concepts, for example, constitutes a semantic shift. It is possible, therefore, that González Holguín's entry "yupana qquellca" is a colonial neologism used to translate from Spanish into Quechua, thus merely reflecting the fact that the semantic field of the term *quilca* had expanded to include alphabetic writing. In this case the pairing of *quilca* with *yupana* would serve to specify the particular type of writing or book. But this would not necessarily explain the pairing of "yupana quipu." The adjective-noun structure of Quechua noun phrases means that the object in question here is a quipu, and the term *quipu* was never used to refer to any Spanish object or practice. Thus, "yupana quipu" may have been a pre-Hispanic term referring specifically to the genre of quipu used to record statistical information such as tribute. Furthermore, in the much earlier *Lexicon* (1560), Santo Tomás also includes an entry for "quillca quippo" defined as "libro de cuentas" (book of accounts).[31] This entry immediately raises the question of which term is being translated into which language. Given that the native Andeans did not use the term *quipu* to translate the idea of alphabetic writing or European books, there would be no reason to pair it with "quilca" in order to refer to "books." Thus this entry is probably a translation of the indigenous expression "quillca quippo" rather than a translation of the Spanish "libro." Here again, the adjective-noun structure of Quechua also means that the object in question is a quipu, more specifically a quilca-type quipu. "Quillca quippo," then, would have been an organic Quechua expression, and Santo Tomás's translation was an attempt to settle on the closest equivalent concept in Spanish.

It would be tempting to posit that "yupana quipu" and "quilca quipu" referred to different genres, one primarily quantitative (i.e., statistical) and the other more qualitative (e.g., narrative). Such an argument would have to assume that Santo Tomás's definition of "quillca quippo" is an error. It is almost certain that such errors are present in this and other colonial dictionaries, and "libro de cuentas" is certainly an infelicitous definition. But primarily statistical quipu could employ both numeric conventions, which fall under the *yupana* concept, and color conventions, which correspond to the *quilca* concept. Thus, "quilca quipu" may refer to any quipu that used color conventions, regardless of genre.

Galen Brokaw

If *quilca* originally referred to a kind of color symbolism—whether woven, inscribed, painted, or otherwise—this would serve as the basis for its relationship to the quipu, which employed conventional colors and color patterns. And the numeric nature of the quipu and the yupana clearly establishes a link between them, which is also corroborated by colonial records. But this indirect link by way of the quipu does not explain the direct association between quilca and yupana indicated by the expression "yupana quellca" in Santo Tomás's *Lexicon*. Of course, the adjective-noun structure of Quechua suggests that the referent of this expression is actually quilca, with yupana functioning as an adjective (a yupana-style quilca). This seems to imply that *quilca* refers to a material object similar in function to the quipu. I would argue, however, that this use of the term *quilca* reflects a kind of metonymy, by which the literal meaning of the term referring to a semiotics/aesthetics of color also refers by association to the media that employ it. The adaptation of the term *quilca* by native Quechua speakers to refer to European writing on paper and in books would also constitute this same type of metonymy. Thus, the expression "yupana quilca" may have been merely another way to refer to quipu that employed both knots and color conventions without necessarily implying a relationship between quilca and yupana.

The inverse expression "quilca yupana" would have provided direct evidence of this relationship, but it does not appear in the sources cited above. Archaeological data, however, may provide evidence of a color symbolism employed by yupana devices and related to the color symbolism in quipu. William Isbell explains that the pre-Inca Wari culture (c. 500–1000 CE) produced oversized ceramic urns for use in ritual offerings and upon which appear images of the agricultural produce involved in the offering, an effigy of a god or paired gods, and storehouses or a polychromatic checkerboard design (fig. 5.3).[32] In an extension of his analysis, I have argued that the storehouse and the checkerboard design are analogous elements related to the administration of agricultural tribute and that the checkerboard design is essentially a representation of an early yupana-type object.[33] The

Fig. 5.3. Wari ceramic vessel with checkerboard design. Courtesy of the
Instituto Nacional de Cultura, Museo Nacional de Arqueología,
Antropología e Historia del Perú.

implication of this analysis is that the yupana may have developed originally from a record-keeping device designed as a small-scale representation of a storehouse. John Topic has suggested a similar development in the context of the Chimu state.[34] Of course, yupana practices did not always have recourse to color. Colonial documents indicate that in some cases Native *quipucamayoc* improvised a yupana by distributing small objects such as pebbles on the ground.[35] But quipu did not always use color either. Many quipu consist of undyed monochromatic cords, suggesting that cord color and cord sequence may have been redundancies that rendered the color component optional in many cases. Based on an analysis of colonial transcriptions of tribute quipu, John Murra concludes that many quipu employed a hierarchy of ethnocategories that determined the order of the items recorded.[36] In such cases the color would still be useful for identifying individual items rapidly and for resolving ambiguities, but in highly standardized records it would not have been necessary. Similarly, the yupana may have employed a color symbolism, especially in its early function as a record-keeping device; but as it developed into a technique for calculation, a standardized spatial configuration would have made the colors more redundant than those of a standardized quipu genre. Even when color was not actually present, the relationship itself may have persisted.

The use of color patterns associated with a yupana-type grid during the Wari period would be particularly significant because quipu first appear in the archaeological record at this point.[37] And in many ways, the color conventions of Wari quipu resonate more with the colored grid of what I have argued is a Wari yupana than with the Inca quipu. The quipu that can be reliably dated to the Wari period belong to a type identified by Radicati as "quipu de canutos," whose rather thick pendant cords have colored thread wrappings beginning near the top (fig. 5.4). The wrapped quipu that contain knots tend to deviate from the standard conventions that characterize the majority of Inca-period quipu and may represent an intermediate stage of quipu development. The thread wrappings produce often complex chromat-

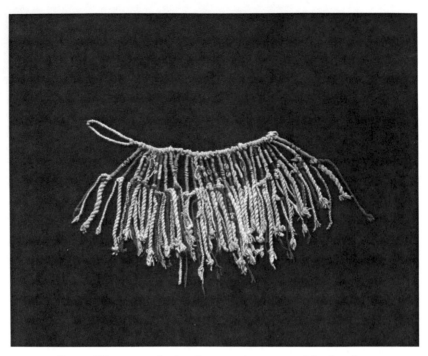

Fig. 5.4. Wari-wrapped quipu. Image #5068, courtesy of the American Museum of Natural History Library.

ic patterns that ostensibly convey the majority of the information. The use of colors in the Wari wrapped quipu, then, appears to be a kind of qualitative semiosis as opposed to the quantitative conventions of the knots, although even the conventions of color wrappings might have had a numeric dimension. When viewed together, the colored bands produce an effect in some ways similar to the checkerboard pattern of the Wari yupana image. One rather unusual, presumably intermediate stage, quipu with both knots and colored thread wrappings, portrays a regular checkerboard pattern (fig. 5.5). Note that this quipu uses uncolored strings wrapped with colored thread, which is consistent with Wari quipu, but it also includes knots, characteristic of Inca quipu. The relationship between the color patterns and the knots is unclear; but it appears that as knots are introduced, the color patterns become simpler, finally giving way to the use of colored cords rather than thread wrappings. But even late Inca-era quipu employ several

Galen Brokaw

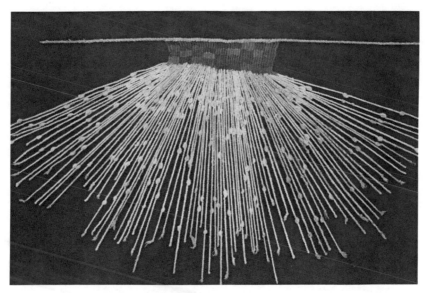

Fig. 5.5. Wrapped quipu with checkerboard pattern. Courtesy of the
Universidad de San Martín de Porres, Lima, Perú. Photograph by Gary Urton.

different techniques in the construction of the pendant cords to produce color variations that may be vestiges of the more complex color system of Wari quipu. In any case, the use of color in these different media exhibits formal affinities.

The yupana checkerboard design on the Wari ceramic vessels also resembles the grid pattern of *tocapu* designs found on Inca tunics and inscribed into wooden cups known as *queros*. These squares often contain complex designs, but many tunics also exhibit monochromatic squares arranged in a pattern that had a particular significance (fig. 5.6). Building on her previous linguistic analysis, Jara enlisted the help of Thomas Barthel in even less rigorous investigations into the possibility that these textile designs functioned as a form of writing or notation.[38] Subsequently, however, other scholars have explored the semiotic nature of tocapu designs in more nuanced analyses. John Rowe argues that differences in tocapu designs indicate status.[39] Tom Zuidema suggests that the tocapu designs that appear in the drawings of Guaman Poma de Ayala's *Nueva corónica* (1615) have both calendrical and historical functions associated with dynastic descent.[40] Tom

Fig. 5.6. Inca tunic, Late Horizon, 1476–1534, Camelid fiber (34.75 x 31.5 in.).
Geographic location: Peru, South America. Dallas Museum of Art, the
Eugene and Margaret McDermott Art Fund, Inc., in honor of Carol Robbins.

Cummins demonstrates that some tocapu may have been toponymic in nature.[41] Carmen Arellano and Rocío Quispe-Agnoli suggest that the tocapu may have represented isolated concepts related to the authority of the sovereigns or nobles and to the administration of the empire.[42] The conventions employed by the tocapu remain obscure, but Rebecca Stone argues that the distinctive tocapu designs on the tunics of each Inca carried special holistic significance derived from the relationships among their constituent components.[43]

References to tocapu in colonial documents are rare and brief, but

Galen Brokaw

several texts refer to the general semiotic significance of clothing in the Inca empire. Polo de Ondegardo states that the Indians wore more or less the same style of clothing but that each region had its unique characteristics, which were preserved in the period of Inca domination.[44] Pedro Cieza de León explains that Inca administrators "went from town to town looking at the dress of the inhabitants and the resources they had and the size of the land or if they had livestock."[45] Antonio Vázquez Espinoza asserts that these differences in dress existed prior to the Inca conquest and that they were allowed to persist in order to facilitate ethnic identification.[46] Cieza de León and Bartolomé de Porras both state that the Incas imposed or at least enforced the use of distinguishing styles of dress for the groups they governed.[47] Of course, these references do not necessarily have anything to do with tocapu. In fact, Cieza de León indicates that tocapu were characteristic only of royal dress.[48] But non-royal clothing often employed geometric designs with color patterns of symbolic significance.[49]

The more complex textiles of Inca dress with their configurations of tocapu designs, then, may represent a more complex form of semiosis. The style of dress of individual Incas appears to have served as an identifying feature. In Guaman Poma's history of the Inca empire, his presentation of each Inca and each *coya* (queen) begins with a physical description that includes the color and design of his or her clothing.[50] Furthermore, the full-body drawings that accompany these descriptions portray each Inca and queen with a distinctive pattern of tocapu. The memory of this information may have been preserved in the ritual conservation and display of Inca mummies, but Guaman Poma's history was also based on quipu sources.[51] Regardless of whether the codification of these dress styles in their relation to individual Incas occurred only postmortem, it indicates the perceived importance of the textile media that made up Inca attire, a significant component of which was the configuration of tocapu designs.[52] We may never know the significance of tocapu patterns, but given their inherent use of color and possible links to the quipu, they would fall under the concept of *quilca* as defined by colonial dictionaries.

If quilca essentially involved the conventional use of color, then a number of other media may have participated in it as well. Jean Pierre Protzen and Craig Morris have investigated the widespread use of horizontal color bands painted on buildings in places such as Tambo Colorado. The number of colors employed at a given site are usually limited to three, but the order of the bands differs in possibly systematic ways, implying some kind of symbolic significance.[53] Radicati identifies a relationship between the thread wrappings of the quipu and archaeological wigs of braided hair that also have the same kind of thread wrappings around the end of each braid.[54] Hugo Pereyra explains that the colored bands on the wigs do not appear to be arranged in any discernible pattern, but he points out that these thread wrappings are similar to the kind of thread wrappings found on quipu from the Middle Horizon period.[55] Museum collections of Andean artifacts often contain numerous examples of sticks, normally in pairs, wrapped with thread to form certain color patterns that often resonate with the kind of patterning created by thread wrappings on Wari quipu (fig. 5.4). And some short staff-like objects exhibit similar thread wrappings.[56]

These striped sticks and staffs or objects related to them may have had a direct link to the quipu. Miguel Cabello Balboa's *Miscelánea antártica* (1586) contains a curious reference to what appears to be a semiotic medium consisting of a bar with color bands that was associated with the quipu. The reference occurs in his account of the death of Huayna Capac in Quito:

[F]eeling close to death, he made a will according to their custom, and in a long stick (like a staff) they went placing stripes of different colors by which they knew and understood his last and final will, which was given for safekeeping to the Quipucamayoc (who was like our Scribe, or Secretary). Through his executors he named Colla Topa and Catumgui and Taur machi and Augui Topayupangui, and three or four more principal captains and close relatives of his and under this testament the good and valorous leader and king Guayna Capac died; having reigned and

Galen Brokaw

ruled the Empire for a little more than 33 years, his death occurred (according to our count) in the year 1525. At the same time, Pizarro, Luque, and Almagro were preparing to explore his kingdom, now already possessed peacefully. His death was kept secret for several days, because those from Cuzco feared some developments and disturbances that often occur at these junctures. But his body having been embalmed (as is their custom) the executors gathered together along with the *quipucamayoc* (or scribe) and they carefully considered that which the *quipu* and knots declared, and being interpreted with the proper and necessary precision, it seemed that he had newly and finally named as sole and universal heir and successor of the Empire a son who he brought with him and whom he loved deeply named Ninancuyuchic, who at this point was sick with fever from which he died a few days later. And Huascar Inca was left with what he had at first. They also discovered from the *quipu* instructions on how they were to carry his body to Cuzco and how they were to enter triumphant.[57]

The beginning of this passage explains that Huayna Capac recorded his last will and testament on a staff using stripes of various colors and then gave it to a *quipucamayoc* for safekeeping. After his death, when the executors of Huayna Capac's will met with the *quipucamayoc*, there is no further mention of this colored staff. The officials meet to examine and interpret what the "quipus and knots" declared. Leaving aside the problem of translating indigenous practices into Spanish legal discourse with terms such as *testamento* (will) and *albacea* (executor), the text offers no explanation as to how, when, or why Huayna Capac's will went from a staff with colored stripes to the knotted cords of a quipu. Nor is there any explanation about the nature of the colored staff. We might assume that the *quipucamayoc* transcribed the will from the staff to the cords, but the nature of the colored staff and why the will was recorded on it instead of directly on a quipu remain unclear. Radicati cites this text in support of his argument that quipu and quilca are two manifestations of a single system.[58]

In *Relación de antigüedades de este reyno del Perú* (1613), Juan de Santa Cruz Pachacuti Yamqui also mentions a staff with colored bands used as a semiotic medium by Huayna Capac's father. In Pachacuti Yamqui's account, Topa Ynga Yupangui appoints Caçir Capac as inspector general of the empire and gives him his commission in stripes on a painted stick: "And at this time, the said Inca dispatches Caçir Capac as inspector general of the lands and pastures, giving him his commission in stripes on a painted stick."[59] This passage is somewhat ambiguous, in that "commission" may refer either to the authority that is granted to carry out a task—in which case the colored stripes on the staff might simply have indicated the office of the inspector general—or to a specific task, in which case the colored stripes would convey more detailed instructions.

This same text, however, contains another, less ambiguous reference to what appears to be a similar staff. Earlier in the account, prior to the advent of the Inca dynasty, a man called Tonapa Viracochampacachan, whom Pachacuti Yamqui identifies as Saint Thomas, arrives in Peru and gives a striped staff to a cacique named Apotampo. This staff contains Tonapa's teachings:

This man, they say that he arrived at the village of a cacique named Apo Tampo who governed the village. And they say that he arrived very tired to a festival in celebration of a wedding. Apo Tampo listened to his reasoning with love and the Indians who were his subjects listened grudgingly. During that day, the pilgrim was a guest, who, they say, gave a stick from his staff to Apo Tampo, reprehending them with affable love, and Apo Tampo listened with attention and received the stick from his hand. Thus, they received on a stick what he preached to them, indicating to them and marking [with stripes] each chapter of his reasoning.[60]

The larger context of this episode evinces clear signs of Andean-Christian transculturation. Nevertheless, the staff in this account appears to be the same kind of object given to Caçir Capac by Topa Ynga

Galen Brokaw

Yupangui. And in this case, it would seem clear that the stripes on the staff convey more specific information suggesting the more liberal reading of Santa Cruz Pachacuti's use of "commission" as referring to "instructions" rather than the conservative interpretation as merely indicating "the authority of an official position." But given the common symbolic use of staffs of office, these two functions may have been interrelated. That is to say, the conventions used to imbue staffs of office with symbolic significance may participate in the same general semiotic tradition.

Of course, this passage from Pachacuti Yamqui's text refers to a past that has been reinterpreted from a Christian perspective; but the rather cursory mention of this color-striped staff may also indicate that such objects were familiar and required no explanation for a Native audience. Pachacuti Yamqui was an ethnic Canchi from an originally Aymara-speaking area in Collasuyo[61] that would have been under Tiwanaku influence during the Middle Horizon period; and he claims to base his history on stories that he heard as a child.[62] The use of such color-striped staffs, then, appears both in Cabello Balboa's Quito-influenced work from the northern Andes and in Pachacuti Yamqui's account from the south. If we accept that these references to color-striped sticks actually correspond to an indigenous semiotic medium, then it appears to have been fairly widespread. Unfortunately, the documentary record of these objects is sparse, but they appear to correlate in one way or another to the various thread-wrapped sticks described above (fig. 5.7).

I would argue that the formal affinity among these various media is phylogenic; that is to say, they exhibit synchronic relationships rooted in diachronic processes. To use a thoroughly felicitous metaphor, the thread that ties all of these media together is the use of color organized into sequences or patterns. The Quechua term translated into Spanish as "color" is *ricchay*, but this term has a much broader meaning than just "color." González Holguín defines the term as "color, o haz de qualquiera cosa, rostro, o imagen, o figura" (color, or face/surface of any thing, face, or image, or figure).[63] It is probably a coinci-

Fig. 5.7. Thread-wrapped sticks. Copyright President and Fellows of
Harvard College, Peabody Museum of Archaeology and Ethnology,
Peabody ID# 75-20-30/8779.

dence that one of the definitions of the Spanish term *haz* is a "bundle of sticks, vines, grass, wheat, and other things that are tied together with some kind of cord or rope,"[64] which resonates with the thread-wrapped sticks discussed above (fig. 5.7). In any case, the derivatives of the term *ricchay* indicate a semantic field that includes the ideas of wakefulness, attentiveness, memory, and similarity in appearance. In the bilingual *Tercero catecismo* produced by the Third Lima Council in 1583, "ricchay" appears in reference to the creation of humans in the image of God and of animals not in the image of God.[65] These passages demonstrate that in addition to similarity of appearance, *ricchay* could refer to similarity of function or nature. This text also employs the term *unancha*, which González Holguín defines as "Qualquiera señal, estandarte, ynsignia, escudo de armas" (any sign, standard, insignia, coat of arms).[66]

In the *Tercero catecismo*'s discussion of religious images, all of these terms also appear in association with quilca. The nineteenth sermon of the catechism focuses on the second commandment, which forbids the worship of images. Of course, the Spaniards were hard put to explain how their own practices did not violate this commandment. The justification for Christian images maintains that it is not the images themselves, but rather that which they represent, that is worshipped. The nineteenth sermon attempts to clarify the metaphysical nature of Christian symbols in opposition to what the Christians saw as a kind of animism that characterized indigenous Andean beliefs:

The Christians do not worship or kiss the images for what they are, nor do they worship that stick, or metal, or painting. Rather, they worship Jesus Christ in the Image of the Crucifix, and the Mother of God, our Lady the Virgin Mary in her Image, and the Saints also in their Images. And the Christians know very well that Jesus Christ, and Our Lady, and the Saints are in heaven alive and glorious, and that they are not in those bundles, or Images, but rather only painted [rickchaynillanmi], and they put their hearts in heaven where Jesus Christ is, and his Saints, and in Jesus Christ they put their hope, and their will, and they revere [yupaychaspa] the Images, and they kiss them, and they bare themselves before them, and kneel down on their knees, and they beat their chests; it is because of what those Images represent, and not for what they are in themselves. Just like the Corregidor kisses the provision and Royal seal [Reypa quellcanta unanchanta] and puts it on his head, not because of the wax or the paper [quillcacta quellca], but rather because it is the King's *quilca* [Reypa quellcan]. And thus you will see that when a bundle is broken, or an Image [imagen quellcapi] is smashed, the Christians do not cry, nor do they think that God has been broken or lost, because my God is in heaven, and he never perishes. And with regard to the Image [imagen] only the stick, or the metal, or the paper [quellca] is broken or lost, which doesn't affect the Christians at all, nor do they take it to be their God.[67]

Here, *ricchay* refers to the painted nature of an image, and *quilca* appears alone in reference to "paper" and in conjunction with "unancha" and "imagen" as renderings of the Spanish "imagen" (image). Furthermore, the passage uses the term *yupay* to describe the veneration shown to Christian images and to the royal seal.[68] As explained above, *yupay* means "to count" but also "to consider," "to esteem," and "to value." I have argued elsewhere that this honorific meaning may have derived from the association between a dynasty of Inca leaders who oversaw the expansion of quipu conventions in conjunction with the expansion and consolidation of the empire and who took on the name Yupanqui by virtue of their roles in this expansion.[69] Of course, the usage here clearly indicates "esteem" or "respect," but the etymology and the larger semantic field of the term may not be completely irrelevant. One of the usages of *yupay* discussed above has to do with the consideration of someone or something not for what it is but for that with which it is associated or for the role it plays. Here, the term is used to translate the verb "to reverence" or "to revere," but whether intentionally or not it describes the metaphysical nature of Christian

Galen Brokaw

symbols: the images are revered not for what they are but for what they represent, which is not present. Thus, the association between this sense of *yupay* and the more explicitly semiotic concepts of *ricchay* and *quilca* would be entirely appropriate. And this relationship may invoke a conceptual link to the yupana and its relationship to the quipu.

Of course, the use of color and even the formal similarities between media does not always mean that they convey the kind of meaning normally associated with semiotic media. As mentioned above, the thread-wrapped braids found on wigs and formally related to the Wari wrapped quipu do not appear to employ explicit semiotic conventions. And the color patterns of Tambo Colorado studied by Protzen and Morris may be primarily aesthetic in nature. But the role color and color patterns played in any given Andean medium may call into question the very distinction that Western thought draws between the aesthetic and the rational. Indeed, the color conventions of the tocapu, the yupana, and the quipu constitute a kind of visual poetry that exhibits both rational and aesthetic features, or rather, a semio-aesthetics and an aesthesio-semiotics.[70]

Such an understanding of indigenous media makes the traditional approach to decipherment highly problematic. Its implication is that Andean media, and I would argue so-called premodern societies in general, do not necessarily rely upon the same kind of codified or predetermined structures that modern thinkers tend to believe characterize their own communicative practices. As Frank Salomon argues in reference to the Andean community of Tupicocha's inscribed staffs of office, which could easily be included in the discussion above, the use of this medium "in different situations yields wordless but unpredictable, nonpredetermined statements about those situations," so that "successive iterations yield not varied messages in a constant code but varying code" whose expression is inflected by the context in which it is performed.[71] This is not to say that in some cases certain media, or certain genres of media, did not develop more rigidly codified conventions or rules. In fact, I would argue that the administration of the Inca empire would have induced a movement in that direction, and many of the archaeological quipu that have survived may be products of this development. But even in these cases, the heterogeneous nature of the medium may have preserved the inherent relationship between aesthetic and "rational" thought to a much greater degree than modern societies. I refer to an "inherent relationship," but this expression reflects the modern mentality that separates the two. The broad concept of *quilca* and its relationship to the various objects and practices discussed above should call into question the status and validity of this dichotomy not only in reference to Andean media but to our own as well.

Notes

1. Martín de Murúa, *Historia del origen y genealogía de los reyes incas del Perú* (Madrid: Instituto Santo toribio de Mogrovejo, 1946 [1594]), 289–90; Felipe Guaman Poma de Ayala, *Nueva corónica y buen gobierno* (Madrid: Historia 16, 1987 [1615]), 359 [361]).

2. Domingo de Santo Tomás, *Lexicon o vocabulario de la lengua general del Perú* (Lima: Instituto de Historia, 1951 [1560]), 61, 155, 98, 131, 157, 158, 216, 357.

3. Antoni Ricardo, *Vocabulario y phrasis en la lengua general de los indios del Perú, llamada Quechua* (Lima: Universidad Nacional Mayor de San Marcos, 1951 [1586]), 172, 143.

4. Diego González Holguín, *Vocabulario de la lengua general de todo el Perú llamada lengua Qqichua o del Inca* (Lima: Santa María, 1952 [1608]), 301.

5. Raúl Porras Barrenechea, "Quipu y quilca (contribución histórica al estudio de la escritura en el antiguo Perú)," *El Comercio*, January 1, 1947, 8, 20; Raúl Porras Barrenechea, "Quipu y quilca," *Mercurio Peruano* Año 22, vol. 27, no. 238 (1947): 3–35; Raúl Porras Barrenechea, "Quipu i quilca (Contribución histórica al estudio de la escritura en el antiguo Perú)," *Revista del Museo e Instituto Arqueológico* 13–14 (Cuzco: Universidad de Cuzco, 1951): 19–53.

6. Carlos Radicati, "Introducción al estudio de los quipus," *Documenta: Revista de la Sociedad Peruana de Historia* 2 (1949–50): 320. See also Victoria de la Jara, *La escritura peruana y los vocabularios Quechuas antiguos* (Lima: Imprenta "Lux," 1964), 366; Victoria de la Jara, "La solución del problema de la escritura peruana," *Arqueología y Sociedad* 1 (1970): 27–35.

Galen Brokaw

7. Jara, *Escritura*, 28. Although Jara does not discuss the second book of Fernando de Montesinos's *Memorias historiales*, presumably she bases this assertion in part on his account, which identifies the *quilca* as a pre-Inca medium. See Fernando de Montesinos, *Memorias antiguas historiales del Perú* (London: The Hakluyt Society, 1920 [1644]), 64.

8. Galen Brokaw, "The Origin of Inca Painting," unpublished manuscript.

9. Juan de Betanzos, *Suma y narración de los Incas* (Madrid: Ediciones Atlas, 1987 [1551]), 96.

10. Jara, *Escritura*, 13.

11. Jara, *Escritura*, 16.

12. Guaman Poma, *Nueva corónica*, 381 [383].

13. Guaman Poma, *Nueva corónica*, 191 [193]. For a discussion of the meaning of the term *camayoc*, see Gerald Taylor, "Camac, camay y camasca en el manuscrito quechua de Huarochirí," in *Camac, camay y camasca . . .* (Lima: Institut Français d'Etudes Andines, 2000).

14. Guaman Poma, *Nueva corónica*, 814 [828]–815 [829].

15. Francisco de Toledo, *Francisco de Toledo: Disposiciones gubernativas para el virreinato del Perú*, 2 vols. (Seville: Consejo Superior de Investigaciones Científicas, 1986–89 [1569–80]), 2:218; see also Galen Brokaw, *A History of the Khipu* (Cambridge: Cambridge University Press, 2010), 205–6.

16. Santo Tomás, *Lexicon o vocabulario*, 357.

17. Thomas Cummins, *Toasts with the Inca: Andean Abstraction and Colonial Images on Quero Vessels* (Ann Arbor: University of Michigan Press, 2002), 190, 211.

18. Rocío Quispe-Agnoli, "Escritura alfabética y literalidades amerindias: Fundamentos para una historiografía colonial andina," *Revista Andina* 34 (2002): 247–48; Rocío Quispe-Agnoli, "Cuando Occidente y los Andes se encuentra: Quellcay, escritura alfabética, y tokhapu en el siglo XVI," *Colonial Latin American Review* 14.2 (2005): 262–72; Rocío Quispe-Agnoli, *La fe andina en la escritura: Resistencia e identidad en la otra de Guaman Poma de Ayala* (Lima: Universidad Nacional de San Marcos, 2006), 185–87.

19. Carlos Radicati, "El secreto de la quilca," *Revista de Indias* 44.173 (1984): 11–60. For a more recent statement along these lines see Fernando Prada Ramírez, "El khipu incaico: De la matemática a la historia," *Yachay* 12.21 (1995): 17.

20. Santo Tomás, *Lexicon o vocabulario*, 61.

21. Santo Tomás, *Lexicon o vocabulario*, 357.

22. *Diccionario de autoridades* (Madrid: Grecos, 1990 [1726–39]), 2:344; Sebastián de Covarrubias Horozco, *Tesoro de la lengua Castellana o Española* (Madrid: Universidad de Navarra/Iberoamericana Vervuert, 2006 [1611]), 1157.

23. González Holguín, *Vocabulario*, 371–72; Santo Tomás, *Lexicon o vocabulario*, 680–82.

24. Fernando Achacata and Luis Conba, "La quenta y razón de lo que pagaron al dicho don Alonso de Montemayor y a sus mayordomos por sus quipos," in *Textos andinos: Corpus de textos khipu incaicos y coloniales*, ed. Martti Pärssinen and Jukka Kiviharju (Madrid: Instituto Iberoamericano de Finlandia/Universidad Complutense de Madrid, 2004 [1578]), 1:299–335; Gary Urton, "From Knots to Narratives: Reconstructing the Art of Historical Record Keeping in the Andes from Spanish Transcriptions of Inka Khipus," *Ethnohistory* 45.3 (1998): 409–38; Inca Garcilaso de la Vega, *Comentarios reales de los Incas* (Caracas: Biblioteca Ayacucho, 1985 [1609]), 1:112.

25. Guaman Poma, *Nueva corónica*, [360] 362.

26. González Holguín, *Vocabulario*, 371.

27. Jara, *Escritura*, 7.

28. González Holguín, *Vocabulario*, 371.

29. González Holguín, *Vocabulario*, 312–13.

30. Simeon Floyd, "Rediscovering the Quechua Adjective," *Linguistic Typology* 11 (2011): 30.

31. Santo Tomás, *Lexicon o vocabulario*, 357.

32. William Isbell, *The Rural Foundation for Urbanism: Economic and Stylistic Interaction between Rural and Urban Communities in Eighth-Century Peru* (Urbana: University of Illinois Press, 1977), 49–54.

33. Brokaw, *History of the Khipu*, 78–83.

34. John Topic, "From Stewards to Bureaucrats: Architecture and Information Flow at Chan Chan, Peru," *Latin American Antiquity* 14.3 (2003): 243–74.

35. Achacata and Conba, "La quenta y razón."

36. John Murra, "Las etnocategorías de un *khipu* estatal," in *La tecnologia en el mundo andino*, ed. Heather Lechtman and Ana María Soldí (Mexico: UNAM, 1981), 433–42.

37. William Conklin, "The Information System of Middle Horizon Quipus," in *Ethnoastronomy and Archaeoastronomy in the American Tropics*, ed. Anthony F. Aveni and Gary Urton (New York: Academy of Sciences,

1982), 267–68; Ruth Shady, Joaquín Narváez, and Sonia López, "La anti-güedad del uso del quipu como escritura: Las evidencias de la Huaca de San Marcos," *Boletín del Museo de Arqueología, Universidad Nacional Mayor de San Marcos* 3.10 (2000): 2–23.

38. Jara, "La solución"; Thomas Barthel, "Erste Shritte zur Entzifferung der Inkaschrift," *Tribus* 19 (1970): 91–96; Thomas Barthel, "Viracochas Prunkgewant (Tocapu-Studien 1)," *Tribus* 20 (1971): 63–124.

39. John Howland Rowe, "Standardization in Inca Tapestry Tunics," in *Junius B. Bird Pre-columbian Textile Conference*, ed. Anne Pollard Rowe, Elizabeth P. Benson, and Anne-Louise Shaffer (Washington DC: The Textile Museum/Dumbarton Oaks, 1979), 239–64.

40. R. Tom Zuidema, "Guaman Poma and the Art of Empire: Toward an Iconography of Royal Dress," in *Transatlantic Encounters: Europeans and Andeans in the Sixteenth Century*, ed. Kenneth Andrien and Rolena Adorno (Berkeley: University of California Press, 1991), 195.

41. Cummins, *Toasts with the Inca*, 134–35.

42. Carmen Arellano, "Quipu y tocapu: Sistemas de comunicación Inca," in *Los Incas: Arte y símbolos* (Lima: Banco de Crédito del Perú, 1999), 215–62; Quispe-Agnoli, "Escritura alfabética," 247, "Cuando Occiddente," and *La fe andina*.

43. Rebecca Stone, "'And All Theirs Different from His': The Dumbarton Oaks Royal Inka Tunic in Context," in *Variations of Expression of Inka Power*, ed. Richard Burger and Ramiro Matos (Washington DC: Dumbarton Oaks, 2008), 372–422.

44. Polo de Ondegardo, *El mundo de los Incas* (Madrid: Historia 16, 1990 [1571]), 117.

45. "iban de pueblo en pueblo mirando el traje de los naturales y posibilidad que tenían y la grosedad de la tierra o si en ellas había ganados" (Pedro Cieza de León, *El señorío de los Incas* [Madrid: Historia 16, 1985 (1553)], 74).

46. Antonio Vázquez Espinoza, *Compendio y descripción de las Indias occidentales*, 2 vols., ed. Balbino Velasco Bayón (Madrid: Historia 16, 1992 [1630]), 743.

47. Cieza, *El señorío de los Incas*, 163, 166; Bartolomé de Porras, Francisco Cocamaita, and Francisco Quiqua, "Testimony of Bartolomé Porras, Francisco Cocamaita, and Francisco Quiqua," in "Instrucción hecha en el Cuzco, por orden del Rey y encargo del Virrey Martín Enríquez acerca de las costumbres que tenían los Incas del Perú . . . ," *La imprenta en Lima*, ed. José Toribio Medina (Madrid: Juan Puego, 1904 [1582]), 1:198;

Stone, "'And All Theirs'"; R. Tom Zuidema, "Bureaucracy and Systematic Knowledge in Andean Civilization," in *The Inca and Aztec States, 1400–1800: Anthropology and History*, ed. George A. Collier, Renato I. Rosaldo, and John D. Wirth (New York: Academic Press, 1982), 446–47.

48. Cieza, *El señorío de los Incas*, 42.

49. Rebecca Stone-Miller, *Art of the Andes from Chavín to Inca* (London: Thames and Hudson, 2002), 212.

50. Guaman Poma, *Nueva corónica*, [85] 85–[119] 119, [120] 120–[143] 143.

51. Galen Brokaw, "The Poetics of Khipu Historiography," *Latin American Research Review* 38.3 (2003): 111–47.

52. For an interesting analysis of Inca tunics and the Andean ideology of dress in general, see Stone, "'And All Theirs.'"

53. Jean Pierre Protzen and Craig Morris, "Los colores de Tambo Colorado: Una reevaluación," *Boletín de Arqueología* PUCP 8 (2004): 267–76; Jean Pierre Protzen, "Max Uhle and Tambo Colorado a Century Later," *Ñawpa Pacha* 28 (2006): 11–40.

54. Radicati, "El secreto," 20–26.

55. Hugo Pereyra, personal communication.

56. Jeffrey Splitstoser has been working on a particularly interesting group of wrapped sticks from the Ica Valley (publication forthcoming). William Conklin attempts to analyze Splitstoser's photographs in "Antes del quipu inca: La evolución de los sistemas informativos basados en cuerdas," *Atando Cabos* (Lima: Ministerio de Cultura/Museo Nacional de Arqueología, Antropología e Historia del Perú, 2011), 77–93.

57. The original reads, "sintiendose cercano de la muerte hizo su testamento segun entre ellos era costumbre, y en una vara larga (a manera de baculo) fueron poniendo rayas con distintas colores en que se conocia y entendia su ultima y postrimera voluntad, lo qual le fue dada en guarda á el Quipo-camayoc (que era como entre nosotros el Escriuano, ó Secretario) dejó nombrados por sus Albaceas y Testamentarios á Colla Topa y a Catumgui y a Tauri machi y Auqui Topayupangui, y a otros tres o quatro Principales Capitanes y deudos cercanos suyos y debajo deste testamento murio el valeroso y buen Caudillo y Rey Guayna Capac auiendo señoreado y mandado el Ymperio poco más de 33 años subcedio su muerte (a nra cuenta) año de 1525. Por el mismo tiempo que Pizarro, Luque y Almagro se andauan aprestando para explorarle su Reyno ya pacificamente poseido su muerte se cayo por algunos dias temiendose todos los del Cuzco de algunas novedades y alteraciones que suelen acudir á tales coyunturas mas

siendo embalsamado su cuerpo (como entre ellos era costumbre) juntar-
onse los testamentarios y albaceas juntamente con el Quipo Camayoc (o
Escribano) y atentamente consideraron lo que los Quipos y ñudos de-
clarauan, y interpretado con la deuida y necesaria fidelidad parecia auer
hecho nuevo y ultimo nombramiento de unico y universal heredero y sub-
cesor del Ymperio en un hijo que consigo traia a quien amava mucho llamado Ninancuyuchic, que en esta coyuntura estaua enfermo de calenturas
de las quales en pocos días murio, y quedose Guascar Ynga con lo que
primero tenia. Hallaron también por los Quipos el orden que se auia de
tener en llebar su cuerpo á el Cuzco, y como se auia de entrar triumphan-
do." Miguel Cabello Balboa, *Miscelánea antartica* (Lima: Universidad Nacional Mayor de San Marcos, Instituto de Etnología, 1951 [1586]), 393–94.

58. Radicati, "El secreto," 49–51.

59. "En este tiempo el inca despacha a Caçir *cápac* por visitador general de
las tierras y pastos, dándole su comisión en rayas de palo pintado." Juan
de Santa Cruz Pachacuti Yamqui, *Relación de antigüedades de este reyno del
Perú* (Mexico: Fondo de Cultura Económica, 1995 [1613]), 85 [f. 28v].

60. "Este varón dicen que llegó al pueblo de un cacique llamado *apo* Tampo,
a quien estaba sujeto el pueblo. Dicen que llegó muy cansado a una fiesta,
cuando estaban en unas bodas. Por el *apo* Tampo fueron oídos sus razon-
amientos con amor y los indios a él sujetos los oyeron de mala gana. Por
aquel día fue huésped el peregrino, el cual dicen que dio un palo de su
bordón al *apo* Tampo reprendiéndolo con amor afable y el *apo* Tampo lo
oyó con atención recibiendo el palo de su mano. De modo que en un palo
recibieron lo que les predicaba, señalándoles y rayando cada capítulo de
las razones." Pachacuti Yamqui, *Relación*, [f. 4r] 9, 11.

61. Pachacuti Yamqui, *Relación*, 2–3; Ludovico Bertonio, *Vocabulario de la lengua aymara* (La Paz: Radio San Gabriel/Instituto Radiofónico de Pro-
moción Aymara, 1993 [1612]), 80; Alfredo Torero, "Lingüística e historia
de la sociedad andina," in *El reto del multilinguismo en el Perú*, ed. Alberto
Escobar (Lima: Instituto de Estudios Peruanos, 1972), 69; Ana Sánchez,
Introducción, in *Antigüedades del Perú*, ed. Henrique Urbano and Ana
Sánchez (Madrid: Historia 16, 1992), 126.

62. Pachacuti Yamqui, *Relación*, 178.

63. González Holguín, *Vocabulario*, 315.

64. *Diccionario de autoridades*, 2:132.

65. *Tercero catecismo* (Lima: Concilio Provincial de Lima, 1773 [1583]), 13, 68,
78, etc.

66. González Holguín, *Vocabulario*, 355.

67. "Los christianos no adoran ni besan las Imàgenes, por lo que son, ni adoran aquel palo, ò metal, ò pintura: mas adoran à Jesu Christo en la Imàgen del Crucifixo, y à la Madre de Dios nuestra Señora la Vírgen María en su Imàgen, y à los Santos tambien en sus Imàgenes: y bien saben los Christianos que Jesu Christo, y Nuestra Señora, y los Santos estàn en el cielo vivos, y gloriosos, y no estàn en aquellos bultos, ó Imàgenes, sino solamente pintados [rickchaynillanmi], y así su corazon lo ponen en el cielo donde està Jesu Christo, y sus Santos, y en Jesu Christo ponen su esperanza, y su voluntad: y se reverencian [yupaychaspa] las Imàgenes, y las besan, y se descubren delante de ellas, é hinca de rodillas, y hieren los pechos, es por lo que aquellas Imàgenes representan, y no lo que por en sí son, como el Corregidor besa la provisision, y sello Real [Reypa quellcanta unanchanta], y lo pone sobre su cabeza, no por aquella cera, ni por el papel [quillcacta quellca], sino porque es quillca del Rey [Reypa quellcan]: y asi vereis que se quiebre un bulto, ò se rompa una Imàgen [imagen quellcapi], no por eso los chritianos lloran, ni piensan que Dios se les ha quebrado, ò perdido; porque mi Dios està en el cielo, y nunca perece: y de la Imàgen [imagen] solo se quiebra o pierde el palo, ò el metal, ò el papel [quellca], de lo qual à los christianos no se les da nada, ni lo tienen por su Dios." *Tercero catecismo*, 259–61.

68. The Quechua passage is a bit longer and more detailed than the Spanish. The passage that employs the term "yupay" in reference to the veneration shown toward the royal seal by the Corregidor has no counterpart in the Spanish version. It is an elaboration and explanation of the act of kissing the seal.

69. Brokaw, *History of the Khipu*, 102–6.

70. I borrow these terms from Katya Mandoki, *Everyday Aesthetics: Prosaics, the Play of Culture and Social Identities* (Hampshire, U.K.: Ashgate, 2007).

71. Frank Salomon, *The Cord Keepers: Khipus and Cultural Life in a Peruvian Village* (Durham: Duke University Press, 2004), 96–98.

6

"Take My Scalp, Please!"

COLONIAL MIMESIS AND THE FRENCH
ORIGINS OF THE MISSISSIPPI TALL TALE

Gordon M. Sayre

Southwestern humor, including the tall tale, emerged into U.S. literary history in the Jacksonian period, as white anglophone backsettlers gained political influence among East Coast metropolitans. It reached canonical status, of course, with Mark Twain, whose pen name came from his career on the Mississippi, the conduit of regional commerce and the home waters for the tall tale. In researching the history and literature of eighteenth-century Louisiana, I have found evidence that the Mississippi tall tale has French origins that long precede Anglo-American literature in the region. In this essay I offer two tales that might satisfy such a search for origins. Let me explain at the outset, however, why I do not see an easy continuity between these tales and the nineteenth-century anglophone genre of southwestern humor.

As Neil Schmitz has written, "the tall tale enters American literature inside the genial anthropology of the sketch, a form designed to civilize the strange," much as the canonical short stories in Washington Irving's *Sketchbook of Geoffrey Crayon, Gent.* presented Dutch folktales from the Hudson valley.[1] Schmitz points out that many of the best-known instances of the southwestern humor genre, such as Thomas Bangs Thorpe's "The Big Bear of Arkansas" and George Washington Harris's Sut Lovingood tales, were published in New York City in *Porter's Spirit of the Times*, a Whig publication that targeted conservative male readers with not only fiction but also horse racing and baseball news. Moreover, Thorpe's famous story, which in some American literature anthologies is the sole exemplar of the southwestern humor genre, "is no folktale, but a literary invention. Jim Doggett's elaborate narrative has no counterparts among our thousands of field-collected texts."[2] What is often obscured in the popular association of Mississippi River tall tales with Twain is the strong class and regional divide that is built into the form of the genre. "The tall tale is thus conventionally framed. A native speaker appears to tell his tale within the genial gaze of a literary observer."[3] The author is literate, speaks standard English, and has connections to metropolitan publishers. The tale teller—Thorpe's Jim Doggett, Harris's Sut Lovingood, or Joseph G. Baldwin's Ovid Bolus—is a coarse southern backwoodsman who speaks in an eye dialect sometimes barely intelligible. In Jacksonian America the two figures came together. Union officers (such as Thorpe) and Confederates (such as Harris), Democrats and Whigs alike manipulated southwestern humor to prove their authenticity and win votes from the yokels, and Davy Crockett even did so for both parties.

The down-home regional authenticity of the tall tale's heroes— backsettler caricatures like Crockett and Mike Fink—was a myth. The actual population of the frontier lower Mississippi was a blend of Native Americans, French, Spaniards, French Canadians, and Africans. The process through which southwestern humor became popular literature, such as by publication in *Porter's Spirit of the Times*, was predicated on an effacement of many of these people and on an ethnographic distance and contrast between the frontier and the metropole, oral and literate, rural and urban, lowbrow and highbrow. In contrast to the eastern cities, French Louisiana did not afford this distance. My analysis of two eighteenth-century French Louisiana tall

Gordon M. Sayre

tales will conclude with some reflections on how the treatment of folklore in American literary studies might move beyond these regional and rhetorical divisions.

Eighteenth-century French Louisiana has attracted little attention in American literary studies, and it might appear to have little to offer. During the period from the founding of the capital city of New Orleans in 1718 until the loss of France's North American colonies in 1763 there was no printing press or publishing business in New Orleans, even though literacy rates were not so low, at least in the capital, as one might expect.[4] With no periodicals, no established theater, and scarce evidence of literary salons, it is no surprise that in the eyes of the Paris elite (and of modern scholars), Louisiana was a pestilential backwater. From 1717 to 1721, when Louisiana was heavily promoted as part of the financial boondoggle led by John Law, a large portion of the colonists sent there were "forçats," involuntary transportees including salt smugglers, prostitutes, vagrants, and petty criminals. The colony acquired a particularly bad reputation. Many of the military officers and soldiers assigned to maintain order among these rogues—including Dumont de Montigny, author of one version of the second tale discussed below—were younger sons who had been shipped off by parents unable or unwilling to finance schooling or purchase positions for them in France. After Law's Mississippi bubble burst in 1720, the flow of supplies to the colony quickly dried up, and food shortages were so severe that many soldiers were told to go live with local Indian tribes. Add to this mixture the initial boatloads of African slaves, some of whom fled to live with the Indians, and the result was a diverse, colorful, yet violent culture, rich in rumor and legend.

In this setting, the two stories I present here circulated among the military officers and early planters who constituted the colonial elite, yet also among their soldiers, servants, and laborers, all of whom had frequent interaction with Native Americans and Africans. The tales were neither emanations from nor parodies of a coarse backsettler class, printed for consumption in a distant metropole. Instead, these two tales of colonial soldiers' encounters with Indians circulated as

Colonial Mimesis and the Tall Tale

real wisdom with practical import. And, more significant for the themes of this collection on early American media, the tales challenge myths of an opposition between literate and oral cultures, between modern and primitive, highbrow and lowbrow, urbane and vulgar, or European colonial and Native American modes of representation or media technologies.

"Lose Your Hair, Not Your Head"

The first tale involves a French officer and explorer named Claude-Charles Dutisné. The most elaborate version of it comes from the three-volume *Histoire de la Louisiane* (1758) by Antoine-Simon Le Page du Pratz.[5] But thanks to the recent discovery of a manuscript account from New Orleans recorded almost thirty years prior to Le Page's book, we know that the story had circulated as folklore. Dutisné, or "du Tissenet," as Le Page spells it, was born around 1690 in Paris and came to Quebec in 1705 with a commission as an ensign (officer-in-training). In 1708 he married Marie-Anne Gaultier de Gaudarville, who brought Dutisné the title of seigneur de Gaudarville from her first husband, and left it to him when she died in 1711. Dutisné remarried two years later, and his second wife so "loved to indulge her curiosity" ("aimoit ce qui flattoit sa curiosité") (2:297) that she accompanied him when he was assigned to the post at Kaskaskia in the Illinois country.[6]

Dutisné must have been a charismatic leader and dashing adventurer, the kind of man around whom yarns were spun. In addition to service at Wabash and Kaskaskia, he helped to establish Fort Rosalie at Natchez, Mississippi, in 1716 and served as commandant there from 1723 to 1726, when Le Page lived on a farm nearby. He achieved positions of responsibility, but not without controversy. In 1714 he misled Louisiana governor Antoine La Mothe Cadillac with claims that silver mines were to be found in the Mississippi valley, perhaps as a ploy to get himself assigned to lead an expedition there. In 1726 the prominent New Orleans priest Abbé Raguet suggested that Dutisné was homosexual.[7]

Gordon M. Sayre

Dutisné is best known today for two voyages of exploration he made from Kaskaskia in 1719, the first up the Missouri River and the second overland, south of the Missouri, toward the headwaters of the Osage River. On each journey Missouri and Osage Indians warned him not to continue westward, and on the second occasion he nearly lost his life at the hands of the Panis or Pawnee nation, surviving only by bravely defying his captors. As he described it: "two times the toma-hawk was raised over me, but . . . through the bravery I demonstrated in defying them to break my head open, these men, brutal as they are, consented to become our allies, and treated me very kindly" ("deux fois le casse-test levé sur moy, mais . . . par la hardiesse avec laquelle je m'y suis pris en leur faisant défi de me casser la test, tout brutaux que sont ces sortes de gens, ils consentirent de faire alliance avec nous, et me traitèrent fort bien").[8] His bravery epitomizes the colonizer's savoir faire, the kind of blustering overconfidence that may have soothed the fears of French soldiers who had seen their comrades scalped by angry Chickasaws. Dutisné himself set down this story in a letter to the Governor Bienville, and we also find it in two brief nar-ratives transmitted to us by Jean-Baptiste Bénard de la Harpe, who explored the Arkansas and Red Rivers from 1719 to 1721.[9]

This letter and the two brief reports constitute the "official" archive of Dutisné's voyages, texts that were supplied to French superiors and forwarded to Paris, but they were not printed until the nineteenth-century antiquarian efforts of Pierre Margry. I am concerned instead with the folk version of Dutisné's brave defiance of Indians, which fi-nally reached print in Le Page's *Histoire de la Louisiane*.[10] Although the story Le Page records may be an exaggerated version of Dutisné's defiance of the Panis, there is no reference to his encounter with that tribe, nor to his exploration along the Missouri River. Le Page opens the tale by remarking: "The adventure that this officer underwent is so extraordinary, that I do not think I will be at fault if I pass it on. I heard it from several Canadians, and it was confirmed by the man himself" ("L'avanture qui a élevé cet Officier, est si extraordinaire, que je ne crains point d'être blâmé en la rapportant; je la tiens de plusieurs

Canadiens, & m'a été confirmée par lui-même") (2:297–98). He concludes it by emphasizing again the sensational nature of the tale:

> The talk of this adventure spread and reached even the Governor, who summoned M. Dutisné. The latter confirmed for him the truth of the tale, such as it had happened to him. The Governor decided that by virtue of this act he deserved to be an officer, and made him an ensign. He wrote to the Court and Dutisné was made a Lieutenant, then later he became Captain. He went down to Louisiana, where he has been my Commandant and my friend in Natchez.

> [le bruit de cette avanture se répandi & parvint jusques au Gouverneur qui manda M. du Tissenet; il lui confirma la vérité du fait tel qu'il lui étoit arrivé. Le Gouverneur jugeant par cette action qu'il méritoit d'être officier, le fit Enseigne; il écrivit en Cour & on le fit Lieutenant; il fut depuis Capitaine: il a passé à la Louisiane, où il a été mon Commandant & mon ami au Natchez.] (2:305)

The story itself lacks the kind of circumstantial details one would expect of a historical, verifiable account and which are provided in many of Le Page's relations of battles and negotiations elsewhere in the *Histoire de la Louisiane*. Le Page was not an eyewitness to the tale, and could not have been, as the events begin in Quebec, where Le Page never traveled, and conclude among a remote and unnamed Indian nation. The story does come with important prefatory remarks, however. Due to a childhood ailment Dutisné was nearly bald, and he wore a wig (unlike most Canadians). In Quebec he won the confidence of a fur trader who hired him to lead an expedition to obtain beaver pelts from a distant nation that had not previously traded with the French, but whose people spoke a language known to the trader, and in which he instructed Dutisné. We are never told the name of the "Marchand" who finances Dutisné's expedition, nor the "Traiteur" who goes with him, nor the region nor tribe they wish to visit. Stripped of these circumstances, the tale resembles an elaborate lead-up to a joke's punch line, the climax of the story when Dutisné at last reaches the Indian village he was seeking.

The villagers there want to obtain all of his large supply of merchandise, but, as one Native man laments to another, "we have no pelts" ("nous n'avons point de pelleteries"). He thus decides that "There is no other way to get these goods except to take their scalps, kill them, and throw them in the river, and we will have it all" ("Il n'y a pas d'autres moyens pour avoir leurs Marchandises que de leur lever la chevelure, les tuer, les jetter dans la Riviere, & nous aurons tout") (2:302). Dutisné overhears this conversation and quickly plots his response. He knows that the Indians have no idea that he has listened and understood their plot against him, and so he tells his men to take up their arms, and then says to the Indians, or "Naturels," as Le Page calls them: "'So you want my scalp? Okay, here it is, take it, if you dare.' While saying these words he threw down his wig, and his head, freshly shaven, appeared as though it had never had hair" ("'Tu veux donc ma chevelure? Tiens, la voilà, ramasses-la, si tu oses le faire': Il jetta sa perruque en prononçant ces paroles, & sa tête pelée & fraîchement râsée parut n'avoit jamais eu de cheveux") (2:302). The Indians are shocked speechless, and Dutisné repeats his challenge: "Take my scalp then, since you want it so badly" ("Prens donc ma chevelure, puisque tu en avois tant d'envie") (2:303). "We believed that you are men like us," the Indians finally reply, "but we see now that you are spirits" ("Nous avons crû que vous étiez des hommes comme nous, mais nous voyons bien que vous êtes des esprits") (2:303). Much as Columbus, Cortés, and so many other colonizers claimed, the Natives in this tale believe the colonizers to be from heaven or endowed with divine powers. They are awed into submission and release Dutisné, much as he wrote that he was freed by the Panis.

Dutisné does not use a gun or any other tool of violence or domination, nor does he claim any divine protection. He does, however, enjoy a profit. The story amounts to a tall tale of depilatory colonialism. Due to his clever deception, Dutisné and his men "were possessed of beaver robes, those known as greasy beaver, the kind of beaver that is used by the Naturals as clothing" ("étoient chargés de robes de Castors que l'on nomme Castors gras; ce Castor est celui qui a servi aux naturels pour les couvrir") (2:305), and which was even more valuable for hat felt than the fresh beaver pelts trapped along streams and ponds. By substituting another's hair for his own, he is able to pull the wool over the eyes of the Indians and make off with the pelts of the beavers that the Indians had used, wig-like, for their own garments.

The fascination Native Americans had for wigs is corroborated by an account of the Fox chief Miskouensa at the great peace conference in Montreal in 1701, which Dutisné would likely have heard about when he arrived there some five years later. Miskouensa covered his head with an old wig "heavily powdered and poorly combed . . . an ornament to make himself appear French . . . and wishing to show that he knew how to live in that manner, he saluted the Chevalier de Callières as with a hat" ("fort poudrée et très mal peignée . . . un ornement pour se mettre à la Françoise . . . & voulant faire voir qu'il savait vivre, il en salua le Chevalier de Callières comme d'un chapeau").[11] As we will see, Dutisné's feat may have been practiced in front of the same Fox tribe that Miskouensa hailed from. The mocking use of wigs both by Miskouensa and Dutisné, and the latter's assimilation of the wig to the *chevelure* (scalp), suggest that French and Native peoples each mimicked the other, and the mimicry lay not only in the manipulation of the hair as a costume but also in the recitation of the feat to others. Dutisné told his tale of successfully outwitting and escaping from the Indians in much the same manner as Indians of the Great Plains told "coup tales" of sneaking into an enemy village and killing or stealing a horse or simply touching an enemy and escaping. It is a tale of manly exploits but not of violent conquest. Dutisné plays the role of a morphing trickster, unabashedly manipulating his body and revealing his foibles in order to outwit his foes and survive for another day.

This story first attracted my attention when I was writing my dissertation in 1992. But only recently did I uncover evidence to prove that the story was neither Le Page's own invention nor necessarily a historical fact, but that it had circulated as a folktale in Louisiana. In 2005 the Historic New Orleans Collection purchased a manuscript narrative of Louisiana dated 1731. It runs to more than one hundred pages, is written in a neat hand, and is accompanied by several stunning color illustrations of ships, fish, and plants as well as copies of maps from French archives. The author, Marc-Antoine Caillot, sailed to Louisiana in 1729 as an employee of the Company of the Indies, which until 1731 held a monopoly on trade in the Louisiana colony. Part of the text is devoted to recounting the news that reached New Orleans immediately after the Natchez uprising of November 29, 1729. But Caillot devotes the bulk of his manuscript to his own adventures, observing the weather and the fish as he sails from Lorient to New Orleans, and courting women and going to parties after he arrives. His text includes what I believe is the earliest account of Mardi Gras celebrations in New Orleans, culminating in a romantic tryst with a young Frenchwoman. Caillot clearly was not writing a draft of a report he planned to send to an official in France. He was spinning his own yarns, and one tale he tells is the story of Dutisné. We know that Dutisné died in 1730 in the Illinois country, so it is unlikely that Caillot knew him personally, as Le Page did. But the fact that he nonetheless tells the story of the removable scalp, nearly thirty years before Le Page published it, suggests the popularity of the folk legend in Louisiana.

There is a man in this colony who found himself in a great deal of trouble, having been surprised by the Foxes and close to being scalped. This is how he was able to get himself out of that situation and at the same time make himself feared by those wretches: Monsieur Dutisné, captain in Plantin's company, being at the head of a detachment that he was leading to the Illinois and taken with the desire to go in to the woods, accompanied only by his manservant, had gone a distance of only three musket-shots when he was attacked by about twenty Foxes. (This is a nation as cruel as it is carnivorous, especially for the flesh of the French, which they prefer over all others, and they eat their own people.) These savages began by stripping off his clothes until he was completely naked, and divided the spoils among themselves. One got a sleeve, another the breeches, another the other sleeve, etc. After this, they set themselves to the task of scalping him. You decide whether he was in a difficult situation, finding himself so close to death.

In the meantime, he resolved himself to risk death, since he was going to die anyway, and intended to try to execute a plan that came to him. To that effect, as they were going to put their hands on his head, he said to them in their native tongue, "Envna," which means "wait," and then he made them an oration in which he made them see that there was no value in taking his scalp. To give them proof of this, he told them he would do it himself. At that moment, he threw his hat on the ground, and, since he was wearing a wig, he took it by the knots and, pretending to be making an effort doing this, threw it at their feet. As soon as these barbarians saw that, they remained completely speechless, but what surprised them the most about this was not seeing any blood running down his head, which had just been freshly shaved. They could not keep from crying out, all of them trembling, that this was a man of great valor, and, for its rarity, they took that wig, which they have preserved in their village as a prodigious thing.

[Il y an un homme dans cette colonie qui s'est trouvé tres embarassé ayant etés surpris par les renards, prest a avoir sa chevelure levée. Voila dequelle maniere il a scu s'en debarasser, et en même tems de faire redouter de ces miserables.

Le Sr. Dutisné Capitaine dans la compagnie de Blontin, etant a la teste d'un detachement qu'il conduisoit aux Islinois, l'envie luy ayant pris d'aller dans le Bois seulement accompagné de son valet, il ne fut pas à 8 portés de fusil qu'il fut attacqué par une vingtaine de renards (c'est une nation aussy cruelle que carnassiere sur tout de la chere du françois qu'ils preferent a toute autre, et ils se mangent eux mêmes). Ces sauvages commancerent par le désabille tout nud et partagerent entre eux sa depuille, l'un avoir une manche l'autre la culotte une autre une autre manches etc. apres cela ils se mirent son devoir de luy lever la chevelure; Jugez s'il se trouvoit embarassé etant si pres de la mort, cependant il prit sa resolution et mourier pour mourir il voulut essayer d'executer ce qui luy vint dans l'idée, et pour cet effet comme ils alloient mettre les mais sur sa teste, il leur dit en sauvage "euxoua" qui veut dire "attend", et ensuitte il leur fit une harangue ou il leur faisoit voir qu'il n'etoit point de valleur de luy lever la chevelure et que pour marque de ce qu'il leur disoit il faloit se la lever luy même, et en même tems il jetta son chapeau a terre, et comme il portoit la peruque il la prit par les noeuds et en feignant de faire un effort il la jetta a leurs pieds. Aussitot que ces barbares eurent vu cela ils demeurent tous interdits, mais ce que leur surprit infiniment ce fut de ne point voir de sang coulée de dessus cette teste qui venoit d'estre fraichement rasée. Ils ne purent s'empescher tous tremblans de s'ecrier que c'estoit un homme de grand valeur et pour tres grand rareté ils prirent cette peruque qu'ils ont conservez chez eux comme une chose prodigieuse.][12]

Caillot does not bother with the prefatory context that Le Page added so as to integrate the tall tale into his historical and ethnographic publication. But the climactic scene is much the same. Dutisné speaks the native language, specifically, "Renard" or Fox, people who along with the Chickasaws were the most redoubtable enemies of the French during the first half of the eighteenth century. The striking visual comedy of his throwing the wig to the ground is precisely the same, and the shaved head beneath needs no elaborate alibi.

A third version of the Dutisné legend appeared in *Nouveaux Voyages aux Indes Occidentales* (1768) by Jean-Bernard Bossu. The book's title and Bossu's background as a young officer who served in Louisiana in the 1750s appear to place his work in the same genre as Le Page's, but the similarity is misleading. As John Carpenter observes, the book is "une collection des anecdotes drôles."[13] Bossu was a tale teller of a tall order. He shamelessly copied from earlier authors about Louisiana, including Le Page and Dumont, and drew upon tales he heard orally. In fact, one cannot tell for sure what is based on eyewitness observation, what is copied, and what is folklore; and as indicated above, the coexistence of the three modes characterizes the pluralist oral culture of French colonial Louisiana. Here is his version of the adventure of the man whose name he spells as Le Page did, in the published translation by Seymour Feiler:

> Monsieur du Tissenet told me what happened to his father, one of the first officers to come to Louisiana with Monsieur de Bienville. While Monsieur du Tissenet was visiting an Indian tribe with some traders, the natives wanted to scalp them. In his travels, Tissenet had learned the language of these Indians and, therefore, understood their discussion. He pulled off his wig, threw it on the ground, and said to the Indians, "Do you want my scalp? Pick it up if you dare." The astonishment of these people is indescribable. They were even more petrified because his head had been shaved the evening before. Monsieur du Tissenet then told them that they were wrong in wanting to hurt him, that he had come to be their friend.[14]

> [M. du Tissenet m'a raconté l'histoire qui est arrivée à son pere, qui étoit un des premiers Officiers venu à la Louisiane, avec M. de Bienville. M. du Tissenet étant chez une Nation Sauvage avec des traiteurs; les naturels du pays vouloient leur lever la chevelure; M. du Tissenet avoit apris la langue en route, il entendit tout ce discours, & comme il portoit perruque, il l'arracha de dessus sa tête, & la jetta par terre, en disant en même-temps dans la langue des Sauvages: Tu veux donc ma chevelure? ramasse-là si tu oses la faire. L'étonnement de ces Peuples ne peut s'exprimer, ils de-

Gordon M. Sayre

meurerent comme pétrifiés; il s'étoit fait raser la veille. M. du Tissenet leur dit ensuite qu'ils avoient grand tort de vouloir lui faire
du mal, qu'il venoit pour faire alliance avec eux.][15]

Bossu, like Le Page, opens by explaining his folkloric source, saying
that he heard the story from the son of Dutisné, although Louis-
Marie-Charles Dutisnet, the one son who appears in contemporary
documents, died in 1736. It seems certain that Bossu read Le Page, for
he calls the Indians "naturels" and copies some lines from his book,
notably, "Tu veux donc ma chevelure? Tiens, la voilà, ramasses-là, si
tu oses le faire," and it appears that he may have also read Caillot, for
he uses some of the same words, such as "Gamelle," meaning lunch
box or canteen, and his text continues with shorter versions of two
more tall tales of colonial domination that Caillot recounted but which
I do not have space to quote in full. Dutisné uses a magnifying glass
to burn a piece of cloth, then to burn the skin of one of the curious
Fox Indians. Then he uses it to set afire some brandy that he has
poured onto a puddle of water. We don't know if Bossu met Caillot
or read his manuscript, but I believe both were setting down an oral
tale about how Frenchmen could use techniques of representation to
awe the Indians. Native Americans of the plains are renowned for
their coup tales, and those of the Northeast (more familiar to the
French colonials) for the *chanson de mort*, a warrior's litany of his courageous exploits, which he was expected to sing if he were captured
and tortured by his enemies. Both emphasized masculine boasting,
bluster, and exaggeration. The tall tale of Dutisné fulfills all these characteristics and yet also relies upon peculiarly European devices, such
as the wig and the loupe or magnifying glass.

Erasable Tattoos

A wig is a form of bodily mimetism, a prosthesis or supplement for
one of a person's most identifiable features, the hair. A tattoo is a quite
different technology of corporeal representation. The wig substitutes
for, enhances, or imitates one's hair, while the tattoo inscribes or de-

faces one's skin. The wig is sophisticated and French; the tattoo, savage and primitive. Each carried considerable status in its respective society, yet whereas the wig connoted ascribed class status, the tattoo denoted, or inscribed, an individual's achievements. French colonial ethnographers all agreed that, to use Bossu's concise words about tattoos, "The more brave deeds a warrior does, the more such marks of distinction he bears on his body" (95) ("Ces marques de distinction se multiplient à mesure qu'ils font des actions d'éclat à la guerre" [102]). This practice appeared in many tribes and was characteristic of what I have called "meritography," for as Bossu put it, "it confers a type of knighthood on only those who have done extraordinary deeds" ("c'est une sorte de chevalerie où l'on n'est admis que pour des actions éclatantes" [102]), unlike the hereditary titles conferred on those of gentle birth, who in that era commonly wore wigs.[16] Tattoos are meritographs or texts recording noteworthy deeds permanently attached to the authors.

This system of meritography fascinated Frenchmen who lived both among the American Indians and under the ancien régime. While some Anglo-American captivity narratives (like that of the Oatman girls) sensationalized the notion of tattoos as the mark of savagery upon the white body, this paranoid repulsion was not occurring in Louisiana.[17] There are many reports of French soldiers and officers getting tattoos. Governor Bienville himself wore a tattoo of "a serpent that wound all around his body" ("un serpent qui lui faisait le tour du corps"), a design reported many times in Louisiana, and which may be the source of the name of the famous chief of the Natchez, Serpent Piqué.[18] Tattoos, unlike wigs, were a language spoken (or written) by both Indians and colonists. And our second legend explores another contrast. Wigs, such as the high and heavily powdered monstrosities of the ancien régime, are temporary and change with fashions. Only a primitive would believe otherwise. Tattoos are permanent and purport to be the antithesis of fashion, which may explain their recent popularity. Only a Frenchman would believe otherwise. Bossu tells the story:

Gordon M. Sayre

If anyone should take it into his head to have himself tattooed without having distinguished himself in battle, he would be disgraced and considered a coward, unworthy of the honor due only to those who risk their lives to defend their tribe. Even the sons of chiefs are not held in special consideration unless they are as brave and virtuous as their fathers and their ancestors.

I knew an Indian who, although he had never done anything outstanding in defense of his tribe, decided to have himself tattooed with one of these marks of distinction in order to impress those who judge others by outward appearances. This show-off wanted to pass himself off as a valiant man so that he could marry one of the prettiest girls of the tribe, who was ambitious even though she was a savage. Just as the match was about to be concluded with the girl's relatives, the warriors, who were indignant upon seeing a coward display a symbol of military merit, called an assembly of war chiefs to deal with the bit of audacity. The council decided, in order to prevent such abuses which would remove the distinction between courageous men and cowards, that this false hero who unjustly decorated himself with the tattoo of a tomahawk, without ever having struck a blow in battle, would have the design torn off him, skin and all, and that the same would be done to all others like him.

Since there was no hope for a pardon in the form of a verdict decreed by this Indian senate, which jealously protected the honor of the tribe, I offered through pity to make French medicine. I assured the Indians that I could remove the skin and the tattoo without hurting the patient and that the operation would turn his blood into water. The Indians, not knowing my secret, thought that I was making fun of them. Imitating their medicine men, I gave the false hero a calabash bowl full of maple syrup, into which I had put some opium. While the man was asleep, I applied some cantharides to the tattoo on his chest and then added plantain leaves, which formed blisters or tumors. The skin and the tattoo came off and a serous fluid was secreted. This type of operation amazed the medicine men, who knew nothing of the properties of cantharides, although they are very common in North America. (95–96)

[Si quelqu'un d'entr'eux s'avisoit de se faire piquer sans s'être distingué dans les combats, il feroit dégradé, & regardé comme un lâche, indigne de l'honneur qui n'est dû qu'à ceux qui exposent généreusement leur vie pour la défense de la patrie. Ils n'ont même de considération pour les fils des Caciques, qu'autant qu'ils sont braves, vertueux à l'exemple de leur pere, & de leurs ancêtres.

J'ai vu un Sauvage qui, ne s'étant jamais signalé pour la défense de la Nation, s'avisa néanmoins de se faire piquer, ou calquer une marque de distinction, pour en imposer à ceux qui ne jugent que sur les apparences. Ce fanfaron vouloit passer pour un homme de valeur, dans l'intention d'obtenir en mariage une des plus jolies filles de sa Nation, qui, toute Sauvage qu'elle étoit, ne laissoit pas d'avoir de l'ambition. Comme il étoit sur le point de conclure avec les parents de sa prétendue, les guerriers indignés de voir un poltron faire trophée d'une marque qui n'est due qu'au mérite militaire, tinrent une assemblée de Chefs de guerre, pour réprimer une telle audace. Le Conseil arrêta qu'afin d'obvier à de pareils abus qui confondroient les gens de cœur avec les lâches, le faux brave qui s'étoit induement décoré d'un Casse-tête sur la peau, sans jamais avoir *fait coup* à la guerre, auroit l'empreinte arrachée, c'est-à-dire, la place écorchée, & qu'on en feroit autant à tous ceux qui se trouveroient dans le même cas.

Comme il n'y avoit point de grace à espérer, & que sa condamnation étoit prononcée par un arrêt de se Sénat Sauvage, jaloux de maintenir l'honneur de la Nation, je m'offris, par commisération pour ce malheureux, de faire la médecine Françoise en sa faveur; j'assurai que je lui enleverois la peau & la marque sans lui faire mal; & que par la vertue de mon remède, son sang se changeroit en eau. Les Sauvages ignorant mon secret, croyoient que je me mocquois d'eux; contrefaisant donc les *Jongleurs*, je fis avaler au faux brave une dose d'opium: & dans l'intervalle de son som-

Gordon M. Sayre

meil, j'appliquai, sur l'empreinte du Casse-tête qu'il portoit sur sa poitrine, des mouches cantarides, puis des feuilles de plantin qui lui causerent des ampoules ou tumeurs; la peau & la marque tomberent, & il n'en sortit qu'une eau séreuse. Cette façon d'operer surprit beaucoup les *Jongleurs*, qui ignoraient les propriétés des mouches cantarides, fort communes dans l'Amérique Septentrionale.] (190–91)

Readers who have tattoos may try this experiment of applying a poultice of firefly paste and plantain leaves. I think you run little danger of erasing your tattoos. Bossu may have heard this tale in Louisiana, or in Paris in the 1740s, or he may have read it in a manuscript by another Louisianan, the 1747 memoir of Jean-François-Benjamin Dumont de Montigny. Dumont was a contemporary and rival of Le Page, and in 1753 he published his own book about the colony, *Mémoires historiques sur la Louisiane*. Only in his manuscript autobiography, however, does he include the tall tale that resembles what appeared in Bossu's book twenty years later. The anecdote appears in a section devoted to describing the Natchez Indians:

> The flesh of their body is tattooed with various designs. Some have a series of dots; others, snakes or suns. The Indian men, the chief and the honored men who are like their officers, will also be tattooed. The tattoos that they make on their bodies are done in this way: They take seven or eight needles; the finest points are best. They lay them out along a small flat stick. Then they dissolve cinnabar or vermillion in water, or perhaps charcoal of willow wood that has been finely ground. There are even some who use gunpowder, but this causes an itchy rash in the flesh or on the skin. They draw upon the skin the design that they wish to inscribe. If it is red, they use vermillion; if it is black, the charcoal or gunpowder. Then they dip each needle into either of these two colors and lightly prick the skin with them, as quickly as possible. The color enters into the holes made by the needles

and incorporates itself into the flesh, marking the design. This lasts for life, although I myself, having had a Croix de Saint Louis tattooed on my left arm when I was young, found the secret to erase it. At the time, it nearly cost me my arm, but nonetheless I did succeed and removed it, although there remain a few lines, almost imperceptible. This is how I did it: with the needles, as I have described above, I re-tattooed the outline of the design upon myself using the milk of a woman who was nursing a boy. This caused a most violent fever that lasted for eight or nine days. My arm became swollen with palpitating lumps that became scaly, but at the end of nine days, this subsided, and the skin flaked off like wheat germ, leaving behind a fresh, new skin with the design nearly entirely effaced. Ordinarily, all those who have themselves tattooed get the fever. But in any case, among these nations, it is only the warriors and men of valor, and even the wives of chiefs and the honored men, who are thus tattooed.

[piqué sur leur chaire des desseins selon leur idée. Les unes auront des pointes, les autres des serpents ou des soleils. Les sauvages hommes, chef et considérez, qui sont ainsi que des officiers, seront pareillement piquées. Cette piquure qu'ils font sur leur corps se fait ainsi. On prend 7 à 8 éguilles; les plus fines sont les meilleures. On les arrange sur un petit bâton plat, bien posées horizontallement. Ensuitte on détrampe du cinabre ou vermillion dans de l'eau ou bien du charbon de saule que l'on écrase finement. Il y en a même qui se serve de poudre à canon, mais celle-cy donne ou cause sur la chaire ou dans la peau une démangaison. On desine sur le corps le dessin qu'on veut imprimer. Si c'est en rouge, c'est le vermillon; si c'est en noir, c'est le charbon ou la poudre. Alors on trempe ces éguilles ainsi rangées dans une de ces deux couleurs, et on pique légèrement et le plus vitement que faire ce peut la peau avec ces éguilles. La couleur entre dans les troux des piquures et s'imcorporent dans la chaire et marquent le

Gordon M. Sayre

dessin. C'est pour toutte la vie, quoique moi-même qui avoit fait sur mon bras gauche, étant jeune, piqué une croix de Saint Louis, j'ay trouvé le secret de l'éffacer. Il m'en a coûté dans ce tems-là l'heure et le moment de perdre le bras, mais enfin j'ay réussy et l'ai ôté, quoiqu'il en reste quelque petits rayons, mais presque imperceptibles. Voicy comme je l'ai fait. Avec des éguilles rengées, comme je l'ai dit cy-dessus, j'ay repiqué moi-même les traits du dessin avec du laict d'une femme nourissant un garçon. Cela m'a causé pendant huit à neuf jours une fièvre des plus violente. Mon bras en est venu montreux avec des batements d'altère furieux. Cet endroit est devenu comme galeux, mais à la fin des neuf jours cela s'est dissipé et a tombé comme en farine, et il est revenu une peau fraîche qui a éffacé presque tout le dessein. Ordinairement tous ceux qui se font piquer, ils ont la fièvre. Mais enfin, il n'y a parmi ces nations que les hommes de valeurs et gueriers, et même les femmes des chefs ou considérés qui sont ainsi piqués.][19]

As Arnaud Balvay has observed, the two officers may have considered their tattoos a good means of assimilating into or at least gaining credibility among the Indians, but when returning to France they wished to reverse the process. Erasing the tattoos marked "the end of their lives at the margin of civilization."[20] The clue that Bossu was retelling this story after hearing it or after reading Dumont's manuscript comes just after the text quoted above:

In 1749, an officer of the Ile de France regiment fell in love with a girl in Paris. The young lady's mother said that she would approve the marriage only if the officer were decorated with the Croix de Saint Louis. He was spurred on by love and a desire to be married as quickly as possible to award himself this honor, which only the King can grant.

[Un officier du Régiment de l'Isle de France, étant devenu amoureux d'une Demoiselle à Paris en 1749, la mere de cette fille, dit

qu'elle la lui accorderoit voluntier s'il étoit décoré de la Croix de
Saint-Louis. L'amour le porta aussi-tôt pour accelérer son marriage, à prendre de lui-même cette distinction, que le Roi seul
peut donner.] (96)

Another officer sees the imitation medal and notifies "Monsieur
d'Argenson," who investigates and then arrests the "false chevalier"
who is "brought before the Tribunal of the Marshals of France. Marshall de Belle-Isle presided at the court martial . . . the accused was
found guilty and sentenced to have the cross taken from him, to be
degraded, and to be imprisoned in a fortress for twenty years" ("va
aussitôt trouver M. D'Argenson . . . traduit au Tribunal de Maréchaux
de France, On tint, à ce sujet aux Invalides, un conseil de guerre où
présida le Maréchal de Belle-Isle. Le faux Chevalier fut jugé à avoir
la Croix arrachée, & condamné à être refermé pendant 20 ans dans un
Citadelle").[21] Dumont's two protectors, the dedicatees of his manuscript works, were Marc Pierre de Voyer de Paulmy, Comte d'Argenson,
and Charles-Louis-Auguste Fouquet de Belle-Isle. Dumont was never awarded the Croix de Saint Louis, a military honor that many of
his comrades in Louisiana eagerly sought, and it does not seem likely he sought to marry an aristocratic girl in 1749, as he was then fifty-
two years old and already married. Bossu uses this tall tale to mock
the elder Louisiana soldier-author for his efforts to rise in status
through flattering his powerful patrons.

The two tales together suggest that as French Louisianans came to
understand Native American societies, they saw how contingent and
ephemeral were the marks of status in their own French society. A
wig, a medal, a fine suit of clothes—these things would not endure
or would not be recognized in America. Rather than mocking or stig-
matizing the people of the Mississippi frontier, these two tales expose
the failings and faux pas of French and Indian, officer and soldier
alike. To deliver this message to metropolitan French readers, however, was not the original motive for telling the tales; it was other
Louisiana colonists who wanted and needed them, and the manu-

Gordon M. Sayre

script sources prove that they circulated orally in the colony before ever being printed in France. The anglophone Mississippi tall tales, on the other hand, were disseminated in urban markets and for distinctly metropolitan reasons.

From a semiological perspective, wigs and tattoos are media of signification, on the same spectrum as quipus, hieroglyphs, handwriting, and printing, and it is worth considering this spectrum as an alternative to the divisions between orality and literacy, performance and textuality. To draw a larger theoretical significance from these two French Louisiana folktales it helps to differentiate them from two concepts that have become commonly used in postcolonial cultural theory: "mimicry," associated with Homi Bhabha, and "mimesis," as used by Michael Taussig. Bhabha wrote in "Of Mimicry and Man: The Ambivalence of Colonial Discourse" that "colonial mimicry is the desire for a reformed, recognizable Other, as a subject of a difference that is almost the same, but not quite."[22] The "colonial discourse" is one of comprehensive domination and bureaucratic control, as in British India in the nineteenth century, and the desire operates upon both the colonized and the colonizers; the latter want to imitate the language, religion, and ceremonies of the colonizers, and the colonizers want them to do so, so long as the imitation is not so perfect as to successfully counterfeit the original, and thereby threaten the Europeans' privileges of race and power. Bhabha's concept of mimicry does not really anticipate instances of the colonizers imitating the colonized. Moreover, mimicry is a human performance; it does not rely on any single technique or technology of reproduction. Taussig, by contrast, writes in *Mimesis and Alterity* of the modernist "age of mechanical reproduction" (a phrase he fondly adopts from Walter Benjamin). "Mimesis" for Taussig refers not so much to performances as to mimetic technologies, machines such as the photograph and phonograph, which become emblems of the vast gap between primitive and modern:

What seems crucial about the fascination with the Other's fascination with the talking machine is the magic of mechanical reproduction. In the West this magic is inarticulable and is understood as the technological substance of civilized identity-formation. Neither the prospector filming in the early 1930s in the New Guinea highlands nor Fitzcarraldo in the jungles of the Upper Amazon in the early twentieth century could make a phonograph, or an electric lightbulb switch for that matter. . . . Taking the talking machine to the jungle is to do more than impress the natives and therefore oneself with Western technology's power . . . it is to reinstall the mimetic faculty as mystery in the art of mechanical reproduction, reinvigorating the primitivism implicit in technology's wildest dreams.[23]

Many scenes in seventeenth- and eighteenth-century colonial encounters with American Indians deploy the same trope using earlier machines, such as the compass and the clock, which were not *mimetic* or reproductive technologies, but were Europe's technological pride at that time, and which the missionaries and colonizers were equally incapable of constructing. Scholars of early America have pointed out many other scenes in this literature where the trope of "shock and awe" is described as Indians are introduced to writing. This of course is a large topic unto itself, and these stories may incorporate a healthy dose of folklore—they may be tall tales. What I wish to emphasize here is that treating alphabetic writing as a mimetic technology monopolized by the European colonizers is also a myth, an anachronistic reinscription of the modernist reproductive technologies onto the early modern period.[24] These eighteenth-century Louisiana tales nuance Taussig's claim, because the wig or "chevelure" and the tattoo do not appear to us to be "modern" technologies and so we can more easily see the mimetic faculty at work.

The colonialist myth Taussig so brilliantly deconstructs holds that the primitives are awed by mimesis because they have no technologies of mimetic inscription, such as the printing press, phonograph, or camera. But they did have other forms of mimetic inscription,

Gordon M. Sayre

such as hieroglyphs and tattoos, and at the same time some colonists lacked certain techniques of mimetic inscription, as for example there was no printing press in French Louisiana. The colonialist myth implies that the Indians have no fact, only rumor; no history, only myth; no permanence, only evanescence. But the French Louisianans knew better. Tattoos are permanent, and the Indians used them to endow social status with a consistent and verifiable basis. The miraculous technology in our second legend was to use local ingredients to remove tattoos, to restore the state of rumor, myth, and impermanence. In the first tale it was a means of mimicking the human hair. If scalping is a permanent scar, and a scalp a counterfeit-proof mark of military valor, then Dutisné discovered the way to undo it, much as Bossu and Dumont removed the permanent inscription of the tattoo.

As an alternative to mimicry and mimesis, I would propose the concept of "mimétisme" as it has been applied to French colonial materials by historian Gilles Havard. Havard treats encounters of cross-cultural imitation as performances, but he does not pigeonhole them as either mocking or flattering the power of the other: "Indians rationalized European 'difference' by appropriating it symbolically, as if otherness were simply not conceivable."[25] Frenchmen could likewise appropriate Indian piquage, at least until the point they wanted to erase it. I propose to extend the concept of mimetism to include the process of imitating, that is, of repeating and circulating, oral tales such as these two that circulated in eighteenth-century Louisiana. Dutisné and the faux brave Dumont functioned as tricksters of French Louisiana, (anti-)heroes of humorous tall tales whose foibles delivered subtle messages about proper behavior among the Indians. Revealing the folkloric roots of these tales can, I hope, move us beyond a monolithic concern for the veracity or authenticity of such accounts of colonial contact, toward a discursive understanding of how folktales both shaped the moral universe of the colonists and constituted the communications media of a world not so isolated, not so "other," as we might have assumed.

Notes

With the exception of Feiler's translation of Bossu, all the translations are my own.

1. Neil Schmitz, "Tall Tale, Tall Talk: Pursuing the Lie in Jacksonian Literature," *American Literature* 48.4 (1977): 471–91, quote on 472.
2. Richard Dorson, "The Identification of Folklore in American Literature," *Journal of American Folklore* 70 (1957): 1–24, quote on 7–8. A database search of scholarly articles will demonstrate that research on the southwestern tall tale peaked in the mid-twentieth century.
3. Schmitz, "Tall Tale," 483.
4. Emily Clark provides literacy figures in New Orleans in 1731–32 of 36 percent for women and 53 percent for men, based on a small sample of marriage registers. Clark, *Masterless Mistresses: The New Orleans Ursulines and the Development of a New World Society, 1727–1834* (Chapel Hill: University of North Carolina Press, 2007), 115.
5. Antoine-Simon Le Page du Pratz, *Histoire de la Louisiane, contenant la Découverte du ce vaste pays, sa Description géographique, un Voyage dans les Terres, l'Histoire Naturelle; les Mœurs, Coutûmes & Religion des Naturels, avec leurs Origines; deux Voyages dans le Nord du nouveau Mexique, dont un jusqu'à la Mer du Sud; ornée de deux Cartes & de 40 Planches en Taille douce*, 3 vols. (Paris: De Bure, Veuve Delaguette, et Lambert, 1758). Hereafter cited parenthetically in the text.
6. See C. J. Russ, "Ditisné, Claude-Charles," in *Biographical Dictionary of Canada*, http://www.biographi.ca, accessed August 17, 2006.
7. See Dumont and Raguet in Dunbar Rowland, A. G. Sanders, and Patricia K. Galloway, eds., *Mississippi Provincial Archives: French Dominion*, 4 vols. (Jackson: Mississippi Department of Archives and History, 1927–84), 2:525–30.
8. Pierre Margry, ed., *Découvertes et établissements des Français dans l'ouest et dans le sud de l'Amérique Septentrionale, 1614–1698*, 6 vols. (Paris: Jouast 1879–88), 6:309–15, quote on 314.
9. These three texts were first published by Pierre Margry and have been translated in various places. For a thorough study of du Tisné and his sensational encounter with the Indians, see Mildred Mott Wedel, "Claude-Charles Dutisné: A Review of His 1719 Journeys," *Great Plains Journal* 12.1 (Fall 1972): 4–25, and 12.2 (Winter 1973): 146–73. The text attributed to Bénard de la Harpe, *Journal historique de l'établissement des Français à la Louisiane* (La Nouvelle-orléans: A.-L. Boimare; Paris: Hec-

tor Bossange, 1831), has been attributed by other scholars to Jean Beau-
rain, but Wedel believes it is the work of Bénard de la Harpe.

10. Because the *Histoire de la Louisiane* has never been translated in its entirety, I have prepared English translations of portions of it and published them at http://darkwing.uoregon.edu/~gsayre/LPDP.html. The
first of the five selections (vol. 1, chapters 16–19) constitutes an even better instance of a tall tale than the du Tissenet story, but Le Page himself
is the author of it, and I have not found evidence of oral circulation for it.

11. Claude-Charles Le Roy Bacqueville de la Potherie, *Histoire de l'Amerique
septentrionale, contenant le voyage de Fort de Nelson, dans la Baie d'Hudson
à l'extrémité de l'Amérique, le premier établissement des Français dans ce vaste
pays, le prise dudit Fort de Nelson, la description du fleuve de Saint Laurent,
le gouvernement de Québec, des Trois-Rivières & de Montréal, depuis 1534
jusqu'à 1701*, 4 vols. (Paris: J. L. Nion et F. Bidot, 1722), 4:247, quoted in
Gilles Havard, "Le rire des Jésuites: Une archéologie du mimétisme dans
la rencontre franco-amérindienne (XVIIième–XVIIIième siècle)," *An-
nales* 62/63 (2007): 564.

12. Marc-Antoine Caillot, "Relation du voyage de la Louisiane ou Nouv.lle
France fait par le Sr. Caillot en l'année 173," New Orleans, The Historic
New Orleans Collection, Catalog No. 2005.11. Translated as *A Company
Man: The Remarkable French-Atlantic Voyage of a Clerk for the Company of
the Indies*, trans. Teri F. Chalmers, ed. Erin M. Greenwald (New Orleans:
Historic New Orleans Collection, 2013), 108-109.

13. John R. Carpenter, *Histoire de la littérature française sur la Louisiane de
1673 à 1766* (Paris: Nizet, 1966), 315.

14. Jean-Bernard Bossu, *Travels in the Interior of North America*, 2nd ed.,
1769, trans. Seymour Feiler (Norman: University of Oklahoma Press,
1962), 115. Hereafter cited parenthetically in the text.

15. Jean-Bernard Bossu, *Nouveaux voyages en Louisiane (1751–1768)*, ed.
Philippe Jacquin (Paris: Aubier Montaigne, 1980), 117. With the exception of note 21 below, all further quotations from Bossu in French are
from this source. Hereafter cited parenthetically in the text.

16. On "meritography" see Gordon M. Sayre, *Les Sauvages Américains: Representations of Native Americans in French and English Colonial Literature*
(Chapel Hill: University of North Carolina Press, 1997), 175–89.

17. Olive and Mary Ann Oatman were captured by Yavapai Indians in Arizona in 1851. See Royal B. Stratton, *Captivity of the Oatman Girls: Being
an Interesting Narrative of Life among the Apache and Mohave Indians* (San

Francisco: Whitton, Towne, 1857); and a photograph of Olive tattooed in Kathryn Zabelle Derounian-Stodola and James A. Levernier, *The Indian Captivity Narrative, 1550–1900* (New York: Twayne, 1993), 123.

18. Arnaud Balvay, *L'epée et la plume: Amérindiens et soldats des troupes de la marine en Louisiane et au Pays d'en Haut (1683–1763)* (Québec City: Presses de l'Université Laval, 2006), 183–84.

19. Jean-François-Benjamin Dumont de Montigny, *The Memoir of Lieutenant Dumont, 1715–1747: A Sojourner in the French Atlantic*, trans. Gordon M. Sayre, ed. Gordon M. Sayre and Carla Zecher (Chapel Hill: University of North Carolina Press, 2012), 348. French original from Dumont de Montigny, *Regards sur le monde atlantique*, ed. Carla Zecher, Gordon Sayre, and Shannon Dawdy (Sillery, Québec: Septentrion, 2008), 367–68.

20. Balvay, "Tattooing and Its Role in French-Native American Relations," *French Colonial History* 9 (2008): 1–11, quote on 11.

21. The Jacquin edition of Bossu's 1768 book is badly abridged, with no indication of the passages excised. The original, however, is extremely rare. This quotation is the only one I reference from the first edition, Bossu, *Nouveaux Voyages aux Indes Occidentales; Contenant une Relation des différens Peuples qui habitent les environs du grand Fleuve Saint-Louis, appellé vulgairement le Mississipi; leur Religion; leur gouvernement; leurs mœurs; leurs guerres & leur commerce* (Paris, 1768), 1:192; translation from Feiler's edition, *Travels in the Interior of North America*, 97.

22. Homi Bhabha, "Of Mimicry and Man: The Ambivalence of Colonial Discourse," in *The Location of Culture* (New York: Routledge, 1994), 85.

23. Michael Taussig, *Mimesis and Alterity: A Particular History of the Senses* (New York: Routledge, 1993), 207–8.

24. Among many instances of this myth, the most familiar may be two scenes in the film *Black Robe*. In the first, the Huron Indians who have come to Quebec sit patiently watching a clock until it strikes the hour. They call it "Mr. Clock." In the second, Father Laforgue and his lay servant Daniel demonstrate the use of writing to the Huron guides. For a critical analysis of these myths of the impact of writing on Native Americans see Peter Wogan, "Perceptions of European Literacy in Early Contact Situations," *Ethnohistory* 41.3 (1994): 407–29.

25. See Gilles Havard, "'So amusingly Frenchified': Mimetism in the French-Amerindian Encounter (XVIIth–XVIIIth c.)," *Le Journal* 24.1 (Naperville IL: Center for French Colonial Studies, 2008): 6. The strength of the concept of "mimétisme," I believe, lies in its pluralism:

Gordon M. Sayre

"mimetism . . . needs to be interpreted in a double context: the context of the interaction, of course; but also the context of the culture in which it was produced" (3). Havard avoids the unidirectional understanding of colonial power implied in Bhabha's "hybridity." I am not so convinced, however, by Havard's notion that the purpose of mimetism "arise[s] from a principle and a rationality consisting, for the natives, of denying the new and reducing otherness" (5).

PART III
SENSORY NEW WORLDS

7

Brave New Worlds

THE FIRST CENTURY OF INDIAN-ENGLISH ENCOUNTERS

Peter Charles Hoffer

How do we deal with novelty, the unexpected, the unforeseen? When our senses alert us that we face a new situation, how do we respond? Insofar as senses are tutored by our culture, our reaction to the unfamiliar is scripted. The intonations are our own; the words are those that every other actor in the same role recites. Such pre-set cognitive patterns are psychologically necessary. In every culture and for every individual, cognitive frameworks do not operate willy-nilly on novelty. Our minds work hard to fit the new into the old.[1]

To avoid cognitive dissonance, the mental friction produced by discordant perceptions, we play tricks on sensuous novelties. We can, for instance, deny novelty by categorizing the new as something we already knew about. Or we might denigrate the new as inferior and so reduce its power to force reordering of old perceptions. We can perceive the novel in a particular or partial way, altering our interpretation of what we sensed to make it less disturbing. Or we may handle dissonance in reverse fashion, by making the new an immediate and catastrophic threat, demonizing what we cannot immediately place in a reassuring perceptual category.[2]

In general, modernity welcomes novelty and embraces change. But our early modern predecessors did not share our optimistic view of change or our sangfroid in its presence. Originality was frightening, and the unknown could be deadly. The European explorers of the New World and the Indians who inhabited that world gave the highest priority to a swift and reliable reading of novelty. In this essay we will ask what novelty meant to English and Indian men who met one another for the first time on the coast of North America. How did they handle the singularity of their encounters? How did sights and sounds dictate their conduct toward one another?

Some of the English who came to the Americas at the end of the sixteenth century and the beginning of the seventeenth century had already traveled abroad, and more of them had read accounts of other European travelers' experiences. But much of this literature was from the Spanish, French, or Portuguese, England's rivals for empire, and was treated with suspicion and derision in England.[3] European scholars and naturalists tried to make sense of the new plants, animals, and peoples brought back from the Americas.[4] But European demands and expectations—including the need to prove European superiority over Native cultures—structured these perceptions.[5] The Europeans approached the problem of explaining the new in terms of the basic ethnocentric assumptions of European culture. The new was to be fit into already-prepared niches.[6]

The Native Americans who greeted the English had either already met Europeans or had heard about them. Systems of trade up and down the coast were also news networks. Stories about Verrazzano in 1524 and the Spanish slave incursions in the same decade, followed by word from the interior of the invasion of hundreds of haughty men riding tame animals as fast as deer (de Soto's expedition), all merged into a composite picture. The men with shiny, hard vests and crested headdresses walked or rode in packs like wolves, spoke in harsh gutturals, and were easily offended. They demanded tribute and called

Peter Charles Hoffer

themselves sons of the one true god.[7] The coastal Indians conceded that the newcomers had spiritual power—they were "manitou."[8] But the newcomers looked and sounded unlike any newcomers the coastal peoples had known.[9] Indians turned to sensory managerial skills different from those the Europeans employed to fit the new into the familiar. Thus a contest of the senses began.

When they met, what would the two groups do? Over and over, simple divergences in perception would lead to larger errors in social intercourse. But not always, and not at first. For novelty has a charm as well as a cutting edge.[10] The English and the Indians were capable of genuine wonder and even delight in the recognition of differences. But the English soon came to regard the Indians as dangerous and acted in aggressive anticipation of the Indians' savage nature.[11] For their part, the Indians' amiable curiosity quickly turned to injured bewilderment at the demeanor of some of the English. Some Indians tried to remain accommodating; others took flight, and many chose to resist with arms.[12]

Indian Perception: Making the World Whole

For the Native American, making sense of what was seen and heard was a skill taught to children as soon as they could walk and mastered in hard schools of hunting and raiding. Studies of modern oral cultures including the Mbuti of the African rain forests, the Inuit of Alaska, the Saami of Finland, and the Maori of New Zealand suggest how peoples living in close accord with nature integrate the various aspects of the senses. They process the sensory in its totality, with the result that the data "possess" the observer. Hunters can mimic the natural sounds and see the almost invisible trails of their prey. The wind and the odors it brought became part of this dynamic whole. The senses capture relationships, not objects. Space and form are not abstract calculations of fixed measure, but part of living mental maps. Re-creations of such holistic experiences in song and dance were not artistic performances but rather literal extensions of the sense data itself.[13]

Indians' perception was communal—individual Indians heard, saw, smelled, touched, and tasted, but meanings emerged from collective deliberation. For example, Indian shamans healed the sick utilizing shared sensory experience. "The parties that are sick or lame being brought before them," William Wood reported of New England Indians, "the powwow [shaman] sitting down, the rest of the Indians giving attentive audience to his imprecations and invocations, and after the violent expression . . . of hideous bellowing and groaning, he makes a stop, and then all the auditors with one voice utter a short canto."[14] On and on they went, the shaman bellowing and writhing, the Indians replying in chorus. Healing was a communally visible and auditory process—group primal therapy, for want of a better description. Indians made no sharp distinction between sensations of the everyday and perceptions that came from the spirit world. When the Delawares first observed a European ship, "their conjurers were set to work" and "all idols and images were examined and put in order." The Indian was a sensory animist. The animals he hunted, the seeds she planted, the fish in the sea and the birds in the sky—all were alive in multiform ways.[15]

Indians believed that weather and animal behavior provided warning of future events. Powwows or spirit chasers could gain knowledge of the future from visions and dreams. The eastern Algonquians, for example, believed that every Indian had two souls—a clear soul, resident in the heart, which guided Indians while awake, and the "dream soul," which traveled abroad while the body was asleep. Leaving the body behind, the dream soul could know future and past, paradise and evil.[16] Joseph-François Lafitau, a Jesuit missionary among the Mohawks of Kahnewaka, said of his charges: "The soul of the Indians is much more independent of their bodies than ours is" and "take[s] long journeys" during sleep. In dreams, the soul reports on its travels.[17]

The Powhatan people of the Chesapeake were warned by one such powwow's dream, before the English arrived, that "a Nation should arise [in the Powhatan land] which would dissolve and give end to his empire."[18] When the Pilgrims defaced a Massachusett Indian grave

Peter Charles Hoffer

site, the Indian sachem whose mother was interred there had a dream: "Before mine eyes were fast closed, methought I saw a vision, at which my spirit was much troubled. . . . A spirit cried aloud 'Behold my son, whom I have cherished, see the paps that gave thee suck, the hands that lapped thee warm, and fed thee oft. Canst thou forget to take revenge of those wild people, that hath my monument defaced in despiteful manner?'" The dream seemed so real that the sachem called his warriors to his side, told them what had happened, and led them to seek vengeance.[19] Another Plymouth-area Indian found an explanation in a dream for the sudden sicknesses that had beset Indians years before. As he told minister Thomas Shepard in 1647, "Two years before the English came over into those parts there was a great dying." At the time, he had a dream "in which he did think he saw a great many men come to those parts in clothes, just as the English are now apparelled, and among them arose a man all in black, with a thing in his hand which he now sees was a book . . . this black man stood upon a higher place than all the rest . . . and told the Indians that God was angry with them." Only by renouncing their sinful ways would the Indians find safety.[20]

The Indians managed sensory novelties by fitting them into holistic frameworks of natural behavior. No thing stood alone, just as no sensation existed by itself. Perception demanded integration. Whatever could not fit into the whole must be outside of nature, hence dangerous. Just as the nonconformity of an individual Indian imperiled his kin, so the ill-fitting cognition endangered the people.

English Perception: Calculation and Categorization

The English did not regard themselves as part of nature, nor did they regard nature as simultaneously material and spiritual. Eyewitness testimony from English voyagers to America conclusively demonstrates that the English travelers and settlers were overwhelmed by the novelty of what they sensed.[21] William Bradford, elected governor of the Plymouth colony in 1621, feared the novelty: "What could they see here but a hideous and desolate wilderness, full of wild beasts and wild men—and multitudes there might be of them they knew not. . . . All things stand upon them with a weather-beaten face, and the whole country, full of woods and thickets, represented a wild and savage hue."[22] Others, equally awed, found delight where Bradford espied danger. Sir Walter Raleigh, journeying up the Orinoco River in search of gold, reveled in the strange scenes and sounds. "Some of the most beautiful country that ever mine eyes beheld . . . the grass short and green and in diverse parts groves of trees by themselves as if they have been by all the art and labor in the world."[23] Arthur Barlow, piloting one of the two barks that Sir Walter sent in 1584 to explore the coast of what is now North Carolina, recalled the odors as the boats neared land: "and was so strong a smell, as if we had bene in the midst of some delicate garden, abounding with all kind of odoriferous flowers."[24]

Feared or embraced, the novel had to be manipulated. It had to be fit into familiar English perceptions through easy-to-envision comparisons that narrowed the gap between the new and the old and reduced the cognitive anxiety of discovery. The dunes of the Carolina barrier islands were like the hillocks of the Downs in southeastern England. George Percy, bathing himself in a natural spa on Guadalupe, recorded that he "found it to be of the nature of baths in England, some places hot and some colder."[25] The comparisons extended to the Indians' technology. Although the English generally disparaged Indian tools, they made an exception for the bows and arrows. No doubt with England's traditional reliance on its longbow men in mind, English visitors to the New World admired the craftsmanship of the Indians' bows and their skill as archers. Another comparison was in order: the bows were in form "like ours."[26]

But the delights that the English imagined in the novelties of the New World were tempered by later experience. Some wonders were not welcome precisely because they seemed to indicate the difficulty of extracting wealth or establishing English control of a region. English perception needed boundaries, markers, and definite ends. What had no extent could not be calculated, and that without markers could not be categorized. Distance and impenetrability frightened the English because it prevented aural and visual communication. Too far off, too dense, meant out of earshot. The Elizabethan Englishman lived in a world full of sounds—rural "soundscapes" of birdsong, insect noise, and the bleating and lowing of domestic animals, to which the yelping of dogs added staccato notes. Town soundscapes of traffic were punctuated by the cries of peddlers, the clank of wagons, and the gurgle of running water. Cannon reports and ringing bells struck the ear and compelled attention wherever they occurred. Ships at sea were just as loud, the rigging and sails moaning and snapping, the cargo in the hold banging about no matter how well trussed, sailors grumbling, snoring, coughing, sneezing, and sometimes shouting at the wind. When storms roared, they drowned out all normal sound. In the city one heard a constant blur of voices mingled; in the countryside farmers working side by side in common fields chatted constantly; at the dockside and in the roads, dory men bawled at the top of their lungs. Elizabethan and Jacobean England were talky places. The English had nothing against noise.[27]

When the English found themselves unable to hear or see one another, they panicked. Novelty became unbearable. The screeching and howling sounds of the American forest and the Atlantic approaches terrified the travelers. Much of the forestland of England was gone by the late 1500s. The remaining forests were home to witches and sprites.[28] Lost in the woods, fearful of a dark bend in the river or a patch of fog-daubed forest, the English quivered with anxiety. Imagination filled in the pictures that strange sounds outlined. So when two of the Plymouth Pilgrims got lost chasing a deer in 1620, "another thing did mightily terrify them; they heard, as they thought, two lions roaring exceedingly for a long time together, and a third, that they thought was very near them."[29] The sounds of the "huracan" (Carib for hurricane) were equally frightful for their novelty to the voyagers to Virginia in 1609. William Strachey, shipwrecked after one such storm's "swelling and roaring as it were by fits," admitted that "the ears lay so sensible to the terrible cries and murmurs of the winds" that even the "best prepared" of the ship's company were shaken.[30]

Out of sight of one another, nervous Englishmen in America relied on trumpets and gunfire to signal position and status.[31] Even music was pressed into service in emergencies. When John White returned to Roanoke after a three-year absence and set about finding the 130 men, women, and children he had left as colonists, he and his comrades "sounded with a trumpet a call," no doubt a military trumpet tattoo, and then "many familiar English tunes of Songs," but the colonists could not be found.[32] When the infamous "Sea Dog" Sir Francis Drake attacked Spanish St. Augustine in 1586, a musical tune saved a man's life. As Drake's men rowed up the river toward the town, "forthwith came a French man being a fifer (who had been a prisoner [with the Spanish]) in a little boat, playing on his fife the tune of the Prince of Orange his song." Hearing this, Drake's men spared him.[33]

The demands of English perception required that auditory and visual signals not blend into the landscape, as Indians' signs did, but stand out from it in sharp relief. Thus the trumpet blast identified the English to one another rather than the imitation of birdsong or animal call the Indians adopted. The same was true of visible signals like fire. The Indians routinely used fire to clear their fields. In their store of images, fire was natural. The English regarded fire as an unnatural event that required immediate attention. The Elizabethan English used bonfires to celebrate special events. Such fires were "dangerous and exciting."[34] White reported that the English used lanterns—controlled fire—to keep fleets of privateers together as they chased down stragglers from the Spanish treasure fleets.[35] The English colonizers also used fire as a signal of peril. When the Pilgrims foraging on Cape Cod feared that they were about to be attacked, they set fires to indicate their position to their shipmates.[36] "One special great fire" on the barrier island of "Haterask" summoned Drake to the rescue of Ralph Lane's men in 1586.[37]

Trumpet blasts, songs, lanterns, and signal fires were temporary expedients to manage the sensation of unknown distance and direction. The English managed sensory novelty by calculating advantage and categorizing differences. They accepted the notion of discrete mate-

Peter Charles Hoffer

rial existence and clearly demarcated the human from the natural. They could tolerate individual divergences in men but not competing material aims. What could not be fit into their promotional scheme had to be subjugated or removed from their perceptual field.

Sensory Imperialism: Roanoke and Jamestown

Thus far we have traced a mutuality of sensory enterprise among the English and the Indians. They both confronted novelty, and although their methods of processing sensations differed, they both tried to see and make sense of the novelty of the other's presence. But within a short time the story changed from one of genuine curiosity, mixed to be sure with some anxiety, to one of asymmetry. Both sides could have striven for generally evenhanded relations based on trade, intermarriage, and selective cultural assimilation. As one modern Indian visionary put it, "there was unlimited potential for harmony. The newcomers could have adapted to the hosts' customs and values or at least understood and respected them."[38] Sometimes this happens in history, though the story of empires is one of dominance rather than mutuality. The former is what happened on the North American coast. Why it happened comprises the three-hundred-year-long story of colonization, a story of competing cultures, mass migrations, epidemics and wars, and the ultimate supremacy of European over Native. At its outset, however, it was a story about sensory imperialism.

All the stories of the imposition of sensory imperialism lead back to Roanoke. The model the English had in mind was Ireland. Richard Hakluyt, a promoter, scholar, and sometime spy for Queen Elizabeth, clearly had Ireland in mind, as had Raleigh himself.[39] Raleigh served in the English army sent to suppress the rebellion in 1579, and he saw firsthand the effectiveness of the English program to turn the Irish into tenants or landless laborers. First, the English established armed camps. Then the Natives were given the choice of accepting English ownership of the land or fleeing. Either way, the English triumphed. Raleigh intended to put the lessons of the reduction of Ireland to use in his American colony. Hakluyt was one of Raleigh's publicists.[40]

Even Thomas Harriot conceded that "some of our company towards the end of the year, showed themselves too fierce, in slaying some of the people, in some towns, upon causes that on our part, might easily enough have been born withall."[41] Ralph Lane, leader of the settlement, grew worried about the Roanokes' hostility and wrote to Raleigh that their leader, Wingina, was plotting against the English. But Lane could not see into the forest on the mainland, where Wingina rallied his kinsmen. Lane literally could not see at all, for the warm days of early spring, followed by the cold of the evening, brought mist. Lane had arrived in the summer, and the all-blanketing fog turned his fear into paranoia. Desperate, he sought a safer place for the colony—perhaps somewhere on the mainland. He gathered a company and rowed across the sound to the mouth of the Roanoke River. The Indians, hoping to be rid of him, revealed the secret of their copper ornaments. They came from high in the mountains, at the beginning of the river. Into its dark corridor he rowed.

The Roanoke is the second-oldest river in the world, according to the curators at the North Carolina aquarium, carrying its brown and red sediments from the Blue Mountains all the way down to the Albemarle Sound. It floods every spring, resembling then a rain-forest waterway on whose banks the hardwoods overhang the water. From their protection, Indians set upon Lane by firing down into his boats. When he and his men landed on the shore to battle the attackers, they "betook themselves to flight." Lane reported, "We landed, and having fair and easily followed for a small time after them, who had wooded themselves we know not where." Fleeing from the mist, Lane and his men were overwhelmed in the forest, beset with sounds they could not decipher and sights they could not arrange or order.[42]

How then to impose the English will on the North Carolina countryside? How to make the Indians see the superiority of the English? The answer was sensory imperialism. Change the way the land looked, alter the terrain, levy an English scenery upon the wild settings of the New World. Begin with fortification: As George Waymouth, who would lead a foray into Indian lands in Maine in 1605, wrote in his

Peter Charles Hoffer

manual for colonization, "for that country being as weakly planted with the English, and they more weakly defended from the invasions of the heathen, among whom they dwell . . . subject unto manifold perils, and dangers whereas it being so fruitful a soil, so goodly rivers and things necessary for fortification." Forts were an absolute necessity.[43] Even when the local Indians had welcomed the English, as they did the first settlers to Lord Baltimore's colony of Maryland, a fort was prudent. So in the fall of 1634 the colonists laid aside their garden tools and English seeds "to finish their fort, which they did within the space of one month; where they mounted some ordinance . . . and such other means of defense as they thought fit for their safeties, which being done, they proceeded with their houses and finished them."[44]

Lane would have preferred to construct a permanent fortress not on Roanoke Island, which had little commercial use except as a base camp, but at the head of the Roanoke River on the mainland. If, as his Indian informants had told him, its ores were "worth the possession, I would there have raised a main fort." Between the island and the main fortress he would have erected a series of small bastions, "a sconce [i.e., a small fort or earthwork] with a small trench and a palisade upon the top of it, in the which, in the guard of my boats, I would have left first the twenty or thirty men," and at a march beyond, on some "convenient plot," he would have built another sconce, "according to the former, where I would have left 15 or 20."[45]

As he had neither the time nor the men to construct or man these outposts, he had to rely on a fort on Roanoke. He and his troop laid out the structure in the northwest corner of the island, using earthworks and timber palisade. Outside of the ditch and wall stood cottages and workshops, as well as houses for the principal men. Apart from grassy mounds, there is no certain evidence today of the exact shape or construction of the main bastion. At the foot of the wooden walls, Lane probably filled in a firing step, so that his men could see over (or through firing ports in) the walls.[46] Lane's own description of the fort is not especially revealing. He merely mentioned the "new fort in Virginia."[47] David Beers Quinn, relying on early archaeological researchers, thought the fort was some forty to fifty yards square, in a star shape.[48] But the dimensions of the star were too small to hold the 108 men landed with Lane, and archaeologist Ivor Noël Hume suggests that the star may have been one of the bastions at the corners of the curtains of wall. Hume believes that the fort must have had a rectangular or triangular shape.[49]

Lane's fort-building enterprise had Native precedents, and the Roanokes would not have been surprised by the idea of a fort. Indians on the mainland had fortified some of their towns. White visited one of these, Pomeiooc, and drew its palisade. Lane's fortress was different from the Indians' constructions in three significant respects. First, Lane's works stood out from the land, altering its shape and design. Indian horticulturalists altered the surface of the land but not its shape, and Indian settlements did not deface the land so thoroughly or thoughtlessly as did Lane's. Indian forts surrounded Indian towns.[50] Lane's fort did not surround a town or village. There were barracks and workshops within it, but it was a European redoubt or refuge, a kind of Norman "keep," rather than part of a settlement for families. Like any medieval keep, its visible imposition upon the landscape was essential to its purpose. Keeps were not only safe places in time of sudden assault or ambush; they established the authority of the lord of the manor over the terrain. Keeps symbolized the authority of the nobility by imposing themselves on the eye. In building a fort, Lane was telling the Indians, look and see: this place is ours, not yours.

Second, by claiming the landscape in such an aggressive and artificial manner, Lane did what no Indian fortification would dream of doing: he imposed upon a spiritual landscape an alien structure. Such effrontery would surely drive off the spirits that dwelled in the land. The Native landscape, whether town, village, former settlement, woods, or littoral, was a plenum, full of natural spirits. The remains of things, people, prey, crops, fallow, were treated with respect because all were part of the whole, and the whole was alive. There was no separation between the material and the spiritual, the human and the not-human. The two infused one another.[51] But the Indians could see that the

Peter Charles Hoffer

English had no respect for the spiritual landscape. The English might speak of their God and their Savior, and the Indians might be willing to add these gods to their own, but nothing could excuse what the Indians saw the English doing to the places where the Indians' demigods resided.[52]

The closing off by light earthworks and palisade violated a basic tenet of Native religious life. Indians believed that almost everything important took place outside of the artificial space of buildings, in nature, where the spirit world and the everyday world came together. The Indians lived, danced, sang, worshipped, and tended their gardens in these open spaces. There were exceptions—mausoleums for the dead, sweat lodges for purification, and council fires within the chief's wigwam—but these were exceptions. Lane's fort, with its closed-up verticals and clapboard walls, denied sight. At best, that was bad manners; at worst, it might conceal all manner of skulduggery. Wingina made sense of what he and the other Indians saw happening, or rather what they could not see, by attributing the maladies to the intentional English manipulation of the spirit world. He professed that the English had reinforcements coming through the air, "yet invisible and without bodies." That made the English powerful, but that power was dark, akin to witchcraft. The Indians feared witches, and this made them suspect the English, even as they put themselves under the colonists' protection. Perhaps Lane and his men turned into witches behind their walls, after driving away the Indians' guardian spirits.[53]

Third, Lane's works suggested that the English had more in mind that simply keeping their secrets hidden from the Indians. They brought with them a heritage of thinking about material things completely alien to the Indians. The fort owed its design to a mathematical revolution in fortification theory and practice then taking place in Europe. The origin of that revolution was the introduction of artillery, and with it came new technological and tactical ways of organizing siege warfare that destroyed natural landscapes and replaced them with artificial planes, ramps, and redoubts.

From all evidences, Lane's fort at Roanoke looked out of place in the landscape to the Indians; it hurt the Indian eye, disturbed whatever natural spirits lived on the island, and violated the natural shapes of dune, marsh, grassy park, and woods on the island. But in Lane's mind, the fort was a comfort. Nearly two hundred years later, on the upper reaches of the Susquehanna, another Englishman approached another English fort to await a parley with Indians. James Merrell describes the scene:

> To [Turbutt] Francis, that fort must have been a pleasant sight. Its palisades and blockhouses, barracks and magazine, officers' quarters and commandant's house symbolized his colony's success in turning back the savage foe and imposing a new order on the frontier. The fifty-five Indians approaching the Forks [of the river] from the other direction on the morning of August 19 [1756] would have seen things differently. . . . [Fort Augusta] was a magnet for "vast numbers" of the intruders, people bent on creating a "very considerable settlement" with no place for Indians.[54]

It was as much this visual comfort as the matter of security that set Lane to work.

Against the visual imposition of the fort, Wingina hurled words. These he used well throughout the winter of 1585–86, building an Indian confederacy to wipe out the English. Wingina had "given" other villages "word" to assemble, and at a gathering of warriors, into which Lane barged, the Indians were working out their plan to "destroy" the English. Wingina had not struck yet, hoping perhaps that Lane's quixotic journey up the Roanoke would finish him off. Lane's unforeseen reappearance in Wingina's bailiwick, as if "dead men returned to the world again," dissuaded the werowance and his allies from carrying out their plan in the spring.

Readying himself for combat with Lane, Wingina changed his name. The Algonquians of the coast were patrilineal, like the English— one's clan membership passed through the father's line. But names could be changed to reflect a person's character, an event in one's life,

Peter Charles Hoffer

or a particular deed.[55] When his brother, Granganimo, who had first welcomed the English to the area in 1584 (and warned them not to truck with his brother on Roanoke Island), died, Wingina changed his name to Pemisapan. "Wingina" may have meant he "who looks at things with equanimity," a good name for a trading partner or a host. "Pemisapan" means "he looks out for" or "he inspects" or perhaps "he suspects."[56] Names tell a story, and the story that Pemisapan was telling his allies was that they must wash the dust from their eyes. They must see clearly that the English purpose had always been conquest.[57]

Pemisapan could not look into the fort—the planks or slats the English used to span the vertical posts prevented the Indians from viewing the interior. Still, Lane knew that he was being closely observed, "for in truth they, privy to their own villainous purposes against us, held as good espial upon us, both day and night, as we did upon them."[58] In response, Lane no doubt posted "sentinels and courts de guard [guardhouses, or huts]" when they went hunting or camped in Indian country.[59] In every encounter with the Indians, the English kept a sharp lookout.[60]

The Indians did not have the benefit of written reports, but they were superb at tracking game and human prey, and the Roanokes tried to keep tabs on every Englishman in their territory. Pemisapan often joined his warriors as they canoed across the sound to hunt deer and wildfowl in the reeds that fringed the island. In the middle of May 1586, Pemisapan ordered the dismantling of the fish weirs he had built for the English. But the English refused to depart. From concealment, the Roanokes watched the English plant another corn crop.[61] They counted numbers. As if the English were prey, the Indians studied their habits. Did they put aside their swords to carry firewood? How long did it take them to reload their matchlocks? How good were they with their longbows? The Indians could smell the lighted matches— without them the muskets were useless—but the bows were another matter. Indian archers respected the effects of the longbow. The war of nerves continued until Lane, never a patient man, could no longer stand the waiting. He sent word that he wished to meet with Pemisapan on the mainland on June 1, arrived at dawn, and assassinated the chief and his councillors.[62] Pemisapan had put words ahead of visions, listened to Lane once too often, believed his ears instead of his eyes, and died for it.

After Lane left North Carolina, the Indians reduced his fort to rubble. Its ruins would no longer trouble the spirits; its walls would no longer offend the eye. The settlers that John White brought in 1587 rebuilt the fortifications, but when he returned to Roanoke in 1590 to look for his "lost" colonists he found that the Indians had once more burned the buildings and dug up the foundations. The fort's outlines were barely visible when Carolina trader John Lawson passed through in the early eighteenth century; grassy mounds marked where ramparts had stood. The Indians had deliberately wiped all visual traces of the English occupation.

One might, in charity to Lane and the English with him, regard his quarrel with Pemisapan as the struggle of two self-willed warriors. It would then have no more general meaning than the circumstances around it required. The English, hungry and virtually besieged, saw the Indians as fiends. The Indians, put upon and disrespected, saw the English as thieves. No need to talk about perceptual strategies or sensory imperialism. What happened at Roanoke Island was precedent confined to its narrow fact pattern.[63] But events at Jamestown twenty years later prove that Roanoke was no fluke.

The same conflicting perceptual processes, the same miscoding of sights and sounds that had caused friction between the English and the Indians at Roanoke exploded in a series of crises during the first two decades of English settlement at Jamestown. By the close of this era of crisis, both sides would have taken their own measure of the other. After the demise of the Powhatan confederation and the transformation of the Jamestown settlement into the colony of Virginia, neither side would ever see the other for what it was. It was the triumph of sensory imperialism, a template for the rest of English settlement in North America.

In 1606 the newly chartered Virginia Company of London hired

Peter Charles Hoffer

Christopher Newport, an experienced ship captain who had taken part in the Roanoke voyages, as commander of an expedition to the Chesapeake, north of the Roanoke site. In November 1606 the company of 105 gentlemen, laborers, craftsmen, and 4 boys set sail, including in its number Gabriel Archer, George Percy, and John Smith, a veteran of Europe's wars against the Turks.

On April 26, 1607, Newport brought his little fleet safely to Cape Henry, at the mouth of the Chesapeake Bay, then sailed up the James River to find a site for the new settlement. The mouth of the river is so wide that Newport must have hoped that he had found the "Indrawing Sea" geographers had predicted would lead to the Pacific. The directors had instructed him to find a place that he could defend against Spanish attacks from the sea and Indian assaults from the land. In effect, the company's conception of the ideal fort was visual—the ability to see the enemy from whatever direction he came. There was no instruction on what the settlement was to look like from the ground up—nothing on the vegetation, the water supply, the lay of the land, none of the features that the Natives would immediately have weighed when deciding where to lay out a village.[64]

Newport chose a potato-shaped peninsula of marsh, woods, and grass connected to the mainland by a narrow isthmus, calling it James Island, after King James I of England. It looked appealing. The water at the river's edge was deep enough for the ships to tie lines to trees onshore, and the land was already partially cleared. On May 14 the colonists and sailors alit on the northwestern edge of James Island and began to build the shelters and storehouse of Jamestown. They constructed a "half moon" redoubt, probably a version of a "demilune" with triangular sides, the point aimed at the mainland, and a half circle at the rear. Behind the first fort they threw up thatch-roofed shanties much as one would find in poorer rural districts of England. The familiar sights comforted them. After a week, Newport set sail upriver with twenty men to trace the river, look for indications that rare metals might be mined, and open trade negotiations with the Indians further along the James.[65]

The English on the James River used the same set of rudimentary signs to communicate with the Indians as had Harriot and White at Roanoke. "By our word of kindness" and "by signs" Newport's men haled Indians in a canoe, one of whom took from Archer a pen and paper and drew a map of the course of the river. The local chief was the vassal of the powerful Powhatan, whose village was further up the river at the falls and whose confederation spread over the entire region. Powhatan arrived, his subordinates forming an honor guard. The Newport crew offered gifts, received offerings from Native peoples on both sides of the river, and sailed on to the seat of the mighty Powhatan himself, "whereon he sows his wheat [i.e., corn], beans, peas, tobacco, pumpkins, gourds, hemp, flax, and etc., and were any art used to the natural state of this place, it would be a goodly habitation." Brought before the seat of the Powhatan himself, once more the English were feasted, but their "best entertainment [was a] friendly welcome." Powhatan indicated by signs that all the Chesapeake Indians gave him tribute, and Newport "signified" that the English would regard all Powhatan's enemies as their own enemies. "Hereupon he (very well understanding by the words and signs we made, the signification of our meaning) moved of his own accord a league of friendship with us, which our captain kindly embraced." By giving gifts of food, Powhatan was telling the English that he viewed them as allied dependents. The dominant partner gave. The English, reading the gifts as tributes of subordinates, accepted the gifts as proof that the Indians would become the willing subjects of King James. A mistaken view, but surely a harmless one?[66]

Following Richard White's notion of a middle ground of European-Indian accommodation defined by creative misperceptions, this James River ceremony should have established a means for the two peoples to live and work together in some semblance of harmony.[67] But the very effort to bring consonance to so many novel sensations was already leading the two groups in different directions. Powhatan had just completed a furious thirty-year process of consolidation of his confederation of villages.[68] He regarded Jamestown as another town

Peter Charles Hoffer

to be assimilated into the confederation. If the English resisted, he knew how to impose his will on them. The English saw an Indian king who was still a savage. Surely he would soon recognize the might of the English nation. If he wavered in his promises of friendship and refused to supply the colonists with victuals, the English knew how to subdue him. This was a volatile middle ground, and it soon shook with violence.

Both sides' desires and needs had bent their perceptions of the encounter and its prospects. The Powhatan was overconfident and short-sighted. He had brought the entire region under his personal dominion. How much trouble could a few newcomers pose? Unused to such novelty as they represented and accustomed to handling novelty in a holistic, communal way, he was unable to comprehend the dimensions of the English threat. The English were even more perceptually inept. They had, for example, let military considerations dictate the site of their encampment, and immediately suffered for it. Jamestown sat on a natural wetlands crossed by two sluggish streams. The eight hundred acres were mosquito-ridden, and the English suffered from malaria that the mosquitoes carried from man to man. Worst of all, the isthmus was situated at the confluence of the fresh and the salt water on the James River, causing the groundwater on the island to retain just about all the waste the colonists produced. In no time at all, they were drinking and washing in their refuse, and falling ill from typhoid fever, dysentery, and other ailments.[69]

Jamestown had been in place but two weeks when its sensory history duplicated that of Roanoke. There were no creative misperceptions, although misperception abounded. The Indians mounted an all-out assault on the little fort. The English drove off the attack. And neither side learned the lessons it might have, because both sides' sensations of the events fit preexisting, pre-encounter models. We have three versions of the little battle from the English colonists. They differed in outlook and purpose, but together they indicate how English perspectives governed English observations.

Archer's financial prospects depended on the success of the colony.

He did not see the battle, but he recast what others had told him in heroic terms. Newport and the councillors had outsmarted the Indians. The future would be bright. Even before the Newport party returned to Jamestown, he read the countenances and gestures of the Indians correctly and rushed back to Jamestown. A day before they returned, some two hundred Indians assaulted the fort, overrunning the tents outside the redoubt and killing a man and a boy. But four of the council chosen by the Virginia Company to run the colony stood in front of the fort and discharged their muskets, much as Indian leading men might have stood in front of their company, defying the enemy.[70] The Indians carried their wounded and dead away. "A little after they made a huge noise in the woods, which our men surmised was at the burying of their slain men."[71] The next day, the English busied themselves "palisading" the fort. On June 8, emissaries of the werowances from upriver arrived, laid down their bows to show they meant no harm, and called "Wingapoh," a friendly greeting, but were driven off by mistake. On June 14 they returned, and Newport recognized one of his hosts from the falls of the James. The two men parleyed, the Indians promising to intercede with the Paspaheghs and their allies, or join the English to fight against their enemies. All would be well, he was certain.

George Percy kept his own account of these events, an educated gentleman's modulated and literary journal. It was Percy who went off gathering flowers in the woods the day after the Paspaheghs' demonstration of their collective anger. Later that day he joined in teasing the Indians when their arrows could not pierce a steel target. He had little to say of the actual fighting. He had seen enough of combat in Europe to know that the Paspahegh incursion was merely a skirmish. He did not see the Indians as villains, but adversaries. The world was full of conflict. Who could expect anything less in this howling wilderness? There is in fact a bit of the cynic in his journal. He never liked the site that Newport picked for the settlement and did not regard Newport as a hero. Instead, he took a professional pride in the construction of the fort. On June 15, "we had built and finished our fort

Peter Charles Hoffer

which was triangle wise, having three bulwarks at every corner like a half moon, and four or five pieces of artillery mounted in them, we had made ourselves sufficiently strong for these savages."[72] An English Renaissance gentleman like Percy, who had traveled through the Low Countries at the height of the religious wars, had nothing to fear from the savages.[73]

Where Archer trusted heroes and Percy trusted himself, Smith trusted no one. He offered an account based on hearsay, but it was the most sensuously cogent of the three. He opined that there could be no sensate compromise between Indian and English. The English acted in plain sight. The Indians skulked. The English reached out in friendship. The Indians hid their feelings and emotions. "Had not God (beyond all the [Indians'] expectations) by means of the ships at whom they [the crews] shot with their ordinances and muskets, caused them [the Indians] to retire, they [would have] entered the fort with our own men, [who] were then busied in setting corn, their arms being then in [boxes] and few ready but certain gentlemen." The colony had survived by a whisker, though thirteen or fourteen were hurt and one killed. At last the English had the dust cleared from their eyes, and "with all speed we palisaded our fort."[74]

Smith regarded the Indians as opponents from the first, and the defining characteristic of that enmity was sensory divergence. He was not the only Englishman to declare sensory war. The English regarded the naked savage as a mere brute, "vile and stinking" in custom. The Indians saw the English as thieves without manners, intruders who refused to leave when they had overstayed their welcome.[75] Even the English understood the animosity of the Indians at "what may be the issue of these strong preparations, landed in their coasts, and yearly supplied with fresher troops . . . to which they open their ears wide, and keep their eyes waking, with good espial upon every thing that stirs, the *noise of our drums of our shrill trumpets and great ordinance . . .* have bred strong fears amongst them."[76] The Indians feared thunder. Perhaps the sound of cannon would cow them as well. The English were waging sensory warfare.

From afar, Smith envisioned the Indians' chagrin and predicted that they would rise up in anger. He was right. Opechancanough, who had succeeded his half brother Powhatan as paramount chief, plotted the expulsion of the English from the first time he laid eyes on Smith.[77] Only Powhatan's hesitancy to wage open war, accompanied by the ability of the company to restock the colony with men and material, deterred Opechancanough from carrying out his plan. But by 1622 the werowance had seen enough. His half brother dead, his allies driven from their villages, he had become the Powhatan, and wanted but the occasion to recover the native landscape and welcome the spirits back to their home.

Opechancanough wanted the attack on the English to be a sensory event that any surviving colonists would never forget. It must be visible, audible, and tactile. But to succeed, the attack must camouflage itself. The werowance knew that the English had grown careless, "their houses generally opened to the savages, who were always friendly fed at their tables, and lodged in their bed-chambers."[78] He set the plan to begin in the early morning of March 22, 1622. The plan was simple; at breakfast time enter the homes of the unsuspecting Virginians carrying no weapons but those concealed on their person, engage in friendly conversation over the first meal, then use the English people's tools to murder their hosts, "not sparing either age or sex, man woman or child . . . neither did these beasts spare those amongst the rest well known unto them, from whom they had daily received many benefits." To enforce the message of the Indians' fury on the minds of the settlers, victims would be mutilated and then displayed. For example, Nathaniel Powell and his entire family were hanged and decapitated in plain sight.[79] Some of the gruesome details in Smith's account resulted from hysterical reports; some were propaganda, but the decapitation of enemies was a common sensory tactic to heighten the terror of the carnage.[80] Torture of the captives served the same purpose. It was always highly visible, auditory, and even olfactory. What is more, it "worked" in terms of the way that Indians processed the report of the senses. Its performance and meaning were communal. The whole

Peter Charles Hoffer

village participated. The strong, comely, and hardy might be deemed worthy of incorporation into the village—a confirmation of the importance of the immediate sensory information in determining the value of a person (and proof of the highly empirical Indian understanding of the senses).

Three hundred and forty-seven Virginians, a fourth of the total number of settlers, died in the massacre; the rest would always remember what they had seen and heard.[81] Opechancanough's sensory warfare had worked too well, however, for the English had a sensory answer for the "massacre of 1622" that went beyond burning Indian villages and crops. Typically, after the massacre, the Indians suing for peace begged to be able to plant their corn.[82] They wanted to restore their old scenery of village and garden plot. But the English had another vision of the colony. The English would forever change the scenery of Tidewater Virginia. In the English landscape the Indian would forever be a foreigner.

Changing the Scenery

In the years after the massacre, the speed and thoroughness of English occupation intensified. House construction and clearing fields for planting were even more important in the sensory campaign to establish English dominion over Virginia than the sound of cannon or war whoops. The plow was the pen with which the English husbandman wrote his name on the land, the furrow the proof of his productivity.[83] When English plows replaced Indian hoes and English furrows Indian hillocks, sensory imperialism would have its victory ensured. That is what, albeit somewhat haphazardly, the Virginia Company finally achieved, by transforming itself from a merchant venture into a real estate development firm. In early 1609 the company reorganized itself to increase its capital, and the new organization determined that the follies of the past two years would end. Armed with a revised charter that gave to the new "governor general," Thomas Gates, the powers of a military dictator, the company dispatched seven hundred settlers to Virginia. Under its new government, the colonists began to spread themselves up and down the river.[84] Jamestown avoided the fate of Roanoke because the Virginia Company of London, before its demise in 1624, provided sufficient resources to populate a large area of the James River shoreline and encouraged the planting of a commercially viable export crop—tobacco. Tobacco cultivation in the end would do what trumpets and artillery could not: make Virginia look like a little England. A boom time in tobacco production, corresponding to widening demand in England and Europe, enabled the company to recruit emigrants. In 1615 the colony sent home two thousand pounds of tobacco; by 1629 that figure had risen to 1.5 million pounds. Everyone from governors to servants devoted themselves to the new crop.[85]

The scorched-earth policy the English adopted against the Indians after 1622 should thus be seen as part of a war the English waged against the land itself. When the English arrived the environment had supported a great diversity of species, in part because Indian farmers' methods of clearing land did not exhaust the subsoil nutrients. They turned forest into garden by "girdling" the trees (slashing and removing the bark of the tree) and firing the underbrush. The old field turned to "park land"—grassy meadows—perfect for browsing animals like deer, then back to forest.[86] Colonial herds of cattle, sheep, and pigs further damaged local environments. English domestic animals ate their way into Indian gardens and competed with deer for forage. One of the first acts of the Indian raiders during the 1622 massacre was to kill cattle. The terms of the peace accords of 1628 specified that no English cattle were to be harmed in the future.[87] The colonists left the trapping of beaver and other fur bearing animals to the Indians, but by inducing the Natives to overhunt fur-bearing animals, colonists further disturbed New World ecology. Untended beaver dams collapsed, spilling rich soils. Clear-cutting of timber, deep plowing, allowing domestic livestock to range freely over the land, and the extinction of many mammalian species left Virginia far poorer in diversity of plants and animals.[88]

The Powhatan chiefdom, after a decade of English retaliation, was in no position to contest the transformation of the Virginia country-

Peter Charles Hoffer

side from park lands and woods to tobacco and wheat farms and cattle runs. The Indians had become a minority in their own land, and what is more, an impoverished minority. In 1644 Opechancanough would attempt a last full-scale rebellion, but it was crushed. Surviving Indian villages were soon hedged by English farms.[89] In 1645 and 1646 the House of Burgesses provided for the construction of a line of blockhouses along the frontier—to keep the Indians in sight. In the meantime, the Indian tribes were relocated behind the falls of the James and the York Rivers, allowing the colony to confiscate over three hundred thousand acres of Indian land.[90]

The first English arrivals at Jamestown had put themselves in peril by not knowing which Indian village occupied which plot of land, but like the "posted" notices that today warn trespassers not to enter, the colonists' hedge and fence required no local knowledge. They did not fit into the landscape but struck the viewer—as they were intended to—by standing out from the surrounding fields and woods. These artificial land markers did not distinguish between one claimant and another. Deed books and plot books in the county courthouse would do that. It was enough that the eye could tell "this land is mine." Pemisapan and Opechancanough had learned the lesson—the English eye had defeated the Indian eye. English sensory imperialism had turned the novel into the familiar and had introduced into the natural landscape a perception of absolute individual ownership taken from across the sea. In the meantime, sensory imperialism taught the English that novelty was dangerous. Better to rearrange what one saw and heard to reproduce what one remembered of the Old World. The Indians, too late, perceived the inverse lesson. The novel encounter with the Europeans ended in death. In this light, Opechancanough's rebellion was a last, desperate gamble born of a sense of irrevocable loss—the loss of a sensate world.

There would be times when the English and the Indians would have common interests.[91] But they would never—could never—see eye to eye or hear one another truly. By the beginning of the nineteenth century, the original clearings of the peregrinating coastal Natives had vanished from the settlers' accounts, just as surely as the remnant of the original villagers was melting into memory. As James Fenimore Cooper wrote in 1823, recalling his youth in the Otsego country, "a dreary and dark wood, where the rays of the sun could but rarely penetrate, and where even the daylight was obscured and rendered gloomy by the deep forests" had greeted the settlers in his father's generation. They transformed natural landscape into pastoral scenery. "The green wheat fields were seen in every direction, spotted with the dark and charred stumps that had, in the preceding season, supported some of the proudest trees of the forest. Ploughs were in motion."[92] What had been a "timeless, wild land of pure nature"[93] became "schools, academies, churches, meeting-houses, turnpike roads, and a market town . . . neat and comfortable farms . . . and beautiful and thriving villages."[94] Because the eye and ear could no longer perceive them, the sounds and sights of Indian habitation and cultivation vanished as if they had never existed.

Notes

1. See, e.g., Leslie Brothers, *Friday's Footprint: How Society Shapes the Human Mind* (New York: Oxford University Press, 1997); and Howard Gardiner, *The Mind's New Science: A History of the Cognitive Revolution* (New York: Basic Books, 1987).

2. See, e.g., the lessons from diplomats faced with novelty in Robert Jervis, *Perception and Misperception in International Politics* (Princeton NJ: Princeton University Press, 1976), 117–202.

3. One of the reasons for the explosion of travel anthologies in England in the 1580s was that the works of the Spanish and French were not trusted and that England's rivals kept much of what they found secret. The English publications were part of a propaganda war against Spain. David Beers Quinn, *The Roanoke Voyages, 1584–1590* (New York: Dover, 1991), 1:5–9, 2:718–25.

4. See, e.g., Anthony Grafton, *New Worlds, Ancient Texts: The Power of Tradition and the Shock of Discovery* (Cambridge: Harvard University Press, 1992); John F. Moffit and Santiago Sebastián, *O Brave New People: The European Invention of the American Indian* (Albuquerque: University of New Mexico Press, 1996), 266–336; Jack P. Greene, *The Intellectual Con-*

struction of America: Exceptionalism and Identity from 1492 to 1800 (Chapel Hill: University of North Carolina Press, 1992); and the essays in Karen Ordahl Kupperman, ed., *America in European Consciousness, 1493–1750* (Chapel Hill: University of North Carolina Press, 1995).

5. Anthony Pagden, *The Fall of Natural Man: The American Indian and the Origins of Comparative Ethnology* (Cambridge: Harvard University Press, 1982), 12: analogy, description, samples, and classification all depend on what "could be seen."

6. Grafton, *New Worlds, Ancient Texts*; Stephen Greenblatt, *Marvelous Possessions: The Wonder of the New World* (Chicago: University of Chicago Press, 1991); Tzvetan Todorov, *The Conquest of America: The Question of the Other* (New York: Harper and Row, 1984); Eric R. Wolf, *Europe and the People without History* (Berkeley: University of California Press, 1982).

7. Charles Hudson, "The Hernando de Soto Expedition," in *The Forgotten Centuries: Indians and Europeans in the American South, 1521–1704*, ed. Charles Hudson and Carmen Chavez Tesser (Athens: University of Georgia Press, 1993), 74–103; David Ewing Duncan, *Hernando De Soto: A Savage Quest in the Americas* (New York: Crown, 1995).

8. Neal Salisbury, *Manitou and Providence: Indians, Europeans, and the Making of New England* (New York: Hill and Wang, 1982), 34–39; Daniel Richter, *Facing East from Indian Country: A Native History of Early America* (Cambridge: Harvard University Press, 2001), 14. A convention in lowercase, manitou is spiritual power. Every living being has it. In uppercase, Manitou is demigod, the visible embodiment of power.

9. James H. Merrell, *The Indians' New World: Catawbas and Their Neighbors from European Contact through the Era of Removal* (Chapel Hill: University of North Carolina Press, 1989), 12.

10. See, e.g., Alden T. Vaughan, *Roots of American Racism: Essays on the Colonial Experience* (New York: Oxford University Press, 1995), 34–54.

11. With all due respect to three magnificent essays, it is clear that I do not agree with the late dating of mutual mistrust in Joyce Chaplin, *Subject Matter: Technology, the Body, and Science on the Anglo-American Frontier, 1500–1676* (Cambridge: Harvard University Press, 2001); Karen Ordahl Kupperman, *Indians and English: Facing Off in Early America* (Ithaca NY: Cornell University Press, 2000); and Michael Leroy Oberg, *Dominion and Civility: English Imperialism and Native America, 1585–1685* (Ithaca NY: Cornell University Press, 2001). It did not take generations for the process of sensory degradation and perceptual derogation to begin. I do

not, however, subscribe to the extermination-from-the-outset thesis in Richard Drinnon, *Facing West: The Metaphysics of Indian Hating and Empire Building* (Minneapolis: University of Minnesota Press, 1980); and Francis Jennings, *The Invasion of America: Indians, Colonialism, and the Cant of Conquest* (New York: Norton, 1975). There was a time of genuine wonder at sensory novelties.

12. See, e.g., John Smith, *Generall History of Virginia* (1624), in *The Complete Works of Captain John Smith*, ed. Philip L. Barbour (Chapel Hill: University of North Carolina Press, 1986), 2:296.

13. See Colin M. Turnbull, *The Human Cycle* (New York: Simon and Schuster, 1983), 50–51; and Paul Rodaway, *Sensuous Geographies: Body, Sense, and Place* (London: Routledge, 1994), 108–13.

14. William Wood, *New England's Prospect* (1634), ed. Alden T. Vaughan (Amherst: University of Massachusetts Press, 1977), 101.

15. Åke Hultkrantz, *Belief and Worship in Native North America* (Syracuse: Syracuse University Press, 1981), 120, 123, 139; Timothy Silver, *A New Face on the Countryside: Indians, Colonists, and Slaves in South Atlantic Forests, 1500–1800* (New York: Cambridge University Press, 1990), 41.

16. Kathleen Bragdon, *Native People of Southern New England, 1500–1650* (Norman: University of Oklahoma Press, 1996), 190–91.

17. John Demos, *The Unredeemed Captive: A Family Story from Early America* (New York: Vintage, 1994), 240.

18. Quoted in Kupperman, *Indians and English*, 129.

19. Thomas Morton, *New English Canaan* (1637), ed. Jack Dempsey (Scituate: Digital Scanning, 2000), 107.

20. Thomas Shepard, *The Clear Sun-Shine of the Gospel Breaking Forth Upon the Indians of New-England* (London, 1647), 10. "Black coat" was a "disparaging term for a minister." Richard M. Lederer Jr., *Colonial American English* (Essex CT: Verbatim Books, 1985), 31. It is entirely possible that the Indian relating the dream to the black-coated ministers is subtly teasing them.

21. Pagden called it the "autotopic"; *European Encounters with the New World: From Renaissance to Romanticism* (New Haven: Yale University Press, 1993), 51–87.

22. William Bradford, *Of Plymouth Plantation (1620–1647)*, ed. Samuel Eliot Morison (New York: Modern Library, 1966), 62.

23. Raleigh quoted in Simon Schama, *Landscape and Memory* (New York: Vintage, 1995), 314.

Peter Charles Hoffer

24. Arthur Barlow, "Discourse of the First Voyage to Virginia" (1584), in Quinn, *The Roanoke Voyages*, 1:94.

25. Percy, "Discourse," in Barbour, *Jamestown Voyages*, 1:131.

26. On bows and arrows see Chaplin, *Subject Matter*, 102.

27. Bruce Smith, *The Acoustic World of Early Modern England: Attending to the O-Factor* (Chicago: University of Chicago Press, 1999), 40–95.

28. Schama, *Landscape and Memory*, 142–58. The 1612 trial of the witches of Pendle Forest, in Lancashire, was perhaps the most noteworthy English witchcraft case. In it, the forest itself was a leading character—people in the village were afraid to go into the woods.

29. [Edward Winslow], *A Relation or Journal of the Beginning and Proceeding of the English Plantation Settled at Plymouth* [London, 1622], ed. Dwight B. Heath (New York: Corinth Books, 1963), 46.

30. William Strachey, "A True Reportory," in *A Voyage to Virginia in 1609*, ed. Louis B. Wright (Charlottesville: University Press of Virginia, 1964), 4.

31. Quinn, *Roanoke Voyages*, 2:585.

32. White, "Narrative of the 1590 Voyage," in Quinn, *Roanoke Voyages*, 2:613.

33. Drake, "A Summary and True Discourse of Sire Frances Drake West Indian Voyage," in Quinn, *Roanoke Voyages*, 1:297. On trumpets and other devices to warn of danger and signal position see Richard Cullen Rath, "Worlds Chanted into Being: Soundways in Early America" (PhD diss., Brandeis University, 2001), 112–13.

34. David Cressy, *Bonfires and Bells: National Memory and the Protestant Calendar in Elizabethan and Stuart England* (Berkeley: University of California Press, 1989), 80–81.

35. White, "Voyage," 1590, in Quinn, *Roanoke Voyages*, 2:585.

36. See, e.g., [Winslow], *Relation*, 33, 43, 23.

37. Drake, "Summary and True Discourse," 1:300.

38. George Horse Capture quoted in Frederic W. Gleach, *Powhatan's World and Colonial Virginia: A Conflict of Cultures* (Lincoln: University of Nebraska Press, 1997), 106.

39. On Hakluyt see David Armitage, *The Ideological Origins of the British Empire* (New York: Cambridge University Press, 2000), 72–81.

40. From 1580 to 1583, Ireland writhed in the grip of civil war. See Nicholas P. Canny, "Identity Formation in Ireland: The Emergence of the Anglo-Irish," in *Colonial Identity in the Atlantic World, 1500–1800*, ed. Nicholas P. Canny and Anthony Pagden (Princeton NJ: Princeton University Press, 1987), 159–212; Nicholas P. Canny, "The Marginal Kingdom: Ireland as a

Problem in the First English Empire," in *Strangers within the Realm: Cultural Margins of the First British Empire*, ed. Bernard Bailyn and Philip D. Morgan (Chapel Hill: University of North Carolina Press, 1991), 35–66; and John McGurk, *The Elizabethan Conquest of Ireland* (Manchester: Manchester University Press, 1997).

41. Harriot, *Report*, in Quinn, *Roanoke Voyages*, 1:381.

42. Lane, "Discourse," in Quinn, *Roanoke Voyages*, 1:271.

43. Waymouth, "The Jewel of Artes," in *The New England Voyages, 1602–1608*, ed. David Beers Quinn and Alison M. Quinn (London: Hakluyt Society, 1983), 233.

44. "A Relation of Maryland" (1635), in *Original Narratives of Early American History: Narratives of Early Maryland*, ed. Clayton Colman Hall (New York: Scribner, 1910), 76.

45. Lane, "Discourse," 1:263, 262.

46. Ivor Noël Hume, *The Virginia Adventure, Roanoke to James Towne: An Archaeological and Historical Odyssey* (New York: Knopf, 1994), 32–79.

47. Lane, "Report to Walsingham, September 3, 1585," in Quinn, *Roanoke Voyages*, 1:210.

48. Quinn, *Roanoke Voyages*, 2:903–10.

49. Hume, *Virginia Adventure*, 60–63.

50. John B. Jackson, "In Search of a Proto-Landscape," in *Landscape in America*, ed. George F. Thompson (Austin: University of Texas Press, 1995), 48.

51. Gleach, *Powhatan's World*, 36–37.

52. Kupperman, *Indians and English*, 141.

53. On witchcraft and Indians, see Alfred W. Cave, "Indian Shamans and English Witches in Seventeenth-Century New England," *Essex Institute Historical Collections* 128 (1992): 239–54; and Harold E. Driver, *Indians of North America* (Chicago: University of Chicago Press, 1961), 517, 523, 540.

54. James H. Merrell, *Into the American Woods: Negotiators on the Pennsylvania Frontier* (New York: Norton, 1999), 309.

55. Bragdon, *Native People*, 170; Driver, *Indians of North America*, 373; Helen C. Rountree, *Pocahontas's People: The Powhatan Indians of Virginia through Four Centuries* (Norman: University of Oklahoma Press, 1996), 73. Deeds in war and preparations for war were both occasions to change a personal name.

56. Quinn, *Roanoke Voyages*, 2:899, 893–94.

57. Merrell, *Into the American Woods*, 20, 49.

Peter Charles Hoffer

58. Lane, "Discourse," 1:286.

59. As did the English at Jamestown. Percy, "Discourse," 1:131.

60. Chaplin, *Subject Matter*, 99–100.

61. Oberg, *Dominion and Civility*, 44.

62. Lane, "Discourse," 1:265, 278, 286.

63. Oberg, *Dominion and Civility*, 45: "For Lane, Roanoke must in many ways have seemed Ireland all over again."

64. A vivid account of these first days is Philip L. Barbour, *The Three Worlds of John Smith* (Boston: Houghton Mifflin, 1964).

65. On the Jamestown fort, see William M. Kelso, *Jamestown Rediscovery* (Jamestown: Association for the Preservation of Virginia Antiquities, 1997), 3:27–39, 4:29–42; Hume, *Virginia Adventure*, 143–89.

66. Archer, "Relation," in Barbour, *Jamestown Voyages*, 1:83, 84, 85, 86.

67. Richard White, *The Middle Ground: Indians, Empires, and Republics in the Great Lakes Region, 1650–1815* (New York: Cambridge University Press, 1991), 50–53.

68. Oberg, *Dominion and Civility*, 55, estimates that 14,000 of the 20,000 Indians in the region were under Powhatan's dominion.

69. See the introduction by Barbour in *The Complete Works of Captain John Smith, 1580–1631*, ed. Barbour, 3 vols. (Chapel Hill: University of North Carolina Press, 1986), 1:5–10; Alden T. Vaughan, *American Genesis: Captain John Smith and the Founding of Virginia* (Boston: Longman, 1976), 29–33; Carville Earle, *Geographical Inquiry and American Historical Problems* (Stanford: Stanford University Press, 1992), 25–58; Rountree, *Pocahontas's People*, 11, 30–31, 34.

70. See, e.g., French Canadian descriptions of the traditional Huron-Iroquois battles that they witnessed in 1609. Mark Lescarbot, "The Voyage of Monsieur de Monts into New France" (1603–11), in Samuel Purchas, *Hakluytus Posthumus, or Purchas His Pilgrimes* (1625) (New York: AMS Press, 1965), 18:292–93; Gordon M. Sayre, *Les Sauvages Américains: Representations of Native Americans in French and English Colonial Literature* (Chapel Hill: University of North Carolina Press, 1997), 74–77, 249–58.

71. Archer, "Relation," 1:95, 97–98. The English noted more than once the Indians' wailing at the death of any of their number.

72. Percy, "Discourse," 1:142.

73. Percy, Smith, and other members of the Jamestown council fought in the Low Countries before they signed on for Virginia. Kelso, *Jamestown Re-*

discovery (Jamestown: Association for the Preservation of Virginia Antiquities, 1996), 2:28, 15, 31, 33.

74. John Smith, "A True Relation" (1608), in Barbour, *Jamestown Voyages*, 1:170, 172.

75. Quotations from Alden T. Vaughan, "'Expulsion of the Salvages': English Policy and the Virginia Massacre of 1622," *William and Mary Quarterly*, 3rd ser., 35 (1978): 60, 61, 63, 65.

76. Emphasis added. William Strachey (1611) quoted in Vaughan, "'Expulsion of the Salvages,'" 66n29.

77. Or perhaps a little later, when Smith had insulted Opechancanough. J. Frederick Fauz, "Opechancanough: Indian Resistance Leader," in *Struggle and Survival in Colonial America*, ed. David G. Sweet and Gary B. Nash (Berkeley: University of California Press, 1981), 26.

78. Smith, *Generall History*, 2:293, 294.

79. Smith, *Generall History*, 2:294.

80. Wood, *New England's Prospect*, 103. The Algonquians believed that the body travels to the afterlife entire; thus decapitation denied the enemy eternal rest. See Jill Lepore, *The Name of War: King Philip's War and the Origins of American Identity* (New York: Knopf, 1998), 180.

81. Smith, *Generall History*, 2:297.

82. Gleach, *Powhatan's World*, 153.

83. Andrew McRae, *God Speed the Plow: The Representation of Agrarian England, 1500–1660* (New York: Cambridge University Press, 2002), 1–2.

84. Vaughan, *American Genesis*, 98–112; Joseph C. Robert, *The Story of Tobacco in America* (Chapel Hill: University of North Carolina Press, 1949), 6–10.

85. Vaughan, *American Genesis*, 99; Edmund S. Morgan, *American Slavery, American Freedom: The Ordeal of Colonial Virginia* (New York: Norton, 1975), 108–30.

86. William Cronon, *Changes in the Land: Indians, Colonists and the Ecology of New England* (New York: Hill and Wang, 1983), 19–33; Bragdon, *Native People*, 55–79.

87. Rountree, *Pocahontas's People*, 74, 80.

88. Calvin Martin, *Keepers of the Game: Indian-Animal Relationships and the Fur Trade* (Berkeley: University of California Press, 1978); Shepherd Kretch III, ed., *Indians, Animals, and the Fur Trade: A Critique of Keepers of the Game* (Athens: University of Georgia Press, 1981).

89. Rountree, *Pocahontas's People*, 81–127.

90. Sylvia Frey, "Rethinking the American Revolution," *William and Mary Quarterly*, 3rd ser., 53 (1996): 369.

91. Merrell, *Into the American Woods*, 52.

92. James Fenimore Cooper, *The Pioneers, or the Source of the Susquehanna, A Descriptive Tale* (1823), ed. James Franklin Beard (Albany: State University of New York Press, 1980), 239, 242.

93. Alan Taylor, *William's Cooper's Town: Power and Persuasion on the Frontier of the Early American Republic* (New York: Vintage, 1996), 32.

94. Cooper, *Pioneers*, 235; William Cooper, *A Guide in the Wilderness*, quoted in Taylor, *William Cooper's Town*, 32–33.

8

Howls, Snarls, and Musket Shots

SAYING "THIS IS MINE" IN COLONIAL NEW ENGLAND

Jon Coleman

Woath woach ha ha hach woath. The great and hideous cry jerked the landing party awake. "Arm, arm," yelled a sentinel. Muskets boomed and fell silent. Men traded whispers in the dark. One, a sailor, had heard the cry before. Companies of wolves, he reported, often sung to him and his mates on the cod-fishing boats off the coast of New-foundland. Convinced that wolves "or such like wild beasts" had made the noise, the men slept, rousing themselves in the morning to pack their shallop (the small boat sent from the *Mayflower* to search for a settlement site) and eat. A group hauled the party's armor down to the boat; the tide was low. They would have to wait to launch the craft until the shallow waters surrounding Cape Cod rose. The armor-bearers headed back to break their fast. Near the encampment, they heard the sound again: *woath woach ha ha hach woath.* "They are men, Indians, Indians." Arrows flew. Miles Standish fired his snaphance. More blasts followed. The Indians' captain stepped from behind a tree and shot three arrows. He uttered "an extraordinary shriek," and the Indians slipped away.[1]

Sound and fear permeated the Plymouth colonists' first encounters with New England's "wild beasts and wild men." Lacking a common language, the English and the Indians communicated their unease by making a ruckus. Fear underlay the shots and shouts. The midnight howl alarmed the landing party. The colonists answered the cry with musket shots intended to scare the beasts that had scared them. Again, in the morning, a hideous sound frightened the English, and, again, they answered with their most potent noisemakers. (Cumbersome and inaccurate, the English guns were more loud than lethal.) The Indian leader ended the conversation with a yell. His shriek epitomized the double meaning of all the shots and shouts. He screamed after a musket ball hit a tree next to his head, making "the bark or splinters . . . fly about his ears." The cry registered the Indian's fright at nearly being decapitated. The shriek expressed terror; but it also induced terror. The "great and strange" noise filled the English with "dread." *Woath woach ha ha hach woath* was the sound of a colonial encounter. It captured the confusion, violence, and shared apprehension of two peoples that could not speak to one another but could scare the hell out of each other.[2]

Animals, including human ones, squeak and bellow for reasons, and their outbursts carry messages. Chirps beckon mates, roars announce physical vigor, and bleats help mothers locate wayward young. Noises strengthen group cohesion, coordinate hunting and travel, and express emotions. Birdsongs, elk bugles, rhinoceros snorts, and leopard purrs fill the air with affection, lust, anger, and elation. Animals also use sound to create and maintain territories. A territory consists of the area an animal or group of animals occupies exclusively by repelling interlopers. Territory is space with teeth, and the promise of violence arranges spatial relations among similar species. The key word here is *promise*. Most species try to avoid fights to the death, turning instead to ritualized displays of dominance, vocal signaling, and scent marking to keep competitors at a proper distance. Animals need space to survive, and they acquire this space through communication as well as bloodshed.[3]

Human beings claim a mastery over communication not shared by their nonbipedal brethren. Animals make noise; people manipulate language. The human song of plosives, nasals, fricatives, and vowels carries sophisticated data no grunt, cluck, or moo could articulate. Yet while a pig may never grasp the nuances of Shakespeare, people have overestimated their own prowess as communicators. When comparing ourselves to other creatures, we continually mistake difference for superiority. Human language differs from, say, the chirps and whistles of chipmunks by being flexible, interchangeable, and infinite. Like many nonhuman animals, chipmunks communicate through a limited set of signals. The meanings of their sounds and gestures are genetically fixed. An aggressive posture that warns "stay away from my acorns" always means "stay away from my acorns." By contrast, human beings monkey with meaning. They rearrange sentences, invent words, and concoct metaphors, puns, and double entendres. The astonishing elasticity of language allows humans to express complex ideas, but all this creativity comes at a price. Over thousands of years, people have mixed and matched sounds and symbols to generate thousands of languages. Alone among the earth's animals, human beings have fashioned a communication system that can make members of the same species incomprehensible to one another.

The 1620 fight between the Plymouth colonists and the Cape Cod Natives illustrated the advantages and the pitfalls of linguistic creativity. Indians and colonists possessed the amazing ability to learn and devise new languages, but they still managed to ignore, misread, and remain oblivious to each other's signals. The English-speaking colonists and Algonquian-speaking Natives yelled, blasted, and wailed across a cultural chasm. The humans' inventive communication system generated confusion when they needed clarity most. The European invasion of New England not only rearranged the spaces humans and animals claimed as their own but also disrupted the flow of information that created and maintained peaceful distances between ecological rivals. The Cape Cod episode demonstrated just how frightening, haphazard, and violent establishing new lines of communication and

Jon Coleman

territory would be for the region's top predators—Indians, colonists, and wolves.[4]

Wolves participated in the Cape Cod skirmish, if only as figments of overheated imaginations. Even disembodied, their presence was telling. To bridge their cultural differences, New England's humans often borrowed other animals' signals. These signals included noises and gestures that communicated a simple yet crucial idea. Howls, growls, and yelps expressed territoriality on an emotional level both Natives and newcomers could understand. Animal noises and postures inspired dread, and dread was an effective space-creating emotion. All the shrieks and shots of early colonial encounters represented humans' attempts to use the clarity of other beasts' vocalizations and dominance displays to extricate themselves from the muddle in which their language had trapped them.

As the 1620 fight exposed the downside of the humans' flexible communication system, it also confirmed the resilience of language. The meanings of words may break down over long distances, but a record of the Cape Cod incident managed to travel across several centuries intact. The English wrote the episode down, verbalizing a confrontation notable for its inarticulateness. The written record was the last act in the clash. Equally engrossed in fear and befuddlement at the time, the invaders reclaimed their mastery of the situation later, describing it in print. Their history made the skirmish intelligible—from their perspective. The English emerged from the incident with a document that by its continued existence proclaimed them the region's dominant communicators.

It is hard to argue with this assessment. The colonists left a written record, whereas New England's other top predators—Native Americans and wolves—scribbled little or not at all. Writing secured the invaders' conquest, filling archives with scripts that enshrined their vision of territorial expansion as the prime interpretation of the experience. Or did it? Writing is not the only form of communication that withstands time; it is merely the form with which historians feel most comfortable. Europeans dominated the transcribed record of the past, but other time frames impinged on history. Both European and Native American humans preserved narratives and rituals in folklore, and wolves exchanged information through gestures, scents, and sounds that adhered to a time regime far slower than those of folklore or history. Wolf communication was simple, rigid, and slow to change, and while these qualities may tempt some to see the animals' exchanges as inferior, their system accomplished goals similar to humans' nimble language. Like people, wolves colonized, and their unpretentious signals proved an effective aid to their adventures in territorial acquisition.

Like humans, wolves traveled long distances in search of fresh territories to inhabit. They colonized, and, while their conquests differed in sophistication and purpose from human voyages of aggression, wolves shared a dilemma with imperialist people: to avoid bloodshed, they had to communicate territoriality (that is yours, this is mine) with Native inhabitants who neither agreed with nor fully comprehended their notions of property. Wolves developed a set of communications that minimized bewilderment and violence. Unlike humans, they colonized with little confusion, and a close look at wolf dispersal reveals an alternative history of colonialism in which animals traveled long distances and expressed territoriality with the help of a simple, rigid, and slow-changing collection of signals.

Wolves were born to lope. With long legs and narrow, "keel-like" chests, wolves move in a fluid stride, hind and forelegs swinging in line like pendulums. This trot carries the animals far. Wolves may trek between ten and twenty miles a day within their territories searching for and hunting down prey, and every so often lone wolves leave their home range and set off on extended journeys. Wildlife biologists call these wolves dispersers, and their travels demonstrate the effectiveness of wolf communication.[5]

Dispersal remains one of the more mysterious wolf activities. Scientists noted the phenomenon only after radio collars allowed long-distance monitoring of individual animals. The number of miles covered by these trekkers surprised their human observers. In one famous instance, the biologist L. David Mech lost track of a female wolf in a Minnesota study area. The wolf turned up five hundred miles away, shot dead by a Saskatchewan farmer. A recent study of wolves in the Rocky Mountains straddling the American and Canadian border followed the movements of forty-two wolves. Seventeen (40 percent) left their home range, and fourteen of these traveled a hundred miles or more. One, a young female, roamed 840 miles, a journey that took her from Banff National Park, Canada, across the international boundary through northwest Montana and into Idaho. A pack of scientists trailed this radio-collared pup via ground triangulation, aircraft, and orbiting satellites. The female, however, kept her motivations hidden. Researchers suspect that competition and aggression prompt dispersal. Wolf packs grow each breeding season through the addition of new pups. Disease, rival packs, and food scarcity encircle the inflating family unit like barbs surrounding a balloon. Lack of meat is by far the sharpest threat, and wolves feel the stab in their stomachs and social relationships. As hunger increases, so do the numbers of fights and dominance showdowns. At some point, the pressure becomes unbearable, and individuals leave, reducing the stress on the group.[6]

Whatever triggers the urge to ramble, the decision to disperse has serious consequences. Territories and packs benefit wolves, so much so that the abandonment of familiar hunting grounds as well as familiar hunting partners borders on lunacy. Unlike most predators, wolves subsist on animals larger than themselves. Wolves kill with numbers, and they depend on each other to procure a daily calorie allowance equal to four pounds of flesh. (Wolves dine irregularly. They may go for days without a meal, then bolt down twenty pounds of meat, marrow, gristle, and hide at one sitting.) Dispersers may snack on the occasional beaver or rummage through the leftovers of another pack's kill, but they will enjoy fewer engorgements. Without feasts to break their famines, the travelers risk malnutrition, if not starvation. Even with hunger gnawing at their guts, dispersers must outrun the bite of another lethal adversary: the prime enemy of lone wolves is other wolves.[7]

Lone wolves must pass through a landscape organized on wolf principles, not human ones. Wolf territories would flummox a real estate agent. They shrink and advance, blossom and collapse in accord with the seasons, the size of packs, and the migrations of prey. Wolves mark their territory, but unlike cartographers, they do so without parameters. They do not own, control, or care about land. Wolves' territorial obsession is spacing, not space. Neighbors howl, fight, snarl, stick up their tails, raise their back fur, and secrete a cornucopia of bodily fluids in order to create and maintain a socially acceptable distance between one another. "Territorial behavior," writes the ecologist Paul Colinvaux, "is explained as a process of 'keep away from me' not of 'this dirt is mine.'" Actually, wolf territories function on a "keep away from us" basis. Packs organize wolf landscapes through violence, scent marking, vocalization, and dominance displays. As packs change over time, so do territories. Social fluidity begets spatial flux, and dispersing wolves must navigate a territorial map under constant revision.[8]

Communication plays such an essential role in dispersal because of the behavior's paradoxical goals. The survival of long-distance travelers depends on avoiding wolves as well as on finding them. Dispersers continually weigh their need for hunting partners, sexual mates, and social companions against their desire to escape the snapping teeth of hostile packs. The stakes of this balancing act are incredibly high. In a recent study of wolves in Alaska's Denali National Park, scientists found "that widespread intraspecific strife . . . is a normal consequence of wolf territoriality in the absence of extensive human interference." In other words, free from the ravages of human traps and bullets, wolves ravage one another. In Denali, neighboring packs killed 52 percent of the thirty-one radio-collared wolves in the study group. Approach or run? Long-distance travelers confront a tough choice when they encounter strangers. Wolves are fierce creatures, but dispersers must rely on social grace to save them, not brute force. They gather and interpret social cues, betting their lives on their skill at discerning friend from foe.[9]

Wolves have evolved into formidable communicators. From nose

Jon Coleman

to tail, their bodies have become complex signaling devices. Take the animal's charismatic grin, for instance. Americans have grown to love this smile. Today, wolf faces grace calendars, greeting cards, magazine covers, coffee cups, place mats, and print ads. The popularity of wolf images is due in part to the species' importance as a symbol of endangered wildness. But wolves have achieved supermodel status for another reason: humans find the predator's mug attractive. Many wolves appear to be wearing makeup. Their eyes, mouth, and ears are outlined in black. Their muzzles are often a lighter color than the rest of their faces, making their dark lips stand out further. (Wolves come in a wide spectrum of colors. The images in popular culture, however, tend to overrepresent gray wolves, which have the most distinctive facial markings.) The color contrasts, slightly upturned mouths, and overall fuzziness of wolf faces communicate nobility, friendliness, and intelligence. The consumers of wolf kitsch react to the expressiveness of wolf faces, but they misread the animals' markings. Wolves use their faces to signal each other, and this dialogue, while intelligent, has little to do with nobility or friendliness. Snarls, furrowed brows, squints, stares, and drawn-back ears indicate social rank. The dark outlines around wolf eyes, ears, and mouths enhance facial gestures that advertise dominance and submission. Within packs, dominant members appear more relaxed and confident than submissive ones. Dominant wolves may look gallant, but a snapshot of the behavior their regal stare inspires would sell few calendars. A full-blown display of submission contorts wolves into ghoulish postures. Submissive wolves bare their teeth and lick their lips obsessively while dropping their eyes, ears, tails, and buttocks. They crouch, whimper, and roll on their backs in order to urinate on themselves. The markings and expressions human consumers find so attractive belong to a social world most of them would find bizarre and repulsive.[10]

The social order of wolves revolves around an endless contest over food, space, and sex. Wolf packs are hierarchical, and a pack's dominant male and female (wildlife biologists have labeled this ruling couple the "alpha pair") eat the choicest morsels, slumber in the comfiest spaces, and copulate with the sexiest partners. Dominant wolves take the initiative during group activities. They confront strangers, lead attacks on prey, defecate first on scent posts, and decide the day's travel itinerary. The dominance system of wolf packs resembles the cutthroat politics of a junior high school gym class: the strong bully; the weak cower. Yet while aggression and humiliation remain bedrock realities of wolf life, the species would not have survived for as long as it has with a social order based solely on bluster and cringing. Dominance and submission arrange social relations within groups, but affection keeps wolf packs together.[11]

Wolves establish affective relationships with packmates first as pups and then again as sexual partners. Puppies are exempt from the adult dominance system. They can nip, growl, and stare down their elders with impunity. During most years, packs rear one litter, and every member helps care for the whelps. The young therefore form bonds with all the adults in a pack. All this changes as the pups mature. Around the age of three months, juvenile wolves become wary of strangers. They stop forming social attachments to new individuals, and their world hardens into a circle of intimates surrounded by a host of dangerous outsiders. Adults rarely make new friends. In studies of captive wolves, scientists have clocked the slow thaw of wolf xenophobia. The socialization of strangers takes at least six months. While stingy with their affection toward outsiders, adult wolves do have another opportunity to create and renew emotional bonds after puppyhood. Like all canines, wolves experience a "copulatory tie" during sexual intercourse. Swelling at the base of the male's penis, combined with the constriction of the sphincter muscles in the female's vagina, stops sexual partners from uncoupling after ejaculation. This tie can last as long as thirty minutes. While the ultimate purpose of this phenomenon remains a mystery, Mech has a theory. The tie, he suggests, "may be important in completing the psychological bond between two newly mated animals." If Mech's surmise is true, then the copulatory tie works as a form of biologically enforced cuddling. The tie bonds the mating pair, ensuring

Jon Coleman

that pups have at least two adults to care for them. The pups, in turn, bond with their parents and other pack members. The copulatory tie may be crucial to the emotional reproduction of the pack.[12]

Long-distance dispersers live on the fringe of a social world that rivals human societies in dynamism and complexity. Dispersers leave behind the emotional attachments of their natal packs. There is no need to romanticize this break. Cruelty and affection intermingle in wolf packs. A subordinate position in the pecking order may be the reason some wolves migrate. Whatever prompts their departure, once dispersers abandon their packs they must deal with other wolves' aversion to outsiders. In order to find a mate or enter another pack, a disperser needs to socialize with other adults. As we have seen, socialization among adult wolves is a long and tortuous process involving months of cautious advances and retreats. The fact that traveling wolves may be killed if they encounter a hostile pack makes the business of establishing affective bonds even trickier.

Dispersing wolves survive on the fringe of wolf society by gathering and interpreting signals. Long-range and long-term information help long-distance travelers avoid unfriendly groups, while short-range gestures, postures, and vocalizations help them negotiate a socialization process that can turn strangers into sexual partners and wanderers into packmates.

Wolves emit long-range and long-term signals from the orifices located at their bodies' polar extremes. Currently in the United States, people pay fees to enter captive-wolf parks or trek hundreds of miles into roadless wilderness to hear the sonorous howls that pass through wolves' mouths, but no one opens a wallet or laces a hiking boot to watch the animals spray urine on a twig or deposit feces on a rock. For dispersing wolves, however, critical information flows equally from both ends. Wolves advertise territory through scent marking. They defecate, unrinate, and rub themselves on familiar landmarks, creating scent posts. These stations receive careful attention and repeated dousings. Packs check and refresh them as they travel along the paths they have worn in their territories. Biologists can only speculate at the messages contained in a whiff of wolf excrement, but they know the olfactory prowess of canines. Dogs can distinguish identical twins by their scent, and they can detect a human fingerprint on a glass slide six weeks after the initial smudge. Scent posts give wolves a way to deposit long-term signals. With territories of many square miles to maintain, wolves need warning signs that transmit data long after the departure. Smells linger, guarding space, while the scent makers go about wresting a livelihood from that space.[13]

Scent posts alert dispersing wolves to the presence, the activity, and, perhaps, the strength of unknown packs. The information gleaned from these fragrant landmarks, however, has a drawback: the news is all past tense. Scent posts indicate that a pack exists, considers a space its territory, and travels past a spot from time to time. The freshness of the scent records the interval since a group last visited a landmark. While helpful, this is not the information a dispersing wolf needs most. Its health depends on knowing where hostile wolves are, not where they were. Howling reveals the current location of packs.

Wolves howl for several reasons. Within groups, howls help locate and call together pack members spread across a territory. At times, packs howl in chorus. These communal outbursts may refresh social attachments in the same way drinking songs bond saloon mates. Howling also functions as an early warning system. Packs communicate their strength and proximity to rival groups through strategic wails. The wolf expert Fred H. Harrington has studied the role of howling in territory maintenance. Over two years in the early 1970s, Harrington and his colleagues monitored the response rates of wolf packs in Minnesota's Superior National Forest. The scientists hiked into the woods, let loose with their best imitation wolf howl, and recorded the reaction. The wolves answered only 29 percent of the time. The low response rate underscored the major findings of the study. The researchers discovered that the Minnesota wolves howled from a position of strength. Alpha males howled more than their beta companions; larger packs howled more than smaller ones; and lone wolves

Jon Coleman

howled rarely, if ever. The presence of food and puppies also affected response rates. Faux howls elicited more replies from packs near kills and rendezvous sites (temporary summer headquarters of packs whose pups remain too young to travel). Howling, the scientists concluded, was a calculated behavior that balanced the risks of exposure to attack against the benefits of keeping rivals away from a critical, and relatively immobile, group resource. The haunting cries that have fired human imaginations throughout American history may actually be songs intended to protect infants and carcasses.[14]

Howls and scent posts guide dispersing wolves through social spaces where trespassers court death. Violence organizes wolf landscapes. Howling and scent posts work as signals because they inspire anxiety. Humans have cloaked these markers in the language of science and fantasy. But wolves neither perform a cost-benefit analysis nor express a dreamy longing when they howl. Like all forms of nonhuman communication, wolf signals are simple, clear, and rigid. Wolves communicate through basic dichotomies: present or absent, approach or retreat, fight or flee, trust or fear. They have no talent for nuance or novelty. Wolves' minimal vocabulary exposes the fallacy of some people's Doolittleian yearning to talk to the animals. If wolves could speak, they would say next to nothing.

Yet while the predators would kill the banter at a cocktail party, their signals and marks suit long-distance migration better than human language. Wolves' communication system minimizes confusion, distortion, and misinterpretation over distances. A scat in Manitoba confers the same type of information as a scat in Colorado. Dispersing wolves communicate with an ease dispersing people could never achieve. As we will see, language could be an irritant as well as a balm. When long-distance travelers entered a rival's territory in colonial New England, the resulting confusion, distortion, and misinterpretation damaged both humans and wolves.

Human language may dwarf animal communication in sophistication and ingenuity, but for nearly a century the level of discourse between

Algonquians and Europeans in southern New England rarely surpassed the eloquence of a yowl, chirp, or squeal. The 1620 fight between the Cape Cod Natives and the Plymouth colonists demonstrated the problems the humans faced. Unable to communicate with words, the combatants shrieked and blasted at one another. This episode was extraordinary for two reasons: first, it showed people communicating like beasts; and second, the incident took place ninety-six years after the Algonquians first spotted Europeans. Decades before the English dispersers beached their shallop on Cape Cod, Europeans and Natives traded along New England's coast. Brief and sporadic, these early encounters featured humans borrowing animal noises and gestures to communicate ideas their disparate languages could not. The Plymouth colonists entered an ongoing dialogue about territory and power conducted without words.

In 1524, Giovanni da Verrazzano, a Tuscan sailing for the French, entered Narragansett Bay. After spying fires on an island "about the bignesse of the Ilande of Rodes," Verrazzano weighed anchor, hoping to trade and replenish his supplies. Twenty small boats met the vessel. The Indians halted fifty paces from the larger craft and screamed at the crew. Verrazzano interpreted their "divers cries" as signs of wonder and gratitude: "They stayed and behelde the artificialnesse of our ship, our shape and apparel, they al made a loud showte together declaring that they rejoiced." The French sailors encouraged the Natives to move closer by mimicking their gestures. When they came within throwing distance, the sailors tossed "bells and glasses and many toys" to the canoes. The gifts broke the impasse. The Indians "lookte on them with laughing and came without feare aborde our ship."[15]

Verrazzano's sojourn with the Narragansett Bay Indians marked the first recorded encounter between Europeans and Algonquians in southern New England. It was a happy beginning. The humans exchanged gifts, traded information, and seemed genuinely amused by each other. The Natives shared their food and pointed out safe harbors. The Europeans welcomed Indian representatives aboard their ship. Both sides communicated through gestures and signs. Smiles and laughter were especially prominent signals. In his report to the French king, Verrazzano noted the "great pleasure" the Indians took "in beholding our apparel and tasting our meates." A "King" of a small island in the bay entertained the sailors by "drawing his bowe and running up and downe with his gentlemen." The Indians arrived at the ship with their faces "all bepainted with diverse colours," explaining through gestures "that it was a signe of joy." While Verrazzano emphasized the congenial aspects of his two-week visit, his report also captured an undercurrent of suspicion below the grins and chuckles. The Indian men kept their wives and daughters away from the ship. The women either stayed in the canoes or were dropped off on nearby islands while the men explored the French vessel. Despite "all the intreatie we could make, offering to give them divers things, we could never obtaine that they would suffer them to come aborde our ship." Verrazzano interpreted the Indians' smiles and laughter as symptoms of their innate jolliness. They were "the goodliest people" he had met. But their cheer had limits. The Indian men drew the line at sailors fraternizing with Indian women. Verrazzano and his crew enjoyed their visit because they never tested their hosts' good humor.[16]

Nobody growled during Verrazzano's stay. The absence of animal noises and gestures was due to the absence of discord. Over time, the meetings between European traders and Southern Algonquians became less pleasurable, and as the friction rose so did the human barking. The source of the tensions was hair. The Europeans wanted beaver hides, and the animal's coat grew long and luxurious in the North's cold winters. The traders refused to swap their best goods (guns) for the South's beavers. For the Southern Algonquians, the fur trade brought political dishonor as well as economic frustration. The Europeans not only withheld items the Southern Algonquians desired but also insulted them with low-quality gifts.

In 1606 Jean Biencourt de Poutrincourt led a French expedition to establish relations with the Indians living on the shores of Massachusetts Bay and Cape Cod. The mood had changed among the Southern Algonquians since Verrazzano's visit. Smiles and laughter gave way to anger and violence. The French stopped in Gloucester harbor, only to cast off in the face of a sizable group of riled-up warriors. Next they sailed to Monomy, an Algonquian village near Pleasant Bay. Again the presence of hundreds of Indians rattled Poutrincourt's nerves. He ordered a display of power. The French fired their guns, waved their sabers, and planted a man-sized wooden cross on the beach. The Indians responded by dismantling the village and moving back into the woods, an action Poutrincourt correctly read as a precursor to an attack. The French retreated to their ship, but five stragglers missed the boats. The Indians hit them at dawn, killing one and injuring three. A rescue party chased the attackers back. The French buried their comrade and left. Sailing out of the harbor, Poutrincourt watched the Indians dig up the body and tear down the cross. They also performed their own dominance display. The warriors turned their backs to the ship, bent over, and proceeded to take "sand in their two hands" and cast "it between their buttocks, yelping all the while like wolves."[17]

Conflict summoned the beast in the humans. At a loss for words, Europeans and Indians tried to communicate through a medley of dominance signals. The presence of so many warriors made Poutrincourt anxious. He fought fear with fear, directing his men to signal the group's martial and spiritual power. The Natives, however, did not prostrate themselves before the French cross or guns. They fled. An experienced trader, Poutrincourt recognized the retreat as a sign of aggression, not submission. He fled, leaving the unlucky dawdlers behind. The Indians displayed their strength by attacking the stragglers; the French displayed their strength by chasing the attackers back into the woods. The yelping warriors on the beach continued the exchange by defiling a cross, a corpse, and the Europeans' dignity.

By comparing the warriors to wolves, Poutrincourt added a final round to the dominance showdown. As the author of the report, he controlled the depiction of the Algonquians' behavior. He used print to insult those who had denigrated him in person, calling them beasts. European colonists loved this slur. They repeatedly contrasted their humanity with the Indians' animality. William Bradford wrote of "the

Jon Coleman

vast and unpeopled countries of America . . . where there are only savage and brutish men which range up and down, little otherwise than the wild beasts of the same." "They run up and down as roaring lions," wrote John Underhill, "compassing all corners of the country for a prey, seeking whom they might devour." Reversing the predator metaphor, William Hubbard described the final days of King Philip, the famous Wampanoag leader: "Philip, like a salvage and wild Beast, having been hunted by the English forces through the woods . . . at last was driven to his own den." Mary Rowlandson, a war captive of the Narragansetts, likened her kidnappers to "hell-hounds," "ravenous bears," and "wolves." Like Poutrincourt, these authors wielded animal metaphors like machetes. They cut their adversaries down to level of brutes while reassuring themselves of their superiority as humans.[18]

Europeans wrote endlessly about Indians. They filled sheaf after sheaf with portraits, ruminations, observations, compliments, and slanders. Arrogance runs through most of these texts, even the friendly ones. As Christians and civilized persons, the authors felt superior to pagan savages. Colonization, however, was more than a linguistic exercise. Ascendancy on the page did not mean power on the ground. Europeans and Indians struggled for supremacy. Words were critical factors in these contests, not as marks on paper but as wellsprings of confusion. Neither side could convince the other of its dominance through language, so they employed dominance signals and gestures. European observers interpreted the Natives' yelling and sand flinging as signs of their animal nature. But the enlightened Christians also used animal communication to get their ideas across. They may have resisted the urge to utter howls and growls themselves, but they commanded animals that had no such modesty.

European crews often sailed with very large, very mean dogs. Mastiffs were the choice of many expeditions, and the English displayed a special affinity for the breed. Today's mastiffs are jowly, barrel-chested giants. A full-grown male can weigh 230 pounds, the size of a linebacker in the National Football League. The animals accompanying the European traders may have looked different. In the seventeenth century, dogs were defined by their work, not their appearance. A bulldog, for example, was a dog that fought bulls. The size, shape, or color of the canine did not matter as long as he could sink his teeth into a bovine's nostrils and hang on. Mastiffs fought bulls as well as bears and lions, but their primary occupation was biting people. They labored as guard animals and dogs of war. In England nobles raised mastiffs to protect their estates, and Henry VIII presented four hundred mastiffs to the Spanish king Charles V to deploy in battle. In America the dogs served as emissaries of terror. "Good Mastiffs are singular defenses to plantations," wrote William Morrell, "in terrifying or pursuing the light-footed Natives."[19]

In 1620 two English ships under the command of Martin Pring sailed into Provincetown harbor near the tip of Cape Cod with two mastiffs on board. Financed by Bristol merchants, the Pring expedition sought a fortune not in precious minerals but rather in prized vegetables. The explorers constructed a shack to protect them at night and spent their days searching for and cutting sassafras. The plant gatherers soon drew the attention of the local Nausets. The two groups exchanged gifts, and a sailor entertained the Indians with a guitar. Long trading and get-to-know-you sessions, however, frustrated Pring, who wanted the sassafras harvested quickly. When the Nausets loitered at the shack, he unleashed Fool and Gallant, the expedition's mastiffs. Pring described the animals as "great and fearefull," and they were an awesome sight, especially Fool. He had acquired the habit of lugging around a half-pike in his mouth like a ham bone. "When we would be rid of the Savages company," Pring wrote, "wee would let loose the Mastives, and suddenly with out-cryes they would flee away."[20]

One afternoon, seventy Nauset warriors armed with bows and arrows approached the shack. Most of the Englishmen were hunting sassafras, and they had taken the dogs with them for protection in the woods. Inside, the four sentries guarding the barricado "utterly refused" when the Indians asked to "come downe unto them." Watching the action from the harbor, the shipmaster ordered a volley fired in

Jon Coleman

hopes of frightening the warriors away. But no one budged. A second volley thumped overhead. Then, off in the distance, the Indians spied the pickers running toward the beach, led by Fool. Confronted with "the Mastiff which they most feared," the Nausets "turned all to a jest and sport, and departed away in a friendly manner." A giant dog clutching a spear in his jaws could inspire more congeniality than a fusillade of cannon. At least, according to Martin Pring.[21]

English traders, explorers, and colonists tested Pring's claims and found them mostly true. George Waymouth sailed with two mastiffs in 1605. His Indian trading partners so feared the animals that they demanded the brutes be shackled "whensoever any of them came aboard us." The Indians may have never met canines as daunting as Waymouth's, but they were familiar with dogs. Both Indians and Europeans raised the animals. Indeed, dogs were the only domesticated beasts common to both cultures. Dogs, therefore, provided a cross-cultural bridge. Both sides understood the species' sounds and postures, and it appears that both sides exploited these signals. During a trading visit to Pemaquid, Waymouth encountered a Micmac war party that included "two hundred eighty three Savages, every one with his bow and arrows, with their dogges, and wolves which they keepe tame at command." The inclusion of canines in Waymouth's list of Micmac weaponry suggested that he saw the animals as markers of the Indians' power. Dogs and wolves added to the Micmacs' ferocity just as mastiffs enhanced the might of Waymouth's expedition.[22]

A question lingers after these dog tales: did the Indians truly fear mastiffs to the extent Europeans asserted? The Natives, after all, lived with dogs, and they tangled with dangerous beasts on a regular basis. Young warriors proved their valor by jumping on the backs of bears and drowning them as the animals swam to coastal islands in search of deer.[23] Would bear wrestlers fall apart at the sight of a large canine? The perspective of the sources makes gauging the Indians' reaction impossible. Pring and his associates did not conduct exit interviews with their foes after a tussle. They based their reports on appearance, not understanding. The reports tell us more about the Europeans' biases and assumptions than about the Indians' thoughts and feelings. Yet even benighted sources can be educational, and Pring's account demonstrates how animals could break through cross-cultural bewilderment. From Pring's vantage point, the mastiffs expressed his group's dominance more forcefully and clearly than words or gunpowder. Fool and Gallant created space when confusion threatened to explode into violence. Whether the Nausets truly feared the dogs or not, they retreated in the animals' presence, and that was all the cultural awareness Pring desired.

The European conquest of North America began with territorial contests more like animal brawls than human battles. European explorers and traders planted crosses and flags, claiming vast regions for God and country. But these were fantasy empires. The humans conducted the actual work of claiming territories through the exchange of gifts, smiles, shouts, insults, and cannon blasts. In southern New England, these early encounters ran the gamut from Verrazzano's pleasant sojourn to Poutrincourt's angry stopover. Whether happy or violent, these episodes shared a key ingredient: miscommunication. The humans' language foundered on its own complexity. During congenial encounters, grins and laughter muted linguistic differences. During conflicts, however, both the Indians and the Europeans expressed their dominance through noises and gestures rather than words. Their repertoire of signals included sounds (gunshots and howls), pantomimes (saber waving and sand flinging), and proxies (slobbery mastiffs and tame wolves). These noises and gestures carried a clear and simple message. In moments of crisis, howls and blasts exclaimed: "Keep away from us." Vocalizations and dominance displays inspired fear, and fear created space. Thus the humans established territories a wolf could appreciate.

But these territories satisfied neither the Algonquians nor the Europeans. Unlike wolves, the humans based their territoriality on social custom as well as physical dominance. Both Indians and Europeans shared an assumption that rules backed by forces, not sporadic out-

Jon Coleman

bursts of anxiety, should organize territories. As soon as the Europeans and the Indians learned more of each other's languages, they began contesting these rules. They battled for the right to determine whose customs would govern the demarcation, ownership, and transference of territory. These battles differed from wolves' territorial conflicts. Whereas wolves growled, howled, and squirted to keep rivals at a distance, people fought over a set of abstract principles as well as parcels of land. Laws, customary or codified, may seem a more dignified approach to territory maintenance, but the humans splattered as much blood over their laws as wolves spilled over their buffer zones. In fact, the violence of human territorial conflicts engulfed other species.

Wolves became casualties in a struggle beyond their comprehension. With time, colonists and Natives cobbled together enough linguistic commonality to converse, trade, argue, evangelize, and negotiate. Unlike the creatures they mimicked, human animals could expand their repertoire of signals with startling speed. Yet even as colonists and Indians talked more and howled less, wild animals continued to facilitate human communication in colonial New England. The region's humans transformed animals into cultural symbols, and no species better served the quarreling bipeds' need for shared symbols than wolves.

Perched atop the food chain, wolves competed with humans for space and calories. Although blessed with jaws that cracked moose femurs, wolves' weapon of choice in this competition was information. The fearsome predators used their keen senses to locate their enemies and run away from them. Wolves' shy behavior highlighted the critical role of communication in territorial creation and maintenance. In a perfect world, ecological rivals acquired living space through advertisement first, violence second. Colonial New England, however, was not a perfect world; it was a communication disaster. Wolves had enough sensibility to retreat from people, but they had no way of knowing that some humans' notion of territoriality extended to the exotic beasts they imported. When they sank their teeth into cows, goats, pigs, and sheep, wolves committed sins unimaginable to them.

Wolves attacked livestock and people attacked wolves with such enthusiasm in colonial New England that a battle to extinction would seem as predictable as the tides. Yet enamored as the English colonists were of the idea of predestination, the annihilation of wolves was not inevitable. All the region's top predators exhibited a talent for conflict avoidance. Wolves had coexisted with the Algonquians for centuries despite hunting the same prey. Even after the English invasion, wolves and colonists generated enough mutual trepidation to keep the species apart. Why, then, did humans and wolves fight, and what explained the conflict's savage violence?

The English colonists' concept of territory—the idea that land, animals, and even people were property—ambushed wolves. The English colonists marked their territory, but wolves could not imagine the significance of the notches and half-moons the humans cut into their beasts' ears to indicate their ownership. Humans killed wolves to safeguard animal property, but another territorial conflict endowed wolves' trespasses with a second, more sinister meaning. Wolves became symbolic participants in the humans' escalating conflict over land and political ascendancy. The English and the Algonquians used wolves to communicate. The Algonquians modeled their war cries on wolf howls; colonists and Natives employed wolves as metaphors in diplomatic negotiations; and finally, the severed heads of Indians and wolves decorated English towns, serving as the ultimate markers of territory. Wolves died by the thousands for their inability to understand humans any better than humans understood each other.

Notes

1. The yell in this episode comes from *A Relation or Journal of the Beginning and Proceedings of the English Plantation Settled at Plymouth in New England* (London, 1622), reprinted as *Mourt's Relation* (Boston: John Kimball Wiggin, 1859), 53. William Bradford also recorded the incident. Bradford, *Of Plymouth Plantation*, ed. Samuel Eliot Morison (New York: Knopf, 1952), 69–70.
2. Bradford, *Of Plymouth Plantation*, 70, 62.

Jon Coleman

3. For animal communication see W. E. Lanyon and W. N. Tavolga, eds., *Animal Sounds and Communication* (Washington DC: American Institute of Biological Sciences, 1960); and R. G. Busnel, *Acoustic Behavior of Animals* (New York: Elsevier, 1963). For a definition of territory see Edward O. Wilson, *Sociobiology: The New Synthesis*, 25th anniversary ed. (Cambridge: Harvard University Press, 2000), 256–76.

4. For a comparison of human and animal communication see Wilson, *Sociobiology*, 177. For the role of miscommunication in colonization see Stephen Greenblatt, ed., *New World Encounters* (Berkeley: University of California Press, 1993); Tzvetan Todorov, *The Conquest of America: The Question of the Other* (New York: Harper Perennial, 1982); and Jill Lepore, *The Name of War: King Philip's War and the Origins of American Identity* (New York: Knopf, 1998).

5. See L. David Mech and Luigi Boitani, eds., *Wolves, Behavior, Ecology, and Conservation* (Chicago: University of Chicago Press, 2003), 11–19; Nathaniel Valière et al., "Long-Distance Wolf Recolonization of France and Switzerland Inferred from Non-Invasive Genetic Sampling over a Period of Ten Years," *Animal Conservation* 6 (2003): 83–92; L. David Mech, Steven H. Fritts, and Douglas Wagner, "Minnesota Wolf Dispersal to Wisconsin and Michigan," *American Midland Naturalist* 133 (April 1995): 368–70; and L. David Mech, *The Wolf: The Ecology and Behavior of an Endangered Species* (Minneapolis: University of Minnesota Press, 1970), 13, 159.

6. Mech and Boitani, *Wolves*, 13–14. Mech's Minnesota wolf story is retold in Peter Steinhart, *The Company of Wolves* (New York: Vintage, 1995), 99. Scientists do know one of the prime benefits of dispersal: genetic diversity. See Pär K. Ingvarsson, "Conservation Biology: Lone Wolf to the Rescue," *Nature*, December 5, 2002, 472; and Diane K. Boyd et al., "Transboundary Movements of a Recolonizing Wolf Population in the Rocky Mountains," in *Ecology and Conservation of Wolves in a Changing World*, ed. L. N. Carbyn, S. H. Fritts, and D. R. Seip (Edmonton: Canadian Circumpolar Institute, 1995), 135–40.

7. For wolf eating habits see Mech, *The Wolf*, 170.

8. Paul Colinvaux, *Why Big Fierce Animals Are Rare: An Ecologist's Perspective* (Princeton NJ: Princeton University Press, 1978), 177.

9. Thomas J. Meier et al., "Pack Structure and the Genetic Relatedness among Wolf Packs in a Naturally-Regulated Population," in Carbyn, Fritts, and Seip, *Ecology and Conservation of Wolves*, 301.

10. See M. W. Fox, "A Comparative Study of the Development of Facial Expressions in Canids: Wolf, Coyote and Foxes," *Behaviour* 36 (1970): 49–73; Mech, *The Wolf*, 82; and Randall Lockwood, "Dominance in Wolves: Useful Construct or Bad Habit?" in *The Behavior and Ecology of Wolves: Proceedings of the Symposium on the Behavior and Ecology of Wolves*, ed. Erich Klinghammer (New York: Garland, 1979), 225–41.

11. Rolf O. Peterson et al., "Leadership Behavior in Relation to Dominance and Reproductive Status in Gray Wolves, Canis Lupus," *Canadian Journal of Zoology* 80.8 (2002): 1405–12.

12. G. B. Rabb, J. H. Woolpy, and B. E. Ginsburg, "Social Relationships in a Group of Captive Wolves," *American Zoology* 7 (1967): 305–11. See Mech, *The Wolf*, 114.

13. For scent marking see Mech, *The Wolf*, 93–95; and C. S. Asa and L. D. Mech, "A Review of the Sensory Organs in Wolves and Their Importance to Live History," in Carbyn, Fritts, and Seip, *Ecology and Conservation of Wolves*, 289–90.

14. For an overview of howling see John B. Theberge and J. Bruce Fall, "Howling as a Means of Communication in Timber Wolves," *American Zoologist* 7 (1967): 331–38; Z. J. Tooze, F. H. Harrington, and J. C. Fentress, "Individually Distinct Vocalizations in Timber Wolves, Canis Lupus," *Animal Behavior* 40 (1990): 723–30; Erich Klinghammer and Leslie Laidlaw, "Analysis of 23 Months of Daily Howl Records in a Captive Grey Wolf Pack," in Klinghammer, *Behavior and Ecology of Wolves*, 153–81; and Fred H. Harrington and L. David Mech, "Wolf Howling and Its Role in Territory Maintenance," *Behaviour* 68 (1979): 239–41.

15. "The Visit of Verrazzano," in *Documentary History of Rhode Island*, vol. 2, ed. Howard M. Chapin (Providence: Preston and Rounds, 1919), 1, 2.

16. "The Visit of Verrazzano," 3, 4.

17. For Poutrincourt's visit to southern New England see Samuel de Champlain, *The Works of Samuel de Champlain*, vol. 1, ed. H. P. Bigger (Toronto: Champlain Society, 1922; rpt. ed., Toronto: University of Toronto Press, 1971), 407–31; and Neal Salisbury, *Manitou and Providence: Indians, Europeans, and the Making of New England* (New York: Oxford University Press, 1982), 63–66. Salisbury describes the sand-flinging episode (66).

18. Bradford, *Of Plymouth Plantation*, 25; John Underhill, *Newes from America* (London, 1638; rpt. in *Collections of the Massachusetts Historical Society*, vol. 6, 3rd ser., Boston: American Stationers' Company, 1837), 15; William Hubbard, *The Present State of New England*, vol. 1, ed. Samuel D. Drake

(Roxbury MA: Eliot Woodward, 1865), 205; Amy Schrager Lang, ed., "A True History of the Captivity and Restoration of Mrs. Mary Rowlandson," in *Journeys in New Worlds: Early American Women's Narratives*, ed. William L. Andrews (Madison: University of Wisconsin Press, 1990), 33.

19. William Morrell, *New-England or A Briefe Narration of the Ayre, Earth, Water, Fish, and Fowles of That Country* (Boston: Club of Odd Volumes, 1895). For dogs as warriors see Marion Schwartz, *A History of Dogs in the Early Americas* (New Haven: Yale University Press, 1997), 162–63. For modern mastiffs see Dee Dee Andersson and Luana Luther, *The Mastiff: Aristocratic Guardian* (Phoenix: Doral, 1999). Harriet Ritvo discusses the shifting definitions of breeds in *The Animal Estate: The English and Other Creatures in the Victorian Age* (Cambridge: Harvard University Press, 1987).

20. George Parker Winship, ed., *Sailors Narratives of Voyages along the New England Coast, 1524–1624* (Boston: Houghton Mifflin, 1905), 61, 57.

21. Winship, *Sailors Narratives*, 61, 62.

22. Winship, *Sailors Narratives*, 122, 127.

23. See William Wood, *New England's Prospect* (London: Thomas Cotes, 1634), 20.

9

Hearing Wampum

THE SENSES, MEDIATION, AND THE LIMITS OF ANALOGY

Richard Cullen Rath

In 1756, Virginia citizens were feeling anxious and vulnerable to the threat of the Catawbas and Cherokees joining the French in the war against the English. Relations with the Indians were already strained on a number of fronts. Catawbas had successfully played internal colonial interests off against each other, so that Virginia had only recently been vying with South Carolina and North Carolina for their loyalties. Virginia had also skipped the unsuccessful Albany Conference, but it had been no more successful in its independent negotiations. With the French and Indian War looming large in their thoughts, the Virginians were now anxious to shore things up with the Catawbas and Cherokees, so they sent messengers to both nations to set up treaty councils.[1]

The Virginia delegation had prepared for Catawba protocols as best they could. They had difficulties obtaining enough wampum to make the treaty hold. They decided to try to be frugal with it in the hopes that more would be brought, but in the meantime they had to substitute other presents for the usual number of belts and strings of the patterned beads made from seashells.[2] Wampum was central to treaty negotiations. It made sounds significant and impressed those sounds upon the minds of those present.

For their part, the Virginians began the negotiations by reading their commissions aloud, thus verbally establishing their legitimacy to be speaking for the whole of the colony. Lieutenant Governor Robert Dinwiddie's instructions concerning his speech reveal interesting notions about Catawba and Virginian beliefs about where sounds came from. He told the commissioners, "(as the Custom of the Indians is) you are to tell them their Brother, the Governor of Virginia, is going to speak to them." The commissioners then read aloud a speech that Dinwiddie had written and marked it by presenting a belt of wampum to the Catawbas.[3] The idea that one person's or a group's speech could come from the mouth of another, a form of ventriloquism perhaps, is a sonic trait that distinguishes indigenous soundways from Anglo-American ones and seems always to have been marked by a present of wampum.

The speeches that followed were carefully framed, but in the discourse of the Catawbas rather than the Virginians. Treaty councils were gendered, age-differentiated spaces, with women and children generally excluded and elders speaking first, perhaps followed by some of the younger warriors. Each statement or proposition was accompanied by a string or belt of wampum, hides, or some other item presented to the listening party. This held for both sides of the negotiations, not just for the indigenous nations. When one side or the other had finished its speeches, the Virginians wrote down their records while the Catawbas entered the speeches into their official record with the wampum that the Virginians presented and a loud shout that the Virginians called the "Yo-Hah."

The sounds that the Virginians and Catawbas made and the wampum they presented each other were in some respects as important as their words. According to the published account of the treaty, the Virginians read Dinwiddie's commission out loud in English, a language that most of the Catawbas did not understand. William Giles, the party's interpreter, then reread the commission in Catawba. The commissioners then spoke a few words connecting the Virginians—and, they hoped, the Catawbas—to "our common Father, the Great King of England." Indigenous societies, often matrilineal with family relations where the father was like an uncle who visited the household rather than a patriarch, placed a different valence on that paternalistic statement than the British and colonial readership of the account would have. In an earlier treaty, when the English asked "How came you to call him [the French governor] Father?" the Oneida Indians replied, "For no other Reason . . . but because he calls us Children. These Names signify nothing." The commissioners then prepared the way for the governor's written speech to be read aloud by giving a belt of wampum. Heigler, king of the Catawbas, answered that the ears of the Catawbas were properly ready to hear what the governor had to say, now that the message of the presented belt had opened up their hearing. The Virginians read aloud the governor's speech in English, framing it as if it were the governor himself speaking, a practice accommodating Indian rhetorical styles. This was largely a vocal but nonverbal act to Catawba ears, so it was next translated into Catawba. Upon its completion, a belt of wampum "confirmed" it, the interpreter translated it, and the Catawbas "*gave the* YO-HAH," in the words of the Virginians' account. The commissioners went on to ask the Catawbas to commit warriors to the English cause. Perhaps to accommodate Indian customs of a person or people speaking through another, the Virginian account has them speak throughout as a single entity, "the commissioners" only once mentioning that the actual reader was the secretary. The Catawba king Heigler then repeated the speech to the interpreter to ensure its accuracy, taking it to council that evening along with an interpreter and promising an answer in the morning, at which time he agreed in substance and "*Gave a Belt of Wampum.*" After that, some warriors spoke out with no wampum presented, indicating that these were just opinions, not binding agreements. The commissioners then responded with a speech, duly translated, and the presentation of

Richard Cullen Rath

their presents, which served a different function altogether from the wampum. Finally, King Heigler verbally accepted the treaty for the Catawbas. The treaty was then read aloud and translated once more, then signed by the commissioners, King Heigler, and a number of the warriors, the Indians signing with marks. Upon this, the Catawba warriors once more confirmed its delivery with the "YO-HAH." Documents and signatures made it real for the colonists, wampum and vocalizations for the Catawbas, but the two sets of practices were not interchangeable.[4] For the Catawbas, wampum stamped the meaning of the speeches on the minds of the listeners, and the whole event was framed and validated by mutually understood nonverbal cries.

The Limits of Analogy

The treaty between the Catawbas and Virginia was typical of most such negotiations in early America. Native Americans throughout the Eastern Woodlands and Great Lakes regions used wampum as part of a multimedia method for capturing proposals, including their performative aspects, making them real, binding, and lasting and impressing them onto communities and nations both present and afar. Attending to the sonic dimension of wampum opens new avenues for discerning its uses. The analogies through which scholars have long understood wampum emphasize its visual aspects and tend to miss sonic ones.

The approach taken in this essay is not so much a replacement for such analogies as it is an extension, a way past the limits that by definition all analogies impose. One working proposition used here is that all media are multimedia, involving some kind of sensory transformation. Writing, for example, captures the sounds of the medium of speech and synesthetically renders them as silent, visible marks. In contrast, wampum binds a much larger portion of the soundscape to the realm of the visible and the haptic than can be captured by analogies with reading, print, or writing, which only transform the sounds of spoken language. The method of getting past the limits of analogy is, first, to consider mediation as process—or more simply, ways—

rather than making an analogy to a particular, perhaps more familiar, medium; and second, to use a working definition borrowed from Marshall McLuhan, that media are extensions of the senses, and that we must attend to how those extensions work.[5]

Framing media as sensory extensions allows us to think about mediation as two linked processes, representation and communication. Representation takes place at either end of mediation (expression and perception, respectively), connecting it to the senses. Representation is the means of mediation, while communication is the ostensible goal. Representation in this sense is a process for the most part internal to but not limited to individuals, a socially constructed representational self. For any notion of actual communication or shared meaning—what theorists call intersubjectivity—to be entertained, social and cultural relations need to be considered. The representational self is thus relational, contingent on others, and sometimes plural to perceivers. The role of the senses is to mediate between the representational self and the larger world, however that is assumed or constructed. One consequence of thinking about mediation this way is that there is no space outside the senses for anything resembling an unbiased understanding or an outside view of mediation, or for that matter, media.

If we entertain the idea that the senses are historically and culturally situated rather than universal facts of nature, then we need to find out, quite literally, how people made sense of their worlds in order to understand them on anything like their own terms. To do that well, we need to discover the sensory biases of our own time and read them against the biases of the past. While all the senses are integral to the understanding of media and mediation in any time and place, present-day scholarly attention has focused largely on visual mediation to the exclusion or attenuation of the other senses, even in situations described as multimedia.[6] One explanation is that writing, literacy, and print cumulatively shifted the ratio of the senses in literate people away from hearing and toward vision.[7] Thus, thinking about wampum in the visually oriented terms of books, literacy, or writing tends to focus discussion on the seen at the expense of other sensory channels.

Richard Cullen Rath

Much of the academic understanding of wampum comes from the use of visual analogies: wampum is "like money," "like writing," "like a gift," or "like a book," to name a few. This is a useful approach, rendering the unfamiliar in terms familiar to the assumed readers.

Analogies, however, take us only part of the way and in the process constrain the historical imaginary. Once a certain threshold is passed, the discussion becomes more and more about the thing wampum is like—money, gifts, writing, or book—than about wampum. Analogy tends to make the indigenous practices appear to be never more than a subset of the thing they are compared to, a pale shadow regardless of the capaciousness of the containing ideas.

Scholars from multiple disciplines and subfields have enriched our understanding of Native Americans' ways of representing themselves both to Europeans and to each other. In recent years, some have made a cogent case for the inclusion of indigenous systems of making durable symbols as writing. Others have resisted this notion, arguing that writing specifically excludes indigenous practices. They limit the meaning of writing to inscription that is linked to the sounds of speech. Depending on one's definition, then, Eastern Woodlands uses of wampum or Anishinaabe bark drawings might—or might not—be considered writing.[8]

Another, older debate lurks around the fringes of this one. The question of whether literate cultures think differently than those that are not has divided and rankled scholars since it was first posed in the late 1950s and early 1960s by scholars such as Marshall McLuhan, Walter Ong, Jack Goody, and Albert Lord.[9] The problem with the theory was that the old divide between civil and savage societies sneaked into the proceedings in the guise of literate and oral cultures. Implicit in the claims for indigenous people's symbol usage being considered as writing is that it then broaches the great literacy divide and places indigenous cultures on the same footing with the colonial invaders, at least cognitively, at least to adherents (conscious or otherwise) to the Great Divide theories of literacy.

Germaine Warkentin advocates considering durable symbol making not only in terms of writing but also in the terms of book history, and she argues that rather than containing indigenous practices within these subfields, we should broaden our notions of writing and the book to make them capacious enough to account for indigenous practices. This solves the cultural baggage problem by admitting indigenous people to the club and showing that they are in fact literate after all. It solves the question of cultural appropriation by expanding the Western notions of writing and the book rather than shoehorning wampum into them.[10] This approach is valuable, moving Western scholars' treatment of indigenous wampum use out of the categorical other and into consideration as a valid form of inscription. Using those visual media takes us further along in understanding wampum use, but it runs into the limits of books as an analogy, because books are, at least on their surface, silent, self-contained, and disembodied things that have been thoroughly decontextualized, and without these features, they somewhat cease to be books.[11] Wampum use, on the other hand, was embedded deeply in a different set of social and cultural protocols that never come up in the study of books or literacy.

Anthropologist Frank Salomon has made the case for graphic pluralism, the idea that different kinds of writing or inscription can coexist within the same society and do their work of symbolic processing in different ways, yet at the same time.[12] Where, then, does graphism end? Galen Brokaw advocates dispensing with graphism altogether and replacing it with the more generic idea of media—in general, if not specifics, the approach I take in this essay. Heidi Bohaker marks the category of graphic pluralism as too narrow to account for all the significant phenomena she finds for Anishinaabe visual representation. She calls for new ways of understanding that challenge Western definitions and categories.[13] Margaret Bender points to a compromise position by pointing out the problem with making Western categories (which in this case are all rooted in analogies) more inclusive:

> If we expand our focus to include material symbols of identity as Heidi Bohaker suggests . . . through her inclusion of symbolic

Richard Cullen Rath

elements of dress (e.g., furs used to express clan identity), then is there any limit to the graphic? That is, is any object deliberately created, manipulated, or modified to serve as a sign, a graph? . . . While we probably do not want to expand our definition of the graphic so broadly that it becomes synonymous with the whole orbit of signs, pushing at the boundaries of the graphic may be helpful in forcing us to think through how graphic systems and texts are and are not like other signs.[14]

Once the category—whether graphism, inscription, the book, or writing—is sufficiently broadened, it dissolves into meaninglessness.

In effect, the analogy of writing that lies at the core of graphism has subtly colonized the conversation. The discussion shifted from Native Americans' ways of expressing themselves—mediation—to what the definition of graphism is and how useful it remains when extended to take into account indigenous practices. The problem will be perhaps clearer if the terms are reversed and writing or reading is treated as being like wampum: "Well yes, but . . ."

Adopting analogies such as currency, writing, books, reading, inscription, or graphism—all of which in their particulars Bohaker correctly marks as Western categories—focuses attention almost solely on the visual at the expense of other sensory modalities, particularly hearing. This ocularcentrism is at least partially the result of our own text-based, vision-oriented habits as literate scholars and writers in the modern academy. It extends even into considerations of sonic practices. When noticed at all, consideration of sound is limited to orality, the linguistic part of the soundscape: just the part reducible to the visual medium of writing. Thus with reading wampum, or treating it like inscription of a book, connections to spoken language might be noticed, but non-verbal vocalizations and non-vocal sounds are not.[15] But analogies can be transcended, and ocularcentrism is a tendency, not a sentence, one that can be recognized and accounted for with some attention to how media and mediation work.

"Media pluralism" might be a more useful term than "graphic pluralism," as mediation takes place in every society without succumbing to the dissolution of meaning Bender signals. This also opens up consideration of the senses as factors in shaping media, providing an escape from ocularcentrism with a little work. Paying attention to the senses, particularly hearing in addition to vision, rewards us with a "thicker," context-specific way of understanding what people meant and did when they used wampum in early America. While listening to wampum use does not reveal the indigenous emic with no intervening mediation, it does take us a little further by giving us another tool with which to shuttle back and forth between emic and etic approaches. Let me reiterate, I am not rejecting the use of analogy—in fact, thinking about wampum and sound opens up some new possibilities in that regard—just suggesting a way to further our understanding that provides the woof to the visual analogy's warp.

Hearing Wampum

First Nations people used sounds to imbue things with meanings. The place where this becomes most apparent is in the uses of wampum in treaty negotiations. There, the punctuation of a speech with a string or a belt of wampum rendered the spoken words effective. In the terminology of linguist J. L. Austin's seminal work, *How to Do Things with Words*, the wampum provides the speech act with its "perlocutionary force," its performativity.[16] In turn, the speech entered into the wampum, leaving traces of its meaning. The vocal but nonverbal communal shout then fixed or set the speech belts, as they were often called, demonstrating that the message had been received. By getting beneath the analogy of reading wampum, we can arrive at a clearer understanding not of an essential meaning but of what wampum meant to Native Americans on their terms at particular historical moments. Perhaps as importantly, by considering wampum in its full sensory context and as one part of a complex system of mediation, we can recover a bit more of that meaning than otherwise possible from considering wampum alone, visible and silent.

We need to interrogate the historical accounts of wampum use that

Richard Cullen Rath

have come down to us in texts (setting aside indigenous oral histories just for the moment). After all, they are the work of biased white participant-observers more interested in getting a particular job done than in any modern sense of ethnographic accuracy. It was precisely the jobs they needed to do that give us some confidence in the reports. While they may not have been able to write from a Native American perspective, an approximate understanding of that perspective was necessary for the business at hand to be transacted, whether Jesuit conversions or French, English, or Dutch treaty making. Competing interests sometimes recorded the speeches and wampum exchange with different words attributed to the speakers, as in the example of the Delaware Indian Teedyuscung in the Easton, Pennsylvania, treaty negotiations of 1756, confounding any objective attempt to reconstruct exactly what was said. James Merrell, reviewing inconsistencies in reports of Teedyuscung's speech, concludes that if we attend to what was shared across all the documents, or if we are able to figure out the biases of a particular amanuensis or two and factor that in (or out), then we can still learn much from these flawed accounts once we give up demands for facsimile.[17]

Although not the focus of Merrell's article, much of what was consistent among the accounts was the frame of the negotiations, for to get that wrong would signal to a knowledgeable colonial reader as well as to the indigenous party that the author did not know how such negotiations worked. The exchange of wampum pegged to speech acts, the shout of the gathered Indians when they agreed to something, the turn taking: each of these tells us something about the negotiations as a whole and wampum in particular.

In order for treaties in the vast Eastern Woodlands region to be binding, negotiations had to follow indigenous people's protocols to some degree. Broad congruences existed between how different Indians perceived wampum. Otherwise, it would not function as a mediating device between nations with different languages and cultural systems. It had to be capable of crossing cultural and linguistic boundaries. Although an agreement could be made in multiple languages, the tracks of its sounds were stored as an underlying meaning that was not constrained by language, like pictographic or logographic writing. The attention to indigenous protocols shifted with the balance of power relations between colonists and Indians. The treaty negotiations at the Albany Congress of 1754 provide a representative example. The colonists' speech to the Six Nations was divided into short sections. At the end of each section, looking much like a signature, was reference to a string or belt of wampum being presented. To resemble Iroquois ways, there needed first to be a ritual address ("brethren . . ."), then a section of a speech given, a gift presented, and a loud, tuneful shout on the part of the Indians, which indicated that the proposal was received for consideration.

According to Peter Wraxall, a New York colonial Indian agent who participated in the Albany Congress, all of this was necessary to negotiate with the Six Nations without being "obnoxious" to them. Wraxall does not even say it was a satisfactory way, perhaps indicating that he and the colonists felt as if they did not quite understand everything themselves. Since the negotiations were between state entities rather than simply within them, this performative system of mediation—of associating words with things to invest them with meaning—must have been spread across all the nations, including Native ones, who maintained diplomatic relations with the Iroquois, not just the Iroquois and the English or the French.[18]

The shout was more than symbol or ritual. Sounds sealed proposals and treaties, making them real, whether between Indian nations or between Indians and colonists. First Nations people structured treaty councils in part through vocal but nonverbal responses to speeches. The shout, which, according to Jonathan Carver, "they repeat at the end of almost every period, is by uttering a kind of forcible aspiration, which sounds like an union of the letter OAH." Not coincidentally, "almost every period" would be an apt description for when wampum was presented too. Eighteenth-century Virginians referred to the shout without comment as "the Indians gave the Yo-Hah," indicating it was something known to their audience and without need of explanation.[19]

Richard Cullen Rath

Perhaps the best description of the shout is Conrad Weiser's 1744 account of treaty making between the English and the Six Nations:

> When they make treaties with whites, the wholle council and all the warriors perform the "shout of approbation," the "Io—hau." It is performed in the following manner: The Speaker, after a Pause, in a slow tone pronounces the U—huy; all the other Sachems in perfect Silence: So soon as he stops, they all with one Voice, in exact Time, begin one general Io' raising and falling there Voices as the Arch of a Circle, and then raise it as high as the first, and stop at the Height at once, in exact Time; and if it is of great Consequence, the Speaker gives the U—huy thrice, and they make the Shout as often. It is usual, when the white People speak to them, as they give a belt or string of Wampum, for the Interpreter to begin the U—huy, and the Indians to make the Shout.[20]

As late as 1780, a Hessian chaplain noted that Creeks accepted a speech by a British colonel for consideration, "as indicated by their mutual Ha!" These vocalizations were not a rhythmic mnemonic device, as was often the case with African American antiphony. Nor were they a repetition, as in white hymnal antiphony. Instead, when combined with the wampum, they served as a communal embodiment of the speech. In effect, Indian antiphony meant that the words were heard and spoken by the whole community. Communal speaking was not merely a metaphor either, as witnessed by a Naudowessie sachem who began a speech by claiming that "I am now about to speak to you with the mouths of these, my brothers, chiefs of the eight bands of the powerful nation of the Naudowessies."[21]

The vocal, nonverbal sound of the shout served as a liminal space marking passage between the proposing of it and its consideration in council. Only attention to mediation, rather than just media, brings this out. The fact that the shout was nonlinguistic was crucial. It bridged communication gaps in situations where all but interpreters (though sometimes not even them) found some part of the proceedings unintelligible. Coming only after translation, it was a way of acknowledging across languages and cultures that the other party had been heard and understood.

Chanting and singing provided another arena linked to wampum use where things that were heard beyond the speech sounds representable in writing played an important cross-cultural and international role, both among Indian nations and between Indians and Europeans.[22] Treaties and alliances had a sonic performative element, literally chanted into being—enchanted. In 1685, at a council in Albany among Virginia, New York, and the Five Nations, the Mohawks responded to Virginia's complaints that the Iroquois had not kept up their part of the treaty. In his response to the Virginians, a Mohawk orator "sang all the Covenant Chain over," thus both chanting it back into being and renewing it. He then concluded with a song "by way of Admonition to the Onnondagas, Cayugas and Oneydoes, and concluded all with a Song to the Virginia Indians."[23] In part, the song's melody and rhythm may have served as a mnemonic device, but in cultures where identities were sung, the chanting had a much more immediate and active role too, in this case making the covenant chain present at the council.[24]

Sound and wampum could be used in contexts other than treaty councils as well. The Haudenosaunees sang and presented wampum, which the French called "porcelain beads," at the arrival of the Jesuits Joseph Chaumonot and Claude Dablon at the Onondagas' main town in 1655. In response to a half-hour speech by one of the missionaries,

The Chief began the song of response; and all commenced to sing, in wondrous harmony, in a manner somewhat resembling our plain-chant. The first song said that it would take all the rest of the day to thank the Father for so good a speech as he had made them. The second was to congratulate him upon his journey and his arrival. They sang a third time to light him a fire, that he might take possession of it. The fourth song made us all rela-

Richard Cullen Rath

tives and brothers; the fifth hurled the hatchet into the deepest abyss, in order that peace might reign in all these countries; and the sixth was designed to make the French masters of the river Ontiahantagué. At this point the Captain invited the salmon, brill, and other fish, to leap into our nets, and to fill that river for our service only. He told them they should consider themselves fortunate to end their lives so honorably; named all the fishes of that river, down to the smallest, making a humorous address to each kind; and added a thousand things besides, which excited laughter in all those present. The seventh song pleased us still more, its purpose being to open their hearts, and let us read their joy at our coming. At the close of their songs, they made us a present of two thousand porcelain beads.

While this was not a treaty in European terms, the Onondagas treated it in much the same way as other alliances. To them, spiritual and earthly politics were not necessarily distinguishable, and both were mediated through song.[25] The visual medium, the porcelain beads (wampum), came last, playing a crucial role in making sounds hold and in rendering linguistic symbols durable and effective.

The "enchantment" of treaties, whether through singing or the Yo-Hah, played a part in making agreements count and in making them present. "Present" is an interesting word, with odd interlocking fields of meaning that usually pass unnoticed. A present, as in a gift, takes its meaning through the fact that it has been or will be presented to someone or some group or community. And to "present" something (the verb) is to make it present to the recipient. While there is a massive literature on "the gift," colonial negotiators were as or more likely to call them presents than gifts.[26] Not to imply that all the analysis of gifts is off target in particular, but the absence of the present seems to be something worth considering. The present, usually treated as a gift in the anthropological sense and lumped together with wampum and pelts, was actually a separate but related part of treaty negotiations, taking place near the end of the proceedings. It served as a tribute, a sign of respect, or a cost of keeping the Indians on the side of the colonists. The importance of the presents grew in the settler accounts of treaty making over the eighteenth century as Indian-colonist power relations shifted in favor of the colonists and indigenous people grew more dependent on English or French manufactured goods.

In the discourse of Indian treaty protocols, the distinction between presents and wampum could be used to make pointed statements. In 1693 negotiations at Albany, the Oneidas made a series of proposals alleging their steadfast support of the covenant chain and the English cause against the French and asking New York's and Pennsylvania's governor, Colonel Benjamin Fletcher, where English support was. The Oneidas "made the Governor a considerable Present of Furs, to shew their Respect to his Person; but they did not give one Belt to confirm any one Article; so that the whole of it is, according to their Stile, only argumentative."[27] This also tells us that the speech acts *accompanied* by wampum were serious, if not yet binding, proposals: to rectify past damages, sort out present power relations, and prescriptively map the future of those relations.

Nonetheless, wampum was presented even though it was not a present per se. It was this presenting that tied together words, threats, and promises—in short, power relations—with wampum. For many First Nations people besides the Iroquois, a relationship of identity existed between speech acts (the content of treaties, for example) and wampum. The presenting of it did not so much stand for the words or sentences; it made their traces present—by presenting it—in the wampum. And when speech, wampum, and nonverbal vocalizations went together, speech took on its performative aspects, the enactment of all three together making the propositions hold. Wampum embodied the speech acts and nonverbal vocalizations of treaty proposals as visible tracks, the patterns of the shells. Wraxall quotes the Mohawks as saying, "By this belt we desire you to consider what we have said, and by the same we inform you that the Five Nations have something to say to you."[28] A string of wampum and a sentence in isolation were two different things. Only when they were put together in the proper

Richard Cullen Rath

Fig. 9.1. Naudowessie sachem holding a belt of wampum and speaking to Anishinaabe neighbors, represented as a deer. Carver used this as a pass to travel through Anishinaabe lands. Jonathan Carver Journal, Add. 8950 folio 169, British Library. © British Library Board. Used by permission.

way along with the necessary shout in a public setting did they come into a relationship of identity that made the treaty real and present. Wampum belts and strings were thus interdependent media—the visible forms in which sonic utterances left their traces—as well as messages. As such, the intent was more immediate than would be captured by calling it "representation," another term, like "gift," with an immense body of writing dedicated to it.[29]

Taking this approach, strung or belted wampum, as well as pelts, were like the tracks of a speech event, with the paths of those tracks as well as the content of the speech embodied in the strings and belts. Take, for example, a drawing that served Carver as a passport up the Chippeway River to Lake Superior (fig. 9.1). It shows a Naudowessie sachem giving a speech and a belt of wampum to an Anishinaabe sachem (represented as a deer) asking for safe passage from all Anishinaabeg along the river. The speech sounds of both parties were represented as tracks from the mouth of each to the ears of the other. Both the drawing and the wampum were the manifestations of those tracks, the visible effects of the speech sounds. In this case, the drawing communicated the message and the power relations while the wampum indicated that it was binding. The Jesuit Joseph-François Lafitau claimed that Indians could recognize ethnicities, even particular people, by their tracks.[30] It is likely that wampum marked similar differences, with belts and strings having slightly variant designs and styles from one nation to another, although in the Carver drawing the picture does at least some of that work.

The identities expressed in the Anishinaabe drawing are good examples of the fluidity of the notion of representational selves discussed above. In the drawing, sounds of a voice did not necessarily belong to the speaker. Groups could speak as an aggregate turned into an individual, like the deer. In the Catawba treaty, one individual could use another's voice without being present, and the aggregate "the commissioners" could be used to represent the actual speaking of the secretary, who was himself not one of the two people who were members of the group of commissioners. Messengers were said to be the sender speaking. Groups, aggregates, and individuals were mixed together in a meaningful, complex way in indigenous practices, and parts of that discourse seeped into the communications of the settlers as well.

The emphasis in the Carver drawing is on the relations as much as the people, places, and things, and there is a sense of action and movement. Many other examples of both voice tracks and animal and human tracks appear in Indian creative expression, from rock art to ledger drawings, that visually illustrate the tracking of speech as well as sounds from a much wider scope than could be expressed through writing. Visually, the tracks, whether on the ground or on a page, take a static medium and put it into narrative form, moving through time. They could be seen and felt as a story and a set of relations in the held belt and the drawing rather than as a speech being read.

Colonial accounts taken individually often missed the performative aspects of wampum use. Dutch accounts tended to focus on wampum as currency. When a band of Delaware Indians returned various stolen shirts and blankets to New Amsterdam city officials in 1656, the officials responded with a speech through an interpreter, saying that

Richard Cullen Rath

Tachpausan, the Indians' sachem, had been wise to return the goods, "for else it might create disharmony and quarrels." In order for the words to have meaning, the New Amsterdam officials sent the Indian messengers back to Tachpausan bearing "a pound of powder" for him that was intended as "a *sign* [my emphasis] of our good heart." The Dutch treated it as a sign, with a signifier (the powder) and a signified (the speech). To the Indians this would not fully make sense, for powder was meant to be used up, and the tracks of the speech event could not be seen. Instead it served as a gift given in exchange.[31]

How was wampum used, particularly in relation to sound? Cadwallader Colden described wampum and its use in treaties this way: "With this [wampum beads], put upon strings, they make these Belts, which they give in all their Treaties, as signs of Confirmation, to remain with the other Party. The Wampum is of two sorts, viz. White and Black; the Black is the rarest, and most valuable. By a regular mixing of the Black and White they distinguish their Belts with various Figures, which they often suit to the Occasion of making use of them." While Colden understood enough for an outsider, and elsewhere in the same book showed a more nuanced understanding, here his treatment of wampum as a sign was perhaps an imposition.

The French might have had a better understanding of wampum than the Dutch and English. In 1684 a French agent of Governor de La Barre spoke to Garangula, an Onondaga orator. De La Barre threatened to declare war against the Iroquois. He punctuated each statement of his threat with wampum belts and the words "*This Belt Confirms my Words.*" In turn, Garangula responded to de La Barre that the Five Nations were not averse to war with France, marking his paragraphs with "*This Belt preserves my Words.*" At the end of his reply, he provided a final belt that "*preserves . . . the Authority which the Five Nations have given me*" from speeches at a preparatory council among Iroquois leaders.[32] Regardless of the lacunae in understanding, a better provisional understanding of wampum use is still possible by reading across many sources and listening for indigenous accounts in the way Merrell prescribed for Teedyuscung's speech.

George Washington, on a trip to the Ohio River in 1754, showed a sharp understanding of the sonic dimension of wampum belts when he called them "speech-belts." A Shannoah (Shawnee) sachem, Half King, offered a French speech belt to him, along with other strings and belts, if only he would wait a day. Washington agreed because he "knew that returning of Wampum was the abolishing of Agreements; and giving this up, was shaking off all Dependence upon the French."[33] Although he already knew the content of the speech that would be given, he waited for the giving of it out loud in council, accompanied by the appropriate shouts, strings, and speech belts. Once the tracks of the speech were left and the French speech, in the form of the speech belt, was turned over, the agreement of Shawnee allegiance to the British became real.

Washington felt it was worth his wait to ensure this accountability. Speaking in a public setting without laying down pelts or belts was the equivalent of trackless speech, the meaning of which would not hold. Three Oneida sachems excused their public slander of the New York governor Edmund Andros during treaty negotiations in 1679 by saying that "it was said after your Answer, and without laying down either Bever or any Belt or Wampum, as we always do when we make Propositions; Therefore we desire that if it be noted, it may be blotted out, and not made known to Corlaer [the governor]; for we hold firmly to our Covenant, as we said in our Propositions." As mentioned above, the Oneidas a few years later made a present of furs to the governor but presented no wampum, indicating that nothing being said or done was binding.[34]

Often, the speeches of Native American orators were quoted directly, as when Colden provided the words of the Mohawk orator, Odianne, who referred to a belt of wampum as a "Remembrancer" that would "Stamp Understanding" into its recipients, the other Iroquois, in a council with the English colonists at Albany in 1684.[35] Here was a perfect example of perlocutionary force and a much more immediate process than could be conveyed by analogies to reading or signification.

Richard Cullen Rath

Understanding the role of wampum as a remembrancer that stamps understanding requires a rethinking of the relationship of sound to preservation held by many media scholars. Writing, in this view, extends memory in time, overcoming the ephemerality of sound, which is susceptible to the introduction of errors, as shown in the children's game of telephone, where a message is whispered from child to child around the room, with the end result often quite different from the start. The analogy is flawed, however, in that it likens the privacy of reading silently to oneself to the community relying on oral histories. Knowledge transmission in Native American oral cultures took place not in this individualistic way but communally. No doubt rhyming and metric patterns, repetition, and other strategies help individuals remember, but the individualistic nature of literary culture and the modern private act of reading should not blind us to the communal context of Native American remembering. As shown here, though, that idea of sound as evanescent is the product of a literate, visual set of mind that mistakenly applies a model of decontextualized information transmission as it occurs in reading, print, and written media to indigenous practices of rendering memory durable using hearing and sound as the representational and communicative paths of mediation.

According to Weiser, after a Haudenosaunee council had deliberated a proposed treaty and reached consensus, its "resolution is imprinted in the Memory of the One chosen from among them, of great Reputation and Elocution, who is appointed to speak in Publick. He is assisted by a Prompter, who puts him in mind of anything he forgets." Colden reported a similar Iroquois method in 1727:

They commonly repeat over all that has been said to them, before they return any Answer, and one may be surprized at the Exactness of these Repetitions. They take the following Method to assist their Memories: The Sachem, who presides at these Conferences, has a Bundle of small Sticks in his Hand; as soon as the Speaker has finished any one Article of his Speech, this Sachem gives a Stick to another Sachem, who is particularly to

R. West inv.   *Grignion sculp.*

The Indians giving a Talk to Colonel Bouquet in a Conference at a Council Fire, near his Camp on the Banks of Muskingum in North America, in Octr 1764.

Fig. 9.2. The Indians giving a talk to Colonel Bouquet in a conference at a council fire near his camp on the banks of the Muskingum in North America in October 1764. A warrior seated next to the wampum-holding orator is smoking a calumet, an improbable happening during the speech. Perhaps Grignion or West, not realizing the significance of the prompter's stick in the hands of an elder, changed it into a pipe to fit his own expectations. Engraving by Charles Grignion of a drawing made by Benjamin West, first published in William Smith and Henry Bouquet, *An Historical Account of the Expedition against the Ohio Indians in the Year MDCCLIV under the Command of Henry Bouquet* (Philadelphia: Bradford, 1765). Image courtesy of the Library of Congress.

remember that Article; and so when another Article is finished, he gives a Stick to another to take Care of that other, and so on. In like Manner when the Speaker answers, each of these has the particular Care of the Answer resolved on to each Article, and prompts the Orator, when his Memory fails him, in the Article committed to his Charge.

This was probably the same method used by the Esopus Indian sachems in complaining to the Dutch in 1659. They "showed 17 staves of wood, with which they signified, that our people had at different places wrongfully beaten and injured their tribe." Communal memorization was still practiced as late as the Revolution on Long Island. Phillipp Waldeck, a Hessian chaplain, described the Long Island Indians' way of keeping track of laws and customs: "Nothing is recorded in writing. When a new law is decreed, the eldest of each family sit together as a court. To each is told what he is to remember, he dare not forget it for fear of death."[36]

Such communal systems of memory had a built-in accountability system of redundancy that made them robust through time in ways that get literally "over-looked" when we focus only on the visual aspects of mediation. Communal memory operated then and now on principles more similar to today's World Wide Web than to books or inscription. I am not making a case for the Internet as a better analogy, just one that takes us to a different place than print and writing. A body of knowledge on the web can comprise the "memories" of many different servers. These servers, like individual humans, are "alive" only as long as they have been paid for and kept up—otherwise their contents are gone. Within a server, or server farm, a RAID array, or more recently, a cloud, there might be overlapping, redundant representations of the data. A network of this type depends on redundant, distributed knowledge, much like the sound-based ones described above. The changing of memories to suit current needs is often seen as a flaw in "oral" cultures. On the web and in communal memorization, however, "continuously updatable content" is thought of as a feature rather than a weakness, and—barring massive destruction—is an option, not a foregone conclusion. And if printed and written texts were really definitive storehouses of memory incorruptible by time, historians would certainly be out of business by now.

These distributed networks can survive the loss of any single server or person, recovering data or memories from the built-in redundancy. In fact, the Internet architecture was a Defense Department project designed to withstand catastrophic loss on a scale few other than Native Americans have survived. In the case of so-called cloud storage, different overlapping sets of data are held on many separate servers. The loss of even multiple servers is self-healing up to a point with minimal to no loss of data. In the First Nations example on Long Island, the whole family was responsible for one proposition, so the loss of any member, or even several, would not corrupt the memory. This communal model of memorization is different from the individualistic mnemonic devices to which oral memory is usually attributed.

Catastrophic change, on a scale that would have disrupted the transmission of knowledge even in any literate society, did take its toll on Indian knowledge and memory. The ravages of constant war and disease strained their ways of using sound to mark and preserve important narratives, ultimately breaking them in many instances, which led to havoc and loss when it came to dealing with land-hungry, ever-growing European American settlers. When the majority of a population died young, no group could converge upon the meanings and narratives and agreements tracked in a belt of wampum. They were lost, having lost, as it were, their communal memory as a result of the breakdown in the redundancy and robustness that made a self-healing network. In fact, the same broad process of catastrophic change wiped out the histories of one *literate* Native American people, the Aztecs, who lost not just a huge proportion of their population but their written records to the Spanish colonial onslaught. But we must not exaggerate this process, for while it happened in a most destructive way, other agreements that were preserved were run over roughshod by whites once a trend toward dispossession was established. In fact, some

Richard Cullen Rath

of the wampum belts—and their meanings—remain with Indian nations, their stories intact to this day. For example, the U.S. government still honors the treaty of Canandaigua, made and recorded in wampum in 1794, by distributing bolts of cloth to the Six Nations each year.[37] The Haudenosaunee (Iroquois) marked the four hundredth anniversary of an agreement made with the Dutch in 1613 with a reenactment of the meaning of the Two-Row Wampum, which says that the Dutch and the Haudenosaunee will each travel in the same stream but in different canoes, indicating that they will live together but keep separate ways. The written record has been lost, but a fair amount of circumstantial evidence points toward an agreement having been made between the two nations at about that time. In 1968, a document purporting to be the 1613 treaty surfaced, but it is probably a forgery, or less likely, an untrue copy. Western scholars who argued that the treaty was forged have undertaken a public campaign to undermine the State of New York's and the Onondaga Nation's efforts to celebrate the agreement, which the Onondagas keep alive with the Two-Row Wampum that is in their possession. The critics, with support from Dutch scholars, argue that since the treaty has been forged, the whole celebration of the agreement is a sham, completely ignoring the meaning carried in the wampum. This small group of scholars implies that if the document is forged then the oral history is false, as if the latter, which long precedes the forgery, is dependent on the former, even though the two are unrelated. If the metric is certainty about a Western treaty being recorded, then the historians have a point, but if we go instead with the probability that the Haudenosaunee and the Dutch made an agreement about four hundred years ago, then the argument seems to go to the Onondagas, who say they do not rely on the written record but on the meaning of the wampum for their historical memory. In this case, in other words, the wampum is the more reliable source than the document, a fact that the scholarly critics have roundly ignored in their attacks.[38]

The decimation of Indian populations through disease and escalating warfare associated with European conquest ultimately overwhelmed many communal systems of memory. Scaticoke Indians lamented the difficulties of staying "true and faithfull to the thing [an old belt of wampum denoting territorial boundaries]" in light of "our ancient people being almost all dead."[39] In practical terms, the failure of communal memory led to more land loss. This failure was not intrinsic to the medium, though. It was the result of the tremendous trauma incurred upon audible ways of remembering through the loss of vast proportions of the remembering population.

Considering wampum as the visible inscription of signs or a silent indexical form of book, with images pointing to things in the world but not able to store ideas as words and language, hinders understanding of wampum as it was actually embedded in the multiple indigenous ways of robustly mediating ideas through time. The analogies, to the extent they become an overarching way to understand wampum, serve to occlude the durability of knowledge passed on through it and communal memory. It is better to use a generic, non-culturally specific category such as mediation, taking into account the full sensorium of ourselves, indigenous people, and the colonists as best as possible, always keeping in mind the certainty only of our own uncertainty in interpreting across cultures and time.

Conclusion

The Catawba treaty, Carver's pass to travel through Anishinaabe territory, and the other examples used here underscore the differences between the relation of writing and print to sound and that of wampum to sound. Alphabetic writing and print point specifically and only to the sounds of the language of the text. While nonlinguistic sounds can be represented alphabetically, as I have been doing in this essay, they are filtered through writing and print's limitation to the linguistic. In contrast, wampum referenced a wider soundscape, directly triggering the Yo-Hah in a successful negotiation and thereafter implying it and calling for it, incorporating pitch characteristics (the circular rising and falling of the Yo-Hah, for example), and conveying multiple simultaneous contexts and relations (the Naudowessie sachem both

Richard Cullen Rath

speaking to and listening to the Deer clan in the presence of the belt of wampum the sachem held). Wampum impressed a whole scene and set of relations, marked by both linguistic and nonlinguistic sounds. It indexed the scene and relations directly, as a gestalt, with each belt representing a whole proposition, language, sounds, and power relations at once. In contrast, print and writing established the scene and relations by linguistic means. For example, the scenes at the Catawba treaty had to be broken down analytically to describe them in this essay, while a surviving belt would evoke the whole scene at once.

Wampum stands in a different relation to sound than anglophone print and writing do, and even the most capacious understanding of graphism, inscription, writing, books, or literacy cannot transcend its visual bias to account for these interrelated mediations that emerge once the soundscape of wampum use is taken into consideration. Crucially, that soundscape must be wider than the habitual linguistically circumscribed orality. Then, when the senses are attended to and a static medium is replaced by the process of mediation, wampum can be properly situated as one part in the complex multimedia system of performative propositions and vocalizations that constituted international relations and treaty making in early America for Europeans as well as Indians.

Wampum served other purposes than treaty making and drew on all the senses, not only sound and hearing. Alliances of war and peace were made and broken with wampum and song, both of which could cross linguistic boundaries more easily than speeches. I have emphasized sound to focus on what are called the distal senses, which, able to operate at a distance, tend to facilitate public interactions. The proximal senses—touch, taste, and smell—may have played a further role in the process of mediation yet to be explored. Wampum use had a definite haptic element, with the holding and passing of the belt a crucial component of the process. Food and drink were often a part of negotiations too, leaving avenues to further extend our understanding of wampum use and treaty making via the senses. Other ways of understanding media than by the senses can surely bring new insights as well, so I make no claims of having the last word on the matter. Instead, I hope the present essay has opened new paths of inquiry, rather than concluding them.

Notes

1. James H. Merrell, *The Indian's New World: Catawbas and Their Neighbors from European Contact through the Era of Removal* (New York: Norton, 1989), 160–64; Francis Jennings, "Iroquois Alliances in America History," in *The History and Culture of Iroquois Diplomacy: An Interdisciplinary Guide to the Treaties of the Six Nations and Their League*, ed. Francis Jennings et al. (Syracuse: Syracuse University Press, 1985), 50–52.

2. Virginia, *Treaty Held with the Catawba and Cherokee Indians* (Williamsburg: W. Hunter, 1756), vi.

3. Virginia, *Treaty Held with the Catawba and Cherokee Indians*, v–xii.

4. Virginia, *Treaty Held with the Catawba and Cherokee Indians*, 1–6; Cadwallader Colden, *The History of the Five Indian Nations Depending on the Province of New-York in America* (New York: William Bradford, 1727), 159.

5. Marshall McLuhan, *Understanding Media: The Extensions of Man* (Cambridge: MIT Press, 1994), 3–4; Marshall McLuhan, *The Gutenberg Galaxy: The Making of Typographic Man*, Kindle edition (Toronto: University of Toronto Press, 2012), 3–5, 35, 40, 183.

6. Mark M. Smith succinctly summarizes this literature in "Making Sense of Social History," *Journal of Social History* 37.1 (2003): 165–86, esp. n8.

7. The idea is expressed most famously in McLuhan, *The Gutenberg Galaxy*, 227, 245, 265–66; but perhaps more clearly in Marshall McLuhan, "Report on Project in Understanding New Media," in *Letters of Marshall McLuhan*, ed. Matie Molinaro, Corinne McLuhan, and William Toye (Oxford: Oxford University Press, 1987), 256.

8. These and debates about the history of the book are ably reviewed in Germaine Warkentin, "In Search of 'The Word of the Other': Aboriginal Sign Systems and the History of the Book in Canada," *Book History* 2 (1999): 1–27.

9. Jack Goody and Ian Watt, "The Consequences of Literacy," *Comparative Studies in Society and History* 5.3 (1963): 304–45; McLuhan, *Gutenberg Galaxy*; McLuhan, *Understanding Media*; Walter J. Ong, *The Presence of the Word: Some Prolegomena for Cultural and Religious History* (New York: Simon and Schuster, 1970); Walter J. Ong, *Orality and Literacy: The Technologizing of the Word* (New York: Methuen, 1982); Jack Goody, *The Do-*

mestication of the Savage Mind (Cambridge: Cambridge University Press, 1977); Jack Goody, *The Interface between the Written and the Oral* (Cambridge: Cambridge University Press, 1987); and Albert Bates Lord, *The Singer of Tales* (Cambridge: Harvard University Press, 1960). The problem is reviewed succinctly and clearly in Daniel Chandler, "Biases of the Ear and Eye: 'Great Divide' Theories, Phonocentrism, Graphocentrism and Logocentrism," 1995, http://www.aber.ac.uk/media/Documents /litoral/litoral.html.

10. See Warkentin, "In Search of 'The Word of the Other,'" which also provides a concise overview of the relevant literature on wampum in the notes; another excellent discussion of wampum's meaning can be found in David Murray, *Indian Giving: Economies of Power in Indian-White Exchanges* (Amherst: University of Massachusetts Press, 2000), 116–40; for a close examination of indigenous "books" and the limits of Eurocentric analogies in early colonial Mexico, see Walter D. Mignolo, *The Darker Side of the Renaissance: Literacy, Territoriality, and Colonization* (Ann Arbor: University of Michigan Press, 1995), 10, 69–81, 188–89. For a discussion of metaphor that is akin to my critique of analogies, see Murray, *Indian Giving*, 10–11.

11. Mary M. Slaughter, *Universal Languages and Scientific Taxonomy in the Seventeenth Century* (Cambridge: Cambridge University Press, 1982).

12. Frank Salomon and Sabine Hyland, "Guest Editors' Introduction," *Ethnohistory* 57.1 (Winter 2010): 1–9.

13. Galen Brokaw, "Indigenous American Polygraphy and the Dialogic Model of Media," *Ethnohistory* 57.1 (Winter 2010): 117–33; Heidi Bohaker, "Reading Anishinaabe Identities: Meaning and Metaphor in Nindoodem Pictographs," *Ethnohistory* 57.1 (Winter 2010): 28.

14. Margaret Bender, "Reflections on What Writing Means, Beyond What It 'Says': The Political Economy and Semiotics of Graphic Pluralism in the Americas," *Ethnohistory* 57.1 (Winter 2010): 176.

15. I make the case for a broader, historically situated unpacking of indigenous and colonial soundways than can be done through the notion of orality, which tends to serve as an ahistorical foil for literacy, in *How Early America Sounded* (Ithaca NY: Cornell University Press, 2003); and "Hearing American History," *Journal of American History* 95.2 (September 2008), http://www.historycooperative.org/journals/jah/95.2/rath.html.

16. J. L. Austin, *How to Do Things with Words* (Cambridge: Harvard University Press, 1962); for a concise discussion of where this influential idea

traveled after Searle, see Kira Hall, "Performativity," *Journal of Linguistic Anthropology* 9.1–2 (2000): 184–87. Much of what follows here is drawn from and builds upon Rath, *How Early America Sounded*, 161–72.

17. James H. Merrell, "'I Desire All That I Have Said . . . may Be Taken down Aright': Revisiting Teedyuscung's 1756 Treaty Council Speeches," *William and Mary Quarterly* 63.4 (2006): 777–826.

18. Peter Wraxall, "Proceedings of the Congress at Albany," 1754, 15, codex=Eng 36 manuscript, John Carter Brown Library, Providence, Rhode Island. For a sampling of wampum and pelts used to punctuate seventeenth- and eighteenth-century speeches of English, Dutch, Iroquois, French, and Esopus treaty makers, see B. Fernow, *Documents Relating to the Colonial History of the State of New York* (Albany: Weed Parsons, 1881), 13:72, 104–5, 107–10, 126, http://www.archive.org/details/documentsrelativ13brod; Colden, *History of the Five Indian Nations*, 30–31, 37, 51, 57; Reuben Gold Thwaites, ed., *The Jesuit Relations and Allied Documents* (Cleveland: Burrows Bros., 1896), 42:37, 47, 99, 101, 167, 187, 189; [William Smith], *Some Account of the North-America Indians* (London: R. Griffiths, 1754), 32–33; Wraxall, "Proceedings of the Congress at Albany," 8–9, 20–24, 27–30, 34, 35, 38, 40–42, 69–72, 78.

19. Jonathan Carver, *Travels through the Interior Parts of North-America, in the Years 1766, 1777, and 1778* (London: J. Walter and S. Crowder, 1778), 260–61; Daniel K. Richter, *The Ordeal of the Longhouse: The Peoples of the Iroquois League in the Era of European Colonization* (Chapel Hill: University of North Carolina Press, 1992), 46–47; Virginia, *Treaty Held with the Catawba and Cherokee Indians*, 2.

20. [Conrad Weiser], *The Treaty Held with the Indians of the Six Nations, at Lancaster, Pennsylvania, in June, 1744* (Williamsburg: William Park, 1744). The Tuscaroras were admitted to the Iroquois Confederacy in the 1720s, making the Five Nations six.

21. Philipp Waldeck, "Diary," trans. E. Bruce Burgoyne, 1781 1776, Hessian Ms. 2, typescript, 203b, from Hessian Ms. 28, Bancroft Collection, New York Public Library; [Smith], *Some Account of the North-America Indians*, 27; Carver, *Travels through the Interior*, 90.

22. Rath, *How Early America Sounded*, 152–61.

23. Colden, *History of the Five Indian Nations*, 44.

24. Indian captives were expected to sing their identity to their captors. Capture and warfare are another form of cross-cultural mediation. Rath, *How Early America Sounded*, 152–61.

Richard Cullen Rath

25. Thwaites, *Jesuit Relations*, 42:77, 79.

26. For an excellent summary of the literature on the gift as it relates to Native American history, see Murray, *Indian Giving*, 30–39.

27. Colden, *History of the Five Indian Nations*, 139.

28. Wraxall, "Proceedings of the Congress at Albany," 38.

29. The study of representation falls more or less into five categories: semiotics—see Martin Ryder, "Semiotics: Language and Culture," in *Encyclopedia of Science, Technology, and Ethics*, ed. Carl Mitcham (Detroit: Macmillan Reference USA, 2004), http://carbon.ucdenver.edu/~mryder/ semiotics_este.html; politics—see Suzanne Dovi, "Political Representation," *Stanford Encyclopedia of Philosophy*, Winter 2011, http://plato .stanford.edu/archives/win2011/entries/political-representation/; cultural studies—see Stuart Hall, ed., *Representation: Cultural Representations and Signifying Practices* (London: Sage and Open University Press, 2002); literary theory—see W. J. T. Mitchell, "Representation," in *Critical Terms for Literary Study*, ed. Frank Lentricchia and Thomas McLaughlin (Chicago: University of Chicago Press, 1995), 11–22; and philosophy of mind—see David Pitt, "Mental Representation," *Stanford Encyclopedia of Philosophy*, Fall 2008, http://plato.stanford.edu/archives/fall2008/entries/mental -representation/.

30. Carver, *Travels through the Interior*, 143–44; Joseph-François Lafitau, *Moeurs Des Sauvages Ameriquains, Comparées Aux Moeurs Des Premiers Temps* (Paris: Chez Saugrain l'aîné: Chez C.-E. Hochereau, 1724), 328, cited in Gordon M. Sayre, *Les Sauvages Américains: Representations of Native Americans in French and English Colonial Literature* (Chapel Hill: University of North Carolina Press, 1997), 190–91.

31. Fernow, *Documents*, 14:369.

32. Colden, *History of the Five Indian Nations*, 51, 52, 55 (emphasis in original). All the punctuating quotations are set off in italics in the print version.

33. George Washington, "Major George Washington's Journal to the River Ohio," *Maryland Gazette* (Annapolis), March 21, 1753, http://earlyameri- ca.com/earlyamerica/milestones/journal/ journaltext.html.

34. Colden, *History of the Five Indian Nations*, 23 n. d, 27, 139.

35. Colden, *History of the Five Indian Nations*, 23, 36.

36. [Weiser], *The Treaty Held with the Indians of the Six Nations, at Lancaster, Pennsylvania, in June, 1744*, viii–ix; Colden, *History of the Five Indian Nations*, 89; Fernow, *Documents*, 13:102–3; Waldeck, "Diary," 42b.

37. G. Peter Jemison and Anna M. Schein, eds., *Treaty of Canandaigua 1794: 200 Years of Treaty Relations between the Iroquois Confederacy and the United States* (Santa Fe NM: Clear Light Publishers, 2000); George C. Shattuck, *The Oneida Land Claims: A Legal History* (Syracuse: Syracuse University Press, 1991).

38. I would like to thank Gerald Jamieson and Shirley Buchanan for bringing the Tawagonshi Treaty to my attention. The most thorough analysis is Robert Venables, "An Analysis of the 1613 Tawagonshi Treaty: History of Relations with Our Brothers," *Onondaga Nation*, September 9, 2012, http://www.onondaganation.org/aboutus/history_two_row_wampum .html. In the newspapers, this position is best summarized in Jack Manno, "Two Row Wampum: Made-up Controversy over Treaty Document Belittles Haundenosaunee Oral History," *Syracuse Post-Standard*, February 3, 2013, sec. Your Letters, http://blog.syracuse.com/opinion/2013/02/ two_row_wampum_made-up_controv.html. Other news articles that present the forgery argument unchallenged are Glen Coin, "Onondaga Nation Treaty Celebration Questioned Again by Scholars," *Syracuse Post-Standard*, January 2, 2013, http://www.syracuse.com/news/index .ssf/2013/01/onondaga_nation_treaty_celebra.html; Glen Coin, "400 Years Later, a Legendary Iroquois Treaty Comes under Attack," *Syracuse Post-Standard*, August 9, 2012, http://www.syracuse.com/news/index .ssf/2012/08/400_years_later_a_legendary_ir.html; Nicoline Van Der Sijs, "Letter: Linguistic Proof Questions Treaty," *Albany Times-Union*, January 22, 2013, http://www.timesunion.com/opinion/article/Linguistic -proof-questions-treaty-4212051.php; Glen Coin, "Dutch Scholars Agree with New York Colleagues: Onondaga Treaty Is a Fake," *Syracuse Post-Standard*, January 23, 2013, http://www.syracuse.com/news/index .ssf/2013/01/dutch_scholars_agree_with_new.html; Harrie Hermkens and Nicolien van der Sijs, "Tawagonshi-Verdrag Is Vervalst [Tawagonshi Treaty Has Been Forged]," *Vrije Universiteit Amsterdam*, August 23, 2012, http://dare.ubvu.vu.nl/handle/1871/39593; Ingmar Koch, "Vals of Echt? De Wampum Bewijst Het [Fake or Real? The Wampum Proves It]," blog, *Ingmar bladert en schrijft*, August 23, 2012, http://ingmarbladertenschrijft .blogspot.nl/2012/08/vals-of-echt-de-wampum-bewijst-het.html. The unmasking of the forgery can be found in Charles T. Gehring, William A. Starna, and William N. Fenton, "The Tawagonshi Treaty of 1613: The Final Chapter," *New York History* 68.4 (1987): 373–93; and Charles T. Gehring and William A. Starna, "Revisiting the Fake Tawagonshi Treaty of

1613," *New York History* 93.1 (2012): 95–101, along with the inability to comprehend anything but documents as evidence. Robert Venables, "The 1613 Treaty," *Syracuse Peace Council*, n.d., http://www.peacecouncil.net/NOON/2row/docs/VenablesonTwoRow.pdf, contains the treaty as well as his analysis.

39. Wraxall, "Proceedings of the Congress at Albany," 68.

PART IV
TRANSATLANTIC
MEDIASCAPES

10

Writing as "Khipu"

TITU CUSI YUPANQUI'S ACCOUNT OF THE CONQUEST OF PERU

Ralph Bauer

In 1571 the penultimate ruler of the Inca dynasty, Titu Cusi Yupanqui, collaborated with an Augustinian monk and a mestizo secretary to produce a text unique in the history of early American mediascapes. *Instrucción del Inca Don Diego de Castro Titu Cusi Yupanqui al Licenciado don Lope García de Castro* is an account of the conquest of Peru told not from the familiar perspective of the Spanish conquerors but from the perspective of one of the main actors in the Andean resistance to the European colonial order. It was written down far from the centers of Spanish power, in the tropical Andean foothills of Vilcabamba, where Titu Cusi was ruling over a neo-Inca state that had been founded by his father, Manco Inca, after the old Inca capital at Cuzco had fallen to the Spaniards in 1533. For almost forty years, the rebellious Vilcabamba Incas had been able to keep the Spaniards at bay, reestablishing a regime that functioned largely independent of the colonial state, while launching occasional raids on Spanish merchants and Native ethnic groups under Spanish control.

By the late 1560s, however, it was clear that the Spaniards would be a permanent presence in Peru. There had been several attempts to negotiate an end to the standoff between the Vilcabamba Incas and the Spanish authorities. In 1564 the crown sent a provisional governor general and president of the council at Lima, Lope García de Castro, to take charge of the government until a new viceroy was appointed (the previous viceroy, Diego López de Zuñiga, Count of Nieva, had died unexpectedly earlier that year). The interim governor pursued a reconciliatory and diplomatic approach to the problem still posed by the rebels at Vilcabamba. In 1565 an agreement, the so-called Capitulations of Acobamba, was drafted. Titu Cusi would be granted properties and revenues; in exchange, he would receive missionaries at Vilcabamba, accept baptism, swear loyalty to Emperor Philip II, and agree eventually to give up his stronghold and live in Spanish Peru. In order to negotiate the terms of this arrangement, gifts, promises, messages, and official letters were exchanged, including the *Instrucción*.[1]

Formally, the text is divided into three distinct sections: (1) Titu Cusi's request (*instrucción*) to present his case before the emperor regarding his claim to the status of Inca (ruler) and his entitlement to compensations; (2) a historical account (*relación*), which is intended to substantiate his claims and which presents a devastating critique of Spanish treacheries, greed, and cruelties; and (3) a power of attorney (*poder*) in which he authorizes García de Castro to represent him legally in the courts of Spain in any matter pertaining to his interests, titles, or possessions. The historical *relación*, which accounts for the bulk of the text, highlights the deeds of his father, Manco Inca, during the turbulent events since the Spaniards' first arrival in Peru: the infamous massacre at Cajamarca in 1532; the capture and eventual murder of the Inca Atahuallpa in 1533; the Spaniards' coronation of his youthful half brother Manco Inca as their puppet ruler; the latter's rebellion and unsuccessful attempt to retake Cuzco in 1536; his withdrawal to Vitcos and later to Vilcabamba in the Andean foothills northwest of Cuzco; his eventual murder at the hands of

Ralph Bauer

two Spanish guests in 1545; and finally Titu Cusi's own assumption of rule at Vilcabamba.

The historical account was originally related orally by Titu Cusi himself before an audience that included one of the missionaries at Vilcabamba, the Augustinian fray Marcos García, and then transcribed in Spanish alphabetical script by Titu Cusi's mestizo secretary, Martín de Pando. The product of a collaborative cultural translation, the *Instrucción* evidences intercultural tensions with regard not only to its multiple authorial subjectivities and ideological perspectives but also to its (often unsuccessful) attempt to bridge the communicative gap between Andean and European languages and media. It is because of this gap that the anthropologist Frank Salomon has called texts by Andean authors in the European medium "chronicles of the impossible"—narratives of the conquest era that must be "fully intelligible to Spanish contemporaries, and, at the same time, made from and faithful to Andean materials alien to European diachrony."[2] This essay will address some of these intercultural tensions in Titu Cusi's text, particularly with regard to competing conceptions of historio-"graphy" as evidenced in its attempt to mediate between Andean and European communication systems. As I will argue, despite its translation from an Andean into a European medium, Titu Cusi's narrative retains both formal and ideological elements distinctive of pre-Hispanic Andean semiosis. Though molded into the generic conventions of the Spanish *crónica de Indias* (chronicle of the Indies), it appropriates the European alphabetical medium within the Andean system of communicating across time and space via the *khipu*, material sign carriers on strings of colored knots by way of which the Incas recorded statistical information used for imperial administration and historical information used in public performances in honor of a particular Inca. While much of the anthropological and ethnohistorical debate has focused on the question of whether the khipu represent a sort of "writing," Titu Cusi's text invites us to ask how European writing could function as a sort of Andean "khipu."[3]

Titu Cusi's *Instrucción* and the *Crónica de Indias*

We do not know with certainty the details of how Titu Cusi's text was composed. In one of the authorizing declarations appended to the end of the text, Titu Cusi states: "[Since] I am unfamiliar with the phrases and modes of expression used by the Spaniards in such writings— [I] have asked the reverend fray don Marcos García and the secretary Martín de Pando to arrange and compose the said account in their customary ways of expression" ("no sé la frase y la manera que los españoles tienen en semejantes avisos, rogué al muy reverendo padre fray Marcos García y a Martín de Pando que conforme al uso de su natural, me ordenasen y compusiesen esta relación arriba dicha").[4] Most historians have deduced from this declaration that the account was originally delivered in Quechua by Titu Cusi, translated into Spanish by fray Marcos García, and then transcribed by Martín de Pando.[5] Though the degree of Titu Cusi's own "acculturation" to Spanish norms has been a matter of critical dispute, his text, as it comes down to us as the collaborative product of at least three different agencies, necessarily bears the marks of cultural hybridity.[6]

The designation *relación* heading Titu Cusi's account of historical events, for example, invokes the Spanish generic mold of the *crónica de Indias*. Generally, this designation identified a text as belonging to a genre that originated, as Roberto González Echevarría has shown, in legal discourse, especially notarial rhetoric, denoting an eyewitness account in a legal dispute. A defining characteristic of the genre of the *relación*, as it originated in the Old World context, was its humble, plain, though highly official character, as well as its appeal to the authority of firsthand experience.[7] In the New World context of overseas expansionism during the sixteenth century, however, the term *relación* took on a new meaning, now becoming, as Walter Mignolo has pointed out, largely synonymous with the terms *historia* (history) and *crónica* (chronicle), "in order to refer to a historiographic text."[8] In the context of overseas imperialism, then, law and history became inextricably intertwined. Historical *relaciones* by eyewitnesses of the

American conquests could hereby serve as a sort of legal deposition or testimony in the official courtrooms of imperial policy and legislation. The reasons for this gradual interpenetration of the previously distinct genres of the *historia* and the *relación* must be seen in the context of not only an increasing importance of empirical knowledge during the New World discoveries but also the important socio- and geopolitical changes accompanying the transformation of communication systems in the context of Spanish transoceanic imperial expansionism.

The cultural historian of communication technology Bernhard Siegert has described the Spanish imperial communication system emerging with the founding of the Casa de Contratación in Seville in 1503, the central clearing house regulating all traffic in passengers, goods, and information between the New World and the Old, as an archetypal "modern" quest for "total information." The Casa was at the center of an intricate bureaucratic machine in which every person who set foot on a ship bound for America had to take a ritual passage through the "light beam of power" (*Lichtkegel der Macht*), in the course of which he or she was identified, recorded, and registered, thus becoming an underling subject whose real identity was henceforth inseparable from his or her representation in the paper records—millions of which are now deposited in the Archivo General de Indias in Seville.[9] It is within the quest for "total information" in the socio- and geopolitically stratified communication system of an emergent absolutist state and a transoceanic empire that the *relación* functioned as the primary generic vehicle. Semiotically, the *relación* was characterized by a distinct positionality and directionality in early modern social space, traveling from the private person transmitting it "upward" to the government official at the receiving end. Whereas the authority of the historian in the Old World rested mainly on his noble social standing, few of the chroniclers of the New World, typically of humble social origins, could shore up their trustworthiness with names and titles. While the *relación* retains, in its New World context, the conventions of an appeal to eyewitness experience, it becomes defined by its positionality and directionality not only in social space but also in geographic space: it moves "upward" in social space at the same time as it moves "inward" in geographic space from imperial periphery to center in an increasingly territorialized imperial chain of command. Thus, the New World *relación* might travel from colonial provinces to the viceregal capitals, from the viceregal capitals to Seville, and, ultimately, from Seville to Madrid, which first becomes the fixed imperial capital in 1561 under Philip II, who broke with the long tradition of his ancestors, still observed by his father, of moving the court about the empire.[10]

From what we know about the history of Titu Cusi's text, it appears that it traveled in the same channels of the imperial bureaucracy as the vast majority of *relaciones*. The original manuscript was taken from Vilcabamba to Lima, the viceregal capital. From there it accompanied the governor's entourage on his journey back to Spain and would have passed through Seville and the Casa de Contratación. Although it is unknown whether García de Castro ever presented Titu Cusi's case before the emperor, it did make its way to Madrid traveling in official channels. The original manuscript is lost today, but a copy was produced in 1574 and then deposited at the Biblioteca del Monasterio de San Lorenzo del Escorial, Philip II's quasi-monastic refuge, where it survives today, bound as one section in a volume of several manuscripts relating to the Incas.

It is in this context of Spanish imperial administration and bureaucratic legalism that much of its content can be understood, especially Titu Cusi's critique of the conquerors' avarice and cruelty. Although it may appear odd to the modern reader that a text addressed to the Spanish monarch engaged in an indictment of the Spanish conquest, we should not prematurely attribute this critique to a "subaltern" or anti-imperial subjectivity. Indeed, the language of Titu Cusi's indictment falls squarely within the tradition of influential voices in the Spanish Empire, such as the Dominicans Francisco de Vitoria and Bartolomé de Las Casas, who had argued that the conquest of America had been an "unjust" war by the standards of scholastic law. Their

Ralph Bauer

depositions were used by the crown, in turn, to justify its attempts at centralizing imperial administration in Madrid by stripping the conquerors' neo-feudal status by passing, in 1542, the so-called New Laws, which revoked the conquerors' claim to an *encomienda* (a royal grant of Native tribute and labor) in perpetuity. These "New Laws" caused outrage and defiance among the conquerors throughout the Americas and, in Peru, even led to Gonzalo Pizarro's insurrection against the crown. When the conquerors mobilized a legal counteroffensive, the dispute over the constitution of the Spanish Empire came to a climax in a famous series of debates held in Valladolid in 1551. The conquerors' legal representative, Juan Ginés de Sepúlveda, argued that the Native lords of the Americas, such as the Aztecs or the Incas, had governed their subjects by way of cruelty and tyranny; moreover, such cultural practices as the Incas' habit of polygamy represented violations of "natural law," all of which disqualified them from being considered the legitimate and "natural lords" of the New World. By contrast, Las Casas argued that the local nobles, even though previously pagans, were and continued to be the legitimate rulers and "natural lords" of the American communities who had willingly subjected themselves to the supreme authority of the emperor and the Holy Catholic faith. The Spanish conquerors, by contrast, were foreign invaders, who, in an "unjust" war, not only perpetrated unspeakable acts of cruelty motivated by greed (*codicia*) but arrogated to themselves a status of feudal lords that rightfully belonged only to the Native nobility. This was the thesis put forward by Las Casas's famous *Brevísima relación de la destrucción de las Indias* (1552) (A brief account of the destruction of the Indies), an important prototype for Titu Cusi's *relación*, in which Las Casas portrayed the Indians as "meek lambs" ("ovejas mansas") being torn up by "cruel and ravenous wolves" ("lobos . . . cruelísimos de muchos días hambrientos").[11]

Titu Cusi's emphasis on the hardship and suffering imposed on the Andean communities by the Pizarro brothers' repeated attempts to extort gold and silver as ransom for captured Inca sovereigns is of a piece with this Lascasian discourse of *codicia*:

greed, so powerful in all men, overcame them [the Spaniards] so completely that they were seduced by the Devil, always a friend of all evil, to conspire and plot in secrecy how and by what means they would torment my father and extort a greater amount of silver and gold than what they had already extorted from him. (73)

[como la codicia de los hombres es tan grande, reinó en ellos de tal suerte que engañados por el demonio, amigo de toda maldad y enemigo de virtud, que se vinieron entre sí a concertar y tratar los unos con los otros la manera y el cómo molestarían a mi padre y sacarían de él más plata y oro de la sacada.] (46–47)

The moralizing and now almost iconic image of the conqueror having fallen victim to the devil in the universal struggle between good and evil here clearly bears the mark of Marcos García's missionary discourse. Moreover, it corroborates political arguments that the unduly heavy burden in tribute and labor imposed by the conquerors on the Natives had deprived them of their rightful status as His Majesty's royal subjects and instead degraded them to the status of the conquerors' personal slaves, leading to demographic catastrophes all over the Americas.

Likewise, the emphasis on the uncompromising loyalty of the various local leaders to Titu Cusi's father, Manco Inca's friendly reception of the Spaniards, as well as Titu Cusi's own conversion to Christianity reinforces the political ideal of the Inca as a natural lord *voluntarily* placing himself under the imperial protection of the king. If, admittedly, this political ideal seems somewhat out of touch with historical reality—after all, the Vilcabamba Incas were in an official state of rebellion—the account takes pains to show that Manco Inca made the decision to remove to Vilcabamba and to resist the Spaniards with force only as a very last resort, after his many attempts at accommodation had been frustrated and his boundless good intentions (*voluntad*) to coexist had been exhausted by Spanish treachery and greed. When the Spaniards move to imprison Manco Inca to extort ransom, he "was very upset and exclaimed: 'What have I done to you that you should

Ralph Bauer

treat me in this manner and chain me like a dog? Is this how you reciprocate the favor I have shown by guiding you through my land and by making you many loving presents of things that I owned here?'" (74) ("alteróse en gran manera diciendo:—¿Qué os he hecho yo: por qué me queréis tratar de esa manera y atarme como un perro? ¿De esa manera me pagáis la buena obra que os he hecho en meteros en mi tierra y daros de lo que en ella tenía con tanta voluntad y amor?" [47]). Titu Cusi's conversion to Christianity continues this gesture of *voluntad* for peaceful coexistence, but his father's experiences have made him, understandably, wary of the Spaniards' trustworthiness. For this reason, he requires legal assurances from the monarch that his status as the legitimate Christian prince of Peru will be honored before he can reasonably be expected to consider giving up his refuge at Vilcabamba.

Thus, both the generic designation of the historical narrative as a "relación" as well as some of the key themes developed in the narrative ostensibly point to the Spanish legalistic context in which the text was inscribed. Some critics have therefore suggested that this text seems to betray a thoroughly Eurocentric perspective, a perspective privileging alphabetical textuality generally and the letter of the law particularly that may have originated either with Titu Cusi's own acceptance of imposed European cultural norms or with a manipulation by the Spanish translator.[12] Such an assessment, however, fails to take account of the profoundly intercultural nature of this text, which is indebted not only to European but also to Andean textual and ideological traditions. Despite the mediations through Marcos García's Spanish translation and Martín de Pando's alphabetical transcription, several of the formal characteristics of Inca historio-"graphy" on which Titu Cusi drew when relating his story still survive in the text.

Titu Cusi's *Instrucción* as Inca "Praise Narrative"

The most obvious of these characteristics concerns the nature of Titu Cusi's knowledge of the historical events he relates. Unlike in the Spanish *relación*, where authority depended on the speaker's claim to eyewitness experience, Titu Cusi could not have witnessed most of the events he relates, as they occurred before he was born or while he was in Spanish captivity in Cuzco.[13] Most likely, therefore, he related them as they had been remembered and passed down in a tradition of what Susan Niles has called "praise narratives" and what Martin Lienhard has called "ritual homage" kept by the descent group of his father. In Inca culture, each ruler was the founder of his own descent group or lineage (*panaca*), whose members competed with those of other panacas in rivalries for succession. Each panaca was therefore responsible for keeping the mummy, memory, and reputation of the deceased ruler in an oral tradition of praise songs, which were performed in periodical ritual enactments. During these enactments, it was believed that the deceased ruler "spoke" to his panaca. The Spaniards who observed these performances called them *cantares* (songs) and compared them to *romanceros* or *villancicos* (two poetic genres of the Spanish oral tradition), emphasizing the role that music and dance played in them. As Niles observes, these "praise narratives" had narrative structures that depended heavily on mnemonic devices that could include stimuli external to the narrative—music or war trophies especially kept for this purpose—or elements internal to the literary structure of the performance itself, such as meter and formulaic repetition.[14]

At least equally important to these oral performances, however, were the khipu, the knotted-string recording devices the Incas used to keep statistical information for imperial administration and remembering historical events for later oral performance. These knotted stings were made, kept, and "read" by the *khipukamayuc* ("those who gave order to the *khipu*") (see fig. 10.1). There has been considerable debate in recent years about the nature of the Andean khipu—what sort of information they encoded, the manner in which they could encode that information, and how they functioned within Andean communication systems. While traditionally, scholars assumed that the khipu were merely mnemonic devices—comparable to, say, a Catholic rosary—we know today that their function went well beyond a memory aid and that their capability included recording phonological and logographic data that could provide statistical and narrative information. Gary

Ralph Bauer

Fig. 10.1. A *khipukamayuc*. Felipe Guaman Poma de Ayala, *Nueva corónica y buen gobierno* (1615). Courtesy of Det Kongelige Bibliotek/The Royal Library of Denmark, Copenhagen, GKS 2232 4°.

Urton, the preeminent scholar of khipu semiosis, has recently even conjectured that the khipu could also encode syntactical subject-object-verb sequences (following normal Quechua syntax); however, this must remain conjecture for the moment, as modern scholars understand the numerical codes governing the statistical khipu but have yet to learn how to read what Urton calls the "anomalous" khipu—including those used in ritual homages, as reported in alphabetical historical sources.[15]

Writing as "Khipu"

Regardless of whether Urton's hypothesis will be verified by further anthropological research, what is salient for my purposes here is that, as Galen Brokaw has pointed out, the "dialogic relationship between the structure of Andean discourses, Andean oral traditions, and the khipu was very different from the relationship between writing and orality in modern alphabetic cultures."[16] To be sure, no secondary system, including alphabetical writing, ever replaces or opposes orality; rather, it engages, supplements, and perhaps transforms it.[17] But the difference between Spanish and Inca systems of communicating inheres less in the medium itself (written versus oral, alphabetical versus non-alphabetical) but rather in the way that the material sign carrier (letter and khipu) functioned as social practice in Spanish and Inca imperial historiography (*relación* and praise narrative). Both the Spanish *crónica* and the Andean khipu are highly official in character and similarly embedded in social and geopolitical practices of authoritative performance. However, whereas the production and the reception of a *crónica* may or may not entail an act of oral telling distinct from transcription or reading, Andean communication via khipu always remained inseparable from oral performance. Though always official, a Spanish *crónica* may or may not be "public," that is to say, "performed 'before' the people" (and in fact, the vast majority of the *relaciones* remained "secret" and in manuscript, intended for exclusive perusal by the imperial bureaucrat or sovereign).[18] By contrast, the tactile performances involving the khipu were highly public and collaborative events, as both the encoding and the decoding of khipu by the *khipukamayuc* were accompanied by a "reading out" by a "bard," such as a "poet" or a "philosopher."[19] We might say that, from a sociological point of view, the letter-based *relación* spoke "up to" authority, while the khipu-based praise narrative spoke "with" authority (the khipu being imagined as the voice of the deceased Inca). From the point of view of the cultural geography of imperial power, we might furthermore say that the message of the *relación* was directed "inward" while that of the praise narrative was directed "outward."

The khipu "texts" of Inca praise narratives were usually stored together with the mummies of the deceased Incas and were "read out" during the ceremonial performances of the ritual homage, during which the mummy of a given Inca was also displayed. We know from a sixteenth-century Spanish source—the narrative of Baltasar de Ocampo—that Titu Cusi (and later his half brother, Tupac Amaru) were keeping their father's embalmed mummy in Vilcabamba.[20] It is therefore likely that Titu Cusi's account of his father's deeds was a translation and transcription for a multiethnic audience of such a ritual "opening" of Manco Inca's commemorative khipu that accompanied the performance of a praise narrative. But even if the occasion of the transcription did not coincide with a formal performance of a ritual homage, the tradition of the praise narrative, and its textual basis in the khipu, would have provided the generic and epistemological context in which Titu Cusi would have understood the act of relating the life and deeds of his father—the act of historio-"graphy." It is in the context of this khipu semiosis that we may see the slightly unusual generic designation in the title of Titu Cusi's text—*instrucción*—which does not seem to refer to any particular early modern Spanish discursive conventions or contexts. The alphabetical text sent to Spain was to serve as an extension and translation of the stringed colored knots—an idea of alphabetical writing conveyed by a "word picture" made by Felipe Guaman Poma de Ayala in his *Nueva corónica y buen gobierno* (1615), where the Andean author wrote his first paragraph as a descending triangle and later added the subsequent paragraphs perpendicular to the main text, so that the added lines appear on the page as hanging down like cords on a khipu (see fig. 10.2).

The context of khipu semiosis also sheds light on the multiple layers of collaborative authorship that characterized the production of the alphabetical text at Vilcabamba. Thus, Titu Cusi's charge to García and Pando to "arrange and compose the said account in their [the Spaniards'] customary ways of expression" (136) in the Spanish manner ("que conforme al uso de su natural, me ordenasen y compusiesen esta relación arriba dicha" [115]) is consistent with the way in which the Incas understood the role of the *khipukamayuc* as "those who gave

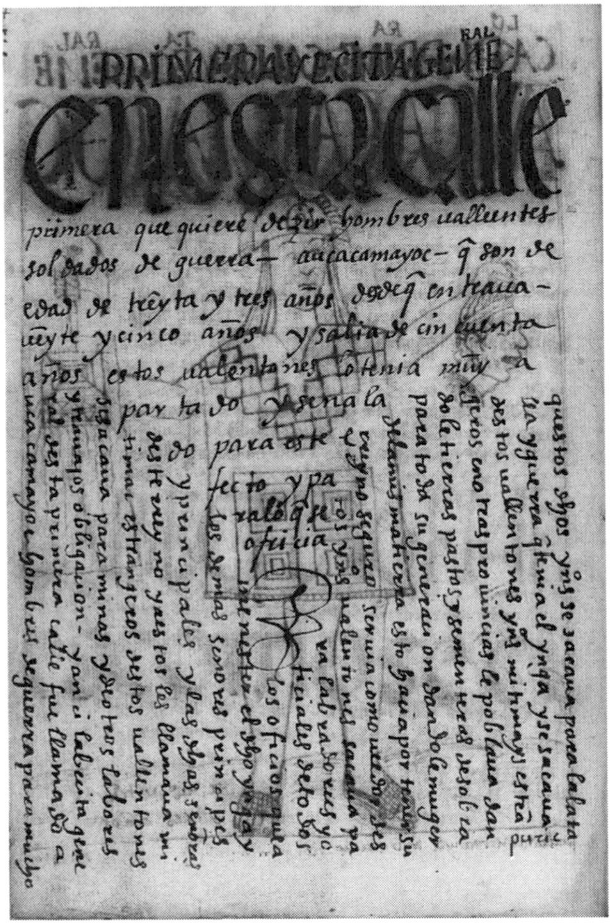

Fig. 10.2. Guaman Poma's paragraph describing the "paths" of men and women in Incan society. Guaman Poma wrote the first paragraph in the form of a descending triangle. Later, he added the subsequent paragraphs in each description perpendicular to the main text, so that the added lines appear on the page as hanging down like cords on a khipu. From Felipe Guaman Poma de Ayala, *Nueva corónica y buen gobierno* (1615). Courtesy of Det Kongelige Bibliotek/The Royal Library of Denmark, Copenhagen, GKS 2232 4°.

order to the *khipu*." Titu Cusi apparently envisioned a similar authorial role for García de Castro as his representative at court in Madrid. In his "Instrucción" to García de Castro, Titu Cusi explains his reasons for relating his story: "As the memory of men is frail and weak, it would be impossible to remember everything accurately with regard

Ralph Bauer

to all our great and important affairs unless we avail ourselves of writing to assist us in our purposes" (58) ("Y porque la memoria de los hombres es débil y flaca y si no nos ocurrimos a las letras para nos aprovechar de ellas en nuestras necesidades, era cosa imposible podernos acordar por extenso de todos los negocios largos y de importançia que se nos ofresciesen" [30]). While at first sight this statement may seem to privilege alphabetical textuality ("letras"), it is clear that Titu Cusi did not conceive of his text in terms of an alphabetical text that would be read verbatim and directly by the emperor. Rather, his "instructions" are cues directed to the departing governor García de Castro—to serve as his emissary and mouthpiece and to present his text in a performance before the king. "It is necessary for me," he says, "being as brief as possible, to call to mind a few important issues. I hope that Your Excellency may favor me by bringing these concerns, which I will momentarily detail, to the attention of His Majesty on my behalf" (58) ("usando de la brevedad posible, me será necesario hacer recopilación de algunas cosas necesarias, en las cuales su señoría, llevando mi poder para ello, me ha de hacer merced de favorescerme ante su magestad en todas ellas" [30]). It is the governor, not the text, who is supposed to act as the primary medium of communication and diplomacy between Titu Cusi and the emperor. He suggests that the governor "begin by giving a testimony about who and whose son I am, so that His Majesty is entirely clear on the reasons why I am entitled to compensation" (58) ("comenzando lo primero por quién yo soy, y cuyo hijo, para que le conste a su majestad por más extenso la razón que arriba he dicho para gratificarme" [30]).

Thus, the "text" of his *Instrucción* is intended to serve the governor mainly as a secondary device when orally representing Titu Cusi's case at court in person—to "assist" his "memory" in Titu Cusi's "purposes." In other words, his text would function as a material sign carrier not in the Spanish sense of a written *relación* but rather in the Andean sense of the khipu, involving as it did two "bards," one in each of Quechua and Spanish (Titu Cusi and Marcos García), and at least one coder (Martín de Pando). From the perspective of khipu semiosis—of communicating across space from Cuzco to the remote parts of the Inca empire by linking transportable material secondary devices with local oral performances—the "hermeneutic chain" connecting Titu Cusi to the Spanish emperor via the "secondary device" of his text could be described like this:

Peru:

> Inka *khipukamayuc*, decoder
>
> Inca "bard" (Titu Cusi)
>
> Spanish "bard" (translator, Marcos García)
>
> Spanish "*khipukamayuc*," encoder (scribe, Martín de Pando)

Spain:

> Spanish "*khipukamayuc*," decoder
>
> Spanish "bard" (Lope García de Castro)
>
> Spanish "*khipukamayuc*," encoder
>
> Audience: King Phillip II

The main difference between the letter-based *relación* and the khipu-based praise narrative lay in the sociology of their respective performances, particularly in their connection to public performance. Indeed, it was the potentially solitary character of Western alphabetical semiosis that, according to Titu Cusi's account, struck the Andeans as extraordinary upon first observing Spaniards with their books: he relates that one of the reasons why the Andean people who first saw the Spaniards upon their arrival in Tahuantinsuyu called the strangers "Viracochas" ("gods") was that "the Indians saw them *alone* talking to white cloths (paños blancos), as a person would speak to another, which is how the Indians perceived the reading of books and letters" (60; my emphasis).[21] Similarly memorable is Titu Cusi's account of the fateful encounter between the Spaniards and Atahuallpa at Cajamarca in 1532. He relates that the Spaniards "showed my uncle

Ralph Bauer

a letter or a book (I'm not sure exactly which), explaining to him that this was the word of God and of the king. My uncle . . . took the letter (or whatever it was) and threw it down, saying: 'What is this supposed to be that you gave to me here? Be gone!'" (60–61) ("le mostraron al dicho mi tío una carta o libro, o no sé qué, diciendo que aquella era la *quillca* de Dios y del rey, y mi tío . . . tomó la carta o lo que era y arrojolo por ahí, diciendo '¿Que sé yo qué me dais ahí? ¡Anda vete!'" [32–33]). The subsequent Spanish attack was triggered when Atahuallpa, in a haughty gesture, flung the breviary presented to him by the priest Vicente de Valverde into the dust.

The encounter between Andean and European semiotic systems haunts the colonial record, which often tends to attribute superior power to the alphabetical medium.[22] Thus, Juan de Betanzos, a Spaniard who was married to Doña Angelina Yupanqui, Atahuallpa's sister and Francisco Pizarro's former mistress, told the story of the conquest as remembered by her family. He wrote that the interpreter had explained to Atahuallpa that he should "obey the captain [Pizarro] who was also the son of the Sun, and that was what . . . the painting in the book said." In response, Atahuallpa "asked for the book and, taking it in his hands he opened it. When he saw the lines of letters, he said: 'This speaks and says that you are the son of the Sun? I, also, am the son of the Sun' . . . Saying this, he hurled the book away."[23] Still, during the early seventeenth century, the indigenous Andean chronicler Guaman Poma de Ayala, who claimed to be a *khipukamayuc* and drew on Native historical traditions, remembered Atahuallpa's response to the book like this: "'Give me the book so that it can speak to me.' And so he [Valverde] gave it to him and he held it in his hands and began to inspect the pages of the said book. And then the Inca said: 'Why doesn't it speak to me?'" before angrily throwing it to the ground.[24] Once in captivity, Atahuallpa reportedly asked the Spaniards to be taught how to "listen" to these texts. From the point of view of Andean mediascapes, there is no "reading" without "listening" and no "writing" without "speaking"; the Western dichotomy between literacy and orality therefore does not apply to Andean semiosis.

In Titu Cusi's text, the intercultural tensions between khipu and alphabetical semiosis are most evident in its narrative structure. As Sabine MacCormack has suggested, while for Spaniards writing about the Native Andean world "the difficulty was collecting and understanding information, not writing it down, the effort that was required of an Andean author writing a book consisted primarily in shaping and sequencing the narrative."[25] One of the most basic features of the Spanish *crónica* is, as its name suggests, its strictly chronological order. And, on the surface, Titu Cusi's *relación* appears to conform to this European convention. Most likely, this narrative structure must be attributed to the translator Marcos García or the scribe Martín de Pando. However, that Titu Cusi's original oral performance of the history of his father's deeds did not subscribe to a strictly chronological order is still evidenced in the alphabetical text by the fact that chronologically distinct "events" tend to happen (in various versions thereof) three or four times. For example, the plot line leading up to the Incas' rebellion and siege of Cuzco is structured into the narration of Manco Inca's being captured and abused by the Spaniards three times. While it is possible that this narrative sequence followed the chronological course of historical events, I have not found any other sixteenth-century sources that present Manco Inca's decision to rebel as the result of a series of three separate captivities. More likely, this threefold repetition is the textual trace of an oral stylistic device that was translated in the alphabetical text as a sequence of three separate events. As Susan Niles has noted, in Inca oral narrative, repetition "served as a formula which facilitated the remembrance of the narratives."[26]

Moreover, the narration of each of Manco Inca's captivities culminates with him giving a speech. His speeches, like the other speeches that occur in the text, are always represented as direct speech, never summarized or reported indirectly, giving the text the overall character of a written record of a dramatic, oral performance. This too was a formal feature characteristic of Inca semiosis.[27] A particularly frequent convention in Inca praise narratives was hereby the representation of deathbed orations that concluded the life history of a

Ralph Bauer

particular Inca. Titu Cusi's narrative about his father follows this convention. It presents not one but two deathbed orations, supposedly delivered after Manco Inca was mortally stabbed by his Spanish guests—one addressed to his subjects and one addressed specifically to Titu Cusi. Each appears as a separate chapter in the narrative with a distinct header.

The syntactical symmetry in some parts of Marcos García's Spanish translation suggests that Titu Cusi's performance may have been metrical, or at least followed a pattern of rhythmical symmetry over certain passages. For purposes of illustration we might represent such a passage here in stanza. It relates the convergence of the various lords and their armies from the different parts of the empire during Manco Inca's siege of Cuzco:

> From Carmenca, which lies in the direction of the Chinchaysuyo,
> Came Coriato, Cuillas, and Taipi, with many others In order to close the city's exit in that direction with their hordes.
>
> From the Contisuyo, Which is the direction of Cachicachi,
> Came Huaman Quilcana, Curi Huallpa, all Superbly equipped and in battle formation, closing a huge gap of more than half a league wide.
>
> From the Collasuyo Came Llicllic and many other generals with a huge number of men, which was in fact the largest contingent That formed the besieging army.
>
> From the Antisuyo, Came Antallca and Ronpa Yupanqui and many others in order to close the ring around the Spaniards. (105)

> [Por la parte de Carmenga, que es hacia Chinchaisuyo, entraron Coriatao y Cuillas y Taipi y otros muchos que cerraron aquel postigo con la gente que traían;
>
> por la parte del Condesuyo, que es hacía Cachicachi, entraron Huaman Quilcana y Curi Huallpa y otros muchos que cerraron una gran mella de más de media legua de distancia, todos muy bien aderezados, en orden de guerra;

> por la parte de Collasuyo entraron Llicllic y muchos otros cap-
> itanes con grandísima suma de gente, la mayor cantidad que se
> halló en este cerco;
>
> por la parte de Andesuyo entraron Antallca y Ronpa Yupangui
> y otros muchos, los cuales acabaron de cercar el cerco que a los
> españoles les pusieron.] (79–80)

The frequent fourfold repetition of narrative sequences such as this one—paying homage to the four parts of the empire, called the Tawantinsuyo (which roughly translates as "the parts that in their fourness make up the whole")—suggests that the *crónica*'s chronological principle is being compromised by a spatial principle in structuring the narrative. In present-day Andean storytelling, as Rosaleen Howard has shown, narrative discourse heavily depends on the naming and ordering of landmarks. For the storyteller, toponymns operate as guides in contextualizing the narrative elements and as memory aids during the act of oral storytelling.[28]

These remnants of Andean semiosis in Titu Cusi's text do not, of course, mean that Titu Cusi himself lacked an understanding of the importance of alphabetical semiosis or even of how it functioned in Spanish culture. While alphabetical semiosis may have been "radically novel" for Atahuallpa and the first Andeans who came in contact with Europeans,[29] it can hardly be assumed to have been novel any longer to Titu Cusi in 1570, when he dictated his text to Martín de Pando. Not only had Titu Cusi himself lived in Cuzco as a child, but he had been employing Pando as a scribe for all his communications with Spanish officials for some ten years. Atahuallpa's successors had quickly learned to use alphabetical writing for their own political purposes in dealing with the Spaniards, some even becoming literate in the foreign medium.[30] The early seventeenth-century *Huarochirí Manuscript*, written by an anonymous Andean person who was probably recruited by the Spanish priest Francisco de Ávila, begins by stating that "if the ancestors of the people called Indians had known writing in former times, then the lives they lived would not have faded from

Ralph Bauer

view until now. As the mighty past of the Spanish Vira Cochas is visible until now, so too would theirs be."[31] Although we must assume that by the 1570s Andeans understood how Spanish writing functioned, this does not mean that alphabetical semiosis had thoroughly replaced khipu semiosis or that Andeans viewed and used alphabetical writing in exactly the same way as Europeans did. Rather, in appropriating the alphabetical medium, khipu and alphabetical poetics fused into an intercultural colonial hybrid.[32]

Titu Cusi's Hybrid Genealogical Narrative

In order for Titu Cusi to succeed in his diplomatic endeavor of securing an encomienda that would enable him to live under Spanish rule as befits Inca nobility, he had to establish his legitimacy as Inca ruler. This legitimacy was challenged by several factors. Although Sayre Topa had left the Inca's royal tassel at Vilcabamba upon his return to Cuzco, and Titu Cusi had assumed his role as Inca, in the eyes of the Spaniards the legitimate ruler was still Sayre Topa. Moreover, in November 1569 a new viceroy, Francisco de Toledo, had arrived in Peru and announced his hard-line approach to the Inca resistance. This policy entailed a new propaganda campaign. Toledo commissioned Pedro Sarmiento de Gamboa to write a new history of the Incas, which was presented to the emperor in 1572. There, Sarmiento de Gamboa claimed that Titu Cusi was "not a legitimate son of Manco Inca" at all but rather a "bastard."[33] While Sarmiento de Gamboa's judgment must be taken with a grain of salt—coming as it does from an unequivocal apologist for viceroy Toledo's new hard-line policies— and while his history was probably not directly known by any of the collaborators at Vilcabamba in 1570, it represented the emerging consolidation of a particular tradition of Spanish colonial historiography unfavorable to claims of legitimacy by Native resistance movements. Even some of the later mestizo and Indian chroniclers were apparently not persuaded by Titu Cusi's claim to legitimacy. He is not mentioned at all by the Inca Garcilaso de la Vega, a mestizo who wrote during the early seventeenth century; nor is he portrayed in Guaman

Poma de Ayala's *Nueva corónica y buen gobierno*, also composed during the early seventeenth century, which portrays every other Inca ruler, including Manco Inca.[34] As Luis Millones has noted, Titu Cusi's account may thus have in part been produced precisely in order to affirm what he could not assume: that he was "legitimate" among the Inca nobility as supreme ruler.[35] Other critics agree, identifying at least three interrelated objectives that Titu Cusi's account was meant to serve: first, to establish his father's authority and legitimacy as Inca, despite the confusions of the pre-conquest civil war and of the conquest; second, to establish the legitimacy of his own claim to the Inca throne; and third, to expose the Spanish conquerors' claim to lordship over Peru as illegitimate.[36]

In his attempt to establish his legitimacy as ruler, Titu Cusi's narrative would naturally have drawn on the conventions of one or both of the historical genres in Inca oral tradition that Catherine Julien has called the "life history" and the "genealogical narrative."[37] Because each Inca founded his own panaca that kept its own khipu and historical tradition, khipu-based Inca historical narratives were not "general" histories of the Inca dynasty or realm, as was commonly aspired to by European chroniclers in sixteenth-century imperial Spain. Rather, they were partisan histories, exalting different founders and different descent groups that competed with one another for prestige. Inca historical traditions could be at great variance with one another and cannot be measured by modern Western ideological standards of historical "objectivity" or "factuality."[38] Titu Cusi's historical narrative is no exception. Aiming to place his own person in relation to that of Manco Inca and at the center of dynastic lineage, the narrative contains many historical assertions that are uncorroborated—even contradicted—by other surviving sixteenth-century sources. For example, his account of the Spanish conquest places his father at the center stage of events from the beginning, even though most histories are in agreement that Manco Inca, being still an adolescent, was a relatively insignificant figure at the time of the Spanish arrival.[39] Similarly, Titu Cusi's claim that his father became ruler by the explicit will

Ralph Bauer

of his grandfather Huayna Capac, and that Atahuallpa merely governed the empire until Manco Inca was old enough to assume the royal tassel, is contradicted by virtually every other contemporary source and is, overall, highly unlikely to be factual. Even less plausible is his claim that Manco Inca ruled Cuzco at the time the Spaniards arrived in Peru. Modern historians generally agree that Huascar ruled Cuzco before he was defeated and captured by Quisquis, one of Atahuallpa's generals, who thereafter ruled Cuzco on behalf of his lord. Finally, Titu Cusi's claim that he was "the one legitimate son . . . among the many sons whom my father Manco Inca Yupanqui left behind" (58–59) [el hijo legítimo . . . que mi padre Manco Inca Yupanqui dejó entre otros muchos (30)], and that his dying father had explicitly determined him as his successor, is disputed by modern historians, who generally agree that after Manco Inca's death, the royal tassel went to his brother Sayre Topa (whose rule is not mentioned by Titu Cusi).

But while none of these claims would have been unusual or problematic by the partisan poetic standards of pre-Hispanic Andean genres, Titu Cusi's text also stands apart from these traditions in various ways. Especially in its attempt to establish his legitimacy as ruler, the text evidences considerable ambiguities, eclectically appealing to a Spanish logic of succession at some times while appealing to Andean notions at others.[40] Consider, for example, his rationale for asserting his own legitimacy relative to that of his half brothers at the narrative's opening, when addressing García de Castro. He says,

> I would greatly appreciate it if Your Excellency could do me the honor of informing His Majesty that I am the one legitimate son, meaning the eldest and first-born, among the many sons whom my father Manco Inca Yupanqui left behind. He entrusted me to take care of them and to look after them as I would of myself. This is what I have been doing from the day he died up to this very day; and this is what I am doing now and what I will continue to do as long as God keeps me alive, because it is right that

sons do what their fathers have ordered them to do, especially during their last days. (58–59)

[me hará su señoría merced de avisar a su majestad de cómo yo soy el hijo legítimo, digo el primero y mayorazgo que mi padre Mango Inga Yupangui dejó entre otros muchos, de los cuales me mandó que tuviesse cargo y mirase por ellos como por mi propia persona, lo qual yo he hecho desde que él falleció hasta hoy, y lo hago y haré mientras Dios me diere vida, pues es cosa tan justa que los hijos hagan los que sus padres les mandan, en especial en sus postrimeros días.] (30–31)

The claim to legitimacy based here on the assertion of primogeniture—that he was "the eldest and first-born, among the many sons whom my father Manco Inca Yupanqui left behind"—is consistent with a Spanish, but not an Inca, logic of succession. In Inca culture (which was polygamous), legitimacy depended not on who was the eldest of the ruler's sons but on the social status of each son's mother. This may be why Titu Cusi's oral history departs from traditional conventions of Inca historical/biographical genres as it would have been recorded in the khipu, and "we learn nothing," as Julien observes, "about his father's principal wife and children, or the name of his lineage, or of the image that served as his surrogate (*huaoque*)."[41] To further Titu Cusi's political interests in the colonial context of viceregal Peru, his text appropriates, then, Spanish conventions of historiography and biography of kings, such as Fernán Pérez de Guzmán's *Generaciones y semblanzas* (1450) and Hernando del Pulgar's *Claros varones de Castilla* (1486), including its conventional understanding of lineage, legitimacy, and "bastardry."[42] By contrast, when he later attempts to establish the legitimacy of his father, Manco Inca, Titu Cusi invokes the Inca logic of succession. Manco Inca was the "legitimate son," he says, because he "had pure royal blood" ("hijo legítimo de sangre real"), whereas Manco's older brothers, Atahuallpa and Huascar, did not because their mothers were "commoners" ("de sangre soez e baja") (61 [33]). Thus,

Ralph Bauer

on a level of both form and content, Titu Cusi *appropriates* the Spanish medium as an extension of khipu semiosis for the purpose of intercultural communication. The result is an eclectic and hybrid text that is fraught with internal contradictions and ambiguities that cannot be fully accounted for by either the Andean or the Spanish cultural context.

Conclusion

It is impossible to determine with certainty to whose agency the contradictions and ambiguities in Titu Cusi's account should most plausibly be attributed. What seems clear enough is that Titu Cusi's text, as it comes down to us, manifests intercultural tensions that originate from the clash of Andean and European early modern mediascapes. Drawing on formal and ideological elements of both khipu-based Inca genres and letter-based Spanish genres, it fuses the two semiotic traditions into a colonial hybrid that ultimately leaves its intercultural contradictions unresolved. Native collaborations in colonial textual productions such as Titu Cusi's can be seen as instances of what Steve Stern has called "resistant adaptation," a dialectic between opposition and accommodation to colonial authority as well as between political opposition and cultural integration, adoption, and appropriation of the act of intercultural textual production.[43] At the same time, however, we may understand Titu Cusi's "instructions" to the departing governor García de Castro to serve as his mouthpiece in the context of Andean mediascapes and in its intertextual relationships to Inca genres of history, as they depended on a dialogical relationship between oral performance and the secondary material recording device of the khipu. While it appropriates the European medium, it reshapes it to function within the logic of Andean semiosis. When seen in this light, Titu Cusi's account of the conquest of Peru invites us to go beyond the scholarly debate about whether or not the khipu represented a form of "writing" and instead to ask how writing could function, in the colonial Andean context, as a sort of "khipu."

Notes

1. For historical background on this text, see Ralph Bauer's introduction to Titu Cusi Yupanqui, Diego de Castro, *An Inca Account of the Conquest of Peru. By Titu Cusi Yupanqui*, ed. and trans. Ralph Bauer (Boulder: University of Colorado Press, 2005).

2. Frank Salomon, "Chronicles of the Impossible: Notes on Three Peruvian Indigenous Historians," in *From Oral to Written Expression: Native Andean Chronicles of the Early Colonial Period*, ed. Rolena Adorno (Syracuse NY: Maxwell School of Citizenship and Public Affairs, 1982), 9.

3. For a theorization of non-written "texts" in terms of a "colonial semiosis" (codexes, *khipu*, drawings, and so on) as part of the totality of cultural production that took place after 1492, see Walter Mignolo, *The Darker Side of the Renaissance: Literacy, Territoriality, and Colonization* (Ann Arbor: University of Michigan Press, 1995). For a discussion of non-alphabetical verbal art as a sort of "writing," see Elizabeth Hill Boone, "Introduction: Writing and Recording Knowledge," in *Writing without Words: Alternative Literacies in Mesoamerica and the Andes*, ed. Elizabeth Hill Boone and Walter D. Mignolo (Durham: Duke University Press, 1994), 3–26.

4. Titu Cusi, *An Inca Account*, 136; *Instrucción del Inca don Diego de Castro Titu Cusi Yupanqui*, ed. Alessandra Luiselli (Mexico: Universidad Nacional Autónoma de México, 2001), 115. All further page references to this translation and edition will hereafter be cited parenthetically in the text. An electronic edition of the *Instrucción del Inca Don Diego de Castro Titu Cusi Yupanqui al Licenciado don Lope García de Castro* is available at the Early Americas Digital Archive (EADA), http://www.mith2.umd.edu/ eada/html/display.php?docs=titucusi_instruccion.xml.

5. More recently, however, Nicole Delia Legnani has argued that Titu Cusi's account would more likely have been related not in Quechua but rather in "the secret language of the Incas," an Aymara with a heavy Puquina substrate, often used in sacred rituals. Legnani, introduction to Titu Cusi, *A 16th-Century Account of the Conquest* (Cambridge: Harvard University Press, 2005), x. By contrast, Catherine Julien has pointed out that Titu Cusi could have related his account in Spanish, considering the fact that he had spent five years in Spanish captivity in Cuzco when he was still a young boy (from age seven to twelve) and probably knew some Spanish. Julien, introduction to Titu Cusi Yupanqui, *History of How the Spaniards Arrived in Peru: Dual-Language Edition*, trans. Catherine Julien (India-

Ralph Bauer

napolis: Hackett, 2005), xiv. Although it is impossible to draw a definitive conclusion on this question, I do not find these recent arguments convincing. On the one hand, if Titu Cusi's text had indeed been delivered in the Incas' "secret language," the making of the Spanish text would have required an additional translator; but none is mentioned in the *poder*. On the other hand, almost thirty years had passed between Titu Cusi's return and the time when he related his narrative in 1570. The language spoken at Vilcabamba was Quechua, and we can assume that fray Marcos García was also proficient in that language, because the church had encouraged the writing of catechisms and the formal training of missionaries in Quechua until the third Provincial Council of Lima (1583). I therefore proceed on the traditional assumption that the text was originally related orally by Titu Cusi in Quechua, then translated into Spanish by Marcos García, and finally transcribed by Martín de Pando, Titu Cusi's scribe, who had lived at Vilcabamba for about ten years. On the politics of language in viceregal Peru, see Bruce Mannheim, *The Language of the Inka since the European Invasion* (Austin: University of Texas Press, 1991), 61–109; Kenneth Andrien, *Andean Worlds: Indigenous History, Culture, and Consciousness under Spanish Rule, 1532–1825* (Albuquerque: University of New Mexico Press, 2001), 106–19; Alan Durston, *Pastoral Quechua: The History of Christian Translation in Colonial Peru, 1550–1650* (Notre Dame IN: University of Notre Dame Press, 2007); Peter Cole, Gabriella Hermon, and Mario Daniel Martín, eds., *Language in the Andes* (Newark: University of Delaware Press, 1994); and Sabine Dedenbach-Salazar and Lindsey Crickmay, eds., *La lengua de la cristianización en Latinoamérica: Catequización e instrucción en lenguas amerindias/The Language of Christianization in Latin America: Catechisation and Instruction in Amerindian Languages* (Markt Schwaben: Saurwein, 1999).

6. For arguments for and against Titu Cusi's "acculturation," see Liliana Regalado de Hurtado, "La relación de Titu Cussi Yupanqui: Valor de un testimonio tardío," *Histórica* 5.1 (1981): 45–62; and Legnani, introduction.

7. Roberto González Echevarría, "Humanismo, retórica y las crónicas de la conquista," in *Isla a su vuelo fugitiva: Ensayos criticos sobre literatura hispanoamericana* (Madrid: José Porrúa Turanzas, 1983), 9–26; see also his *Myth and Archive: A Theory of Latin American Narrative* (Cambridge: Cambridge University Press, 1990).

8. Walter Mignolo, "El métatexto historiográfico y la historiografía Indiana," *MLN* 96.2 (1981): 389; see also his "Cartas, crónicas y relaciones del

descubrimiento y la conquista," in *Historia de la literatura hispanoameri-cana: Época colonial*, ed. Luis Iñigo Madrigal (Madrid: Ediciones Cátedra, 1982), 57–116.

9. Bernhard Siegert, *Passagiere und Papiere: Schreibakte auf der Schwelle zwischen Spanien und Amerika (1530–1600)* (Munich: Wilhelm Fink, 2006), 24; see also his *Passage des Digitalen: Zeichenpraktiken der neuzeitli-chen Wissenschaften* (Berlin: Brinkmann and Bose 2003) and *Relays: Liter-ature as an Epoch of the Postal System*, trans. Kevin Repp (Stanford: Stanford University Press, 1999).

10. See Ralph Bauer, *The Cultural Geography of Colonial American Literatures: Empire, Travel, Modernity* (Cambridge: Cambridge University Press, 2003), 30–76.

11. Bartolomé de Las Casas, *Brevísima relación de la destrucción de las Indias* (Madrid: Ediciones Catedra S.A., 1989), 77. See Lewis Hanke, *The Span-ish Struggle for Justice in the Conquest of America* (Philadelphia: University of Pennsylvania Press, 1965); see also Anthony Pagden, *The Fall of Natural Man: The American Indian and the Origins of Comparative Ethnology* (Cambridge: Cambridge University Press, 1982); and David Brading, *The First America: The Spanish Monarchy, Creole Patriots, and the Liberal State, 1492–1867* (Cambridge: Cambridge University Press, 1991), 70–71.

12. Alessandra Luiselli, "Introducción," in *Instrucción del Inca don Diego de Castro Titu Cusi Yupanqui*, 30n1.

13. See Bauer, introduction; also Legnani, who observes that "the text's dia-logic structure eludes Spanish legal forms for validating testimonies which give more authority to eyewitness over hearsay testimonies" (intro-duction, 18).

14. Susan Niles, *The Shape of Inca History: Narrative and Architecture in an Andean Empire* (Iowa City: University of Iowa Press, 1999), 40, 27, xvii, 28–44; Martin Lienhard, *La voz y su huella: Escritura y conflicto étnico-social en América Latina, 1492–1988* (Hanover NH: Ediciones del Norte, 1991), 186–92. See also Margot Beyersdorff and Sabine Dedenbach-Salazar Sáenz, eds., *Andean Oral Traditions: Discourse and Literature/Tradiciones Orales Andinas: Discurso y Literatura* (Bonn: Bonner Ameri-kanistische Studien, 1994).

15. See Gary Urton, *Signs of the Inka Khipu: Binary Coding in the Andean Knotted-String Records* (Austin: University of Texas Press, 2003), 32, 35, 55, 64; for some highlights in the history of khipu scholarship, see also Mar-cia Ascher and Robert Ascher, *Code of the Quipu* (Ann Arbor: University

of Michigan Press, 1981); and Jeffrey Quilter and Gary Urton, eds., *Narrative Threads: Accounting and Recounting in Andean Khipu* (Austin: University of Texas Press, 2002).

16. Galen Brokaw, "The Poetics of Khipu Historiography: Felipe Guaman Poma de Ayala's *Nueva Corónica* and the *Relación de los Quipucamayos*," *Latin American Research Review* 38.3 (October 2003): 111–47, quote on 113.

17. Brokaw, "The Poetics of Inca Historiography," 113; see also Jack Goody, *The Power of the Written Tradition* (Washington DC: Smithsonian Institution Press, 2000) and *The Interface between the Written and the Oral* (Cambridge: Cambridge University Press, 1987).

18. On the difference between early modern and modern understandings of the "public," see Jürgen Habermas, *The Structural Transformation of the Public Sphere: An Inquiry into a Category of Bourgeois Society*, trans. Thomas Burger (Cambridge: MIT Press, 1996), 18.

19. See Margot Beyersdorff, "Writing without Words/Words without Writing: The Culture of the Khipu," *Latin American Research Review* 40.3 (2005): 299; see also Brokaw, "The Poetics of Inca Historiography," 113.

20. Baltasar de Ocampo, "Account of the Province of Vilcapampa and the narrative of the execution of the Inca Tupac Amaru," in *The History of the Incas by Pedro Sarmiento de Gamboa and the Execution of Tupac Amaru by Captain Baltasar de Ocampo*, ed. Clements Markham (Cambridge: Printed for the Hakluyt Society, 1907), 203–29.

21. The notion of "Viracocha" as a "creator god" appears to be the product of a colonial cultural development; see Pierre Duviols, "Los nombres quechua de Viracocha, supuesto 'Dios Creador' de los evangelizadores," *Allpanchis: Revista del Instituto de Pastoral Andina* 10 (1977): 53–64; see also Arthur Demarest, *Viracocha: The Nature and Antiquity of the Andean High God* (Cambridge: Peabody Museum of Archaeology and Ethnology, Harvard University, 1991).

22. For a discussion of the Andean oral traditions surrounding this scene, see Regina Harrison, *Signs, Songs, and Memory in the Andes: Translating Quechua Language and Culture* (Austin: University of Texas Press, 1989); also Jesús Lara, *La poesía quechua* (Mexico City: Fondo de Cultura Económica, 1979), 92; and Nathan Wachtel, *The Vision of the Vanquished: The Spanish Conquest of Peru through Indian Eyes, 1530–1570*, trans. Ben and Siân Reynolds (New York: Barnes and Noble, 1977), 35. On Andean oral traditions more generally, see also Beyersdorff and Dedenbach-Salazar Sáenz, *Andean Oral Traditions*.

23. Juan de Betanzos, *Narrative of the Incas*, trans. and ed. Roland Hamilton and Dana Buchanan (Austin: University of Texas Press, 1996), 263.

24. Felipe Guamán Poma de Ayala, *Nueva corónica y buen gobierno* (Paris: Institut d'ethnologie, 1936), 357.

25. Sabine MacCormack, *On the Wings of Time: Rome, the Incas, Spain, and Peru* (Princeton NJ: Princeton University Press, 2007), 46.

26. Niles, *The Shape of Inca History*, 40, 27, xvii, 28–44; see also Beyersdorff and Dedenbach-Salazar Sáenz, *Andean Oral Traditions*.

27. Niles, *The Shape of Inca History*, 32–37; see also Julien, introduction, xix.

28. Rosaleen Howard, "Spinning a Yarn: Landscape, Memory, and Discourse Structure in Quechua Narratives," in Quilter and Urton, *Narrative Threads*, 26–52.

29. Constance Classen, *Inca Cosmology and the Human Body* (Salt Lake City: University of Utah Press, 1993), 127.

30. On Andean appropriations of the European alphabetical medium, see Rolena Adorno, ed., *From Oral to Written Expression: Native Andean Chronicles of the Early Colonial Period* (Syracuse NY: Maxwell School of Citizenship and Public Affairs, 1982); and Rolena Adorno, *Guaman Poma: Writing and Resistance in Colonial Peru* (Austin: University of Texas Press, 1986); see also Raquel Chang-Rodríguez, *La apropiación del signo: Tres cronistas indígenas del Perú* (Tempe: Center for Latin American Studies, Arizona State University, 1988); Raquel Chang-Rodríguez, *El discurso disidente: Ensayos de literatura colonial peruana* (Lima: Pontificia Universidad Católica del Perú, 1991); Raquel Chang-Rodríguez, *Violencia y subversion en la prosa colonial hispanoamericana, siglos xvi y xvii* (Potomac MD: Studias Humanitatis, 1982); Raquel Chang-Rodríguez, "A Forgotten Indian Chronicle: Titu Cusi Yupanqui's *Relación de la conquista del Perú*," *Latin American Indian Literatures* 4 (1980): 87–95; and Raquel Chang-Rodríguez, "Writing as Resistance: Peruvian History and the *Relación* of Titu Cussi Yupanqui," in Adorno, *From Oral to Written Expression*, 41–64; and Susana Jákfalvi-Leiva, "De la voz a la escritura: La *Relación* de Titu Cusi (1570)," *Revista de Crítica Literaria Latinoamericana* 19.37 (1993): 259–77.

31. Frank Salomon and George Urioste, eds., *The Huarochirí Manuscript: A Testament of Ancient and Colonial Andean Religion* (Austin: University of Texas Press, 1991), 41. For a discussion of this text, see Sabine Dedenbach-Salazar, "El arte verbal de los textos quechuas de Huarochirí (Perú, siglo XVII) reflejado en la organización del discurso y en los medios estilísticos,"

Ralph Bauer

in Beyersdorff and Dedenbach-Salazar Sáenz, *Andean Oral Traditions*, 21–50; for historical context see Karen Spalding, *Huarochirí: An Andean Society under Inca and Spanish Rule* (Stanford: Stanford University Press, 1984).

32. For a more general discussion of the hybridity of Titu Cusi's text, see Bauer, introduction. For a similar discussion with regard to Guaman Poma's text, see Brokaw, "The Poetics of Khipu Historiography."

33. Pedro Sarmeniento de Gamboa, "History of the Incas," in *History of the Incas by Sarmiento de Gamboa and The Execution of the Inca Tupac Amaru by Captain Baltasar de Ocampo*, trans. and ed. Sir Clements Markham (London: Hakluyt Society, 1907), 193. This is repeated during the early seventeenth century by Baltasar de Ocampo, who wrote that Titu Cusi was not "the natural and legitimate Lord of that land (he being a bastard) having no right." Ocampo, "Account of the Province of Vilcapampa and the Narrative of the Execution of the Inca Tupac Amaru," in Markham, *History of the Incas*, 213.

34. El Inca Garcilaso de la Vega, *Obras completas del Inka Garcilaso de la Vega*, ed. P. Carmelo Saenz de Santa María, Biblioteca de Autores Españoles desde la formación del lenguaje hasta nuestros días, vol. 133 (Madrid: Real Academia Española, 1960).

35. Luis Millones, "Introducción," in *Ynstrucción del Ynga Don Diego de Castro Titu Cusi Yupangui*, ed. Luis Millones (Lima: Ediciones El Virrey, 1985), 7. For an extended discussion of these historical inaccuracies, see Carlos Romero, "Biografía de Tito Cusi Yupanqui," in Urteaga, *Relación de la conquista*, xxii–xxiv.

36. Chang-Rodríguez, "A Forgotten Indian Chronicle," 88.

37. Catherine Julien, *Reading Inca History* (Iowa City: University of Iowa Press, 2000), 49–90.

38. For a history of the rise of this modern ideology of history as a "science," see Peter Novick, *That Noble Dream: The "Objectivity Question" and the American Historical Profession* (Cambridge: Cambridge University Press, 1988); on the prehistory of this notion during the sixteenth and seventeenth centuries, see Bauer, *Cultural Geography*, esp. chapters 2 and 3; on the eighteenth century, see Jorge Cañizares-Esguerra, *How to Write the History of the New World: Histories, Epistemologies, and Identities in the Eighteenth-Century Atlantic World* (Stanford: Stanford University Press, 2001).

39. See, e.g., Guillermo Lohmann Villena, "El Inca Titu Cusi Yupanqui y su entrevista con el oidor Matienzo (1565)," *Mercurio Peruano* 66 (1941): 4.

40. For a more extended discussion of this, see Julien, *Reading Inca History*, 23; also Bauer, introduction.

41. Julien, introduction, xix; also Julien, *Reading Inca History*, and Brokaw, "The Poetics of Inca Historiography."

42. On Spanish conventions of biography, see Robert Brian Tate, introduction to Fernán Pérez de Guzman, *Generaciones y semblanzas* (London: Tamesis, 1965), xxii–xxiii; see also Brokaw, "The Poetics of Inca Historiography," 121.

43. Steve J. Stern, "New Approaches to the Study of Peasant Rebellion and Consciousness: Implications of the Andean Experience," in *Resistance, Rebellion, and Consciousness in the Andean Peasant World, 18th to 20th Centuries*, ed. Steve J. Stern (Madison: University of Wisconsin Press, 1987), 3–25, 11.

Ralph Bauer

11

Christian Indians at War

EVANGELISM AND MILITARY COMMUNICATION IN THE ANGLO-FRENCH-NATIVE BORDERLANDS

Jeffrey Glover

In the fall of 1710, the French Jesuit Louis d'Avaugour wrote to his superior Joseph Louis-Germain to report on the town of Lorette, located on the bank of the Saint-Charles River just northwest of Quebec. After briefly describing his evangelical endeavors among the "holy savages" (Christian Indians) living in the town, d'Avaugour quickly turned to the topic of France's precarious relationship with neighboring Huron military allies.[1] In the face of growing English control over trading routes, he worried that the Hurons might "flock to the neighboring [English] heretics, from whom they make a much greater profit." Yet d'Avaugour also had a solution to the colony's uncertainty about the hearts and minds of its Huron allies. Though the trade had faltered, d'Avaugour suggested that missionary outreach might secure the political allegiance of the Hurons. "Nothing else than religion retains the savages in their fidelity to the French," he insisted (66:173).

The problem of monitoring and tracking political loyalties had a long history in the French, English, and Native borderlands. New France and New England had made many friends and enemies among Native groups since the appearance of permanent settlements on the North Atlantic coast in the early seventeenth century. Wars and skirmishes among tribes and colonies involved constantly shifting alliances, and d'Avaugour's anxieties about "retain[ing] the savages in their fidelity" paralleled those of many European, Algonquian, and Iroquois leaders, who had conflicting systems for recording alliances. Within the chaotic world of borderland diplomacy, Christian Indians were a particular source of anxiety. As multilingual individuals who could switch sides rather easily, Native converts were often involved in controversies over alliances and allegiances.[2] In this essay, I examine missionary accounts of political loyalties during King Philip's War and the first decades of the French and Indian Wars. In the past few decades, many scholars have done important work on the complexity of missionary identity in North American settlements.[3] This work has dispelled the notion that Native converts were merely passive recipients of religious instruction from doctrinaire evangelists. European evangelism combined concepts from tribal and European religions, and Natives played an active role in seeking out Christianity and merging it with Native religious concepts. Yet with a few important exceptions, scholarship on colonial evangelism has focused on particular national and religious cultures, looking at John Eliot's mission to praying Indians in New England, for example, or at French Jesuit missions in Canada or Louisiana.[4] As I will try to show here, missionaries were also involved in the systems of military and diplomatic correspondence that connected tribes, colonies, and imperial crowns. While most missionary publications were religious in nature, these political networks involved many other kinds of genres and media, including the petitions and treaty papers of colonial states as well as the rituals and non-alphabetic writings of Native peoples. In what follows, I compare two texts by colonial missionaries, Daniel Gookin's *An Historical Account of the Doings and Sufferings of the Christian Indi-*

Jeffrey Glover

ans in New England (1677), a report on the role of praying Indians in King Philip's War, and d'Avaugour's letter on the mission of Lorette in New France (1710), an account of the role of Huron converts in the raid on Deerfield, Massachusetts, in 1704. Although Gookin and d'Avaugour were separated by national and religious differences, they faced many similar challenges as European guardians of Indian converts. Their chief adversaries in the New World were not hostile Indians or imperial rivals but rather military leaders in their own settlements, who viewed Christian Indians as allies of questionable loyalty and often sought to banish or marginalize them.

I examine how missionaries and converts negotiated political and diplomatic communications in order to defend their communities and churches during times of inter-imperial and intertribal conflict. Both Gookin and d'Avaugour tried to persuade other colonists of the military usefulness of converts by publicizing accounts of Christian Indians' battlefield exploits. Such publications were a way of defending missions from opponents who believed that Indian converts were unreliable allies or traitors. And while these defenses were imperialistic in their designs, placing converts in a subordinate role as servants of European military interests, as I will show here, both Gookin and d'Avaugour pay remarkable attention to indigenous practices of war and diplomacy. Rather than attempting to replace Native modes of communication with Christian ones (as missionaries are often thought to do), Gookin and d'Avaugour suggest instead that colonial writing must accommodate Native American practices of political and military communication, even as missionaries eradicate Native religion. Gookin and d'Avaugour articulate administrative procedures for maintaining converts' religious commitments while encouraging their retention of indigenous military and diplomatic practices useful to imperial crowns. These efforts at reconciling religion and war led to radically different outcomes; most of the converts under Gookin's authority were resettled, while many Hurons live near Quebec to this day. Yet read alongside each other, these texts call into question the assumption that Native American politics was confined to the realm of an oral culture that operated outside the domain of writing, print, and other settler technologies.

Tracking Loyalty in Gookin's *Historical Account*

An Historical Account has received little scholarly attention when compared to printed narratives by Mary Rowlandson, Increase Mather, and others. One reason is that Gookin's book expressed profound sympathy for praying Indians at a time when many English colonists viewed them as traitors. Gookin often appears in the historical record as a lonely advocate for praying Indians in a world hostile to their existence. I will suggest here that discussions of Gookin and his book should not be limited to a consideration of colonial missions and their fate on the English frontier. While King Philip's War largely involved the English United colonies and the Wampanoags and their Native allies, French-allied Native groups also joined raids, and the English were constantly suspicious of French-Native alliances. One reason Gookin wrote *An Historical Account* was to argue that evangelism could produce powerful Indian allies that would bolster colonial forces in conflicts with hostile Indians or European rivals. Even as Gookin advertises the Indians' civil comportment and religious devotion, he suggests that the English should learn to understand indigenous military practices and knowledge.

Unlike most Massachusetts Bay Colony leaders, Daniel Gookin traveled widely before immigrating to New England. He was born in 1612 in Kent to a family with connections to a wide variety of overseas enterprises.[5] Gookin's father was involved in numerous colonizing efforts, purchasing lands in Ireland as part of Robert Boyle's Munster settlements as well as shares in the Virginia Company, in which he was active throughout the 1620s. Daniel Gookin first appeared in public records after the 1641 Irish Rebellion, when the members of his family fled Munster after the uprising against Cromwellian rule. After immigrating to Virginia, Gookin pursued many of the opportunities available to him as a member of a well-placed colonial family, joining the General Court as a judge and organizing a militia to pro-

Jeffrey Glover

tect outlying Chesapeake settlements from incursions by Powhatan Indians. Soon after arriving, however, he apparently became troubled by the colony's lack of interest in evangelizing Indians. In 1642 Gookin joined with Puritans in Virginia and began corresponding with ministers in the Massachusetts Bay Colony. After a ban on nonconformist religion in Virginia, he moved to Boston, where he was quickly admitted to the church.

After several years in Boston, Gookin accepted a position as superintendent of Eliot's praying towns, a decision that may have been influenced by his recent experience with Ireland. Gookin's duties placed him in the middle of the political networks that connected New England Indians, the Eliot mission, the Bay Colony magistracy, and London administrators. As Richard W. Cogley has detailed in his account of the mission, the position of superintendent involved many kinds of administrative work, including documenting commercial exchanges, arbitrating disputes about land deals between settlers and Natives, and hearing criminal cases involving praying Indians.[6] Gookin also worked as an advocate on behalf of praying Indians seeking to make claims before the New England magistracy, serving as a liaison between converts and government leaders in the colonies. His work in this position included transcribing testimony from Native plaintiffs and drafting petitions on behalf of aggrieved Native parties.

While many praying Indians enjoyed legal standing in English courts as covenanted members of churches, the outbreak of King Philip's War left them in a vulnerable position. The war pitted the English colonies against a Wampanoag-led alliance of Native groups, and both sides were hostile to the praying Indians. Over the course of the war they faced a number of legal restrictions and civil penalties, including forced resettlement.[7] Despite these sanctions, Gookin and those working in his office made many attempts throughout the war to shelter or rescue praying Indians. Many of his efforts involved helping praying Indians negotiate the colonial legal system. Over the course of the war, Gookin's office published and circulated a number of documentary genres, including affidavits, confessions, and requests for leniency. Gookin also transcribed and drafted petitions aimed at protecting converts whose allegiances had been questioned in the war. After the war, he petitioned to have praying Indians freed from enslavement and other sentences meted out on the suspicion of their disloyalty to the English.[8]

After the defeat of King Philip's forces in 1676, the United Colonies passed measures that provided for the resettlement of praying Indians to islands and land reserves, and Gookin lost much of his jurisdiction over converts. Gookin likely began work on *Historical Account* around this time. In an important account of Gookin's publication efforts, J. Patrick Cesarini has argued that the book is an attempt to reconcile a providential narrative of war as a godly test with an empirically verifiable and documented account of praying Indians' "demonstrations of . . . fidelity."[9] And indeed, the book is something of a multimedia document, including certificates, testimonials, eyewitness reports, and other European genres, which show empirical evidence of praying Indian loyalty, and refute reports of their treachery. However, Gookin's engagement with the mediation of political allegiance is not strictly limited to European documents, even though they provide the bulk of his evidence. Gookin's many papers and certificates reference speeches, networks of intelligence and stories, acts of camouflage, and other forms of communication, suggesting that the praying Indians' loyalty can be glimpsed not only in English records but also in indigenous techniques of war and diplomacy that colonial administrators have failed to understand or document.[10]

Many English believed that Native people were unreliable military allies. Algonquian fighters relied heavily on retreat and camouflage, a practice that one colonial leader derisively referred to as a "secret, sculking manner" of war.[11] According to Gookin, such misconceptions have led English leaders to ignore information that might have prevented the worst of the war, including the surprise attacks that initiated the conflict. Describing why the English were taken unawares by the outbreak of hostilities, Gookin claims that English leaders ignored key reports from praying Indian allies:

Jeffrey Glover

In April, 1675, before the war broke forth above two months . . . Waban, the principal Ruler of the praying Indians living at Natick, came to one of the magistrates on purpose, and informed him that he had ground to fear that Sachem Philip and other Indians, his confederates, intended some mischief shortly to the English and Christian Indians. Again, in May, about six weeks before the war began, he came again and renewed the same. Others also of the Christian Indians did speak the same thing, and that when the woods were grown thick with green trees then it was likely to appear, earnestly desiring that care might be had and means used for prevention, at least for preparation for such a thing; and a month after the war began. (440–41)

The English refuse to take Waban seriously and disregard his knowledge of military timing and seasonal cover. After fighting commences, however, they quickly reverse course, embracing Waban and his way of war. In their initial approach to King Philip's groups, Gookin writes, "The English at first thought easily to chastise the insolent doings and murderous practices of the heathen," assuming that racial and cultural superiority translated easily into military dominance. However, "it was found another manner of thing than was expected; for our men could see no enemy to shoot at, but yet felt their bullets out of the thick bushes where they lay in ambushments." In response to these unexpected frustrations, "The Council . . . judged it very necessary to arm and send forth some of the praying Indians to assist our forces, hereby not only to try their fidelity, but to deal better with the enemy in their own ways and methods, according to the Indian manner of fighting" (441). Faced with imminent defeat, colonial leaders resort to combining English military strategies with indigenous military knowledge and practice.

Gookin ultimately claims that the military contributions of praying Indians have played a decisive role in the English victory. This fact, proved by documentary certificates from English captains, weighs heavily against English stereotypes of Native allies as ineffective or treacherous. Gookin writes:

I contend that the small company of our Indian friends have taken and slain of the enemy, in the summer of 1676, not less than four hundred; and their fidelity and courage is testified by the certificates of their captains, that are inserted in the close of this discourse. It may be said in truth, that God made use of these poor, despised and hated Christians, to do great service for the churches of Christ in New England, in this day of their trial; and I think it was observed by impartial men, that, after our Indians went out, the balance turned of the English side. (513)

English practices have finally caught up to Indian ones. The documentary record of certificates from English captains dispels superstitions about Native military tactics, showing that praying Indians are brave and loyal soldiers despite the fact that they employ a different manner of fighting. By paying attention to indigenous sources, Gookin's mission makes English documents accountable to Native ways of war, with enormous consequences for the outcome of the fighting.

At the close of the manuscript, Gookin broadens his focus to some of the geopolitical stakes involved in heeding indigenous tactics. One of the most frequent accusations against praying Indians was that they would revert to tribal ways at moments of conflict.[12] Many English leaders and ministers circulated stories about praying Indians abandoning English towns for tribal settlements. Gookin seeks to correct these stories by citing indigenous sources, which reveal that the vanished praying Indians have in reality been taken captive by French-allied tribes. Gookin thus presents evangelism as a way to open international channels of communication that will enable the English to monitor European rivals and their Native alliances.

Gookin is well aware that praying Indians have begun to disappear mysteriously into Indian country. These disappearances, he writes, have been a matter of "scandal and offence, (to such as are ready to take up any thing to reproach the profession of religion among the Indians)" (521). While many colonists have seen the disappearances as a backsliding from religion, or a betrayal of the English, Gookin suggests

Jeffrey Glover

that captivity, rather than the abandonment of Christianity, is the main reason for the vanishing of the Indians. Indeed, in their exposure to attacks from hostile tribes, praying Indians share a common lot with English settlers in the countryside:

> In this month of September, about the 19th day, a party of Indians fell on a village called Hatfield; near Hadley; they burnt some dwelling-houses and barns, that stood without the line, and wounded and killed about twelve persons, and carried away captive twenty English persons, most of them women and children. It was conceived, at first, that this mischief was done by a party of Mahawkes. . . . But it appeared afterward, by an English prisoner that escaped from the enemy, that this party of Indians . . . had fled to the French about Quebec . . . for, on the very same day, another pty of Indians, that came from the French, came to Naamkeke, near Chelmsford; and there, either by force or persuasion, carried away with them Wannalancet, the sachem, and all his company, excepting two men, whereof one was the minister, and their wives and children, and one widow that escaped to the English. (520)

This passage adopts many of the conventions of the English captivity narrative, describing the helplessness of innocents in the face of an Indian onslaught. However, it also dramatically reverses other narratives' assumptions about the religious and cultural commitments of praying Indians. Far from representing a reversion to tribalism, the disappearances of converts can be traced back to the involvement of the French, who direct Mohawks or hostile Iroquois to attack both English settlements and Indian converts. While the English have conceived of King Philip's War in racial terms, as a struggle between white colonials and barbarous Indians, Gookin shows that the conflict is actually part of a broader geopolitical rivalry among European empires in which the captivity and conversion of Indians plays a central part.

For Gookin, the pursuit of indigenous knowledge of warfare is thus inextricably bound up with geopolitical calculation and imperial strategy. The networks of captive bodies, rumors, and stories that link tribes are an important source of information for understanding the threats to English empire in the region. Gookin brings his narrative to a close with a speech by the Christian sachem Waban. In it, Waban delivers an extended oration in which he forgives the English for their many sins against praying Indian communities. However, Waban also calls attention to the importance of information from praying Indians in tracing and interpreting the complicated acts of proxy warfare that are part of imperial rivalry in America. The ability of Gookin and the other evangelists to communicate with praying Indians suggests that organized evangelical efforts are central both to religious redemption and regional security. Asked about the true cause of apparent praying Indian defections, Waban responds:

> That God knew, that they had done their utmost endeavours to carry themselves so that they might approve their fidelity and love to the English. But yet, some English were still ready to speak the contrary of them, as in this matter instanced; and in that business at Cocheco, lately, when the Indians were carried away by the Maquas [Iroquois]; yet the English say, they ran away to the Maquas and were not carried away; yet . . . I know the governor and magistrates and many good men had other thoughts of them and more charity toward them. (522–23)

At this moment, evangelism is given a geopolitical importance, serving as a crucial means of acquiring information about the place of English colonial endeavors in a larger international and intertribal world. Gookin and fellow administrators of praying towns are the only English capable of divining the hand of the French in what appears to be a conflict between the English and the Indians.

While Gookin is eager to show that praying Indians have abandoned tribal traditions that are inimical to English civility and religion, he urges New England colonists to learn to understand and track Native military and diplomatic communications. If the English want to win frontier wars, they must follow the Indians' lead, embracing camouflage, guerrilla warfare, and surreptitious networks of intelligence. By the same token, they must learn to cultivate sources among the praying Indians, who alone are able to expose the involvement of New France in raids against English towns. Rather than transforming Indians into English subjects, Gookin wants to preserve their existing military and diplomatic networks. Gookin's book is undoubtedly a reflection of the interests of English evangelists; while Indians are often quoted, their speech is heavily stylized, and is almost certainly edited. But broadening our focus beyond Gookin's book to the military and political networks of which it was a part enables us to see the pressure that indigenous modes of communication exerted upon English writing. According to Gookin, any account of the war and its consequences must draw upon indigenous sources.

Gookin's *Historical Account* would remain at the margins for many decades. It circulated in copies until 1836, when it was published in the American Antiquarian Society's *Transactions and Collections* series.[13] The book's failure to find a printer suggests the waning of transatlantic financial support for evangelical ventures after the war. Yet Gookin's book was also part of a much broader network of military and diplomatic communication that was not confined to English-speaking readers. Indeed, Gookin's invocation of a shadowy French presence lurking behind the Maqua Indians suggests that similar questions about alliances and loyalty were being raised elsewhere.

D'Avaugour's Holy Savages and the Deerfield Raid

Like their English counterparts, the French were concerned about the loyalty and effectiveness of Native allies, but for different reasons. While French involvement in King Philip's War amounted only to the encouragement of occasional raids, the outbreak of the Nine Years' War (1688–97) and the War of the Spanish Succession (1702–13) forced New France to mobilize against New England and forge formal military alliances with Native groups.[14] While some Native groups, such as the Abenakis and Pennacooks (who had participated in King Philip's War), joined the French in attacks against the English, others were often reluctant to engage in yet another conflict and hesitated to fully commit to the French side. Still others, such as the Hurons, fought alongside the French, but for their own reasons, such as collecting captives, symbolic goods such as scalps, or spoils that could serve as currency in the regional trade.[15] Thus, while the French depended upon Native allies, they were uneasy about the Natives' commitment to their cause and their differing understanding of the ends of war.

As the priest of the Jesuit mission at the Huron town of Lorette, Louis d'Avaugour was at the center of the conflicts over Native alliances and wartime rituals that surfaced after the intensification of war with New England. Lorette was originally established in 1673 by Huron refugees from the Iroquois-Huron War. French Jesuits built a chapel in the town in 1674 modeled after the one at Loreto in Italy, and many Hurons converted to Catholicism, becoming known for their intense piety and regular acts of devotion.[16] While the Lorettans (as converts were called) inspired nothing like the virulent racism directed at praying Indians in New England, they were still a source of anxiety. A French military commander saw them as "the most loyal Indians that we have," but other French leaders were suspicious of such praise and "complain[ed]" of the "excessive scrupulosity" of the converts, especially their unwillingness to drink wine at political summits (66:157).[17] More troubling still from the French point of view was their move in 1697 to a new site (Jeune Lorette) and the persistence of Huron domestic and agricultural customs amid Catholic rituals. These developments raised the suspicion that Hurons were using Christianity to maintain political autonomy. The French were also concerned that the weakness of their own position in the regional trade might drive Indians to seek out alliances with the English.[18]

D'Avaugour joined the mission at Lorette shortly after the conclusion of the Deerfield raid.[19] His work there included many administrative tasks, such as preaching and organizing Huron devotions. Like many Jesuits, he described his activities in written correspondence os-

Jeffrey Glover

tensibly addressed to his French Jesuit superiors but also intended for copying and dissemination among broader audiences of priests, government officials, and colonial investors. While addressed as a private communication to Joseph Louis-Germain, d'Avaugour's letter about the Hurons was composed in Latin, a language of international correspondence, indicating his ambitions for the document's publication.[20] In the letter, d'Avaugour presents Lorette as a model mission, describing the Hurons' faultless dedication to Catholic observances. However, he also argues for the geopolitical importance of Jesuit missions and tries to show how the government at Lorette has retained the loyalty of tribes who might otherwise have deserted New France. D'Avaugour argues that the introduction of Catholic rituals, combined with a respect for existing Huron ways of war, will produce "holy savages" who cling to Catholic faith while fighting France's enemies.

D'Avaugour opens the letter by presenting the Hurons as devoted converts. Lorette, he claims, is a triumph of evangelism. The Indians there "practice piety openly and in security." Their devotion rivals that of any European. "Every day at early morn, as soon as they awake, they repair to the church," he writes, and "neither rigorous December nor the burning Dog-days can deter any from this pious duty" (66:149). "The very children vie in outstripping their seniors," and "[t]heir modesty is so remarkable that the French passing through the village admire it—to their own confusion, when they compare themselves and their behavior with these barbarians" (66:149, 149–51). While many French view Indians as profligate drinkers, d'Avaugour informs his superior that "[d]runkenness" has been "thoroughly abolished and destroyed in the village" (66:149).

According to d'Avaugour's letter, Catholic rituals have entirely replaced those of Huron religion. The Indians show "extreme docility in obeying the priest who presides over the Mission," he reports (66:155–57). However, the abolition of Indian traditions extends only so far. The centerpiece of the letter is a narrative of Huron heroics in the chaos of the Deerfield raid (which d'Avaugour had heard about secondhand). "[T]his piety of the Lorettans does not at all diminish the warlike

Spirit which these savages commonly possess," he reports. "[I]t merely imposes moderation and certain limits upon their Martial ardor" (66:159). Distinguishing between those military practices that should be preserved and those that should be extinguished is one of d'Avaugour's chief concerns in the letter. He wants to show readers that Christian Indians have not only retained their ferocity but are also better fighters than pagans and more willing to follow widely accepted norms of engagement when it comes to taking captives. Huron conduct in the Deerfield raid is the most important evidence of d'Avaugour's claims to this effect. "The French captains enlist no soldiers more willingly than those from the village of Lorette," he writes (66:161). Part of the Hurons' reliability as fighters derives from their devotion to Catholic rituals. After the call to arms is raised, the Hurons insist on performing last rites, "although it was in the dead of night" (66:163). Their trustworthiness as allies also derives from their love of French leaders. "[T]hey revere above all King Louis of France," for his "noble deeds" and for his "zeal for the extension and protection of religion" (66:161). D'Avaugour is aware that to many of his readers the Hurons might appear to be an exception to the norm. The French viewed Natives as unsteady allies, and in the course of the Deerfield raid a number of Indians from different groups had allegedly abandoned French positions at key moments. Acknowledging that some "savages" were "shamefully put to flight," d'Avaugour concedes the criticisms of skeptics of French-Indian alliances, who in the aftermath of Deerfield blamed Indian cowardice for the weakness of French forces in the face of English counterattacks. Yet the Hurons from Lorette were not among the fleeing Indians, d'Avaugour insists. Indeed, they "[a]lone" retained allegiance to the French alliance, and "[s]ustained and repelled the onset" of the English attack (66:159). The Hurons themselves offer the definitive explanation for their courageous behavior, testifying that the assurance of eternal life embodied in Catholic rites has enabled them to fight bravely: "For who can be strong Knowing that he is the enemy of God; and that, after losing this mortal life, he must enter into everlasting death?" they testify (66:159–61).

The spread of Catholicism and the instruction of Indians in the last rites thus has a practical military value, freeing the Indians from the fear of death and enabling them to fight with abandon. According to d'Avaugour, the suppression of Huron rituals only intensifies the Indians' traditionally warlike spirit. However, in emphasizing the Hurons' stalwart actions on the battlefield, d'Avaugour also touched on another source of anxiety among the French military command. French generals were aware that many groups, such as the Hurons, fought for reasons that had little to do with European politics. Though the Hurons had been at war with the Iroquois for many years, they shared Iroquois battlefield customs, such as captivity, torture, and the ritual execution of prisoners as a way to avenge fallen kinsmen. The taking of captives was a key motivation for Indian participation in the Deerfield raid. France's Indian allies seized many Deerfield settlers, most famously John Williams, whose printed captivity narrative later enjoyed wide readership and many reprintings.[21]

In the immediate aftermath of Deerfield, the intentions of the Indians to torture and even burn some captives left French generals in a bind. While they needed Native military support, they had reservations about leaving other Europeans as Indian captives or abandoning them to torture.[22] D'Avaugour argues that Catholicism, and in particular the rituals of devotion his mission has taught the Hurons, will provide a resolution to this dilemma. His letter closes with the story of the great Huron warrior Thaovenhosen, a Christian who is one of the most imposing fighters in the French camp. "Wherever he fought, the enemy was routed, defeated, and slaughtered," d'Avaugour reports. Yet Thaovenhosen, as a Christian, rejects the traditional practice of torturing captives, and the events of the Deerfield raid soon bring about a conflict between him and the other Indians. In the course of the battle the Huron chief dies, and his relatives clamor for an English captive to burn as revenge. At this decisive moment, Thaovenhosen "ris[es] . . . makes a speech in the assembly of the notables, and boldly pleads for the life of the Captive. He prays, he entreats them to remember that they are Christians and citizens of the village of

Lorette; that dire cruelty is unbecoming to the Christian name; that this injury cannot be branded upon the reputation of the Lorettans without the greatest disgrace" (66:169). After Thaovenhosen concludes the speech, "no one dared to decide upon any greater severity toward the captive" (66:171). Thaovenhosen is fully a warrior. "He is all covered with honorable wounds received in battle," d'Avaugour reports (66:167). But his commitment to Catholic faith has led him to reject indigenous rituals of torture that offend European sensibilities. Thaovenhosen's religious scruples bring the Hurons within the orbit of European laws of war. Jesuit missions, and the rituals and devotion they teach, are the key to waging a successful and lawful campaign against France's rivals.

It is striking that d'Avaugour's letter culminates in a speech by an Indian rather than a sermon from a priest. Thaovenhosen does the work of the Jesuits for them. Importantly, though, it is not just his religious authority that enables him to dissuade his tribesmen from traditional practices of torture—it is also his prowess as a warrior, written on his body in scars sustained in battle. The power of priestly homily thus combines with an indigenous form of corporal textuality to provoke a renegotiation of the place of torture in Huron war-making practices. Thaovenhosen's speech undoubtedly reflects d'Avaugour's particular sense of just Christian warfare. The rejection of torture is presented as a triumph of civility and Catholic morality and a reformation of savage Indian ways. But if one considers d'Avaugour's letter as part of a broader network of political and military communication— one that includes practices such as the taking of captives, the delivery of orations at war councils, and the telling of stories through markings on the body—it becomes clear that d'Avaugour's missionary project was part of a broader struggle over the meaning of Native ways of war. D'Avaugour, like Gookin, informs his superiors that they must learn to work through Native channels, listen to Huron councils, and read Huron bodies. Thus, while his text everywhere erases Huron religion, it also points to the power and influence of Native people in political venues beyond French control.

Jeffrey Glover

Both Gookin and d'Avaugour use claims about frontier political media to advance their missionary endeavors, not to make a plea for multicultural inclusion. However, their texts offer new ways of thinking about indigenous communication and the history of colonial writing. The scholar Bernard J. Hibbitts has called attention to the ways that Western traditions have favored written expressions of conscience over gestural, visual, and aural modes of laying open the heart and mind. Hibbitts argues that Western legal systems should revise standards of admissible evidence to include forms of media that may have aural and visual reaches radically different from documentary systems.[23] For early modern scholars, cases like those of Gookin and d'Avaugour suggest that scholars look beyond paper archives to consider the significance of alternative modes of expression such as speech, gesture, and even bodily writings in constructing conscience, allegiance, and loyalty. Focusing on media from the borderlands will offer new ways of comparing colonial texts from different national and religious traditions. Moreover, these texts' engagement with multiple systems of communication suggests ways scholars can move beyond reductive accounts of Native politics as merely an oral culture. For both Gookin and d'Avaugour, the most credible accounts of border wars are from indigenous sources, and colonists must learn to read them.

Notes

1. Louis d'Avaugour to Joseph Louis-Germain, 1710, in *The Jesuit Relations and Allied Documents: Travels and Explorations of the Jesuit Missionaries in New France, 1610–1791*, 73 vols. (Cleveland: Burrows Brothers, 1891–1901), 66:163; hereafter cited parenthetically in the text.
2. For involvement of praying Indians in King Philip's War, see Jill Lepore, *The Name of War: King Philip's War and the Origins of American Identity* (New York: Knopf, 1998), 21–47. For a wide-ranging account of the place of Jesuit missions in building indigenous alliances with New France, see Tracy Neal Leavelle, *The Catholic Calumet: Colonial Conversions in French and Indian North America* (Philadelphia: University of Pennsylvania Press, 2011).

3. For the English context, see Richard W. Cogley, *John Eliot's Mission to the Indians before King Philip's War* (Cambridge: Harvard University Press, 1999); and David J. Silverman, *Faith and Boundaries: Colonists, Christianity, and Community among the Wampanoag Indians of Martha's Vineyard, 1600–1871* (Cambridge: Cambridge University Press, 2005). For the writings of English missions, see Kristina Bross, *Dry Bones and Indian Sermons: Praying Indians in Colonial America* (Ithaca: Cornell University Press, 2004); Laura M. Stevens, *The Poor Indians: British Missionaries, Native Americans, and Colonial Sensibility* (Philadelphia: University of Pennsylvania Press, 2004); and Hilary E. Wyss, *Writing Indians: Literacy, Christianity, and Native Community in Early America* (Amherst: University of Massachusetts Press, 2000). For the French context, see Leavelle, *Catholic Calumet*; and John H. Pollack, "Native Performances of Diplomacy and Religion in Early New France," in *Native Acts: Indian Performance, 1603–1832*, ed. Joshua David Bellin and Laura L. Mielke (Lincoln: University of Nebraska Press, 2011), 81–116.

4. For comparisons of English and French colonial writing, see Gordon M. Sayre, *Les Sauvages Américains: Representations of Native Americans in French and English Colonial Literature* (Chapel Hill: University of North Carolina Press, 1997). See also Susan Castillo, *Colonial Encounters in New World Writing, 1500–1786: Performing America* (London: Routledge, 2005).

5. I draw my account of Gookin's career from Louise Breen, *Transgressing the Bounds: Subversive Enterprises among the Puritan Elite in Massachusetts, 1630–1692* (Oxford: Oxford University Press, 2001), 145–96.

6. Cogley, *John Eliot's Mission*, 224–29.

7. See James D. Drake, *King Philip's War: Civil War in New England, 1675–1676* (Amherst: University of Massachusetts Press, 1999), 140–67.

8. See Breen, *Transgressing the Bounds*, 170–71.

9. J. Patrick Cesarini, "'What Has Become of Your Praying to God?': Daniel Gookin's Troubled History of King Philip's War," *Early American Literature* 44.3 (2009), 489–515. Daniel Gookin, *An Historical Account of the Doings and Sufferings of the Christian Indians in New England, In the years 1675, 1676, 1677*, in *Transactions and Collections of the American Antiquarian Society* 2 (1836): 423–524, quote on 465; hereafter cited parenthetically in the text.

10. Instructive on this point is Nan Goodman, "The Deer Island Indians and Common Law Performance," in Bellin and Mielke, *Native Acts*, 53–79,

which considers the relationship between praying Indians' wartime actions and English common-law concepts.

11. Daniel Gookin, "Historical Collections of the Indians in New England," *Massachusetts Historical Society Collections*, ser. 1, 1 (1792): 164. For more on this idea see Patrick M. Malone, *The Skulking Way of War: Technology and Tactics among the New England Indians* (Lanham MD: Madison Books, 1991). For more on the broader history of the English and Indian military encounter, see Joyce E. Chaplin, *Subject Matter: Technology, the Body, and Science on the Anglo-American Frontier, 1500–1676* (Cambridge: Harvard University Press, 2001); and Wayne E. Lee, *Barbarians and Brothers: Anglo-American Warfare, 1500–1865* (Oxford: Oxford University Press, 2011).

12. Lepore, *Name of War*, 21–47.

13. For Gookin's luckless fortunes in the print market, see David D. Hall, *Ways of Writing: The Practice and Politics of Text-Making in Seventeenth-Century New England* (Philadelphia: University of Pennsylvania Press, 2008), 18.

14. See Evan Haefeli and Kevin Sweeney, *Captors and Captives: The 1704 French and Indian Raid on Deerfield* (Amherst: University of Massachusetts Press, 2003), 78–92.

15. Peter MacLeod describes this as a "parallel war" in *The Canadian Iroquois and the Seven Years' War* (Toronto: Dundurn Press, 1996), 36.

16. Haefeli and Sweeney, *Captors and Captives*, 59–63.

17. Le Roy Bacqueville de la Potherie, *Historie de l'Amérique Septentrionale: Relation d'un séjour en Nouvelle-France* (1722; reprint, Monaco: Rocher, 1997), 2:486; quoted in Haefeli and Sweeney, *Captors and Captives*, 59.

18. Haefeli and Sweeney, *Captors and Captives*, 59–63.

19. Evan Haefeli and Kevin Sweeney, *Captive Histories: English, French, and Native Narratives of the 1704 Deerfield Raid* (Amherst: University of Massachusetts Press, 2006), 191–92.

20. Haefeli and Sweeney, *Captive Histories*, 192.

21. See Evan Haefeli and Kevin Sweeney, "Revisiting the Redeemed Captive: New Perspectives on the 1704 Attack on Deerfield," *William and Mary Quarterly*, 3rd ser., 52.1 (1995): 3–46.

22. Haefeli and Sweeney, *Captors and Captives*, 132–36.

23. Bernard J. Hibbitts, "Coming to Our Senses: Communication and Legal Expression in Performance Cultures," *Emory Law Journal* 41.4 (1992): 873–960.

12

The Algonquian Word and the Spirit of Divine Truth

JOHN ELIOT'S INDIAN LIBRARY AND THE ATLANTIC QUEST FOR A UNIVERSAL LANGUAGE

Sarah Rivett

Over the course of the settlement of the New World in the sixteenth and seventeenth centuries, European missionaries discovered the power and knowledge available to those who learned Indian languages. Spanish missionaries began a massive effort to compile, organize, and record indigenous tongues. In 1547, Pedro de Gante published the *Doctrina Cristiana*, offering a Nahuatl text in which the linguistic knowledge set in black-letter type comes from twenty-nine manuscript leaves, produced by a number of hands (see fig. 12.1). Introduced in Spanish, the purpose of de Gante's *Doctrina Cristiana* was to increase knowledge of Nahuatl among Spanish speakers, many of whom were actively involved in the missionary endeavor in New Spain. What is striking about de Gante's text is that it is not merely functional, designed to give an accessible overview of Nahuatl for the simple purpose of facilitating fluency such that the missionaries could pursue

Fig. 12.1. Page from Pedro de Gante, *Doctrina Cristiana en lengua Mexicana* (1547). Reproduced by permission of the Huntington Library, San Marino, California.

their endeavors of proselytizing and converting more effectively. Rather, the printer took a great deal of care in the production of this text, setting the frontispiece in two different ink colors so that the titular announcement of doctrines "en lengua Mexicana" in red is offset by the inlaid black-and-white image of a Fransciscan friar speaking these truths to a group of patiently attendant indigenous proselytes. The manuscript leaves record how such knowledge had been acquired, recorded, and preserved, emphasizing the process and pious work that went into this rendition of Christian truths. The material form of the book announces something substantial to be conveyed through the representational power of revealed truths in an indigenous tongue.

De Gante's *Doctrina Cristiana* exemplifies a large number of such printed texts coming out of Mexico City in the sixteenth century.[1] The Spanish practice of compiling, ordering, and printing indigenous languages set the stage for parallel endeavors among the French, English, and Germans. Although the Jesuits were not granted the printing press that they requested in the 1660s, manuscript grammars proliferated among them. Jean de Brébeuf was the first linguist of the Huron language, producing a grammar that was then reprinted in Samuel de Champlain's *Voyages in New France* (1632). Paul Le Jeune printed grammars in the *Jesuit Relations*, published regularly in Paris between 1632 and 1672, and Pierre Chaumonot compiled a manuscript dictionary of the Montagnais language.[2] Missionary linguistics proliferated in New France, with manuscript dictionaries and grammars circulating among the Jesuits and Franciscan Recollects stationed in missionary communities, while vocabularies of Montagnais and Algonquian were also printed in Paris. These linguistic efforts instigated sweeping and irrevocable change.

Imperial language projects have long been described by scholars as acts of erasure or techniques of domination and colonial appropriation. Stephen Greenblatt reads "linguistic colonialism" as the pervasive intellectual and popular belief in the sixteenth and seventeenth centuries that American Indian languages were either "deficient or nonexistent."[3] Jill Lepore and David Murray show the detrimental effects

Sarah Rivett

of this ideology throughout the colonial period as literacy and translation destroyed cultural relativity and autonomy.[4] Shifting our focus to Renaissance writing in Latin America, Walter Mignolo demonstrates the semiotic colonization of Amerindian languages.[5] While these interpretations have produced a fascinating discussion, deliberate acts of preservation were also central to the linguistic dimensions of the colonial encounter. European encounters with Native American languages and the Indian grammars that emerged from them focused on retention and—especially in the case of Anglo-America—reinvention. In North America, missionaries confronted the problem of translating Algonquian from oral to written. They began this process by preparing lists of words and expressions and compiling a grammar. The final stage involved the composition and preaching of sermons. This was a crucial phase, integral to the cycle of Algonquian language acquisition. It served the practical purpose of enabling ministers to transmit the gospel to the Native Americans whom they were trying to convert. But sermons preached in Algonquian also completed a tripartite transformation from the fallen, spoken language of heathen savages to the written language of pious Christians, and then back into a redeemed primitive language whose aural quality was believed to capture the essence of God. Finally, Native American proselytes were taught by Anglo missionaries to read Algonquian and then asked to recount their conversion to Christianity publicly in their native tongue.

Each organized project of missionary linguistics in the New World simultaneously celebrated the diversity of tongues and voices through which Christian truths might be uttered and espoused a belief in a universal Christianity that superseded linguistic boundaries. To collect the earth's disparate languages and translate key Christian texts into a variety of tongues both effectively spread the gospel among the earth's inhabitants and advanced humanity toward a collective millennial hope for recapturing the moment described in Genesis 11:1 when "the whole earth was of one language and of one speech." Even though missionary linguistics crossed a range of national, linguistic, religious, and geographic boundaries, seventeenth-century English ministers imagined themselves as engaged in a unique process of translation. The shared goal of figures ranging from Roger Williams to John Eliot to Experience Mayhew to Jonathan Edwards Jr. was to unlock the sacred power of indigenous tongues. For Anglo missionaries, Indian languages served as crucial data in the unfolding of a millennial history that they claimed as uniquely their own.

Through their Indian grammars and the small print industry that developed around them, English missionaries claimed privileged access to the sacred essence of an oral language whose purity and power had been lost in the Fall. A convergence between the production of Anglo-Indian grammars and a specific program developed by the Royal Society in the mid-seventeenth century to implement a universal language that would be common to all humanity helped to underwrite this Anglo notion of privileged access. The hope of such natural philosophers as Cave Beck, John Wilkins, James Delgrano, and others was that a universal language would unlock the secrets of God by recuperating semiotic perfection, where words would be linked to nature and their correspondent referent in the invisible world. The Indian grammars, compiled through the evangelical encounter, not only bore an analogy to but also constituted a central site of fieldwork for this project. Additionally, Anglo missionaries working within Protestant communities trained their Native proselytes to speak Christian truths in a redeemed Algonquian tongue once its sacred essence had recaptured the redemptive power lost in the Fall. The missionary objective correlated directly with the aims of some of the linguistic universalists who also wished to recapture the fallen languages of Babel. Universal language planners influenced such missionaries as Williams and Eliot as each sought to compose Indian grammars that would facilitate this epistemological endeavor, while missionary communities in turn offered the words of Indians speaking within this redeemed tongue as proof of the imminently realizable potential of linguistic recuperation.

This remarkable process of linguistic translation did not survive much beyond the initial phase of seventeenth-century missionary ef-

Sarah Rivett

forts, yet the unique historical convergence between Royal Society and Protestant millennial hopes for sacred languages established an important precedent. Both a fascination with Indian grammar and a belief in its ancient, sacred significance persisted well beyond John Eliot's mission to the Indians as well as beyond the development of a science of language that would eventually come to replace biblical understandings of linguistic dispersal. Algonquian remained a repository for sacred knowledge on the periphery of the Protestant world in the eighteenth century and then became central to the formation of U.S. national identity in the early decades of the nineteenth century. Presidents of the American Philosophical Society such as Thomas Jefferson and Pierre Du Ponceau as well as missionaries such as John Heckewelder revived seventeenth-century missionary linguistics in the 1810s and 1820s in their effort to construct an archive of a national past that was distinctly American. The Indian grammars collected, reprinted, and promoted by these figures contributed to a scientific and literary project of building the U.S. nation-state. Indian grammars functioned as atavistic remnants of a sacred past that infused both the land and its naturally dying-out inhabitants with the prophetic power to forecast the rise of a new empire. In the Anglo-American world, Indian languages were both archive and script for enacting the *translatio imperii*.

The Word and the Spirit

Part of the persistent Anglo-American interest in and knowledge of Indian grammars developed from an archive of Christian texts printed in Algonquian in the 1660s when an English printer named Marmaduke Johnson went to Cambridge to open a printing press. Working alongside a Massachusett Indian named James the Printer, Johnson translated catechistical texts into Algonquian so that they might circulate to the requisite audience in New England. Some of these texts included the *New England Primer*, the *Bay Psalm Book*, *The Holy Bible*, Richard Baxter's *Call to the Unconverted*, and *A Christian Covenanting Confession*.[6] We do not have a lot of information on the circulation of these texts and the reading practices of Native American communities, but a few scholars have carefully sifted through the spotty archive. Hilary Wyss argues that Natives redefined "literacy" to suit their own purposes, voicing their own particular relationship to the divine. Kathleen Bragdon's archival research shows that "sermon delivery was a flourishing vernacular genre among the native Christians" and that "several natives enjoyed reputations as powerful and accomplished preachers."[7] For both scholars, empowerment significantly comes through the reappropriation of Algonquian from a newly written, then *re*oralized, language.

The Indian Library, as the printed works associated with New England missions have come to be called, serviced the creation of a transatlantic culture of spoken Algonquian. Scholars Kristina Bross and Laura Stevens have proposed compelling explanations for the transatlantic circulation of printed missionary tracts in Cambridge, Boston, and London. For Bross, the occasion of the publication of the Eliot tracts in London (1643–70) was a scene of metropolitan politics. She argues that the English Civil War instigated what Puritan ministers hoped would be a commensurate and complementary effort to spread the gospel in New England.[8] Stevens makes a different case for Christian Indians' status as a kind of cultural capital. Her study shows how Indian proselytes became objects of sympathy in a transatlantic British culture of sentiment in which English readers learned the proper affective response to the tears of "poor Indians."[9] We have learned from the interpretive method of these scholars how sweeping currents of Anglo cultural transformation and the missionary program affected each other reciprocally. I add to their studies an account of how Native American proselytes made an indigenous contribution to natural philosophy. In a 1663 letter, Robert Boyle, a founding member of the Royal Society, offered his advice to Eliot that "we desire care may be taken that [the Indians] *retain* their own native Language."[10] What was a natural philosopher like Boyle hoping to discover in the Massachusett words of Eliot's proselytes? In recounting their conversion experiences in Algonquian, the praying Indians (Native converts to

Sarah Rivett

Christianity) made the meeting house a site of sensory, signifying practices, an empirical testing ground for discovering how the language might be heard as the embodiment of divine essence.

Just as some proponents of the universal language argued that the newly redeemed language would lead to universal religious harmony, Thomas Shepard Jr. indicates the harmony produced by hearing Native Americans in a 1673 letter to a Scottish Presbyterian minister. Shepard describes this harmony in a number of scenes: the spread of the gospel among Richard Bourne's Mashpee proselytes, the Natives preaching in Algonquian on Martha's Vineyard, and the system of praying towns established by John Eliot in Massachusetts. Each instances a microcosm of the universalizing Protestant spirit as it descends across sectarian divisions on both sides of the Atlantic. The aural culture of Algonquian communication produced in each setting is evidence of this process. Eliot "begins his prayers in the Indian's language." Then the son of Waban reads the Proverbs from Eliot's Indian Bible, "which [according to Shepard] has been printed & is in the hands of the Indians."[11] A Native named Job prays for half an hour in "the Indian Language" and then preaches from Hebrews 15:1. Several Natives stand up and read from the *New England Primer* or from Eliot's Bible. Shepard emphasizes that the allure of such scenes lies in hearing the aural quality of a divinely redeemed Algonquian tongue. Such scenes serve as proof of God's presence, as the aural sound lifts the spiritual essence from printed Algonquian words. Along with his letter, Shepard sent a copy of the primer to the Scottish minister in an attempt to illustrate the precision with which New Englanders pursued this linguistic path to a universal Protestant spirit.

The scenes thus present Algonquian "grammar" as a medium for accessing divine truth. Popular accounts of the linguistic philosophy of Jan Comenius, such as John Saltmarsh's *Dawnings of Light* (1644), explain that through grammar, man learns to approximate the universal language that links the natural world with the divine. Saltmarsh defines this empirical project as a striving to move beyond "lower and more natural interests" in order to begin to see the divine, "that which is more hidden and secret."[12] Language is the vehicle through which Saltmarsh imagines accomplishing this hermeneutic. Revived with spiritual, sensory significance, spoken sounds and their carefully corresponding written mark achieve a semiotic unity with the divine. Revealing the divine essence encoded in the Algonquian tongue, New England missionaries presented a landscape through which such grammatical spiritualizing was taking place. Redeemed Algonquian words unlocked a secret, invisible divine essence that became immediately intelligible to those witnessing the scene. This goal of semiotic perfection stemmed in part from Augustine's proposal for a language restored from its fallen state to a pure, direct connection to the divine in the moment of conversion.

"Christian translation" is the phrase I use to describe this scene of witnessing. It involved locating the power of Christian, scriptural authority in the heathen other and then reclaiming this authority as an ancient, sacred essence unfolding within the present. Indian grammars began Christian translation by searching indigenous languages for anomalies. The anomaly became both a way of marking the American Indian as different and of framing the utterance in such a way as to suggest the recapturing of something that had been lost through the Fall. Christian translation thus encapsulated the purported wisdom of an ancient and original other in order to rescript it within a presentist eschatological frame. It was this final phase of linguistic transformation that Anglo missionaries in particular hoped to hear echoed by proselytes as they described the effects of divine grace upon their souls. American Indians learned to read in their native tongue in missionary schools, but this was not simply a one-dimensional translation from an oral to a written language, from a pre-literate to a literate indigenous society. Rather, the transformation of Algonquian through the colonial encounter involved a complex, circular process: Native proselytes were first asked to read the Bible or the *New England Primer*, as these texts were translated by missionaries, into their own language. Then they were called upon to narrate their conversion to Christianity orally, in a linguistic idiom that was not European but

Sarah Rivett

was paradoxically believed to be infused with biblical power. Far from simply being the technology of domination that Lepore ascribes to the print industry that accompanied King Philip's War, the printed word was in missionaries' minds a vehicle for recapturing the sacred essence of an oral language whose purity and power had been lost in the Fall.

If Shepard's letter conveys this ideal as the scriptural words uttered from the lips of Native Americans, Eliot's translation of both Testaments into Algonquian grounds such performative sounds within the *sola scriptura* ideal. Eliot's Indian Bible was a novelty. It was the first printed in the colonies, the first printed in a non-European tongue, and the first printed for which an entire phonetic writing system was devised. Eliot's translation bridged the Augustinian ideal with the universal language project. Reflecting on this accomplishment in a letter to Boyle, Eliot wrote, "my work is translation, which, by the Lord's help, I desire to attend unto." This statement conveys the sense of translation as God's work as much as the business of saving souls. Published in Cambridge in 1663, Eliot's Indian Bible was part of a biblical translation effort connected with both the universal language movement and a more general Royal Society practice. Society papers contain several examples of "specimens" of scripture designed to decode and illuminate the hidden meaning within the text.[13] The manuscript table pictured in figure 12.2 gives the elements of the oriental languages and references in Hebrew, Latin, and Arabic. It shows how the ancient languages were studied by members of the Royal Society interested in this project of biblical translation. Translations of scripture into ancient tongues coincided with translations of the Bible into indigenous tongues where the spread of the gospel was taking hold.

Eliot published his Indian Bible with the hope that it would sanctify Indian languages and contribute to this sensible knowledge. Two supplemental texts bookend the scripture to reveal the Bible's status as a connecting thread between two very different audiences. The Indian Bible concludes with "Rules for Christian Living in Algonquian,"

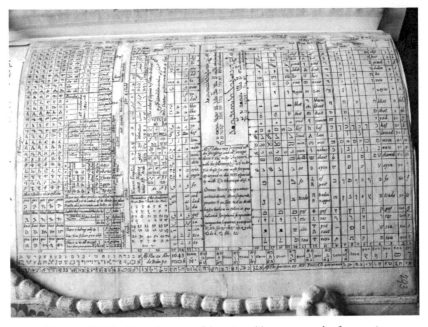

Fig. 12.2. "Table giving elements of the oriental languages and references in Hebrew, Latin, and Arabic." Boyle Papers. © The Royal Society.

reflecting the text's proselytizing and civilizing design in relation to Native people.[14] At the beginning of the book is an Epistle Dedicatory to Charles II that establishes the publication as a valuable commodity within the archive of English nationalism. The copy presented to Charles II in 1664 was a symbol and a gesture of English nationalism rather than something he could read and understand. The dedication explains that this is the "First . . . in this Language or from this *American World*, or from any Parts so Remote from *Europe* as these are, for ought that ever we heard of."[15] Eliot's Indian Bible both conveyed the homogenizing effects of subsuming more of the earth's scattered and degenerate "Sons" under the canopy of English nationalism and announced itself as a New World curiosity: the first of its kind. The Indian Bible may also have appealed to Charles II as a symbol of his agenda for imperial expansion through scientific discovery; his 1660 charter for the formation of the Royal Society outlines an effort to "extend not only the boundaries of Empire but also the very arts

Sarah Rivett

and sciences."[16] The Bible symbolized this vision of empire. By facilitating scriptural translation in multiple Native tongues, the Royal Society perpetuated Charles II's scheme.

Indian Keys to Ancient Wisdom

While philosophers since Augustine have expressed an interest in universal language schemes, the belief in language's recuperative potential reached a high mark in the seventeenth century through the teachings of Czech philosopher Jan Comenius, who theorized that language could be used as a vehicle for unlocking divine essence. Comenius taught that the key to revelation was a linguistic system, or a "universal language," that followed a one-to-one correspondence between language and nature. His theory of linguistic isomorphism suggested that revelation was the result of the proper use of language to unlock the mysteries of the divine. Ultimately, Comenius hoped to promote religious harmony through a universal "character." He saw it "both [as] an attempt to renew contact with divine harmony in the universe and a crucial effort to bring about a reconciliation between men that would lay the foundations for an enduring religious peace."[17] The method for achieving religious peace consisted of a redemptive language that was mathematically and empirically precise. Mathematical exactness compensated for human fallibility by providing principles that were "universal, fixed and subject to no exception."[18]

This reliance on mathematics responded to another problem that theorists of the universal language movement faced. Since the destruction of the tower of Babel and subsequent centuries of misusage, natural languages were corrupt and consequently full of irregularities. The universal character that would emerge out of this movement was necessarily artificial rather than natural, because it was impossible to eliminate the irregular and corrupted elements of natural languages. One of the places that this theory featured was in Richard Verstegan's *Restitution of Decayed Intelligence* (1605), a treatise printed multiple times in the seventeenth century that recounts the story of the Fall in order to issue a proposal for reclaiming the sacred intelligence encoded in ancient languages. According to Verstegan, the development of the universal character involved a complex interplay between the collecting of primitive languages where the gospel was beginning to take hold and the Scholastic tradition of studying languages of the ancients. The goal was to infuse ancient linguistic precedent with the recuperative and transformative powers of newly discovered idioms that could help to recapture "decayed intelligence" or lost power. Verstegan ascribed this process of reclamation and transformation specifically, as his subtitle declares, to "The Most Noble and Reformed English Nation."[19] By discovering the origins of the English language, England could establish a program for collecting linguistic data and securing exclusive access to the knowledge lost in the fall of Babel. Like Comenius, Verstegan advocated a return to the pureness of speech as a way of implementing universal religious harmony. He also saw England as having the divine authority to instigate this pansophic vision.

By the time Verstegan published *Restitution of Decayed Intelligence*, Thomas Harriot and Richard Hakluyt had already begun to encourage the accumulation of primitive languages as an integral component of their writing on how most effectively to build an English presence in the New World. In his *Discourse Concerning Western Planting* (1584), Hakluyt encouraged English preachers to begin their plantation endeavors by first "learning the language of the people." In addition to serving a practical purpose, Hakluyt explains, language acquisition remedies the "gift of tongues" that had long ago been "taken away." Through his focus on preaching in the language of New World inhabitants, Hakluyt proclaims a particular use of missionary linguistics for the English, distinguishing their work in this regard from that of the Spanish. This will put the English on the right path toward millennial fulfillment, Hakluyt promises, unlike the Spanish, who "fling their Bibles and prayer Books into the Sea."[20] On the one hand, this statement reflects a common theme in colonial writing, a component of the "Black Legend"—early English settlers often contrasted the success of their settlement with the failures of Spanish colonization. Yet Hakluyt also references an instance of careless misuse: the discard-

Sarah Rivett

ing of religious texts into the ocean by Catholics who knew how to plant neither the seeds of civilization nor the seeds of Christianity. Here the proper Christian use of both scripture and catechism has been mastered by the English.

Harriot also fostered this link between the proper cultivation of an English plantation and a carefully recorded indigenous tongue. While writing his *Brief History*, Harriot produced a manuscript titled *A Universal Alphabet*, containing thirty-six letters toward the development of this universal alphabet built from the oral expressions of a man's voice, speaking Virginian. Part of Harriot's attempt to represent Virginia as an inviting territory available for cultivation included compiling a "Vocabulary with Several Phrases of Speech in Virginia" that circulated in the seventeenth century. Scholars have speculated that Harriot's "vocabulary" was even used by Francis Lodwick in 1686 when Lodwick devised and published a "universal alphabet" to help missionaries to North American Natives.[21] Lodwick explains the importance of this alphabet in his manuscript essay titled "Of Converting Infidels to Christianity," which describes the importance of being "well skilled in the languages of those [the ministers] address."[22]

Thematically central to the writing of Verstegen, Harriot, and Hakluyt was a connection between an emergent English national identity and the cultivation of Indian grammars in North America. This connection underpinned the pansophic idealism of Comenius's English followers with imperial goals. Comenius's philosophy gained popularity in England in the 1630s and 1640s through his own travels as well as through his collaboration with English linguist Samuel Hartlib. Hartlib promoted Comenius by publishing some of his tracts in English; additional versions of his theory were available in such texts as Hezekiah Woodward's *A Light to Grammar* (1641) and John Saltmarsh's *Dawnings of Light* (1644). Comenius's utopic vision for establishing religious harmony through the stabilizing framework of mathematical science influenced the "Invisible College" that began meeting at Cambridge and Oxford in the 1640s. In addition to Hartlib, members of the "Invisible College" included John Wilkins, Seth Ward,

Robert Boyle, Sir William Petty, Sir Christopher Wren, and Thomas Sprat. This group formed the Royal Society in 1660.[23] Over the course of these discussions, Wilkins and Ward began to formulate their own plan for the discovery of a universal character. They believed that language was the key to empire and hoped to facilitate trade between nations. The consequent expansion of English national territory was justified through the millennial vision of a global Christianity encoded in a universal language.

The pansophic and millennial goals of the universal language scheme, then, facilitated a particular vision of empire. Comenius proposed an educational scheme for realizing this purity through a universal character that uniformly inculcated principles of political, social, and religious reform in the minds of the young. Legend has it that Comenius's educational philosophy resulted in his being invited to New England to oversee the education of Native Americans as they were instructed in their own tongue.[24] Cotton Mather laments Comenius's decline of this offer in his *Magnalia Christi Americana* (1702): "That brave old man Comenius . . . was indeed agreed withall, by our Mr. Winthrop in his Travels through the Low Countries, to come over into New-England, and Illuminate this College and Country in the Quality of a President: But the Solicitations of the Swedish Ambassador, diverting him another way, that Incomparable Moravian became not an American."[25] There is some debate about whether this story is true; nonetheless, the story gestures toward the relationship between missionary linguistics and Comenian theory as it first appears in Roger Williams's *A Key into the Language of America* (1643). The *Key* begins with the following declaration: "This *Key*, respects the *Native Language* of it, and happily may unlock some *Rarities* concerning the *Natives* themselves, not yet discovered."[26] Through the metaphor of a key unlocking the undiscovered, Williams draws upon Comenius's lexical system for intuiting God in nature.[27] Williams applies Comenian linguistics to the concept of the rarity. The "rarity" was a defining category of empirical discovery in the Scientific Revolution from Bacon forward. Yet Bacon also warned that our mind constructs conju-

Sarah Rivett

gates or resemblances of them. In the *Key*, the Native speaker attains the status of a natural object of inquiry through which observers might "discover" unexplored dimensions of the invisible domain. By conjoining the Baconian term "rarity" and the Comenian metaphor of unlocking, the *Key* promotes the study of Indian language as the point of intersection between empiricism and the discovery of divine essence. As the site of this discovery, New England in Williams's text is the "*Land of Canaan.*" Consisting of the geographical as well as national space of Israel's typological descendants, the experimental site must be "attended with *extraordinary, supernatural, and miraculous* Considerations."[28]

This association of New England with the Land of Canaan reflects the typological tradition in New England. But Williams does not simply narrate a story of spiritual fulfillment upon New World arrival. Rather, he explains that the land itself is infused with an indigenous sacred power that is worth observing in its natural state. Through his striking typological association of New England as an "extraordinary and supernatural" Land of Canaan, Williams inhabits a unique position as a kind of spiritual ethnographer. He presents the Natives as exhibiting a special connection to the land that makes them experimental sites for ascertaining the sacred essence encoded in primitive languages. Through its metaphor of the key and its typological claim that New England was the land where such evidence could be claimed, Williams's text marks a transformation in the history of missionary linguistics. Specifically, it adapts Comenian theory to the particular case of America in order to make a claim for the sacred and secret contents of American languages through the idea that one needed a key to access them. As such, Williams's *Key* sets the stage for a history of linguistic encounters by claiming that both the land and its inhabitants contain the potential for recapturing something rare, wonderful, and original in Native languages.

This conflation of typological association and linguistic treasures also speaks to a post-Reformation resurgence of interest in Hebrew. Studies of "the sacred language" coupled with the theory of the ten lost tribes promoted in such tracts as Thomas Thorowgood's *Jews in America* (1660) produced what Shalom Goldman calls "an indigenous American Hebraic occultism [that] emerged in seventeenth and eighteenth-century America."[29] Building upon this Hebraic occultism, Anglo-American missionaries tailored Indian grammars according to two linked goals: proving narratives of Native origins, and unlocking the divine essence encoded within their languages. The theory of the Algonquian Indians as one of the ten lost tribes enfolded them within the Anglo plot to recuperate the language of Genesis. And, as John Eliot indicates in his preface to Thorowgood's *Jews in America*, grammar was integral to this story: "It seemeth to me, by the little insight I have, that the grammatical frame of our Indian language cometh nearer to the Hebrew, than the Latin or Greek do."[30] Eliot's claim for Hebraic originality draws on Thorowgood's theory even as it locates Indian translation practices in relation to the quest for a universal language. Universalists believed Hebrew to be the starting point for the discovery of the universal character, because it most closely approximated the language spoken in Genesis before the confusion of Babel. Hebrew was believed to contain mystical qualities, and it also contained fewer radicals—underived words—than any other language. This grammatical feature appealed to universal linguists, whose basic technique was to minimize the number of radicals in order to simplify and expand communicative intelligibility.

To test his theory of Algonquian and Hebraic grammar, Eliot compiled and published an Indian grammar. The standard interpretation of these grammars by scholars such as David Murray is that early missionaries like Williams and Eliot simply inserted what they perceived as flawed indigenous languages into a Latin grammatical frame.[31] But this is not entirely the case. Eliot dedicates his grammar to Robert Boyle in order to present it for "public use," whereby it could contribute to research for a new, universal language to call forth the secrets of the divine. Like Williams, Eliot sought the linguistic rarity in order to "satisfy the prudent Enquirer [perhaps Boyle, to whom the work is addressed] how I found out these *new ways of Grammar*, which no

Sarah Rivett

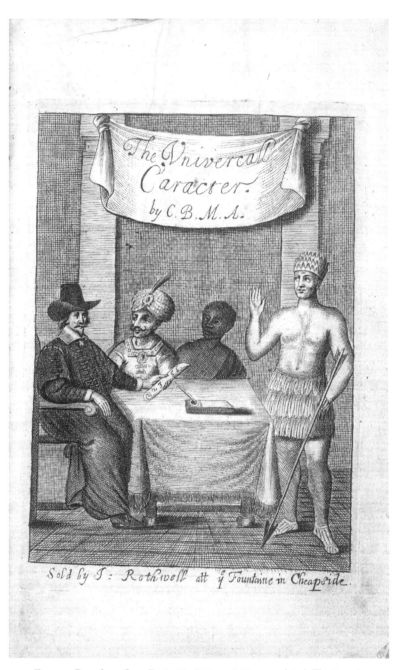

The Univercall
Caracter.
by C. B. M. A.

Sold by J: Rothwell att ẏ Fountaine in Cheapside.

Fig. 12.3. Page from Cave Beck, *The Universal Character* (1657). This item is reproduced by permission of the Huntington Library, San Marino, California.

other Learned Language (so far as I know) useth."[32] Eliot intended a record of linguistic anomalies that might yield a grammatical structure and reveal Algonquian's proximity to Hebrew. While early missionaries were not adept at thinking about grammatical structures outside of a European context, Eliot's goal in pointing to the "rarities" was not to indicate deficiencies, as Murray proposes, but rather to access the epistemological potential encoded therein.

As if anticipating this claim for public use, Cave Beck's 1657 treatise *The Universal Character* explains that philosophers have made great strides toward discovering the universal character by compiling the "new languages of Native North Americans" and comparing these languages to those of the "ancients," including Egyptian symbols and Chinese characters (see fig. 12.3).[33] The frontispiece of Beck's book shows an imperial goal of universal language theory growing out of the epistemological one. In it, a European consigns Beck's project to a Hindu, an African, and an American Indian. The American Indian remains standing and expresses himself with a gesture of his hand. Europe's elected leader seems to be in a position of power that immediately evokes the idea of *translatio imperii*, or the westward course of empire. The scroll he holds visually echoes the scroll above; both uncurl slowly to reveal the unfolding potential of the universal character. But what is the source of this universal character? The Hindu and the African gaze toward the European, suggesting that he wields power over the unfolding scroll. But the European gazes at the American Indian, whose eyes, in turn, are raised toward heaven. A poem opposite the title page refers to his gesture as a "dumb sign," which in the seventeenth century would most likely have meant that he was deaf. The deaf were believed to have certain divinely inspired powers; at the least, an American Indian seems to occupy a position of knowledge within this scene. Beck is invested in the use of the universal character for free trade between nations, and he frames his treatise as a tool for English expansion. But what we see in this image is a striking disruption of the *translatio imperii* narrative. The frontispiece masks—in order to reveal powerfully—Beck's sense that the deaf but

Sarah Rivett

heavenward-gazing Indian supplies the ancient wisdom necessary for this endeavor.

The Lockean Turn toward Linguistic Anthropology

The quest for a universal character came to symbolize a desire for expansion and progress as well as primitivism and recuperation. Comenius's ideal system of names that would signify the essence of things promised enduring religious peace and reconciliation among men. Beck expanded this logic to promote a homologous relationship between commerce and communication. But the most comprehensive attempt to develop a universal language came in 1668, when John Wilkins published his *Essay towards a Real Character and a Philosophical Language*. The *Essay* includes a table that culminates with the first line of the Lord's Prayer written in the universal character. Wilkins sought to classify the whole knowable universe in taxonomic form, construct a written character based on the tables, and generate a spoken language that conveyed an isomorphic relationship to the real character. His table contains more than two thousand "primitives," or natural philosophical species. Arranging them taxonomically, he assigns each group a character that is supposed to signify all of its variations. Wilkins chose his characters arbitrarily, but once inserted into a sequence they were "supposed to mirror the very composition of the denoted thing."[34] Wilkins constructed his table to unite a character uniformly and systematically to the thing or concept it named, thereby eliminating linguistic differences and inconsistencies. The graphic symbol assigned to each universal concept formed a character that could be intelligible in any language. As the basis for this mathematical compilation, Wilkins proposed that the "Hebrew Tongue, consisting of fewer Radicals" than any other language, should "be the fittest ground work for such a design." Hebrew would form the basis for a natural grammar that would not only be understood by all men everywhere but would also reclaim the voice of God in spoken language. At the bottom right of the chart, the first line of the Lord's Prayer is written in the universal character with the pronunciation key below. The ability to translate the first line of the Lord's Prayer into the universal character emblematizes the culminating goal of the universal language movement: to reclaim "the first Language [that] was co-created with our first Parents" who "immediately understood the voice of God speaking to them in the Garden." While Wilkins's chart foreshadows the promise of such reclamation, he cautions elsewhere in the text that the table is not complete. An adequate classification of this original language requires the continued ethno-linguistic efforts of scientists working over vast regions of the globe for a considerable amount of time. Wilkins solicited the collaboration of the Royal Society for this endeavor and observed with praise that "evidence of these languages is starting to be re-collected from histories from all over the Americas."[35]

Wilkins's call for missionary archival work formalizes a relationship between the universal language movement and missionary linguistics that, as I have been arguing, was a constitutive component of the missionary impulse to preserve the spoken language of Native proselytes. But not long after Wilkins made this striking claim for an imminently realizable linguistic utopia, Locke published his *Essay Concerning Human Understanding* (1690). The *Essay* rendered the universal language program scientifically untenable by making a case for words as mere human constructs. Locke challenged the semiotic premise of universal language theory on two counts. First, he decoupled the "nominal essence" of the word from its real essence, highlighting the discrepancy between human ideas of things and the things themselves. Second, he dismissed the idea of language as having scriptural origins. Instead, his *Essay* sought to unite the study of language with the study of human thought and understanding rather than with divine revelation. This strategy challenged the universalists' belief that language might be restored to semiotic perfection in order to achieve a real connection to the divine. Yet despite the transformation in linguistic philosophy proposed by Locke, the *Essay* simultaneously identifies American Indians as sites of a different kind of epistemological plentitude.[36] In his *Essay*, Locke refers to American Indians as "Naturals"

Sarah Rivett

who, having no "universal principles" or "general propositions" "impressed" upon their minds, can be used effectively as a sort of ideal, embodied tabula rasa. Where universal principles are more suited to "artificial argument," Locke finds the thought process that takes place in the "Huts of the Indians" conducive to the "discovery of Truth."[37] Even as Lockean linguistics forecloses the possibility of a universal language scheme, Locke imagines the different forms of knowledge that might be acquired in the huts of Native Americans, building upon a seventeenth-century precedent of indigenous contributions to natural philosophy.

This passage from Locke's *Essay* resonates with a parallel claim made by Robert Boyle in *The Christian Virtuoso* (1690), where Boyle imagines that "an ordinary seaman who traveled along the coast [of America] could learn things that could never be learned in Aristotle's philosophy or Ptolemy's *Geography*."[38] This striking overlap indicates that the two philosophers were of a shared mind on the philosophical value of the American Indian. The evangelical encounter in the New World had a deep impact on the natural philosophical methods of both Locke and Boyle, indicating a reciprocal relationship in the intellectual history that conjoined missionary efforts and universal language schemes. Locke and Boyle were close correspondents for nearly thirty years; Boyle refers to Locke in his *General Heads for the Natural History of a Country* (1692), while Locke issued similar ethnographic questionnaires to travelers in foreign countries.[39] By the end of the seventeenth century, the scientific study of sacred languages had leavened the rise of a science of human nature.

Religious, scientific, and aesthetic interest in Indian languages persisted through the eighteenth century and into the antebellum period. Even as missionary work became increasingly fragmented over the course of the eighteenth century, missionaries continued to look to Indian languages as a means of promoting the belief in language's sacred and millennial powers. David Brainerd, who was Jonathan Edwards's protégé and widely successful in converting Native Americans on the New Jersey and Pennsylvania frontier, was one of the last colonial missionaries to ascribe eschatological importance to Indian words in his missionary writing. Brainerd describes seeing an "Indian woman" who experienced her soul's salvation "like one pierced through with a Dart." Lying flat on the ground, the woman prayed "earnestly" in Algonquian, uttering words that Brainerd interpreted as "Have mercy on me, and help me to give you my heart."[40] This Indian convert, like those recorded by Experience Mayhew or indeed by John Eliot in the generation before, was seen as embodying a kind of scriptural precedence and sacred essence that could be philosophically and theologically useful as long as it was safely contained within a primitive past. Yet even in making this claim, Brainerd positions his ministerial authority on the margins of a much broader Protestant culture. The Indian woman registers religious truth through her position on the periphery rather than within a central scene of Protestant signifying practices.

Indian languages remained peripherally of interest to the Royal Society, which continued to solicit missionary vocabularies and Indian grammars. In 1719, Royal Society member Paul Dudley solicited a request for "accounts of the Peculiarities & Beauties of the Indian Language, and wherein they agree or differ from the Europeans."[41] Experience Mayhew, the descendant of three generations of missionary Mayhews on Martha's Vineyard, responded to this request. In an account of Algonquian that was supposed to be published in the Royal Society *Transactions*, Mayhew moves beyond Williams's and Eliot's claims for linguistic rarities to suggest that Algonquian has a unique grammatical logic. Mayhew's claim hints at a gradual shift through the eighteenth century toward an interest in Indian languages that could not be assimilated into Europe's universal character but rather stood on their own as a distinct system of signification: "To speak the truth I think most of the Indians, not to say all of them betwixt Canada, and New Spain, inclusively, do speak what was Originally one and the same Language; how different soever their Several Dialects may now appear to be."[42] Condensed within this word "originally" is Wilkins's quest to reclaim the lost language of Eden coupled with a

Sarah Rivett

sense that the Indians represent an origin that can no longer be claimed in the present.

The son of Jonathan Edwards also boasted superior knowledge of Mohican by learning it as he did his own "mother Tongue" during time spent as a child on his father's Stockbridge mission. Jonathan Edwards Jr. made a study of the Mohican language, *Observations on the Language of the Muhhekaneew Indians*, published in 1788. This text marks a turning point in the history of missionary linguistics. Edwards makes a structural claim for a kind of continuity across the languages of a number of Indian tribes, including the Delawares, the tribes of New England, and the Mohicans. He also wants to ascribe a sacred, Christian origin to these languages while simultaneously marking them as different from modern European languages. Edwards identifies "specimens of analogy" across a number of Indian tongues. The "analogy," he claims, "is sufficient to show" that the languages "are mere dialects of the same original language." His translation of the Lord's Prayer proves this, for "in no part of these languages does there appear to be a greater coincidence, than in this specimen." His translations of the Lord's Prayer across a range of Native languages not only proves grammatical or analogical continuity but also re-unifies the languages into a cohesive original. After discussing a unique grammatical logic of expressive verbs and adjectival pronouns, Edwards explains that "in this particular the structure of the language coincides with that of the Hebrew, in an instance in which the Hebrew differs from all the languages of Europe, ancient or modern." In contrast to generations of missionaries before him, Edwards points out this Hebraic connection in order to suggest an atavistic element of linguistic origins that is unrecoverable as a workable language in modern life. What links Mohican to Hebrew is also what makes Mohican fundamentally *unlike* European languages. Like seventeenth-century Indian grammarians, Edwards looks for the linguistic anomaly, "the peculiarity in which this language differs from all languages," but Edwards also views this peculiarity as a relic of an ancient and unrecoverable past.[43]

Indian Grammars and Nineteenth-Century American Literature

The turn in missionary linguistics that I am attributing to Jonathan Edwards Jr. set the stage for a parallel use of Indian grammars and vocabularies as archives of American archaeology. By the late eighteenth century, Indian languages were increasingly extolled as transmitters of a kind of ancient, sacred wisdom, while American Indians became thought of increasingly as a race of "Aborigines," existing outside of time. "Aborigines" is the title Thomas Jefferson gives to his chapter on American Indians in *Notes on the State of Virginia*, a text written and published at the same time as Edwards's *Observations*. The term had been used since the sixteenth century to refer to the original inhabitants of a country; by the eighteenth century, it also meant the natives found in possession of a territory colonized by the Europeans. Jefferson's use of this term in 1787 is significant because it reflects the way that his *Notes* both acknowledges the indigenous occupants of America and disavows their continued claim to the land. He accomplishes this through a process of temporal displacement that identifies Native tribes as part of prehistory:

> It is to be lamented . . . that we have suffered so many of the Indian tribes already to extinguish, without our having previously collected and deposited in the records of literature, the general rudiments at least of the languages they spoke. Were vocabularies formed of all the languages spoken in North and South America, preserving their appellations of the most common objects in nature, of those which must be present to every nation barabarous or civilized, with the inflections of their nouns and verbs, their principles of regimen and concord, and these deposited in all the public libraries, it would furnish opportunities to those skilled in the languages of the old world to compare them with these, now, or at a future time, and hence to construct the best evidence of the derivation of this part of the human race.[44]

Sarah Rivett

Jefferson's lament is in fact a call for a national anthropological project of collecting and recording Indian vocabularies. This endeavor, he proposes, would supply the new American nation with an important archive of its past. Once vocabularies are collated and assembled, a comparative philological analysis could scientifically reveal the "derivation" of this part of the human race. Jefferson himself took on this task. He collected a vast manuscript archive of Indian dialects in order to excavate an American Indian prehistory. Only a few survived to be sent to the American Philosophical Society in 1817. Shortly afterward, the Philosophical Society took on Jefferson's project. Pierre Du Ponceau, Jefferson's successor as president of the Philosophical Society, revived Indian grammars in order to make ethnological and philological claims for the superior status of America's "aboriginal inhabitants." He reprinted such texts as Eliot's *Grammar of the Massachusetts Indian Language* to show how "the learned in Europe" had in fact been "deeply engaged" in the languages of American Indians.[45] Du Ponceau saw the revival of this linguistic project as a way of establishing American languages as unique and claiming American sciences as dominant on an international scale. This post-Lockean archive, however, marks a change in the history of missionary linguistics. Far from the American aborigines whose "natural" extinction Jefferson laments, praying Indians stood at the dawn of history in 1660. The Lockean turn in linguistic philosophy did not quell the attempt to discover sacred origins in Indian languages. Rather, it relocated those speaking sacred utterances within a different temporality. After Locke, divine mysteries are archaeological artifacts rather than human utterances of ancient, scriptural wisdom.

James Fenimore Cooper seized upon the aesthetic value that could be constructed from the history of debates about Indian languages. The primary source for *The Last of the Mohicans* was John Heckewelder's *History, Manners, and Customs of the Indian Nations*, published in 1818. Collecting ethnographic information under the auspices of the American Philosophical Society, Heckewelder intervened in a scientific debate about the metaphysical capacity of Indian languages.[46] Some of his contemporaries believed that Indian languages contained no imaginative or spiritual capacity, thus confirming the inferior status of the Indian mind. Heckewelder and his American Philosophical Society colleague Du Ponceau disagreed, explaining that with its musical oral qualities, the Delaware language came much closer to the original language of Adam and Eve than the fallen English language. Cooper attempts to construct an authentic American literary aesthetic from this idea. Throughout *The Last of the Mohicans*, he repeatedly compares the corrupt language of English and French to the pristine language of the Delawares. Following the Anglo missionary precedent, Cooper describes to his English-speaking audience the untranslatable, lyrical anomaly of the Indian tongue:

> It is impossible to describe the music of their language, while thus engaged in laughter and endearments, in such a way as to render it intelligible to those whose ears have never listened to its melody. The compass of their voices, particularly that of the youth, was wonderful; extending from the deepest bass, to tones that were even feminine in softness.[47]

Set in contrast to the comical presence of the character of David Gamut, the pious singing teacher from Connecticut, the Delaware language resonates with Cooper's descriptions of an American landscape that is still, secret, and secluded, "interrupted, only, by the low voices of men, the occasional and lazy tap of a wood-pecker, the discordant cry of some gaudy jay, or a swelling on the ear, from the dull roar of a distant water-fall."[48] Cooper describes the landscape itself as having a lyrical quality, consisting of sounds that must be heard to be known and forming music set to a language that may not be understood. In a novel of violence, death, and rebirth, the language of the Delawares surfaces as a tenuous link between America's past and its future. As the fate of the Indian race—also referred to by Cooper as the "Aborigines of the American continent"—becomes increasingly clear and inevitable, language is what Cooper suggests the next great civilization hold on to:

Sarah Rivett

The imagery of the Indian, both in his poetry and his oratory, is Oriental,—chastened, and perhaps improved, by the limited range of his practical knowledge. He draws his metaphors from the clouds, the seasons, the birds, the beasts, and the vegetable world. In this, perhaps, he does not more than any other energetic and imaginative race would do, being compelled to set bounds to fancy by experience; but the North American Indian clothes his ideas in a dress that is so different from that of the African, and is Oriental in itself. His language has the richness and sententious fullness of the Chinese. He will express a phrase in a word, and he will qualify the meaning of an entire sentence by a syllable; he will even convey different significations by the simplest inflexions of the voice.[49]

Many elements of this passage are familiar aspects of the "noble savage" in early nineteenth-century literature and art: the link between Native people and the natural world; the Asiatic origin that gives historical depth and civilized respectability to a new nation anxious about its lack of both; the elevation of the Indian above the African as a way of simultaneously proclaiming the superiority of American aborigines and complicating the ongoing program of genocide. Yet the ideas about language attached to this image of the noble savage come out of the history of missionary linguistics described in this chapter. Cooper's description of the unique metaphysical capacity of the Indian tongue stems from the Christian idea of the Indian tongue redeemed. Cooper urges his readers to imagine the power and spiritual capacity of the Delaware tongue just as David Brainerd and Experience Mayhew explained to their readers the prophetic significance of a sign uttered in Algonquian. In each case, the Indians described, either fictionally or ethnographically, are supposed to be atavistic remnants of an ancient spiritual world recently brought to light through their position in an unfolding millennial story. Yet paradoxically, the American Indian can only be described this way through the retrospective lens that follows from the evangelical encounter.

The Last of the Mohicans forecasts national rebirth on a biological and spiritual level with a prophetic certainty that derives the inevitability of history from Christian millennialism. Cooper imagines this process occurring on a most elemental level—through language, human sacrifice, death, generation, and regeneration. The Indian word is the sign through which the world of nature is made flesh and spiritually usable for future generations. Yet unlike Thomas Shepard Jr.'s description of praying Indians speaking in a redeemed Algonquian tongue across a range of New England scenes, Cooper does not imagine the American Indian speaking these words. Instead, through his own failure to translate and his celebration of the Delaware tongue, Cooper asks the reader to imagine an American world of sacred significance past the inadequacies of Western languages. The word is made flesh in the reader's mind as a sign of untapped potential. By the 1820s, the "original condition" ascribed to the American Indian was part of a past quickly approaching extinction rather than a Protestant sign of typological fulfillment within the present. Divine mysteries became archaeological artifacts rather than embodied human utterances of ancient, scriptural wisdom. Correspondingly, the image of the Indian had changed from the fruit of an English nation to an ethnographic object of erasure. But in each case, the words spoken by Native people and recorded, translated, and reconfigured by Anglo missionaries, linguists, and anthropologists remained millennial proof of an original, sacred language that helped to write each narrative of progress.

Notes

1. The Huntington Library alone owns twenty examples of such printed texts, all published in Mexico City between 1547 and 1591.
2. Victor Egon Hanzeli, *Missionary Linguistics in New France: A Study of Seventeenth- and Eighteenth-Century Descriptions of American Indian Languages* (The Hague: Mouton, 1969).
3. Stephen Greenblatt, "Learning to Curse: Aspects of Linguistic Colonialism in the Sixteenth Century," in *Learning to Curse: Essays in Early Modern Culture* (New York: Routledge, 1992), 16–39, quote on 30.

Sarah Rivett

4. Jill Lepore, *The Name of War: King Philip's War and the Origins of American Identity* (New York: Random House, 1998); David Murray, *Forked Tongues: Speech, Writing and Representation in North American Indian Texts* (Bloomington: Indiana University Press, 1991).

5. Walter Mignolo, *The Darker Side of the Renaissance: Literacy, Territoriality, and Colonization* (Ann Arbor: University of Michigan Press, 2003).

6. Eliot's Indian Library included, among other texts, the Bible, Bayly's *Practice of Piety*, *The Indian Primer*, Richard Baxter's *Call to the Unconverted*, and *A Christian Covenanting Confession*.

7. Hilary Wyss, *Writing Indians: Literacy, Christianity, and Native Community in Early America* (Amherst: University of Massachusetts Press, 2000), 581; Kathleen Bragdon, "Gender as a Social Category in Native Southern New England," *Ethnohistory* 43.4 (1996): 573–92.

8. Kristina Bross, *Dry Bones and Indian Sermons: Praying Indians in Colonial America* (Ithaca: Cornell University Press, 2004).

9. Laura Stevens, *The Poor Indians: British Missionaries, Native Americans, and Colonial Sensibility* (Philadelphia: University of Pennsylvania Press, 2004).

10. Letter from Robert Boyle in the Connecticut State Archives, Ecclesiastical Vol. 1, Document 7. Transcription in *New England Company Papers*, folder 3, American Antiquarian Society, Worcester, Massachusetts.

11. Letter by Thomas Shepard Jr., September 9, 1673, Wodrow Collection, Edinburgh. The exact addressee of this letter is not known.

12. John Saltmarsh, *Dawnings of Light* (London: R.W., 1644), 17–18.

13. Boyle Papers 11:310–34, Royal Society, London. While Eliot prepared the Indian Bible in Massachusetts, Robert Everingham secured funds for three thousand copies of a Gaelic translation of the New Testament, first printed in 1681 and distributed in Ireland and Scotland. Boyle Papers 11:310–34, Royal Society, London. Comenius also initiated an effort to translate the Bible into Turkish. See Noel Malcolm, "Comenius, Boyle, Oldenburg, and the Translation of the Bible into Turkish," *Church History and Religious Culture* 87 (2007): 327–62.

14. Bragdon and Goddard believe that these Bibles were widely available in praying towns; one copy at the American Antiquarian Society contains marginalia written in Algonquian by a Native American.

15. John Eliot, *The Holy Bible: Containing the Old Testament and the New* (Cambridge: Samuel Green and Marmaduke Johnson, 1663).

16. Quoted in Raymond Phineas Stearns, *Science in the British Colonies of America* (Urbana: University of Illinois Press, 1970), 90.

17. James Knowlson, *Universal Language Schemes in England and France, 1600–1800* (Toronto: University of Toronto Press, 1975), 14–15.

18. G. H. Turnbull, *Hartlib, Dury and Comenius: Gleanings from Hartlib's Papers* (London: University Press of Liverpool, 1947), 344.

19. Richard Verstegan, *A Restitution of Decayed Intelligence: In Antiquities Concerning the Most Noble and Reformed English Nation* (Antwerp: Robert Bruney, 1605).

20. David B. Quinn and Alison M. Quinn, eds., *A Particular Discourse Concerning the Great Necessity and Manifold Commodities That Are Likely to Grow in this Realm of England by the Western Discourses Lately Attempted, Written in the Year 1584 by Richard Hakluyt* (London: Hakluyt Society, 1993), 8.

21. Vivian Salmon, "Thomas Hariot (1560–1621) and the English Origins of Algonkian Linguistics," *Historiographia Linguistica* 19.1 (n.d.): 34, 39.

22. Francis Lodwick, "Of Converting Infidels to Christianity," Sloane Papers, British Library of London, 897, ff. 40r-43v.

23. G. H. Turnbull, "Samuel Hartlib's Influence on the Early History of the Royal Society," *Notes and Records of the Royal Society* 5 (1948): 101–30.

24. Robert Fitzgibbon Young, *Comenius and the Indians of New England* (London: School of Slavonic and East European Studies in the University of London, King's College, 1929).

25. Quoted in Turnbull, *Hartlib, Dury and Comenius*, 344.

26. Roger Williams, *A Key into the Language of America*, in *The Complete Writings of Roger Williams*, 7 vols. (New York: Russell and Russell, 1963), 1:19.

27. Comenius's *Janua Linguarum Reserata* translates as "the gate of languages unlocked."

28. Roger Williams, "The Examiner Defended: In a Fair and Sober Answer to the Two and Twenty Questions Which Largely Examined the Author of *Zeal Examined*," *Complete Writings*, 7:251.

29. Shalom Goldman, ed., *Hebrew and the Bible in America: The First Two Centuries* (Hanover NH: University Press of New England, 1993), xviii.

30. Thomas Thorowgood, *Jews in America, or Probabilities That Those Indians Are Judaical, Made More Probable by Some Additionals to the Former Conjectures* (London: Henry Brome, 1660).

31. Murray, *Forked Tongues*, 15.

32. John Eliot, *A Grammar of the Massachusetts Indian Language*, ed. Peter S. Ponceau (Boston: Phelps and Farnham, 1822), 66.

33. Cave Beck, *The Universal Character by Which All the Nations in the World*

May Understand One Anothers Conceptions, Reading out of One Common Writing Their Own Mother Tongues (London: William Weekley, 1657), B2.

34. Umberto Eco, *The Search for a Perfect Language*, trans. James Fentress (Oxford: Blackwell, 2005), 250.

35. John Wilkins, *An Essay towards a Real Character and a Philosophical Language* (London: Gellibrand and Martin, 1668), 5.

36. For a fuller discussion of Locke's interest in American Indians, see David B. Paxman, "'Adam in a Strange Country': Locke's Language Theory and Travel Literature," *Modern Philology* 92.4 (1995): 460–81.

37. John Locke, *An Essay Concerning Human Understanding*, ed. Peter Nidditch (Oxford: Clarendon Press, 1975), 64.

38. Robert Boyle, *The Christian Virtuoso: Showing That by Being Addicted to Experimental Philosophy, a Man Is Rather Assisted Than Indisposed to Be a Good Christian* (London: John Taylor, 1690), 76.

39. Daniel Carey discusses this relationship in "Locke, Travel Literature, and the Natural History of Man," *Seventeenth Century* 11.2 (1996): 259–80.

40. David Brainerd, *Mirabilia Dei Inter Indicos, or the Rise and Progress of a Remarkable Work of Grace Amongst a Number of the Indians in the Provinces of New-Jersey and Pennsylvania, Justly Represented in a Journal Kept by Order of the Honourable Society (in Scotland) for Propagating Christian Knowledge* (Philadelphia: William Bradford, 1748), 2, 15.

41. Experience Mayhew to Paul Dudley, March 20, 1722, in Experience Mayhew, *Observations on the Indian Language*, Library of American Civilization, ed. John S. H. Fogg (Boston: D. Clapp and Son, 1884), 8.

42. Experience Mayhew to Paul Dudley, March 20, 1722, in Mayhew, *Observations on the Indian Language*, 6.

43. Jonathan Edwards Jr., *Observations on the Language of the Muhhekaneew Indians* (New Haven CT: Josiah Meigs, 1788), 6–12.

44. Thomas Jefferson, *Notes on the State of Virginia*, ed. William Peden (Chapel Hill: University of North Carolina Press, 1955), 101.

45. Ponceau, "The Massachusetts Language," in Eliot, *Grammar of the Massachusetts Indian Language*, 4.

46. See Steven Blakemore, "Strange Tongues: Cooper's Fiction of Language in *The Last of the Mohicans*," *Early American Literature* 19.1 (1984): 21–41.

47. James Fenimore Cooper, *The Last of the Mohicans* (New York: Oxford University Press, 2008), 227.

48. Cooper, *The Last of the Mohicans*, 34.

49. Cooper, *The Last of the Mohicans*, 8.

Contributors

RALPH BAUER is an associate professor of English and comparative literature at the University of Maryland, College Park. His publications include *The Cultural Geography of Colonial American Literatures: Empire, Travel, Modernity* (2003, 2008), *An Inca Account of the Conquest of Peru* (2005), and (coedited with José Antonio Mazzotti) *Creole Subjects in the Colonial Americas: Empires, Texts, Identities* (2009). He is currently completing a monograph titled "The Alchemy of Conquest: Science, Religion, and the Secrets of the New World."

HEIDI BOHAKER is an associate professor at the University of Toronto. Her research interests include Anishinaabe political history in the Great Lakes region; Native American writing, communication systems, and material culture as sources for history; treaty relationships; and federal government policies toward indigenous peoples in Canada. She is also a cofounder of GRASAC, the Great Lakes Research Alliance for the Study of Aboriginal Arts and Cultures.

GALEN BROKAW is an associate professor in the Department of Modern Languages and Literatures at Montana State University. His research focuses primarily on colonial Latin American historiography, indigenous writing, orality-literacy studies, media studies, and the interaction between indigenous media and alphabetic script. He is the author of *A History of the Khipu* (2010).

MATT COHEN is an associate professor in the Department of English at the University of Texas at Austin. He is the author of *The Networked Wilderness: Communicating in Early New England* and a contributing editor at the online *Walt Whitman Archive*.

JON COLEMAN is a professor in the Department of History at the University of Notre Dame. He the author of *Vicious: Wolves and Men in America* (2004) and *Here Lies Hugh Glass: A Mountain Man, a Bear, and the Rise of the American Nation* (2012).

JEFFREY GLOVER is an assistant professor in the Department of English at Loyola University Chicago. He is currently working on a book about Anglo-Native treaties and the early history of international law.

PETER CHARLES HOFFER teaches early American history at the University of Georgia, where he is a distinguished research professor.

ANDREW NEWMAN, an associate professor of English at Stony Brook University, is the author of *On Records: Delaware Indians, Colonists, and the Media of History and Memory* (2012).

BIRGIT BRANDER RASMUSSEN is an assistant professor of American Studies and Ethnicity, Race, and Migration at Yale University. She is the author of numerous articles and a prize-winning book titled *Queequeg's Coffin: Indigenous Literacies and Early American Literature* (2012). She is coeditor of *The Making and Unmaking of Whiteness* (2001).

RICHARD CULLEN RATH is an associate professor of history at the University of Hawai'i at Mānoa. He teaches courses on early America, Native Americans, and the history of media and the senses. He is the author of *How Early America Sounded* and is currently working on two books, one an introduction to the history of hearing and the other comparing the rise of print culture in eighteenth-century North America to the rise of Internet culture today.

SARAH RIVETT is an assistant professor of English at Princeton University. She is the author of *The Science of the Soul in Colonial New England* (2011).

Contributors

GORDON M. SAYRE is a professor of English and folklore at the University of Oregon, where he teaches courses in colonial American literature, autobiography, Native studies, and ecocriticism. He is the translator and coeditor of *The Memoir of Lieutenant Dumont, 1715–1747*, the manuscript narrative of Jean-François-Benjamin Dumont de Montigny, published in 2012 by the Omohundro Institute of Early American History and Culture and the University of North Carolina Press.

GERMAINE WARKENTIN is professor emeritus of English at the University of Toronto and a fellow of the Royal Society of Canada. Her interests cover early modern literature and exploration, with emphasis on manuscript and book history and on aboriginal communication. She is the editor of *The Collected Writings of Pierre-Esprit Radisson* (vol. 1, *The Voyages*, 2012) and editor in chief of *The Library of the Sidneys of Penshurst Place ca. 1665* (2013).

Index

alphabetic scripts (*continued*)
"complete," 83; *Corónica* and, 160; European contexts and, 56; evolutionary approaches to, 88; exclusivism and, 80; "extreme valorization" of, 163n10; Great Lakes region and, 100; Heckewelder on, 92; indigenous literary traditions and, 144; *Instrucción* and, 327, 333, 337, 339, 344; literacy and, 78, 80–81, 93n4; Mexican history and, 12; mimetic technologies and, 224; modernity and, 37n29; non-linguistic sounds and, 314; *Nueva corónica* and, 143; orality and, 116–17; power and, 341; *quipus* and, 145, 152, 156, 180, 342, 345; winter counts and, 59; writing and, 81–82, 90, 91, 170, 197. *See also* books; writing
Amazon River region, 224
American Antiquarian Society, 26
American Languages in New France (Salvucci, ed.), 135n43
American literature, 27, 400–404
America north of Mexico, 77, 81, 85–87. *See also* Canada; United States government
American Philosophical Society, 381, 401, 402
amoxtli, 8
analogies, 295–96, 297, 298, 308, 311–12, 314, 317n10, 399. *See also* metaphors
ancient wisdom, 387–95
Andean society and language: cord systems and, 10; *Corónica* and, 163n15; evolutionary hierarchies and, 81; *grafismo indígena* and, 3; Guaman Poma and, 156; *Instrucción* and, 327; orality and, 353n22; *quipus* and wampum and, 68; semiotic heterogeneity and, 167; social structure and, 147, 149–50; Spaniards and, 149, 164n28; structure of manuscripts and, 161n5. *See also* Incas; Incas, language of; *Nueva corónica y buen gobierno* (Guaman Poma); Peru; *quipus* (*khipus*)

Andros, Edmund, 308
Anglicans, 20–21
animals, 236, 267–68, 269, 278, 279, 280, 281, 287n4. *See also* beaver fur; cattle; dogs; horses; wolves
animation, 105
animikiig (thunderbeings), *120*, 123, 124
animism, 105, 193–94, 236
Anishinaabeg: animism and, 105; cosmic struggles and, *120*, 123–24; defined, 133n26; identity and, 100–101; media diversity and, 54; personhood and, 129n6; pictographs on birchbark and, 118; traveling messages and, 112–13, *114*; travel pass and, *305*, 305–6, 314; visual representation and, 295–96; weaponry, 119–20; writing and, 295. *See also* Chippewas; *doodemag*; Ojibwes
anthropology, 15, 102, 401
Antigüedades mexicanas (Chavero), 14
Apess, William, 28
apocalypticism, 24
Apotampo, 190
Appadurai, Arjun, 5–6, 33, 49, 60, 61, 101, 105, 127
Arabic language, 385, *386*
Arapahos, 57, 59
archaeology: ancient wisdom versus, 401; art and, 131n14; biology and, 60–61; the divine and, 404; Great Lakes region and, 103–4; Indian grammars and, 400; Jefferson and, 25; museums and, 106; pipes and, 124; Roanoke and, 243–44; yupana-type objects and, 181–82
Archer, Gabriel, 249, 251–52, 253
architecture, 7, 168
archives: categorization and, 71n25; Eliot's books and, 22; Great Lakes region indigenous histories and, 99–129; as imaginaries, 11; indigenous uses of, 15; methodology and, 16–17; print media and, 27; U.S., 26–27. *See also* documents
Ardèche paintings, 65

exclusivism, 80–81, 82–83, 85
explanations, 63
"extended phenotype," 67
"external symbolic storage," 67
"extreme valorization," 163n10
eyewitnesses, 328–30, 352n13

fabrics, 7
factuality, 346
Fahrenheit 451 (Bradbury), 55
the Fall, 380, 384, 385, 387–88
fear, 267, 269, 284
federal removal policy, 28
Feiler, Seymour, 214, 228n21
Feister, Lois M., 39n40
Fernow, Berthold, 318n18
"fetishism of writing," 163n10
film, 15
financescapes, 5, 101
Fink, Mike, 204
Finland, 235
firearms, 79
fires, 240
first century of encounter: changing
   scenery and, 255–58; English perception of, 237–41; Indian perception of,
   235–37; novelty and, 233–35; sensory
   imperialism and, 241–55. *See also*
   "contact"
Fischer, Steven Roger, 82
Fisher, Simon, 74n49
fishing, 127
Fitzcarraldo, 224
Five Nations. *See* Iroquois and allied
   Native groups (Five Nations; Six
   Nations)
Fletcher, Benjamin, 304
Florida, 59
folktales, 225, 270
forests, 239, 256
fortifications, 242–48, 249, 252–53, 257
Fort Marion (FL), 59
Fossa, Lydia, 149
Fougquet de Belle-Isle, Charles-Louis-
   Auguste, 222

Fox Indians, 210, 211–13, 215
Francis, Turbutt, 246
Franciscans, 47–48. *See also* missionaries
the French: colonization and, 126; Indian allies and, 290, 357–73; Iroquois-
   allied Native groups and, 22–23; tall
   tales and, 203, 222–23; tattoos and,
   216; wampum and, 302–3, 307; writing and, 117. *See also* Dutisné,
   Claude-Charles (du Tissenet) *and
   other Frenchmen*; Jesuits (missionaries); New France
French and Indian Wars, 290, 358
fur, 304
fur pelts, 256, 305, 308, 318n18

gaming, reservation, 29, 33
Garangula (Onondaga), 307
García, Marcos, 327, 328, 333, 337, 339,
   340, 342, 343, 351n5
García de Castro, Lope, 326, 330, 338,
   339, 340, 347
Garibay, Ángel María, 15
Gates, Thomas, 255
Gaur, Augustine, 88
Gay Head, 26–27
Gee, James Paul, 85, 86
Gelb, Ignace J., 81, 88
genealogical narratives, 346
Generaciones y semblanzas (Pérez de
   Guzmán), 348
*General Heads for the Natural History of
   a Country* (Boyle), 397
geometric designs, 123, 187
Georgian Bay, 115
gestures, 18, 24, 373
gifts, 135n45, 250, 278, 279, 282, 284, 303–
   5, 308, 319n26, 326. *See also* wampum
Giles, William, 292
Ginzburg, Carlo, 62–63, 73n40
Glass, John B., 52
globalization, 6, 33–34, 69n7, 82, 101
Glover, Jeffrey, 98n61
Goddard, Yves, 405n14
Goldman, Shalom, 392

González Holguín, Diego, 169, 177–78, 179–80, 191–93

Good, Battiste (Brulé, Dakota), 58–59, 72nn30–31

Goody, Jack, 13, 78, 295

Gookin, Daniel, 26, 358–59, 360–67, 372, 374n13

government agencies, 27–28

Graff, Harvey, 76–77

grafismo indígena, 3

grammar, 82

Grammar of the Massachusetts Indian Language (Eliot), 401

grammatology, early Americanist, 76–93

Granganimo (Roanoke), 247

graphic pluralism, 56, 130n12, 296–97

GRASAC (Great Lakes Research Alliance for the study of Aboriginal Arts and Cultures), 71n25, 108, *122, 123*, 132n23

graves, 22, 102, 109, 112, 113–14

Gray, Edward, 24

Great Divide theories, 78–79, 80, 295

Great Hare family, 115, 136n53

Great Lakes region: agriculture and, 104, 132n16; alphabetic scripts and, 100; categories and inventories and, 105–9, 119–25; cultural categories and, 105; history and, 103–4; kinship networks and, 54; language families and, 104; map, *103*; mnemonic practices of, 116–19; notational practices and, 109–16, 133n25; sources and, 101–2; writing and, 22–23

Great Lakes Research Alliance for the Study of Aboriginal Arts and Cultures (GRASAC), 71n25, 108, *122, 123*, 132n23

Great Peace of Montreal (1701), *107*, 111, 210

Great Plains Indians, 210, 215

greed (*codicia*), 326, 331–32

Greek language, 24

Green, Lesley and David, 54

Greenblatt, Stephen, 79, 99, 129n2, 378

Greg, W. W., 69n4

Grusen, Richard, 7

Guadalupe, 238

Guaman Poma de Ayala, Felipe: on Atahuallpa's response to books, 341; books and, 141–60; on Incan clothing, 187; *quilca* and, 173–74, 175, 177; *quipus/yupana* and, *178*; scholarship on, 161n3; Spanish genres and, 161n5; *tocapu* designs and, 185; word picture of, 337, *338*. See also *Nueva corónica y buen gobierno* (Guaman Poma)

Guatemala, 52

Gustafson, Sandra, 2

Guthrie, Thomas H., 54

Haack, Susan, 63

Haas, Angela (Eastern Cherokee), 54, 55

Habermas, Jürgen, 35n12

Hakluyt, Richard, 241, 388–89

Hakluytus Posthumus (Purchas), 13

Half King (Shannoah Shawnee), 308

Hall, Kira, 318n16

Hallowell, Irving, 105, 129n6

Handbook of Middle American Indians (Glass), 16, 52

hand signs, 18

harmony: Anishinaabeg and, 124; gifts and, 307; James River ceremony and, 250; Quechua and, 150, 154; *quipus* and, 156; sensory imperialism and, 241; universal language and, 383, 387, 388, 389, 395

Harpe, Jean-Baptiste Bénard de la, 207, 226n9

Harrington, Fred H., 276

Harriot, Thomas, 19, 242, 388, 389

Harris, George Washington, 204

Hartlib, Samuel, 389

Hatfield raid, 365

Haudenosaunees (Iroquois), 104, 111, 118, 122, 132n17, 302–3, 309, 313

Havard, Gilles, 225

Havelock, Eric, 78

Hayles, N. Katherine, 2

healing, 236
Hebrew language, 24, 385, *386*, 391–92, 394, 395, 399
Heckewelder, John, 13, 27–28, 91–93, 381, 401–2
Heigler (Catawba), 292–93
Hemispheric American Studies (Levander and Levine), 43n83
hemispheric treatments, 30, 43n83
Henshilwood, Christopher, 65
hermeneutic chains, 340
Herrera y Tordesillas, Antonio de, 12
Hibbitts, Bernard J., 373
hieroglyphics, 14, 82–83, 91–92, 114, 225
High Hawk, 59
Hindus, 394
Hirschfeld, Lawrence, 74n49
Hispanophone contexts, 10
Histoire de la Louisiane (Le Page du Pratz), 206, 207–8, 227n10
Historia del origin y genealogia real de los reyes Ingas del Pirú (Murúa), 146
Historia de Tlatelolco desde los tiempos más remotos, 9
Historia general de los hechos de los castellanos (de Herrera y Tordesillas), 12
Historia natural y moral de las Indias (de Acosta), 12, 143
An Historical Account of the Doings and Sufferings of the Christian Indians in New England (Gookin), 362–67, 372
historiography, 15, 327, 328–30, 333, 345, 348
historio-"graphy," 337
History, Manners, and Customs of the Indian Nations (Heckewelder), 401–2
history and historians: authority of, 329; conceptions of, 3; "contact" and, 106; contemporary legal claims and, 127; ethnology and, 26; evolution versus, 64; indigenous inscriptions and, 12–13; indigenous representation and, 4–34, 6; *Instrucción* and, 333–34; intelligibility and, 269; Internet and, 312; legal cultures and, 328–30; professionalization of, 15; *quipus* and,

346; *relación* and, 328; science and, 355n38; sources of, 54, 100, 102, 127, 131n13; Western conceptions of, 126–27; writing and, 102, 344–45. *See also* archives; mnemonic practices
History of How the Spaniards Arrived in Peru (Titu Cusi; Julien, trans.), 350n5
The History of the Alphabet (I. Taylor), 1
holistic experiences, 235, 240, 251
"holy savages." *See* Christian Indians at war
horses, 58, 79, 94n11
Howard, Rosaleen, 344
How to Do Things with Words (Austin), 298, 317n16
Huarochirí Manuscript (anonymous), 344–45
Huascar Inca, 189, 347, 348
Huayna (Guayna) Capac (Inca), 188–89, 190, 347
Hubbard, William, 281
Hudson River Valley, 17
human sciences, 11. *See also* anthropology
Hume, Ivor Noël, 244
hunters, 79, 80, 127, 235, 256, 271
Hurons and Huron language, 357, 359, 368–72, 378
Huron-Wendat Confederacy, 111, 116
hybridity. *See* cross-/inter-cultural mediation (fertilization/hybridity)
Hyland, Sabine, 55–56
hypertext and wampum, 55

Ica Valley, 200n56
icons, 62, 81, 82, 101–2. *See also* pictography; semasiographic systems
identities: Anishinaabeg and, 100–101; captives and, 318n24; clothing and, 115; *doodemag* and, *107*, 109–11, 114–15, 116; European, 77; Indian grammars and, 389; paper records and, 329; political, 119; symbols of, 296–97; tracks and, 306; U.S., 381
ideology, 83, 96n44. *See also* Eurocentrism (Western conceptions); politics

legal cultures (*continued*)
  media and, 373; oral-literate divide
    and, 32–33; praying Indians and, 361–
    62, 374n10; Titu Cusi and, 333; wolf
    conflicts compared to, 285; writing
    and, 89. *See also* eyewitnesses
legitimacy, 345–48, 355n33. *See also* sover-
  eignty of tribes
Legnani, Nicole Delia, 350n5, 352n13
Le Jeune, Paul, 378
Lenape, 87
Le Page du Pratz, Antoine-Simon, 206,
  207–8, 211, 215, 227n10
Lepore, Jill, 4, 373n2, 378–79, 385
Levander, Caroline, 43n83
Levine, Robert S., 43n83
*Lexicon o vocabulario de la lengua general
  del Perú* (Santo Thomás), 169, 176, 181
Liberia, 90
libraries as metaphor, 51
"libros," 47–48
Lienhard, Martin, 2, 163n10, 334
lienzos, 9, 14, 37n22, 52
life and mind, 73n39
life history, 346
A Light to Grammar (Woodward), 389
lineages (*panaca*), 334, 346, 348
linguistic isomorphism, 387
linguistic turn, 15
Lipman, Andrew, 94n11
literacy: alphabetic, 78, 93n4; Amerindian, 163n12; Andeans and, 344–45; autonomy and, 379; captivity narratives
  and, 93n5; colonialism and, 144; definitions of, 76–77; the divine and, 382;
  extensions of, 85–90; Great Divide
  theories and, 78–79; inclusivism and,
  93; New Orleans (1731–32), 226n4;
  orality and, 1–2, 56, 78, 341; politics
  and, 76, 83; senses and, 294–95; *Walam
  Olum* and, 97n52; writing and, 80–85;
  86, 296. *See also* reading; writing
literary theory, 319n29
Littlehales, Major, 112, 114
local control, 7, 38n37

localization, 33–34
Locke, John, 24–25, 396–97, 401
Lodwick, Francis, 389
logographic systems, 82
longbows, 238, 247
Longfellow, Henry Wadsworth, 27
Long Island example, 312
loon people, 115
Lord, Albert, 295
Lord's Prayer, 399
Lorette (New France), 357, 359, 368, 369
Louis-Germain, Joseph, 357, 369
Louisiana, 204–5, 211, 216, 222–23, 225, 358
Luxton, Richard, 164n33
Lyon, Patricia J., 84

MacCormack, Sabine, 342
MacLeod, Peter, 374n15
Madrid, 330
Magnalia Christi Americana (C.
  Mather), 390
Magne, Martin, 58
Mahicans, 19
Maine, 242
Mallery, Barrick, 59
*Mamusse Wunneetupanatamwe Up-
  Biblum God* (Eliot), 21
Manco Inca, 325, 326–27, 332–33, 337,
  342–44, 346–47, 348
Mandoki, Katya, 202n70
Mani, 47–48
manidoog, 120, 123–24
manitou/Manitou, 259n8
Mannheim, Bruce, 351n5
Manteo (Powhatan), 19
the manuscript, 141–60
Maoris, 54, 235
mapas, 37n22, 52
maps, 7–8, 9–10, 10–11, 14, 16, 25, 27,
  96n39, 126
Maquas, 366, 367
Mardi Gras, 211
Margry, Pierre, 207, 226n9
Martha's Vineyard, 383
Marvelous Possessions (Greenblatt), 129n2

South America, 15, 16, 102, 136n51, 224
South Carolina, 290
South Kensington Museum, *123*
southwestern (U.S.) humor, 203–4
sovereignty of tribes, 28, 29, 30. *See also* authority; legitimacy
space, 235, 267, 271, 273, 285, 344. *See also* territories
the Spanish: the Andes and, 149, 164n28; Aztecs and, 312; bureaucratic administration and, 329; Christianity and, 193–94, 388; *Corónica* and, 154, 155–56, 158–59; destruction/preservation of documents and, 8–9; England and, 258n3; Incas and, 325–49; *Instrucción* and, 328; Mexican alphabetic writing and, 12; Nahuatl language and, 376; *Nueva corónica* and, 142; Peruvian histories and, 12; *quilca* and, 171, 172; *quipus* and, 10, 162n6, 170; "rasterization" and, 35n7; *relaciones geográficas* and, 9; Titu Cusi and, 350n5; views of Amerindian writing, 11, 12. *See also* Guaman Poma de Ayala, Felipe *and other Spaniards*
speech (spoken language): the divine and, 383–84; icons versus, 82; *Instrucción* and, 342; pictographs versus, 92; politics and, 373; religion and, 379; tracks and, 306; treaty councils and, 291, 293–94; universal religious harmony and, 388; visible effects of, 305; wampum and, 91, 298; writing and, 81
speech acts, 299, 304. *See also* performative systems
speed of communication, 6
Sperber, Dan, 74n49
spirit chasers, 236
spirits and spirit world, 236, 244–45, 246, 254, 259n8, 303, 381–87, 403. *See also* upper (sky) world
Splitstoser, Jeff, 200n56
spoken language. *See* speech (spoken language)
Sprat, Thomas, 390

stage performers, 28
Standish, Miles, 266
St. Augustine, 240
stelae, 12, 52
Stern, Steve, 349
Stevens, Laura, 382
sticks, prompter's, *310*
St. Lawrence valley, 126
Stone, John Augustus, 27
Stone, Rebecca, 186
stone inscriptions, 7
stone objects, 177
Strachey, William, 19, 239
striped sticks, 188–89
subalternity, 16
subjects and objects, 49
substrates, 49
Suma y narración de los Incas (Betanzo), 172–73
superstition, 47–48
Susquehanna, 246
Sut Lovingood tales (Harris), 204
syllabaries, 7
symbol, 62
systems, 33

Tachpausan (Delaware), 307
Tahuantinsuyu encounter, 340
tall tales, Mississippi: American studies and, 203–5, 222–25; erasable tattoos and, 215–22; "Lose Your Hair, Not Your Head," 206–15
Tambo (co), 188, 195
Tardif, Guillaume, 24
tattoos, 7, 19, 40n51, 102, 105, 215–25, 228n17. *See also* body art and writings
Taussig, Michael, 223
Tawagonshi Treaty, 320n38
Taylor, Allan R., 133n25
Taylor, Isaac, 1
technology, 238
technoscapes, 5, 101
Teedyuscung (Delaware), 299, 307
Tercero catecismo (Third Lima Council, 1583), 193

Urton, Gary, 10, 84, 334–35

Vai people (Liberia), 90
Valverde, Vicente de, 341
Van Der Peet decision (Canada, 1996),
    127
"vanishing Indian," 27, 28
Varela, Francisco, 73n39
Vasina, Jan, 131n14
Vastokas, Joan, 131n13
Vega, Garcilaso de la (Inca), 345
verification, 61, 62–63
Verrazzano, Giovanni da, 234, 278–79, 284
Verstegan, Richard, 387–88, 389
Vico, Giambattista, 13, 25
Vidal, Lux, 3
Vilcabamba, 325–26, 327, 332
village identity, 107, 109
villancicos, 334
Viracochampacachan, Tonapa, 190
Vira Cochas, 345
Virginia, 19, 20–21, 25, 29, 239, 290–91,
    300–301, 302, 360–61
Virginia Company, 249, 255, 256, 360
Virginian speech, 389
visions, 236
visual mediation, 10, 82, 294, 306, 315. *See
    also* icons; ocularcentrism
Vitoria, Francisco de, 330–31
vocabularies, 19, 26, 27, 378, 389, 398,
    400–401
Vocabulario (Holguín), 169, 179
*Vocabulario y phrasis de la lengua general
    de los indios del Perú* (Ricard), 169
vocalizations. *See* non-verbal vocalizations
Voyages in New France (Champlain), 378
Voyer de Paulmy, Marc Pierre de, 222

Waban, 363, 366
Wahunsunacawh (Powhatan), 20
Walam Olum, 87, 97n52
Waldeck, Phillip, 311
Wampanoags, 281, 360
wampum: analogies and, 295; carved on
    weapon, 119; commodification and,
56; functions of, 135n45; Great Lakes
    region and, 101, 104; hearing, 290–
    316; as hypertext, 55; Iroquois and,
    89–90, 144; museumification and,
    108; orality and, 117; scholarship on,
    317n10, 318n18; the social and, 67; as
    system, 33; treaty negotiations and,
    130n9; Two-Row Wampum, 313;
    writing and, 23, 88–89, 90, 91, 98n61,
    102, 295. *See also* gifts
Wanchese (Powatan), 19
Wannalancet, 365
Ward, Seth, 389, 390
warfare: assimilation and, 126; Christian
    Indians and, 370; cross-cultural me-
    diation and, 318n24; Indian names
    and, 262n55; and indigenous practic-
    es, 359, 360, 362–64, 365–66, 368–72;
    landscapes and, 245; memory and,
    312, 313–14; mnemonic practices and,
    334; Roanoke and, 242; soundscapes
    and, 253; stelae and, 52; trade and,
    374n15; wampum and, 315; writing
    and, 367, 373. *See also* fortifications;
    weaponry
Wari period, 168, 181–85, 188, 195
Warkentin, Germaine, 50, 87, 104, 130n9,
    295–96, 316n8, 317n10
War of the Spanish Succession (1702–
    13), 367
Warren, William, 28
Washington, George, 308
Watt, Ian, 13
Watts, Pauline Moffit, 85
Waymouth, George, 18, 242–43, 283
weaponry, 102, 112, 119–22, 120, 136n53,
    240, 266–67, 283
weather, 236
Weaver, Jace, 5
Wedel, Mildred Mott, 226n9
Weiser, Conrad, 301, 309
Wendat Confederacy, 111
Wendats, 112, 133n31. *See also* Wyandots
Western conceptions. *See* Eurocentrism
    (Western conceptions)